BETHLEHEM STEEL

BETHLEHEM STEEL

BUILDER
AND
ARSENAL
OF
AMERICA

Kenneth Warren

UNIVERSITY OF PITTSBURGH PRESS

Published by the University of Pittsburgh Press, Pittsburgh, Pa., 15260
Copyright © 2008, University of Pittsburgh Press
All rights reserved
Manufactured in the United States of America
Printed on acid-free paper
First paperback edition, 2010
10 9 8 7 6 5 4 3 2 1

ISBN 13: 978-0-8229-6067-6
ISBN 10: 0-8229-6067-2

CONTENTS

FIGURES AND TABLES

Figures

Tables

PREFACE

It is 150 years since the first iron company was formed in the small town of Bethlehem in eastern Pennsylvania. By December 2004, a century had passed since the incorporation of the Bethlehem Steel Corporation. On both counts it seemed an opportune time to examine the history of what, from very small beginnings, had eventually become America's second biggest steel company. Such a study would be a complement to *Big Steel,* my account of the first century of the United States Steel Corporation. Unfortunately, the distress in the steel industry during recent decades eventually caught up with Bethlehem Steel, and by a short distance it failed to complete the course of its first century. What follows is an analysis of what was achieved, how and why the enterprise grew and succeeded, and the ways in which that expansion passed into contraction and ultimate failure. It is a story not only of industrial vision but also of opportunism, of entrepreneurial risk taking that brought great achievements and wealth, of dogged rearguard actions delaying collapse year after year, and of revived hopes confounded time and again.

The varying nature of the sources I have used requires a brief comment. A few books and a considerable number of articles deal with or include a consideration of Bethlehem Steel. Apart from these important secondary sources, I have drawn extensively on the trade journals that, as sources for the business or company historian, were better in earlier than in later years. The vital primary archival material is frustratingly incomplete. For Bethlehem Iron in the nineteenth century, there are excellent board minutes. For this period too there are letters, including the industrial correspondence of John Fritz and the diaries of Robert Sayre. After 1904, the records of the Bethlehem Steel Corporation are voluminous but in many ways less useful. There are some enlightening letters, especially from Charles Schwab and Archibald Johnston. The engagement diaries of Schwab and Eugene Grace have survived, but the daily entries are minimal, just a few words. For example, one would like to know more of what lay behind the entry in Grace's diary for Wednesday, 23 October 1929: "Winston Churchill and party at Bethlehem." The earlier, simpler, but more informative minute books were replaced by separate records of meetings from various sectors of the company's widening business, and they record nothing of the arguments or passion that lay behind what were sometimes momentous events in corporate history. At the quarterly meeting of directors held on 29 January 1931, Schwab announced the acquisition of the major construction company McClintic-Marshall. The minutes of that meeting are tantalizingly incomplete: "Mr. Grace then stated at some length to the Board the pertinent facts regarding the properties and business of McClintic-Marshall Corporation . . . and the reason why the management thought the acquisition to be desirable." In a general discussion that followed, "Mr. Grace answered a number of questions and discussed various points raised by members of the Board." There is no record of what Grace stated, of the questions asked, or of the answers given.

In the same way, major decisions after World War II had little or no documentation, and certainly the discussions that preceded them are not recorded. Board minutes in the 1950s paid more attention to recording the procedures by which its members decided each other's bonuses (each director left the room while his peers voted on his case). During the 1960s and into the 1970s, a common notation in the minutes of stockholders meetings was: "There followed a discussion of various subjects relating to the business and affairs of the Corporation and the Chairman answered or had answered a number of questions with regard to the annual report and such business and affairs." No fuller record was preserved for posterity. In later years, reports from subcommittees of the board became an important method of exploring and summarizing controversial issues, for instance, the future of the Johnstown operation, but neither the committee proceedings nor their reports to directors seem to have survived or, if they did, they are shut away somewhere.

For the last few decades there is a valuable supplement to written records: the recollections of events, decisions, and decision makers by those who were personally involved. They have shed a good deal of light onto things that otherwise would have remained even more obscure. It is of course always important to recognize that memory is a personal perspective, cannot be other than partial, and, despite the best intentions of the person struggling to recall past events, is therefore probably partisan. To counterbalance that rather depressing conclusion, one should remember that it is said that the passage of time helps put things into perspective. In any case, I was extremely grateful for these recollections.

As those last few paragraphs reveal, in researching the colorful history of the Bethlehem Steel Corporation I have been greatly helped by the resources of a handful of important industrial archives, especially the large collections of Bethlehem Iron and Bethlehem Steel materials at the Hagley Library in

Wilmington, Delaware, and at the National Canal Museum (NCM) in Easton, Pennsylvania. I would like especially to record my appreciation of the help, encouragement, and many kindnesses I received from Lance Metz, historian at the NCM, during my visits. I contacted four of the most recent chairmen of the company and benefited from a two-hour interview with one of them and the written comments of another. Four other former senior executives of the Bethlehem Steel Corporation generously provided me with information and insights into the later history of the company.

Kenneth Warren
September 2007

INTRODUCTION

A PROLIFIC IF RATHER VAGUE early twentieth-century writer began a book with these words: "In the following pages I propose to prove that Business is now being developed into a science." More than 170 pages later he ended with these: "The industrial and commercial contest of the next twenty years . . . will be incredibly vast and magnificent; and the inevitable law of Nature will still hold good—THE FITTEST WILL SURVIVE."[1] The difficulty was knowing which really were the fittest. Was it those who had merely survived? In business, as in other departments of life, difficulties evoke various responses. Some firms fail, others react so positively that this reaction leads to new, higher levels of business success; after all, crises present opportunities as well as problems. Superior plant, the introduction of new technologies, or a switch to more saleable or higher value products, large-scale operations, administrative economy, excellent marketing strategies, or, better still, combinations of all these factors can deliver success that evades less skillful management. Yet all factors important for business success are by no means under the control of an individual company; the wider business environment must also be taken into consideration. The economist E. H. Chamberlain once summed up the complications faced by any company in shaping a competitive enterprise: it "must consider not only what [its] competitor is doing now, but also what he will be forced to do in the light of the change which he himself is contemplating."[2] In short, those directing a firm face very much the same types of problems as a general in charge of a great military campaign, and the reactions required are similar as well. Statistics on production, sales, revenues, and profits are measures of success, but the reasons for that success lie in human decision making and the wisdom of the choices made. In short, the indicators and all the complexities of the production processes are lit up by the interactions and sometimes the clashes of different personalities. As noted by Fritz Redlich, who wrote extensively about the great entrepreneurs, "Figures are quantitative symbols which stand for something, in this case the *results* of a process. By lining these symbols up in the form of a time series, we incorrectly create the impression that they actually represent a process, whereas they merely act as yardsticks, measuring a process."[3]

Any historian should be cautious when he or she criticizes decisions made in the past. In retrospect, looking in from beyond the noise and heat of the fray, it is all too easy to conclude that a wrong choice has been made, but at the time, under pressure, it was not so easy to be right. Yet those in control had to choose some path, even if it was later to prove less than the best. Business decision makers, like politicians, are involved not with ideal solutions but with the art of the possible. What now may seem—or may have proved—a mistake, probably seemed a logical choice at the time. A decision or arrangement that was indeed good at one time may prove unsatisfactory later.

Establishing what happened in the long-term development of a major company like Bethlehem Steel is a laborious but reasonably practicable task. There are numerous secondary sources of book length or in learned journals dealing with industry and company history, and there have been excellent trade journals almost from the earliest days to the present time. Access to company archives permits a much fuller, balanced analysis of what happened. It is true that the business historian is faced with the serious problem of the selection and ordering of the material and that therefore the facts presented and the themes emphasized will differ widely from one history to another. Every student of "the facts" comes to them with a unique perspective and will therefore present the account in a distinctive fashion. No account of what happened can be, whatever the efforts made by its author, fully straightforward and objective; it is necessarily also an interpretation. Some scholars, the theory builders, stress the need to interpret what happened in the light of conflicting hypotheses. More generally, what happened is of such compelling interest that we want to know much more about the reasons. Why did this or that event or development occur? How was a choice made between various possibilities?

Finding a satisfactory answer to the question "why?" is surrounded with all sorts of difficulties. The most obvious is a practical one: evidence is not available or is only partial. Company minute books illustrate this well. From them, it may be possible to trace vital decisions that shaped the course of a company's history, decisions about expansion, contraction, new equipment or new plants, or about technology and personnel. Yet it is rare for the minutes from a board of directors to fully present the range of alternatives and the arguments and costs for each. Memoranda from subcommittees, specially appointed to examine this or that project, may of course do so, but the good fortune to come across one of these comes only rarely to the research worker. Correspondence between principal officers or managers of the company may give invaluable insight, but the availability of this source material is much rarer than that of minute books, and in any case it is not always clear how influential were the views expressed in letters when the time for decision making came. For more recent periods, interviews with senior members of the firm are invaluable, but one always has to remember that recollection may not always be accurate and that, however well disposed, the interviewee will not always find it easy to represent his or her contribution to the choices made in less than a favorable light.

Another, and quite different, range of limitations to the ability to tease out the causes of events has already been mentioned: decision makers are not in command of all the variables. Invariably, they have only partial knowledge of the situation and are constrained by what has been called "bounded rationality" in dealing with what they do know. The drift of wider economic forces in other industries, in the national and even the global economy, though no doubt carefully studied and projected, remains uncertain. Yet such changes will influence the outcome of any important decision, such as the decision to expand an old plant or build a new one, embark on a new line of business, or tear out old equipment and install new technology. Bounded rationality may be extended from restrictions of ability or of judgment to considerations that detract from strictly commercial criteria of what is desirable, such as concern for workers, the environment, or the wider good of society—or indeed anything that allows for even a glimmer of sentiment in business. Yet we know well enough that those engaged in business, like those in any other employment, are not mere automatons and usually have other interests and aspirations than the mere maximization of profits.

There remain the "ifs" of business history, those forgone opportunities that might have made the whole course of development different. The late nineteenth-century history of Bethlehem Iron is particularly rich in these. In the late 1870s, as the rail trade became increasingly difficult, the directors might have heeded John Fritz's advice and the company would then have become a major factor in the structural steel trade a full generation earlier than it did. If this had happened, the company would probably not have entered the armaments business in the mid-1880s as an alternative means of dealing with its trading difficulties. Sometime later, perhaps as Pennsylvania Steel embarked on its Sparrows Point project, and certainly long before Lackawanna chose to tackle its competitive disadvantages by moving to Buffalo, Fritz is said to have sketched out the advantages of and even to have drawn up plans for a works on a new site on the lower Delaware River. In the late 1890s, construction of a fine plate mill promised a successful new commercial trade and might have led to new and viable business groupings, for at that time some important shipbuilders were looking for association with a major steel producer. Instead, Bethlehem lost confidence in the plate project and sold the mill and its ancillaries at a bargain price to a rival. As a final instance, if Charles Michael Schwab had succeeded in securing his vision of the direction of advance for the United States Steel Corporation, rather than being sidelined by Elbert H. Gary, he would not have fully linked his talents and drive to the transformation of Bethlehem Steel. In that case, Bethlehem's twentieth-century history would have taken a different path.

Looked at in retrospect, the course of a company's history is likely to seem a logical progression, almost an inevitable development. It is essential to keep in mind that at innumerable points of decision making along that path there were alternatives. A different choice would have led to further choices and the likelihood of still wider divergence between what happened and what might have been. In short, the idea of inevitability is as inapplicable in business history as in any other branch of historical study.

A final consideration is the ethos of the industry. This differs from one period to another. For instance, the cut-throat competition of the last decades of the nineteenth century was succeeded by the live-and-let-live spirit of the "Gary years," from 1901 into the 1920s. A decade later, government in the form of the New Deal pressed on the industry more heavily than ever before or through most of the decades since that time. There is also the attitude of the American industry to the rest of the metallurgical industry around the world. This may perhaps best be approached by a historical analogy. It was not until 1890 that the United States passed Great Britain to become the world's leading steel producer, but for many years before that American practice had been far superior in most sections of the industry to that in the older economy. In 1890, members of the Iron and Steel Institute—largely but not wholly from Britain—paid an extended visit to the United States. They were warmly welcomed and shown around a large number of iron and steel works. The Britons had been so long accustomed to leadership in the industry that it seemed almost impossible for them to accept that they had now been superseded. For their American hosts, it was a matter of wonder that their guests found it so difficult to acknowledge the fact. As the trade journal *Iron Age* put it in a hard-hitting editorial, "The first impulse of the Englishmen seemed usually to be either to deliberately close their eyes to anything which constituted an improvement over their own methods, or to belittle it." Sixty or so years later, American steel makers seemed as sure as the British had once been that they commanded the iron and steel world as of right. Examination of the trade press during the 1950s will show that little notice was taken of what happened in the industry in the rest of the world. Yet at that very time, the progress of European and Japanese reconstruction from wartime damage, a fresh surge in the industry worldwide, and the application of new technology, especially in bulk steel making, was building up a threat to U.S. hegemony in steel similar in many respects to that the Americans had earlier represented for Britain. Decades later, some representatives of the industry still seemed to assume it was almost in the divine order of things that they should lead in world steel and, as it could now be seen that they no longer did so, that this must be because others had subverted the rules of the game. No clearer illustration of this can be given than the testimony to two congressional committees in 1983 by the chairman of Bethlehem Steel. The attitude survived into the 1990s. Given Bethlehem Steel's large capital outlays for new plant, it would be quite erroneous to suggest that the company did not respond vigorously to the challenge of foreign competition. The fact remains, however, that it espoused the dangerous doctrine that any national superiority in an industry was part of the natural order of the world economy. Both it and many other major steel companies gradually learned the hard lesson that it was not.

I

THE

BETHLEHEM

IRON

COMPANY,

1857–1899

1

THE EARLY YEARS
AND THE DECLINE
OF THE ANTHRACITE
IRON INDUSTRY

THE CONTEXT FOR THE EMERGENCE and growth of Bethlehem, Pennsylvania, as an iron making center at the time of the Civil War was the development of the anthracite coal industry and the application of anthracite to the smelting of iron. Almost thirty years before, Albert Gallatin, by then an elder statesman, had sent a memorial to the Free Trade Convention in 1831. It considered the conditions that might enable American ironmasters to compete with foreign iron in the Atlantic coastal districts. The first item on his list of desirable improvements was "a happy application of anthracite coal to the manufacture of iron."[1] At that time, the mining of anthracite itself was little more than a decade old. There was a large consumption of coal in the towns and cities along the Atlantic seaboard, but their needs were supplied by imports or from American coastal districts where mines were nearer tidewater. The second war with Britain had cut off a major source and provided an incentive for entrepreneurship in the anthracite coalfields, but effective response to the opportunities of the times meant grappling with serious physical obstacles. One instance may illustrate the costs involved. During 1814, Charles Miner of Wilkes-Barre, Pennsylvania, an associate of Jacob Cist, hauled twenty-four tons of coal over rough roads to the Lehigh valley. There, it was placed in an "ark," a primitive type of boat, which carried it down the Lehigh and Delaware Rivers to be sold in Philadelphia. Haulage expenses amounted to fourteen dollars a ton.[2] Further exploitation of anthracite was delayed by the peace with Britain and a consequent revival of shipments of coal from Liverpool. Competition from the small deposits near Richmond, Virginia, was another problem. Challenging such competitors required a reduction in delivery costs, which in turn depended on new infrastructure. Production of anthracite in 1820 was less than four thousand tons. Eventually it would be seen that establishing outlets for anthracite in or nearer the coalfields could be another important help.

River improvement and canalization, canal construction, and later the building of railroads provided the vital keys for the opening and development of the anthracite coalfields. The Schuylkill Navigation Company was incorporated in 1815, and within eleven years it had completed the improvement of river and canalized navigation for the 108 miles from Port Carbon, above Pottsville, to Philadelphia. In 1818, the organization of the Lehigh Navigation Company marked the beginning of commercial growth along that river. By 1820, temporary navigation and coal shipment on the Lehigh was under way, with 365 tons being delivered that year.[3] When shipping increased to the limits of the temporary navigation facilities in this valley, a new phase of development involving canal works took place between 1827 and 1829. By 1832, the Lehigh Valley was shipping about one-fifth of the 380,000 tons of coal carried downriver from the anthracite fields.[4]

Construction of short rail links from coal workings to the Lehigh Canal, starting with a line in 1827 from Mauch Chunk into the coalfield (the second railroad in the nation), led to longer lines to open new areas. In 1837, the Lehigh and Susquehanna Railroad was formed. It was required by its Pennsylvania-issued charter to link the two rivers in its title. Its twenty miles of track from White Haven, over the watershed, into the drainage basin of the North Branch of the Susquehanna, and so on to Wilkes-Barre was not fully operational until 1844. It was designed to capture the coal trade of part of the Wyoming valley field, a revolutionary step when contrasted with Charles Miner's pioneer efforts

PART I. The Bethlehem Iron Company

only twenty-three years earlier. More relevant to the history of Bethlehem, in 1846 the Lehigh Valley Railroad (LVRR) was incorporated to build from the head of the Morris Canal at Phillipsburg, New Jersey, across the Delaware River from the point at which it was joined by the Lehigh, through the length of that valley, and on to Wilkes-Barre. Construction began in 1851, and by September 1855, the LVRR was opened to Mauch Chunk.

Coal production in eastern Pennsylvania by then had reached 8.5 million tons. Much of it was delivered to the coastal cities, but large tonnages were by this time also used in smelting iron. To supply the coastal markets with anthracite fuel had required large-scale investment in infrastructure: the development of the anthracite iron industry depended on a technological breakthrough. As anthracite became more widely available, attempts were made to employ it in various iron manufacturing processes. By 1827, the Phoenix Ironworks in Chester County was reported to have proved the practicability of using it to generate steam; within another eight years, M. B. Buckley of Pottsville employed it in puddling.[5] For many years, Gallatin's dream of using it as blast furnace fuel proved tantalizingly elusive. By 1830, America each year made between 165,000 and 180,000 tons of pig iron, and output was increasing rapidly. All of it was smelted with charcoal fuel. Charcoal furnaces made excellent iron and, as they were widely distributed across the country, were well able to draw on the scatter of iron ore deposits and to serve local markets. But charcoal also had many disadvantages. It was too soft to support a large mass of minerals in the furnace without crushing, which in turn would impede the movement of the blast through the burden. Consequently, the physical dimensions and average annual production of furnaces using charcoal were small. A second problem was that the very success of any furnace rapidly depleted its resource base; the cutting of wood meant that each season the supply of fuel had to be hauled farther, leading either to exhaustion of the holding or an increase in costs. Already, for many decades all but a very small proportion of Britain's much larger output of pig iron had depended on furnaces using mineral fuel, either coke or uncoked coal. As coal is a much more concentrated source of energy than wood, a relatively small acreage of it can supply a furnace for many years. Even more important, as time was to show, coal and still more coke, being physically stronger than charcoal, could support a much heavier burden of materials in the blast furnace, thereby opening up the possibility of higher furnace outputs. By the 1830s, there were incentives to move in this direction. As demand for pig iron for puddling and use in rolling mills increased as the first railroads were built, the prospect of productive and geographically concentrated smelting operations on the British model became more attractive. The increasing output of anthracite coal seemed to offer possibilities.

Unfortunately, anthracite coal is an intractable fuel. Being very low in volatiles, it is not readily combustible, although high temperatures can be attained when burning is under way. As early as 1825, a charcoal furnace at Mount Carbon in the Schuylkill valley south of Pottsville experimented with it, having already proved that, mixed with charcoal, it helped economize fuel consumption.[6] At that time, the air blown into blast furnaces was unheated and the amount of anthracite consumed per ton of iron was high. Three years later, James Neilson of the Clyde Iron Works in Glasgow patented the use of heated air (the hot blast) in smelting, a discovery quickly followed by the mushrooming growth of the Scottish iron industry. The heated blast potentially opened a way of breaking through the problem of slow-burning Pennsylvanian anthracite, but real success in this direction was delayed for another eleven years. Meanwhile, an offer of free water rights for any company that operated a coal burning blast furnace along the canal constructed by the Lehigh Coal and Navigation Company produced no viable outcome. In December 1833, Frederick W. Geisenheimer of New York took out a patent for making iron using anthracite exclusively in a blast furnace with either a cold or a hot blast, but it was not until the following year, and then in a charcoal furnace at Oxford, New Jersey, that Neilson's hot blast was first used in the United States. In 1836, Geisenheimer tried and for a short time succeeded in making anthracite iron in Valley Furnace on Silver Creek near Pottsville. There was another Pottsville area trial that same year, and in 1838, a small furnace at Mauch Chunk limped along for some months before failing. As with the hot blast itself, real success in employing the new fuel depended on the importation of know-how.

Early in 1837, a few months after the Pottsville trials, a practical process for using anthracite in the blast furnace was at last achieved. The innovators were George Crane and David Thomas of the Ynyscedwyn Ironworks, in the anthracite area on the northwestern edge of the South Wales coalfield, and they received a patent for their process. There followed an important instance of individually carried transatlantic technology transfer. At the end of December 1838, following a further round of experiments at Pottsville, Thomas was engaged to bring his knowledge of anthracite iron from the small Welsh anthracite field

Table 1.1 New charcoal and anthracite blast furnaces built in Pennsylvania, 1840–1846

	Number	Annual iron capacity (tons)	Avg. annual capacity (tons)	Avg. investment ($)	Avg. investment per ton capacity ($)
Charcoal	72	78,100	1,085	50,995	47.00
Anthracite	36	107,200	2,978	74,450	25.00

Source: Based on *Journal of the Franklin Institute*, 3rd ser., 12 (1846): 124–36.

to Pennsylvania, where it could be applied in a potentially much larger sphere of operations. On 4 July 1840, the blast furnace he had erected for the Lehigh Crane Iron Company, near Catasauqua in the lower Lehigh valley, produced its first iron, initiating the commercially successful use of this fuel in the United States. Soon after the breakthrough there, six furnaces were using anthracite: two on the Schuylkill River, three on the lower Susquehanna, and the Crane works on the Lehigh. So rapid was the response of entrepreneurs to the new opportunities provided by this technological advance that by autumn the *Philadelphia Commercial List* reported that twenty-one furnaces and six rolling mills and puddling departments were either built or were to be constructed to use anthracite. Already the Lehigh seemed likely to become the major focus, with thirteen furnaces and five of the six mills being either in that valley or along the Morris Canal, in transport terms a continuation of the Lehigh Canal toward the iron ore districts of New Jersey.[7]

Smelting with anthracite caused a veritable revolution in the iron industry, transforming not only commercial circumstances but the industry's size, structure, and location. Within fifteen years, the tonnage of iron made from anthracite surpassed that of charcoal iron, and by 1859–1860 it was 76 percent greater. This runaway growth resulted from higher productivity coupled with lower overheads, an unrivaled combination so long as furnaces could be operated near capacity. The supply of fuel was no longer subject to the vagaries of weather, unlike that used in charcoal furnaces. Anthracite blast furnaces and iron works were larger than those in the charcoal iron industry and were sometimes geared to the manufacture of finished products in associated puddling and rolling operations. For these reasons, their outputs varied less year to year than those of charcoal iron works.

The dominance of the Lehigh valley through the middle years of the century proved to be less than had seemed likely in the development planning of the early 1840s, but even so, this district led in both capacity and production. It accounted for 37.3 percent of the anthracite iron produced in Pennsylvania in 1849, only 31.6 percent in 1854, but by 1860, 39.9 percent. (By this time there was also a substantial output outside Pennsylvania, notably in the Hudson valley and as far west as Buffalo.) As early as 1854 the authors of the British reports on the New York Exhibition recognized that the Catasauqua, Glendon, and Trenton works were "all large concerns and are conducted on a scale and a system quite equal to the best in this country."[8]

Even more impressive than Lehigh valley preeminence in output were two other features of its iron trade, themselves puzzling in the contrasting indications they seemed to give: the valley had the largest iron works, but it was relatively insignificant in iron finishing capacity. By 1857, it contained five blast furnace plants with greater than 15,000 tons' annual capacity; the four other districts into which the anthracite iron industry was divided for statistical purposes had six works of this size. The five Lehigh plants averaged 28,800 tons; the six others averaged 18,500. Yet whereas by 1846, fourteen new "anthracite" rolling mills with a combined annual capacity of 36,500 tons of iron had been built in eastern Pennsylvania, not one was on the Lehigh River, though farther south, on the Delaware, there were three rather small mills near Philadelphia. To some extent, this discrepancy between the valley's position in making and in finishing iron reflected a low-cost, highly competitive position for pig and therefore a lack of need to go further. For instance, a good deal of the iron was shipped to Philadelphia and Reading to be melted and shaped into hardware.[9] A decade later, too, the valley remained of little significance in finishing as compared with the Schuylkill or the upper or lower Susquehanna. However, it was at this time that an important new iron and rolling operation was set up amid the giant operations of the lower Lehigh.[10] Expansion of the rail network, a much less certain increase in domestic ability to supply the demands of that growing system, and the specific requirements of a local railroad provided the context for the establishment of this new operation.

The earliest phase of railroad building in the late 1820s was followed by links between important cities and then by trunk lines, the laying out of branches, and finally the filling out of major regional systems and a gradual emergence of a national network. In mileages built and calls on other industries for supplies and services, a remarkable acceleration occurred. During 1835, as pioneer entrepreneurs in the anthracite coal region struggled to make a success of smelting ore with local coal, the total length of railroad operated in the nation passed

Table 1.2 Annual output of finished iron products in the anthracite districts of Pennsylvania, 1855–1857

	Number of mills	Output (tons)
Lehigh valley	2	1,544
Schuylkill and Philadelphia	23	37,741
Upper Susquehanna	4	34,135
Middle and lower Susquehanna	17	49,155
Totals	46	122,575

Source: Based on J. P. Lesley, *The Iron Manufacturer's Guide to the Furnaces, Forges, and Rolling Mills of the United States* (New York: American Iron Association, 1859).

1,000 miles. By the end of 1845, it was 4,633 miles and ten years later, 18,374 miles.[11] A large part of the iron required for all this construction came from foreign, mainly British, works. Varying import duties on railroad iron, themselves reflecting conflicting business and sectional interests and changes in the balance of power in Congress, largely determined the year-to-year success of the domestic industry in meeting this competition. Recognizing this, the people of Pottsville eventually erected a monument to Senator Henry Clay, whose legislative efforts on tariffs aided their industries. But duties raised by the Tariff Act of 1828 were gradually reduced in the 1830s, and between 1832 and 1839 imports of rolled bar and rail iron almost tripled. The Tariff Act of 1842 reintroduced higher duties, and at this time American rail manufacture became established, the first heavy rails being rolled at Mount Savage, Maryland, in 1844. A new tariff act in July 1846 introduced ad valorem duties of 30 percent, and by the following year another seven rail mills were at work. Four were associated with anthracite iron: the Montour mill at Danville, Cooper and Hewitt at Trenton, New Jersey, the Phoenixville operations of the Phoenix Iron Company, and at Scranton, the Lackawanna Iron and Coal Company. In 1848, there were new works at Danville and at Safe Harbor on the lower Susquehanna. Unfortunately for these ventures, at the end of the 1840s depression in Britain's domestic markets meant that British prices fell and therefore an ad valorem duty became less protective. Imports rose from 13,500 tons in 1847 to 142,000 in 1850; over the same period, the output from American mills fell from 41,000 to 15,000 tons. By early 1850 only two of fifteen rail mills remained at work. After that business revived, national output increased threefold between 1850 and 1856 to more than 160,000 tons, by which time the anthracite iron districts had nine working rail mills, half of the total within the northeastern states.[12]

In terms of its relative standing in the nation's iron trade, the anthracite iron industry was at its peak in the 1870s. Soon after that, it began its decline, and a few years later still it was in full retreat. In 1896, the journal *Iron Age* was in a retrospective mood when it referred to a heroic age in the Lehigh valley, the thirty-odd years from the mid-1850s into the 1880s when "furnace after furnace was erected until from Easton to Parryville the valley was a blaze of light."[13] The national tonnage of iron smelted with anthracite had passed that of charcoal iron in 1855. Already, however, for mineral supplies and markets alike the balance of advantage was visibly shifting westward, to places close to bituminous coalfields, or, more important still, coke. Many years later, Abram Hewitt recalled that it was in about 1858—at the very time the Bethlehem project was taking shape—that he had come to recognize that Phillipsburg and Trenton, New Jersey, were no longer ideal places for making and shaping iron and that it would be well to move to Pittsburgh, only to have his senior partner, Peter Cooper, refuse the support essential for such a move to take place. After 1865, variations in levels of production for anthracite iron were greater than for iron made from other mineral fuels, with tonnages shrinking more in slack periods and barely regaining the old position in succeeding years of revival.[14]

In 1873, anthracite furnaces accounted for 46 percent of the total production of iron; nine years later, their share was 40 percent. Even more decisive as evidence of decreasing competitiveness, after 1875 coke was mixed with anthracite in some furnaces. In short, considerable amounts of what was nominally anthracite iron was in fact anthracite/coke iron. By 1883, when these two classes of "anthracite" iron were first reported separately, the tonnage of anthracite and coke iron was already 95 percent as large as that made using only anthracite. In 1890, those furnaces which used either only anthracite or mixed charges produced 21 percent of the national output and by 1900, 12 percent.[15] Until 1882, the Lehigh valley was America's leading iron district. The next year it was surpassed by Allegheny County. In another five years the latter turned out 50 percent more iron than the Lehigh valley. Moreover, though in 1890 pig iron production in the Lehigh valley was higher than ever before, in output per furnace it lagged well behind districts using coke or uncoked coal. This lower productivity was an important factor in the loss of rank for the fuel and the area. The average weekly output of each of its forty furnaces in 1887 was 303 tons of iron. There were only fourteen furnaces at work in the Pittsburgh area, but each of them could make 986 tons a week. Sixteen coke furnaces in Illinois averaged 1,035

Table 1.3 Pig iron production in the Lehigh valley and Allegheny County, Pennsylvania, 1872–1900 (thousand net tons)

	Lehigh Valley	Allegheny County
1872	450	111
1878	417	217
1883	576	592
1887	723	898
1890	816	1,498
1900	611	2,770

Source: AISA, annual statistics.

tons.[16] Anthracite had given the eastern furnaces impressive advantages over charcoal furnaces, but its nature was now a major factor in the lower productivity of local furnaces compared with those using coke. High temperatures could be reached with anthracite, but it was a slow-burning and dense fuel. The hot blast had made its use possible, but its unsuitability for hard driving brought about its eventual decline. Alongside this technical limitation was a more direct cost consideration. Anthracite was in steady demand along the eastern seaboard for domestic and other heating and for various manufacturing processes, and its use in such fields was spreading more widely throughout the Northeast. As a result, the price to the ironmaster remained high in comparison to that of coke, for which there were fewer competing outlets.[17]

From the mid-1870s, coke, especially the highest grade from the Connellsville district of southwestern Pennsylvania, was used mixed with the local coal in the anthracite districts. First resorted to during strikes in anthracite mines, this mixture was found to increase furnace output and so continued to be used by some firms even when local hard coal was again available. Even so, as late as 1888, only four of seventeen iron making plants in the Lehigh valley were recorded as mixing coke with anthracite. Mixed charges were usually one-third or one-quarter coke and the remainder would be anthracite. After that, the pace of change quickened to a revolution, and by the end of the 1890s, only two of sixteen works in the valley were identified as using only anthracite.[18] Although a partial, or better still, a wholesale transfer to coke could increase furnace productivity, there were two continuing problems. First, unless new plant was installed, coke was being charged into furnaces built and equipped to use a different fuel, so that yields, though higher, were still below those in plants especially designed for coke. Second, whereas anthracite was a local fuel (or at most had to be carried short distances and then often on downhill grades on railroads running out of the coal region), coke had to be hauled from Connellsville. If procured from bituminous districts nearer at hand, the coke was of poorer quality, like the coal lands that the Lehigh Valley Railroad owned near Snow Shoe in Centre County, Pennsylvania, more than 150 miles west of Bethlehem. In 1887, when prices of coke at ovens in Connellsville ranged from $1.75 to $1.80 a ton, one eastern ironmaster considered himself satisfied if he could secure it for $4.50 delivered at lower Lehigh valley works.[19]

There were also serious problems with ore supply. The opening, development, and eventual supremacy of the upper Great Lakes ranges as sources of ore for furnaces west of the Appalachians and the massive investment in bulk transport facilities that made ores reliably available in huge and ever-expanding tonnages and at low unit costs helped highlight the inability of eastern iron manufacturers to provide anything approaching such favorable conditions. They had no access to large ore deposits suitable for direct shipping to the furnaces, the main ores used in Bethlehem furnaces being New Jersey magnetites and hematites. Some ore bodies that had sufficed in the past were now heavily depleted. By the mid-1880s, the scattered brown hematite ore bodies in the Great Valley of the Appalachians were considered so variable in mineral characteristics and geological structure as to be too difficult to mine, and over the previous fifteen or so years there had been so large a decline that "long rows of idle or abandoned ore banks are encountered."[20] Even the biggest eastern deposits were unsatisfactory. The Cornwall ore banks had been controlled by a single family, contained magnetites that were extremely low in phosphorus, and could be cheaply worked, but as the Swedish expert Richard Ackerman found in the mid-1870s, the owners were "said to be uncommonly conservative, and to prefer a high price with a limited sale to the plan otherwise common in America of working on as large a scale as possible." A decade later Cornwall produced about 700,000 tons of ore a year. There was good ore in the Lake Champlain district, but Ackerman described handling facilities at Port Henry and Crown Point, New York, as inferior to those in place on Lake Superior.[21] Technical difficulties were experienced in smelting eastern magnetites, apparently in considerable part because of their silica content. This characteristic of the ore raised the tonnage of the other minerals required as compared with that in furnaces using Great Lakes ores of lower iron content. Dwindling output of eastern ore was accompanied by a lowering of its grade. In 1900, Lake Superior mines produced 20.5 million tons of ore; the combined output of Pennsylvania, New York, and New Jersey was less than 1.7 million tons. Cornwall ore averaged 45.9 percent iron; the iron content of Minnesota's 15 million gross tons of ore produced in 1902 was 56.8 percent.[22]

As raw material supply conditions worsened, the eastern iron industry also suffered from its increasingly marginal location within the national economy. There was a large and growing market for iron within the region, but this section's share of national production and wealth was decreasing because of westward expansion. The Midwest was well on its way to becoming America's economic heartland. The great misfortune for eastern companies was that this shift in consumption was to the area best endowed to make cheap iron.

Finally, there is evidence that, faced with serious challenges, some eastern ironmasters rested on past glories. The *Bulletin of the American Iron and Steel Association (BAISA)* compared two furnaces at one Lehigh valley iron works in midsummer 1857 and midsummer 1892. At first sight, it seemed to be recording a success story. Overall costs of production, excluding standing charges, had fallen from $19.545 per ton of iron at the earlier date to $10.865 in one furnace and $9.46 in the other. This was attributed to "better selection of ores and the management of the furnaces according to the latest scientific methods," but the account continued in less flattering manner: "The furnaces which are here compared are the same furnaces in every respect at which the results were produced which are quoted in the figures for 1857. They are blown by the same power and have the same equipment in other respects."[23] No contemporary Pittsburgh ironmaster would have been able to admit, much less admit proudly, that his operation's furnaces, ancillary equipment, and blowing power were in any way comparable with those of the late 1850s or early 1860s, when that district's first blast furnaces had been brought into operation. It is clear that the example chosen by *BAISA* was not exceptional. Early in 1896, a writer for the *Engineering News* compared the Lehigh valley works he had visited in summer 1873 with the present situation. In this instance, the furnaces had been increased in size, their tops had been closed, and formerly wasted gases were used to heat the blast. As a result, fuel consumption and labor costs per ton of pig had been almost halved and the output of the furnace was more than four times that of two decades earlier. But there was "a struggle for existence and those companies without sufficient capital to modernize had been compelled to suspend operations." Even such a "uniformly prosperous" company as the Thomas Iron Company was being forced to contemplate remodeling its whole plant, for despite its previous success, "its management has been eminently conservative, and to outward appearance even 'old fogy.' But few alterations have been made in the last 20 years. Only one of the furnaces is equipped with firebrick stoves, and the modernizing of the whole plant is only begun."[24]

As late as 1880 the East accounted for 42 percent of national pig iron production; eighteen years later its share was 12 percent. Throughout the Lehigh valley there were signs of collapse. Production and enterprise were moving elsewhere. In 1854, Samuel Thomas had joined his father David and others in the establishment of the Thomas Iron Company of Hokendauqua, Pennsylvania. In the mid-1860s, he succeeded his father as president. Years later, he became interested in coal and iron ore near Birmingham, Alabama, and in 1887, he resigned as head of Thomas Iron for a time to lead the new iron project of the Pioneer Mining and Manufacturing Company of Thomas, Alabama. Although he returned to eastern Pennsylvania in the 1890s, depressed conditions and much lower prices were making for particularly difficult times in the eastern iron trade. In March 1896, the rolling mill operations of the Catasauqua Manufacturing Company at Catasauqua and Fullerton passed into receivership, and a few weeks later the large works of the Glendon Iron Company was taken over by assignees to be run in the interests of creditors. From 1890 to 1898, the number of anthracite works in the Lehigh valley decreased only by one, to sixteen, but furnace numbers fell from forty-eight to thirty-four.[25]

A wide variety of individual company histories produced this broad pattern of growth and decline in the nineteenth-century anthracite iron industry. Not one of those companies could completely escape the generally adverse drift of circumstances. Bigger or smaller operations, some well equipped and well situated, others not, managed well, indifferently, or badly; they followed their individual courses, and eventually, one by one, they were extinguished. Along the lower Lehigh River, a few miles above its confluence with the Delaware, a new iron works was established just before the outbreak of the Civil War. Exceptionally, it would evolve into something much bigger and more diverse and, outliving all its rivals in the region, would survive for almost a century and a half. What began as the small, locally sponsored Bethlehem Iron Company would become the giant, multi-plant Bethlehem Steel Corporation.

2

THE ESTABLISHMENT AND GROWTH OF IRON AND STEEL MAKING IN BETHLEHEM

THE TOWN OF BETHLEHEM, PENNSYLVANIA, was founded in 1741 by Count Zinzendorf, the leader of a group of Moravian settlers. By the mid-nineteenth century, the clearing they had made in the forest by the side of the Lehigh River had become a town of some three thousand people and a service and processing center for the surrounding agricultural area, with flour milling, brewing, tanning, saw milling, agricultural implement manufacturing, and so on. As late as spring 1852, C. H. Schwartz, traveling to Bethlehem from Doylestown, twenty miles to the south, was impressed by its unspoiled surroundings. Of the countryside south of the river he wrote, "Its richness was unsurpassed in my knowledge. The famous Saucon Valley was below me at one time, a veritable paradise."[1] In fact, well before then, bulk transport developments had begun to change the economy and character of the area. The Lehigh Canal had reached the southern edge of Bethlehem in 1829. The business expansion that followed was cut short by the panic of 1837 and then by a general depression of trade until 1844. Local reaction to these threats to the traditional way of life of the town took a form that would shape its future distribution of industry and other urban functions. In 1847, the Moravian congregation sold a tract of land to C. A. Luckenbach. In this area, extending from the Lehigh toward South Mountain, were four large farms. Soon to be known as South Bethlehem, it would receive the larger-scale, nuisance-creating activities encouraged by the new transport facilities, while the old town largely retained its dignified ways. By 1855, the Lehigh Valley Railroad had more decisively altered the spatial relationships of the town, and development soon followed.

The first important manufacturing activity was zinc smelting, which drew on local calamine deposits. It led to bigger things, both in the scale of manufacturing and, much more importantly, in methods and in the entrepreneurial qualities it brought into the area. By 1854–1855, control of zinc mining and smelting operations had been incorporated in the Pennsylvania and Lehigh Zinc Company. This firm was managed by a Philadelphian and member of the Society of Friends who had received some chemical training and, as time was to prove, possessed great abilities in marketing, finance, and industrial promotion. At this time, Joseph Wharton was in his late twenties, a prototype of the new men who would transform the economy of the nation. He would be closely involved in the development of the lower Lehigh valley for half a century. When in the panic of 1857 the zinc company was forced into receivership, Wharton leased it, reconstructed it, and made it profitable. During that year, his commitments also extended into what would become a much bigger project.

During the 1850s, iron ore was discovered in the Saucon valley. An unsuccessful attempt was made to attract a government foundry to the area. Then, on 8 April 1857, the Saucona Iron Company was incorporated to build an anthracite iron works at Bethlehem, near the ore, and also favorably situated at the junction of the Lehigh Valley Railroad and the North Pennsylvania Railroad, the latter providing a link to Philadelphia. The initial idea came from a local merchant who had leased the Saucon ore beds: Augustus Wolle, one of the main investors in the Catasauqua Ironworks seven miles farther upriver. With two other local business leaders, C. Brodhead and C. W. Rauch, he was granted a charter for the new iron company. Wharton and Asa Packer of the Lehigh Valley Railroad Company were also involved. The promoters intended to make pig iron for sale. However, it was soon clear that they had chosen an unpropitious time. The economic depression in 1857 that caused the failure of the zinc company also resulted in that year's production of anthracite iron falling 12 percent below the record level of the previous year. Output fell a further 7.5 percent in 1858. In such circumstances it proved impossible to sell sufficient stock in Saucona Iron, and the project fell into abeyance. As the iron trade recovered in 1859 and then surged on to new heights, the scheme was revived, but it now took a form different from that of the existing large iron works in the valley, a change mirrored in a new title: the Bethlehem Rolling Mills and Iron Company. Its first board, formed in June 1860, was again largely of local men, but with an admixture of regional railroad interests: Alfred Hunt of Philadelphia as president, with directors Asa Packer, who had first served the Lehigh Coal and Navigation Company and eventually was president of the Lehigh Valley Railroad, J. T. Johnston of the Central Railroad of New Jersey, John Knecht of Shimerville, and three Bethlehem men, Augustus Wolle, Charles W. Rauch, and their secretary, Charles B. Daniel.[2]

There seem to have been two reasons for adding finishing operations to the blast furnaces of the original scheme. One was to spread risks rather than be wholly dependent on sales of pig iron; the other, which gave this intention its particular shape, was the inclusion of a new promoter. Packer brought in as chief engineer and general superintendent a former civil engineer with the canal company, Robert Heysham Sayre. The LVRR had purchased rails from the Lackawanna Iron and Coal Company, but that company was associated with rival railroad interests and Sayre decided that his railroad needed a reliable alternate source of supply. He therefore pressed his fellow Bethlehem directors to install rolling mills. In spring 1861, another change of title created the Bethlehem Iron Company. Before this occurred, Sayre had made another vital contribution to Bethlehem Iron by securing for it the services of one of the outstanding men in the iron business.

After learning the trades of blacksmithing and machine work in the late 1830s, in 1846 twenty-four-year-old John Fritz worked on the construction of the new rolling mill in the iron works at Norristown. In 1849, he helped build a new iron plant and rail mill at Safe Harbor on the lower Susquehanna. Then, after a short time in a small foundry and machine shop at Catasauqua, he moved away from the anthracite iron district to western Pennsylvania, where he became general superintendent of the Johnstown works of the Cambria Iron Company, whose blast furnaces would use coke. There, in addition to molding the whole

Robert H. Sayre.
*Courtesy of the National Canal
Museum, Easton, Pennsylvania.*

of a major plant into a viable operation, he demonstrated highly inventive abilities in pioneering the three-high rolling mill, which increased efficiency and reduced costs. Yet, despite successes as plant supervisor and technological innovator, his relations with the Cambria directors were far from harmonious. The latter provided an opportunity that Sayre proved adept at exploiting to the advantage of Bethlehem Iron. In spring 1860, he visited Fritz in Johnstown. Then on 1 May Sayre wrote to him. He explained that he could quite understand how Fritz might find it difficult to leave an establishment he was so identified with, but he believed that the Bethlehem area might suit him far better, and that a move would not affect his reputation: "You say truly that a man's merit is measured by his success." They could offer great opportunities: "The establishment of a good mill at this place producing a first rate quality of rails will establish your reputation in a section of the country that is destined to be in my opinion the most populous and wealthy in this or any other state. . . . I predict a growth for it that will surprise its most sanguine citizens." He mentioned that Rauch and Daniel concurred with Fritz that they needed sufficient capital to purchase their machinery at cash prices and agreed that Fritz should have complete control: "I tell them that a rolling mill is like a man of war, it must have but one captain." Sayre ended on a persuasive note: "Hoping to have the pleasure of seeing you soon and of hearing you say that you are coming to dwell among us, I remain yours truly, Robert H. Sayre." Fritz arrived in Bethlehem on 5 July 1860, and two days later Augustus Wolle sent him the resolution made at a board meeting that day that appointed him superintendent and manager at a salary of four thousand dollars a year. In addition, on 1 July 1861 he would receive forty shares in the company and twenty more on 1 July for each of the three years after that. These shares were in exchange for his agreement to the free use of his patent for a three-high rail mill. It indicated that a vital decision had already been made that would differentiate the new Bethlehem Iron Company from its near neighbors and from the majority of those in the wider anthracite region. Wolle asked Fritz if he accepted the arrangements. He received a positive reply, and on 16 July 1860, only eleven days after Fritz arrived in the town, ground was broken for the plant that he would manage.[3]

The works of the Bethlehem Iron Company was built on the tract of land south of the Lehigh that the quiet Moravians of the old town had sold to Luckenbach thirteen years before. To ensure that their new operation would be the best possible, Sayre and Fritz visited many other eastern operations, paying particular attention to the Lackawanna rolling mill. But the outbreak of the Civil War nine months after construction began delayed work, and it was disrupted again by floods. As a result, the first blast furnace was not blown in until 4 January 1863. It marked an important new departure for the Lehigh valley as it was its first furnace to be plated in iron—a "shell furnace." The manufacture of wrought iron began on 27 July, and on Saturday, 26 September 1863, the mill rolled its first iron rails. Next year Bethlehem made 9,830 tons of pig iron, ranking it a poor eighth among Lehigh valley iron making establishments.[4] A second furnace was in operation by 1867, and a year later the company's absorption of the nearby Northampton Iron Company gave it a third one.

The Bethlehem Iron Company was soon busy supplying the railroads. Many of its outlets were either local or in eastern coastal and interior districts. For example, board minutes of 4 December 1864 recorded the sale of three hundred tons of rails to the Camden and Amboy Railroad at $130 a ton and an order for one thousand tons of fifty-seven-pound rails from the Lehigh and Mahonoy at $125.[5]

John C. Fritz c. 1900. *Courtesy of the Historic Bethlehem Partnership.*

Although its furnaces and rolling mills were of great importance in the locality, they were a small factor in the iron trade of the nation, which was already a highly competitive business. In 1864, Bethlehem's first full year of operation, there were thirty-eight rail mills in the United States, with a combined annual capacity of about 684,000 gross tons. Utilization of this capacity was low, for although at its highest level to date, rail output was only 283,000 tons. Imports accounted for 99,000 tons of rails. Not quite half of the domestically produced rails came from Pennsylvania mills: 40,000 tons from Cambria Iron, 22,000 from Lackawanna, and 20,000 from Pennsylvania Iron at Danville. The remaining 56,000 tons were supplied by a number of mills. Unfortunately, Bethlehem's figures for 1864 are not available, but the next year, an even better one, work over three summer months at its rail mill yielded 3,500 tons, which would be an annual rate of, at the most, 14,000 tons.[6] There is no evidence that over the next few years output rose appreciably above this level. By 1873, the plant's annual pig iron capacity was 30,000 tons, requiring 70,000 to 75,000 tons of coal and 70,000 tons of Pennsylvania and New Jersey hematite ore a year. Most of the iron the plant made was used in its own rolling mills, whose capacity was by now 20,000 tons and whose work force numbered seven hundred. In 1871, 1872, and 1873 (the three record years for iron rails), Bethlehem turned out an average of 18,278 tons. As a contributor to national output, it was even falling behind, one estimate (admittedly a rough one) giving it a share in 1865 of about 4.4 percent and in 1871–1873, 2.5 percent. By the early 1870s, national production was more than double the level of the mid-1860s, but the keenness of the struggle for business had increased as new capacity was built. By 1873, the United States had some fifty iron rail mills.[7] In addition to the cut and thrust between iron firms, by this time another factor was beginning to upset the trade. This disturbing element was growing competition from rails made of steel.

The Bethlehem Iron Company's delayed start in iron making, caused by the adverse reaction of investors to depressed trade and then by uncertainties at the outbreak of the Civil War, meant that by the time it was in operation the company was working with a process and a product that would soon be superseded. During 1862, while the works was still under construction, the Philadelphia merchant house of P. S. Justice handled the first imports of Bessemer steel rails, and steps were taken that would lead to their production in the United States.[8] Early that year, the engineer Alexander L. Holley traveled to Europe on behalf of Edwin Stevens, a railroad man and manufacturer who was planning to build an ironclad and wanting to learn of the latest techniques being used in Old World shipyards and armament manufacture. In his tour of industrial centers, Holley visited Sheffield, saw Henry Bessemer's steel making process in action, and was deeply impressed by its powers. During fall and winter 1863, he negotiated for its use by Griswold and Winslow at Troy, New York. Sometime during 1864, the first full year of operations in the iron plant he had just completed at Bethlehem, Fritz went to Troy to investigate its new Bessemer plant. For a time he was skeptical as to the prospects of the new process, believing America lacked the essential supplies of low-phosphorus iron ore. There were additional reasons for his caution. The rolling of steel required heavier and more powerful mills than those that were satisfactory in dealing with wrought iron and would therefore mean writing off old-style rolling mills, which at Bethlehem had been at work for a mere handful of years. Accordingly, Fritz concentrated instead on trying to improve the quality of iron rails. As with some enterprising "finished" iron makers in Britain, he gave a good deal of attention to production of an iron rail with a steel head. However, there was strong countervailing pressure. As he had done a few years before when the iron works was first planned, Robert Sayre pressed the board to make a more decisive move. The motivation for this came from his experience at the Lehigh Valley Railroad. In 1865, it imported some British steel rails. Operating experience showed they were four times as resistant to wear as iron rails. Consequently, though on grounds of the quality and durability of the product rather than by answering Fritz's doubts about the resource base for its manufacture, Sayre became optimistic about the possibilities in Bessemer rail manufacture.[9]

After further delays, but also after gaining useful experience by helping design a Bessemer plant for the Pennsylvania Railroad Company at Steelton, near Harrisburg, and visits in 1868 to Bessemer works in Britain, France, Germany, and Austria, in the fall of that year Fritz and Holley together began the installation of converters at Bethlehem. They designed a plant of four eight-ton converters, which, like other works at this early stage of the Bessemer steel industry, worked on pig iron remelted in cupola furnaces. New blooming and rail mills were purchased. The plant incorporated many new engineering features introduced by Fritz, and the quality of its product quickly gained a high reputation. In contrast to its relatively minor role in the iron rail trade, Bethlehem's new steel rail mill was immediately acknowledged as a major new factor in the trade. Long before the mill was completed, the *Pittsburgh Evening Chronicle* extolled it as "the largest in the world."[10]

As with the earlier iron plant, though in this instance for unknown reasons, construction and completion was a long drawn out process. One factor seems to have been Fritz's desire to make his new plant the most mechanically efficient of all the American Bessemer works. At last, in early fall 1873, it was ready, and Schropp, the company secretary, communicated to the American Iron and Steel Association news of the successful first blow in the converter plant on Saturday, 4 October 1873. The association's *Bulletin* duly recorded the triumph, typically using it to serve the protectionist cause: "The quality of the steel made was excellent. The whole process of conversion, from cupola to ingot, could not have been carried out more satisfactorily in every particular. This will be gratifying news to the friends of this great company and its hard-working and efficient officers. The Bethlehem Works have hitherto ranked among the very first iron

The rail trade: the Bessemer converter plant at Bethlehem c. 1875. *Harper's Weekly*, 1875.

establishments in the country, and now that their Bessemer plant is completed and in successful operation, they furnish a fresh illustration of what American energy, skill and capital are capable of accomplishing when sustained and encouraged by wise legistlation."[11] There seemed every prospect that Bethlehem would succeed in its new trade. It had a large mill, projected to have a starting capacity of one hundred tons of steel rails a day or approximately thirty-five thousand tons a year—more than double that of the largest mill yet built.[12] The high quality of this plant was suggested by a comparison. When the Edgar Thomson works was commissioned in 1875, it was said that its "rolling mill is more complete than any other, perhaps excepting that at Bethlehem." Three years later, Holley wrote that Edgar Thomson was the best rail mill in the United States, again with the exception of the Bethlehem mill, whose annual capacity was by then put at fifty thousand tons.[13] Fritz was discontented with their rails, however. His was the reaction of a perfectionist engineer. As he later recorded, his attitude was in sharp contrast to that of his directors, which was typical of a capitalist business community; for them, it was sufficient that their rails were as good as those made by others.[14]

Although the longer term prospects seemed good, Bethlehem began to make steel and steel rails at a difficult time. The rail network had been increasing rapidly; over the first five postwar years, 16,174 miles of track had been built and in the next two, 14,099 more were added.[15] Although the share of steel in the national rail system was as yet small, it was rising rapidly. Already by the end of 1869, about 110,000 tons of steel rails had been used, of which a third had been laid down that year. Only small tonnages had yet been supplied by domestic mills; steel rails came principally from Britain and to a small extent from Prussia.[16] But the Schenck Tariff Act of 1871 put a duty of $28 a ton on imported rails, and a larger share of the increasing market fell to domestic rail mills. For a time this was accompanied by rising prices, the average annual price of rails sold by the Pennsylvania Steel Company increasing from $102.50 a ton in 1871 to $112 the next year, and in the first quarter of 1873, to $120.[17] Much of the existing capacity was underused, but Bessemer works and rail mills continued to be added to the lists of producers. Reporting on 1874, the American Iron and Steel Association indicated that at the year's end, eight completed Bessemer establishments had a capacity of 250,000 net tons of steel; production that year, though the highest ever, was only 175,000 tons. Capacity in the rolling mills at these works was at least 20 percent more than their best-ever yield.[18]

The inevitable struggle for business was intensified by the onset of depression, for on 18 September 1873, the major banking house of Jay Cooke collapsed. After its long construction programs, Bethlehem was looking for a steady increase in output and good returns on its capital outlay, but instead near paralysis spread rapidly through large sections of the national economy. Indeed, the same issue of the AISA *Bulletin* that welcomed the new mill also pointed out that hard times lay ahead: "Many of the rolling mills and furnaces throughout the country have suspended work because of the difficulty of making sales and others are preparing to do so. Rail mills especially have but little encouragement to keep running. In very many cases manufacturers of iron are heroically endeavoring to tide over the crisis and the winter by decreasing the cost of manufacture through a reduction of wages, preferring this course, for the sake of their workmen, to putting out their fires."[19] This crisis began a long depression through which, though domestic steel rail output still increased year to year, prices fell sharply, again, year after year. There was also another, associated problem. Although it came into production as conditions worsened, the Bethlehem mill had been installed in a time of high prosperity, which had pushed up capital costs. In contrast, mills brought in a year or so later benefited from reduced overheads because they had been built under depression prices. A leading instance was the Edgar Thomson works in Pittsburgh, constructed between 1873 and 1875. A conservative estimate put its cost at three-quarters what would have been required two or three years earlier.[20] Making the Bethlehem situation even worse, as the new plant was put up, an only partially amortized iron rail mill was largely abandoned.

In terms of railroad extensions, the long depression of the mid-1870s was a rather barren time, a challenging environment for the flowering of the domestic steel rail business. For the five years from 1873 to 1877, not quite two hundred more miles of railroad were built than in the two years of 1871 and 1872. Though they had to cope with falling prices, the rail mills were sheltered from the worst effects of the slowdown in construction by two other changes of the times: a rapid shrinkage in the output of iron rails and, because of the tariff, a spectacular decline, indeed near annihilation, of steel rail imports. Even so, in part because it was distant from main areas of railroad construction, now occurring more and more in the West, Bethlehem suffered badly. Mills in Cleveland, Pittsburgh, or Chicago were well placed to serve the Midwest market; the unquestioned center for serving outlets in the West was Chicago, whose mills by 1875 rolled about 29 percent of the Bessemer rails produced.[21] In supplying rails to the Pacific seaboard, eastern mills again came into their own. Major shifts in the center of production were also under way. In rails of all kinds, iron as well as steel, the share of output from rolling mills in New England, New York, New Jersey, and Maryland mills fell between 1871 and 1879, from 23.3 to 8.4 percent; for Ohio, Indiana, and Illinois, the respective shares rose from 23.2 to 36.4 percent.

From the outset of the panic of 1873, amid fast-changing levels of production and consumption and competing locations for manufacture, Bethlehem made its way. Because of difficult trading conditions, its first Bessemer blow on 4 October 1873 was not immediately followed by commissioning of the rail mill. In fact, it was not at work until March 1874, and in its first three or four months of operation, it made only 1,676 tons of rails though its annual capacity was 30,000 to 35,000 tons. By October, steel rails were selling at prices as low as those that only two years before were being asked for good iron rails. In the year prior to June 1875, it made no more than 13,440 tons of rails. By 1877, rail mill capacity was put at 50,000 tons, but average output from 1876 to 1878 was only 35,000 tons. The price trend was strongly downward. The company did benefit from close connections with some regional railroad companies. In the month the mill started work, it received an order from the Central Railroad of New Jersey, and that fall the Lehigh Valley Railroad contracted to buy 6,000 tons of rails at eighty dollars a ton. Next year the Southern Pacific Railroad contracted for 15,000 tons of rails from Pennsylvania Steel and Bethlehem Steel, but these had to be delivered by the long, costly, and uncertain haul around Cape Horn.[22]

Reports to the Bethlehem board vividly convey the distressed state of its trade. In June 1875, reporting on the first full year of their steel plant and rail mill, Alfred Hunt gave this summary: "The past year has been one of generally unprecedented dullness and depression from which our special interests have suffered, more perhaps than their share." For the next decades, that last phrase became a leitmotif of Bethlehem Iron experience. After another year—one in which national rail output doubled—Hunt reported things had been better, but prices had fallen all the time and if things continued along the same lines, they would have to close the works. Next year his tone was even more somber. Since the last meeting, "there has not been even a temporary improvement in our business, as prices have steadily declined, and the same may be said of the demand for our products—with no present prospect of an early improvement." Dull and unprofitable trading, with little demand for rails, continued in the first seven months of the next fiscal year. Inevitably, times were hard times for their investors. Between 1869 and 1873, as it carried the cost of building the new plant, Bethlehem had paid only stock dividends. From 1873 to 1879, neither stock nor cash dividends were declared, operations being conducted at a loss. Adding to the burden, in 1874, a $1 million bonded debt was created, and three years later more bonds, valued at $278,000, were issued.[23]

Other firms were suffering, too, especially if they hung on too long to iron rails. When the Lackawanna Iron and Coal Company decided to suspend puddled iron operations in mid-May 1874, its yards were crowded with thousands of tons of iron rails for which it could find no buyers. Next, it too began to make Bessemer rails. Steel rail makers were often in serious trouble. In spring 1874, the Troy steel works and mills laid off its work force for some four months. Both Lackawanna and Troy shared Bethlehem's disadvantage of remoteness

Table 2.1 Prices secured for sales of Bessemer rails by Bethlehem Iron, 1874, 1875, and 1877

Year (autumn)	Amount/type of rails	Price ($/ton)
1874	3,000 tons of 66-pound rails (sold to LVRR)	80
1875	62.5- to 66-pound rails (small lots)	70–72
1877	2,000 tons of rails (weight unspecified)	41

Source: Bethlehem Iron Company minute books.

from the areas of most active railroad construction, but the experience at the intrinsically much better placed Joliet Iron and Steel Company and the Vulcan Steel Company of St. Louis seemed to show that success or failure owed more to quality of management than to location. Joliet began to make Bessemer rails in 1873, failed and stopped in 1874, and tried and failed a second time, after making investments totaling $3.7 million. By 1879, when it was sold and began at last to be successful, its original capital had been lost. Vulcan first made steel in 1875, failed soon afterward, ceased production, was revived, and for a long time made serious losses.[24]

Bethlehem's managers tackled their difficulties by emphasizing quality and efficient methods, raising productivity, and attempting to cut costs. As always, Fritz stood out for quality, so much so that at one time even the billets rolled as an alternative product on the rail mill sold at a premium of some four dollars a ton above prices obtained by most other makers.[25] To reduce unit costs, it was essential to increase plant output, and here too there were important successes, as when, on the last night of 1875, one converter turned out what was believed to be the largest heat of steel to date in the United States. The efficiency of Bethlehem operations received warm endorsement in the second half of the 1870s from Andrew Carnegie, though it is not clear how much weight should be given to his words. After a visit, he wrote to thank Fritz for his hospitality and asked for more information about costs: "Nothing during our trip surprised me more than the low cost at which you could handle ores per ton of metal. . . . I might say that everything I saw tended to convince me that, on the Darwinian principle of the survival of the fittest, you have no reason to fear the future."[26] Unfortunately, such a sanguine prediction proved too rosy. The steel operations of the man who made them were a leading cause of the inaccuracy of Carnegie's prediction.

For three years, from late 1874 onward, the prices received for the rails sold by Bethlehem Iron dropped by roughly half, but given the company's circumstances, it was not easy to make comparable cost reductions. One major expense was for purchase of low-phosphorus ores or, alternatively, for iron made from such ores. By 1878, the company operated eleven ironstone mines, in eastern Pennsylvania and New Jersey and extending as far as Staten Island. High-grade ores were imported from North Africa and Spain. A year before it began to produce steel, Bethlehem was also importing considerable tonnages of good-quality pig iron from Britain, in September and October 1872 buying at least 4,500 tons of Bessemer pig from the North West Coast district for between $55.85 and $57.87 a ton delivered in Philadelphia. Rail prices in 1873 left more than enough margin to cover such costly supplies, but the next year's rail price was almost 22 percent lower. By 1879, the price was only 40 percent of the 1873 figure, but the company was still buying Bessemer pig iron, some of it from distant suppliers. In five weeks in late 1879, two-thirds of the 9,140 tons purchased was from English works.[27] Remedying such difficulties would involve searching out other suitable ores within the eastern region and outlay for more blast furnace capacity.

A necessity for more capital spending was a recurrent theme at board meetings. By summer 1877, with rail prices falling sharply (though, as subsequent figures showed, demand was in fact strengthening), it was recognized that more outlay was vital for survival: "Supposing the Company to continue operations, receiving cash for sales as fast as expenses accrue, $200 to $250 thousand would seem sufficient to put the Company into a reasonably comfortable position, but with little or no reserve resources." Nine months later, as things began to look up, the board was gently prepared for continuing calls for money:

> It is not possible, in these times of rapid changes of view as to the superiority of steel over iron for many uses, and the constant demand made for new sizes and shapes in steel, to say when we will be able to cease expenditures for new work, but it will be the aim of the management to make the absolutely necessary improvements from time to time, in such manner as not to embarrass the financial position of the company. In this period of low prices for our product every advantage must be taken of improved machinery and appliances for economizing our work.[28]

As the works expanded and became more complex, it proved difficult to maintain a well-rounded operation. For example, by spring 1879 their annual consumption of pig iron was estimated to exceed production by about 13,000 to 14,000 tons, and the shortfall was expected to double as a result of improvements then being made to the steel plant. Accordingly, that summer, when all products were reported as being in "good demand"—though at prices of which all that could be claimed was "it is believed [they] will afford a slight margin of profit"—they purchased the Northampton furnace and a furnace at Bingen, formerly operated by the North Run Iron Company.[29] Late in 1881, Holley noted that Bethlehem had installed much new equipment since his account of the works in 1877, even including a new Bessemer plant with a capacity of 3,000 tons a week. In fact, from 1877 to 1882, annual Bessemer bloom and rail capacity increased from 50,000 to 135,000 tons.[30]

At last economic revival began. National rail output in 1878 was at least 100,000 tons more than in 1877, and the next year there was a larger increase. Prices strengthened after five years of steady decline. Bethlehem figures are not directly comparable with national ones because its fiscal and production year ended in June, but at 71,000 tons in 1879, output of rails was almost 88 percent more than in 1878. Despite the fears the board had entertained, the company had survived. In 1875, its first full year of operation, Bethlehem had made 5.2 percent of the nation's steel rails; in 1879, its share was 11.5 percent. Over the year and a half to mid-1879, the value of its stock advanced from fifteen to forty-five dollars a share.[31] What was now needed was a period of sustained high operating rates to cover the large capital outlays already made. Unfortunately, after a promising start, the business environment of the 1880s would prove no more congenial than that of the 1870s.

Bethlehem Iron shared many of the problems of the other anthracite iron companies, but it had a better balanced operation. By 1890, all other iron making firms in the Lehigh valley had a rated iron capacity of some 735,000 tons but combined rolling mill capacities of only 104,000 tons; at Bethlehem, the respective figures were 160,000 and 285,000 tons.[32] As an integrated operation it escaped reliance on the uncertain outlets for pig iron and had more valuable products to sell. These advantages were counterbalanced by dependence on a more limited choice of raw materials and by the fact that, whereas eastern iron makers competed with merchant iron works on the Great Lakes and in the South, Bethlehem was engaged in a ruthless struggle for business with Bessemer steel makers and rail mills west of the Appalachians, rivals nearer to superior ore and fuel supplies as well as to the main areas of new railroad construction. The company was fortunate to have access to Lehigh Valley Railroad capital.

In the early 1870s, coke furnaces in western Pennsylvania and Ohio could make about double the amount of iron turned out by similar sized furnaces in eastern Pennsylvania. By increasing the pressure of the blast, Fritz managed to make Bethlehem furnaces equal the tonnages produced by western furnaces using low-pressure blast. However, some western ironmasters responded by raising blast pressures at their own furnaces, and given the raw materials with which he was working, Fritz could not follow suit.[33] Holley, who thought highly of Bethlehem, recognized its mineral supply problems. In the mid-1870s, it was using anthracite from mines in the upper parts of the Lehigh valley, but "it cannot be claimed for anthracite that as a smelting fuel it is equal to coke, for the reason that coke is a more porous fuel, and burns more freely, and sustains its burden better than anthracite, which is compact and liable to splinter."[34] The obvious way of escaping this limitation was to use some coke, or perhaps make a wholesale switch to it, but the Bethlehem furnaces and ancillary equipment had been designed for anthracite. Freight charges on coke would always be a burden. Bethlehem's ore supply problems proved even more intractable than those for fuel supply.

By embarking on steel making, Bethlehem took on a heavier burden in organizing its ore supply than those eastern firms that remained makers of pig iron or, on a much smaller scale, were involved in rolling finished iron. From the time of Fritz's visit to Troy to inspect the experimental plant installed there in 1864–1865 to the decision in fall 1868 to go ahead with steel making, and even apparently in the early period of operations, he had serious doubts as to their command of adequate sources of the low-phosphorus ores needed in the Bessemer process.[35] When Holley and Smith visited Bethlehem a few years later, they found that the local hematites with the lowest phosphorus content were about fifteen miles from the plant. Overall about one-eighth of the furnace charge was made up of hematites procured from within four to twenty miles of the works; another eighth (sometimes up to three-eighths) was brown hematite hauled seventy-five miles from Staten Island. The Cornwall ore banks, fifty miles from the furnaces, provided up to half the charge. Magnetite was brought in an average distance of sixty miles from New Jersey and also from the mines of the Crown Point Iron Company in the Lake Champlain district, a three-hundred-mile journey, mostly by water, but ending with a sixty-mile rail haul inland from Perth Amboy. When ice closed the navigation, the ore had to be hauled by rail all the way. Rather optimistically, Holley and Smith added,

"The ores of Lake Superior may also be delivered at Bethlehem at low cost via the Lakes to Buffalo, New York, and thence over the Erie Railway and Lehigh Valley Railroad."[36] Bethlehem Iron made its ore supply situation worse by failing to organize it effectively. Fritz recalled that the Cornwall ore was good, but they had lost the chance to make long-term contracts for it at favorable prices, preferring instead to purchase in dribs and drabs. Other companies bought their way into this huge reserve to Bethlehem's disadvantage. Similarly, they let slip an opportunity to develop the Tilly Foster mines in the Hudson valley, which a few years later were being developed to supply the Lackawanna works. Eventually, Fritz felt forced to recommend that his company move into higher grade products because "I could plainly see the end of the acid Bessemer process everywhere, and especially with us, as the company had let every ore property that was available and suitable for the Bessemer process pass beyond their control, and the end was in sight."[37] Before they reached that extreme situation and point of choice, they had also been trounced by the competition in steel finishing operations and marketing.

3

FAILURE IN
COMMERCIAL STEELS,
1880–1899

BETWEEN 1880 AND 1899, the national rail network almost doubled, from 92,100 to 163,500 miles. Of this increase, 73 percent occurred in the 1880s. At the beginning of this period, 29 percent of the mileage was laid with rails made from steel; by 1890, the figure was already 80 percent.[1] Supply was now dominated by domestic producers. Rail imports were 259,000 tons in 1880; ten years after that, no rails were brought in, and in 1899, imports were only 2,000 tons. Domestic output at the three dates was 860,000, 1.87 million, and 2.27 million tons. Demand increased, but the struggle between producers became ever keener. The competition between highly capitalized firms, each seeking to "run full" in their mills, depressed prices. At the end of this period, E. C. Potter of the Illinois Steel Company highlighted the problems of costly plant and an ever lower priced product: "The rail is today the cheapest finished product in the whole domain of iron and steel manufacture, and is at the same time the most difficult to make. It requires an expenditure of at least $3 million before a single rail can

Table 3.1 Average annual prices for Bessemer rails at Pennsylvania works by five-year periods, 1880–1899 (dollars per ton)	
1880–1884	49.13
1885–1889	31.83
1890–1894	28.76
1895–1899	23.36

Source: AISA, annual statistics.

be economically turned out." A few years earlier, a Pittsburgh source put expenses even higher, claiming that to build and fully equip a good rail mill might cost as much as $8 million to $10 million and that the Edgar Thomson (ET) and the South Chicago works represented outlays on that scale.[2]

Making conditions less certain, outlays for railroad extensions were particularly sensitive to the trade cycle. The aftermath of the financial panic of 1893 illustrated this well. In 1893, 3,024 miles of new track were built; the next year's figure was 1,760. By mid-1894, more than 190 railroads, operating more than 40,000 miles of track, had failed.[3] General overcapacity, increasing competition, and wide variations in levels of consumption resulted in volatile prices, but their long-term trend was downward. To survive and still more to prosper in such conditions, a producer had to control good mineral resources, have favorable access to markets, and above all operate with first-rate management determined to succeed. Bethlehem proved lacking on both the material and the human accounts.

The westward trend in rail consumption was now more pronounced than ever. A snapshot from a time of high activity in construction brings this out vividly. In October 1882, 1,068 miles of new road was completed. Of this, 892 miles lay west of a line from Lake Erie and then down the Ohio River and along the Mississippi to the Gulf of Mexico; only 176 miles was east of that line.[4] There was also a rapid transfer in the balance of advantage in access to the raw materials. As late as 1880, New York, New Jersey, and Pennsylvania mined 52.7 percent of the merchantable iron ore produced in the United States; by 1890, they accounted for 19.4 percent and ten years later, 6.0 percent. Iron made using coke or raw bituminous coal as fuel already amounted to 45 percent of the total in 1880; that share advanced to 69 percent by 1890 and was 85 percent in 1900. Bethlehem Iron, like other eastern iron makers, could and did obtain both Great Lakes ore and Connellsville coke, but hauls on both were longer than those in the Great Lakes–Ohio River belt, now becoming the core area for the industry. Delivery of Great Lakes ore to Bethlehem involved a longer journey, across Lake Erie and a rail haul from Buffalo at least twice the distance from Lake Erie ports to Pittsburgh. Less than 40 miles separated rail mills in the Monongahela valley from first-rate coke in Connellsville; Bethlehem had to pay for carriage over 240 miles. In 1887, coke that was $1.75 per ton at ovens in Connellsville cost about $4.50 delivered to Bethlehem.[5] Adding to such unavoidable difficulties, Bethlehem failed to acquire and exploit its own large mineral holdings in the way successful companies in the western part of the manufacturing belt had done.

In the rail business, Bethlehem Iron for a time managed to hold its own, in both 1880 and 1890 making 8.9 percent of the national tonnage, but production then fell off sharply. Bethlehem was not alone in falling behind; during the 1890s the share of rails coming from eastern Pennsylvania fell more sharply than that from other sections of the state. In Pittsburgh, the challenge of worsening circumstances was being much more purposefully tackled. Replacement of puddled iron by steel, fuel economy in smelting, and westward movement in economic development had made the old characterization of that district as "the gateway to the West" an anachronism. Yet through the 1880s, the drive to modernize operations at the ET works was unceasing, involving numerous small-scale improvements and occasional bigger steps. In the early 1880s, a small change in the metal used in ingot molds cut the cost of steel by forty-five cents a ton. Molten iron was first used in the Bessemer plant in 1883. Five years later "Captain" William R. Jones was instructed to build a new rail mill on which no expense should be spared to make it the best possible.[6] Equally important, the Carnegie companies spared no effort to push their trade. As a result, the ET works, described a few years before as comparable with Bethlehem in occupying the front rank, drew ahead, eventually also outperforming Chicago mills, which had the advantages of an increasingly favorable location for iron manufacture and a prime position in supplying the rail network. In short, sustained efforts at ET overturned any burdens imposed by location. At Bethlehem, disadvantages were certainly greater, but more importantly, the efforts were fewer. The board minutes reveal the difficult process of adjustment.

In the year to June 1880, things seemed to be going well. Prices had risen, output was at record levels, and the works was fully employed. Although the company had lost money over the first six years of the steel works, by 1879–1880, the directors at last felt able to pay a 6 percent dividend. As they put it, "This result may we trust be considered as satisfactory for the present and as an earnest of future prosperity."[7] Over the next year the works again had full employment and prices, though a shade lower, remained remunerative. In 1881–1882, $119,269 was spent on the Bessemer plant to reduce costs and improve quality, but an even larger sum was reserved in anticipation of possible outlays for entry into fields other than rail manufacture that would use Bessemer steel.[8] The rail mill was stopped in December 1882 for repairs and to compound its engines, so as to add to its power and capacity. In this operating year, the collapse in imports left the market almost entirely to domestic mills, but demand fell, which "has caused keen competition with constantly declining prices."[9] A year later, output had fallen only slightly, but the presidential remarks of Alfred Hunt were pessimistic: "The intimation as to keen competition and declining prices in our report of last year has been fully confirmed by the events of the past 12 months, while the outlook for the coming year is anything but favorable and gives little promise that we will be able to keep the works in full operation."[10]

The report of June 1885 was fuller and more explicit. It acknowledged that the company was unlikely to survive long as a major player: "As foreshadowed to you in our last Annual Report, the ability to manufacture steel rails is so much in excess of the wants of the country that the prices at which they have been sold have not covered their cost of production. A number of steel rail mills have been cold most of the past year, while ours have continued in full operation, with the results which have just been stated." They had decided to operate even at a loss in order not to break up the organization and to avoid disaster to the community, but the prospects looked little if any better: "We can see no immediate relief from severe and trying competition unless we are able to produce rails considerably cheaper than our competitors, which is hardly likely to be expected." Even so, they had almost completed a new heavy rail mill that would enable them to cut costs and also "to put steel in other merchantable forms." They hoped the new mill and other improvements might enable them "to cheapen somewhat our cost of production and possibly to secure a moderate profit on our business," but the report finished with fears that others might have similar ideas for cost reduction.[11] Commenting, the *Bethlehem Times* was shocked by what it saw as an unexpected turn of events: "There is a disappointment to us in this report, because it had been the general impression that in location, in superior machinery, and in other facilities the Bethlehem Iron Company could meet its competitors and would have a small margin left."[12]

For many years longer, the company struggled to stay in the rail trade. In August 1885, at its suggestion, representatives of twelve Bessemer rail makers met to consider limiting output. With three other companies, Bethlehem was allocated 12 percent of the restricted output, the largest share. Orrin Potter of the North Chicago Rolling Mill Company, Luther Bent of Pennsylvania Steel, and Garrett Linderman from Bethlehem constituted the board of control for this rail pool. By early November that year, Bethlehem had sold less than half its allotment.[13] Moderate profits were made in the year to June 1887, but next year the performance was less good in terms of output and profits and in 1888–1889, a "falling off of our products in all departments" was reported as rail prices fell throughout the year. The rail and merchant mills were idle for about a quarter of the time. Wages were cut 8 percent in July 1888. What had become a substantial industrial operation was now threatened. The plant had an annual capacity for 160,000 tons of iron, 225,000 tons of Bessemer steel, and 250,000 tons of rails, billets, and blooms, and in normal times it provided work for about three thousand men.[14]

Through the 1890s, rail consumption and prices would continue to oscillate sharply and Bethlehem's position to deteriorate. It tried pioneering. In 1891, when orders were scarce and prices well below those of the previous year, it rolled for the Boston and Albany subsidiary of the New York Central Railroad ten thousand tons of the heaviest steel rails yet made in the United States. They were made from higher carbon and therefore harder steel than usual.[15] But all the company's efforts to break out of its difficulties failed. In the sharp depression of 1892–1893, prices fell only slightly, but the rail mill was idle for 90 days. The next year prices were sharply lower, the average price being $3.40 a ton below that of the previous year, and the mill worked only 126 days. As the directors put it, the general depression in the national economy was "well reflected" in their own figures.[16] To some it began to seem that the time might be ripe for a takeover of the company. In December 1893, Andrew Carnegie received an interesting letter from F. W. Leinbach, president of the Consolidated SOS Bay Company: "Dear Sir, would you buy the stock of The Bethlehem Iron Company of Bethlehem, Pa in any considerable amounts? If so, I believe I can be of service to you. I reside in Bethlehem, but am engaged in business in New York. I would be pleased to have an interview with you at your convenience if you desired."[17] There is no record of a reply, but in any case, Carnegie was already convinced there was no future in bulk steel for the East. Now and again things looked up, as in 1894–1895, when, though the price obtained was down by another $3.00, business volume rose and the rail mill was at work for 167 days. The next year prices went up, a good deal of work was done to make further economies in rail manufacture, and the mill operated for 223 days—and spent another 105 days rolling billets.[18]

After that brief recovery, conditions again worsened. The operating year 1896–1897 was one of "great and continued depression." In December 1896, the price of rails was cut from twenty-eight to twenty-five dollars a ton. Less than two months later, there was a far more disruptive event: the "sudden and entirely unexpected" withdrawal from the Steel Rail Association of the Lackawanna Iron and Steel Company, which caused the failure of the association and, in less than a week, a price collapse to seventeen dollars a ton. In 1897, Bethlehem turned out rails on only 47 days and rolled billets for 194 days. Wages were reduced 10 percent at the beginning of March 1897. The next year was even worse. The nominal annual capacity of the Bethlehem mill was now said to be 205,000 tons, but it made only 25,006 tons of rails. Prices were so low that the company could only afford to complete old contracts or roll for the Lehigh Valley Railroad. Hope was expressed that if rail prices advanced and they could get their materials cheaper, "it will be possible to again operate this department to advantage." But in 1898–1899, the Bessemer department was idle for eleven months.[19] As a maker of rails, Bethlehem had to face the fact its career was at an end.

In the late nineteenth century, it was clear to all thinking people that railroads had played a key part in the transformation of the commercial world, but a few individuals recognized that the greatest years of expansion might have passed. In a review in 1902, the New York financier John Greenhough marveled at the fact that the tonnage handled by American railroads had increased between 1870 and 1898 from 72.5 million tons to 975 million tons. The editor of the *Railroad Gazette,* Colonel Henry Prout, after acknowledging that railroads had "immeasurably" widened the spheres both of procurement and marketing, concluded with a simple but thought-provoking statement: "They have made modern society possible." But he pointed out that rates of extension were slowing and that this might have major implications: "Probably the railways built in the United States in the four years ending in 1883 cost at least $1,000,000,000 more than those built in the four years ending 1898. The release of this vast capital for other uses must affect profoundly the industries and commerce of the civilized world."[20] Neither Prout nor any other contemporary could foresee another sharp revival of construction that, in its three years of greatest activity

(1902, 1903, and 1906), would add 17,200 miles to the system. For those who stayed in the trade, beset with excess capacity, the keenest of competition, and low prices, a hard struggle for business would continue. In such circumstances, marginal producers would look for ways of reducing their costs and/or try to find alternative, less ruthlessly competitive lines of production.

Eastern firms reacted in various ways to these worsening circumstances. Beginning in the late 1880s with plans for an iron making plant, Pennsylvania Steel over the next few years instead built a completely integrated new works to produce rails on the shore of Chesapeake Bay at Sparrows Point, Maryland. It was excellently placed for access to foreign ores and to foreign and coastal markets. Even so, through the mid- and late 1890s, Pennsylvania Steel's performance was poor. A different approach was adopted by the Lackawanna Iron and Steel Company. After suffering badly in the free-for-all that followed the breakdown of the rail combination, it decided to move toward Great Lakes ore, relocating from Scranton to a virgin site near Buffalo. In the year that this intention was announced, Bethlehem's rail mill was idle. Long before, it had begun to search for alternative products.

One of the important advances in the use of steel in the late nineteenth century was its application to construction. Wrought iron proved an unreliable building material; mild steel was stronger and more uniform in quality throughout each piece. On railroads and in cities, steel bridges began to replace those made from wood or iron. Beginning in about 1883, the availability of cheap structural steel meant that it became common to use a metal frame for the entire construction of multi-storied buildings. The word "skyscraper" was coming into use, though it was then applied to buildings rising to no more than ten to twenty stories. The main columns of these buildings were made up of riveted bars, channels, angles, and plates, but there was also considerable use of I-beams. The early record is very fragmentary as compared with that for rails, but between 1878 and 1889, output of structural iron and steel shapes seems to have increased twofold. After 1892, the first year from which there is a continuous record, there was further rapid advance. In 1900, rail output was 54 percent greater than in 1892, but production of structurals had increased 79 percent. Bridge building was widely scattered, but the market for beams in high-rise buildings was concentrated in the downtown areas of the biggest cities, where land values were rapidly increasing. The first skyscrapers were in Chicago, but mid-Atlantic seaboard cities soon became the main centers for this type of construction. It was evident that the East was suitable for this trade. A structural steel agreement in 1897 involved nine firms, four of them eastern, being located at Passaic, New Jersey, and at Pencoyd, Phoenixville, and Pottsville, Pennsylvania. Together the four eastern firms received one-quarter of the sales tonnages allocated that year.[21] On more than one occasion, Bethlehem Iron considered entering the structural steel business.

As early as the extremely difficult trading years in the late 1870s, it was suggested that the company should make structural shapes. Fritz urged this on his directors, but they refused to take the opportunity, except for making small beams and channels. He later considered this the biggest mistake made by his former employers, but his assessment may in part have been colored by subsequent experience at Bethlehem. In summer 1886, Bethlehem installed a new mill to roll heavy sections in long lengths, and this installation included provision for rolling structural steel as well as rails.[22] More than a decade later, there was some correspondence with Fritz (who had by this time severed his connection with Bethlehem Iron) about structural steel. It is particularly interesting in the light of what was to happen a few years later and as a result of the initiative of others. At the end of December 1897, Henry Grey wrote to Fritz from the Ironton Structural Steel Company, sending him plans for the general arrangement of beam mills—mills having vertical rolls for working the outside of the flanges, in other words, a universal mill. Grey's letter ended, "The size of the train would control the size beam to be made, but I think it would be easy to roll up to 36 or 40 inches with 12 inch and maybe 15 inch flanges, supposing the mill to be built heavy enough." Less than three weeks later, the Union Bridge Company of New York wrote to say that they were sorry not to have been able to talk more with Fritz "about the matter of structural material and its manufacture at Bethlehem."[23] Apart from the puzzling reference to Bethlehem, it seems that both correspondents were reacting to a Fritz interest in what might have been the world's first successful Grey mill.

Another important product for which the East offered not only large but rapidly increasing outlets was plate. Steel plates were used in making built-up beams in general engineering and in shipbuilding. In the mid-nineteenth century, the United States had been both a major shipping and shipbuilding nation, but the operation and output of ships fell off drastically after that. On the eve of the Civil War, America's merchant navy was about 15 percent bigger than that of Great Britain; by 1896, it was only 46 percent as large. Decade after decade, average annual launchings of ships declined, from 366,000 tons in the 1850s to 219,000 tons in the 1880s. By 1900, total U.S. commercial construction was then just over one-fifth as large as that of Great Britain and its empire. In naval terms, it also lagged far behind; in 1890, U.S. ironclad tonnages were 40,000 versus 460,000 for the British.[24] However, in the next few years work began on a new navy, and merchant shipbuilding also increased. A large proportion of the shipyards were on the mid-Atlantic coast. Although a considerable share of the new tonnage was of wood (compared to new ships in Europe), this belatedly expanding shipbuilding industry also consumed large tonnages of steel plate and angles. Outside the Lehigh valley, southeastern Pennsylvania in 1901 contained thirty-six works that had rolling mills. None of them had standard Bessemer plants; they instead depended either on purchased steel or had open hearth furnaces, both acid and basic. Industry authority Harry Campbell computed steel output in this area as 629,000 tons.[25] Plate was an important part of the finished output. Established as early as 1810, the Lukens venture at Coatesville produced steel from 1881 and eleven years later built a universal plate mill. Other examples were the Alan Wood operation at Conshohocken, which had a small output of light plate and sheet, and Chester, where there was a small integrated works rolling plate and angles. Some shipbuilders made efforts to improve their own position by encouraging iron and steel manufacture. As early as the 1870s, the Delaware River Iron Shipbuilding and Machine Works had been one of the two firms that founded the Chester Rolling Mill Company, and shipbuilder Charles Cramp told the U.S. Industrial Commission in 1901 that he had tried, without success, to establish commercial links with steel makers. One of the companies he approached was Bethlehem, and indeed, they did a considerable amount of business with the Cramp shipyard in the 1890s.[26] In plate manufacture, Bethlehem advanced much further than it had with structurals, but having ventured, it then drew back.

When the depressed conditions of 1893–1894 deepened despondency about the future of the rail trade, Bethlehem management decided to evaluate the strength of the opposition and consider whether it could provide any guidance out of their own predicament. During early autumn 1894, the general manager and Fritz's successor as chief engineer traveled to Pittsburgh to visit various rolling mills. After paying particular attention to the Carnegie Steel plate, beam, rail, and billet mills, they reported that what they had seen "demonstrated that this company was unable to compete successfully for rails, billets, and general output with modern-built mills and appliances." In a positive response to this dismal conclusion, the general manager asked his directors for an outlay on plant amounting to a total of $1.5 million. Well over two-thirds of this was to be spent equipping their works to serve the shipbuilding industry. Central to the program was entry into large-scale production of steel plate.

Expenditures approved in fall 1894 included $812,025 for a complete plate mill and new open hearth furnaces, slabbing mill, and related production infrastructure and $243,300 for improvements to the Bessemer plant and modifications to enable the rail mill to roll deck beams and angles. A few weeks later Charles M. Schwab reported to colleagues at Carnegie Steel that Bethlehem's intention was "to make an extensive and modern plant for all sort of plate."[27] Less than three months after resolving to go ahead with the improvements, Bethlehem contracted with the plant and equipment makers Mackintosh, Hemphill of Pittsburgh for a thirty-two-inch slabbing mill, thirty-four-inch plate mill, and twenty-six-inch universal mill.[28] Completed in 1897, the new mills had an annual capacity of some 90,000 tons and were recognized as of high quality, the trade press reporting them as representing "the first step in a comprehensive plan for the production of merchant material."[29] Yet, notwithstanding a promising start, early operating experience was disappointing, and in spite of its newness and quality, for most of the year to June 1898, the Bethlehem mill was idle. In fifty-seven days of operation it rolled only 3,490 tons of plate. Less than eighteen months after its completion, the board concluded that their venture had been less than satisfactory, reporting that "in some ways it was defective, or rather that it was not properly balanced to secure the greatest economy in operation." Accordingly, the plant was provided with new heating furnaces and an extension of the table for the shears. The stacks of the four open hearth furnaces were raised and a charging machine provided.[30]

Even this further outlay failed to prevent the project coming to a speedy and rather humiliating end. At the beginning of 1898, the Carnegie Steel Company was considering installing a universal plate mill at Homestead. Senior officers at Carnegie observed that consumption, already large, was being increased further by the requirements of the growing manufacture of steel rail cars. They reckoned that $2 more per ton could be obtained for universal than for sheared plate. Homestead's superintendent, William E. Corey, and the engineer P. T. Berg were sent to look over various universal plate mills in the East.[31] Early in January 1899, the Carnegie managers approved the purchase of the Bethlehem plate plant—a slabbing mill, by now a 120-inch plate and a 42-inch universal plate mill, two large cranes, smaller cranes, engines, charging machinery, and so forth.

Completing its humiliation, Bethlehem was to dismantle, load, and ship the plant at no cost to Carnegie Steel. The purchase price was $500,000, well under two-thirds of the initial cost as projected little more than four years before.[32]

Charles M. Schwab, Carnegie Steel's president, anticipated that through 1899 the newly acquired plate mills would increase Homestead profits by $675,000, almost a quarter of the increase expected that year for this large, diverse, and commercially successful works.[33] In striking contrast to these upbeat assessments, Bethlehem's own record of the sale stressed that the experience had caused them to conclude "that there was little if any money to be made by operating a Plate Mill in the East in ordinary times." Accordingly, as the buildings housing the mill and the melting shop could be used for other purposes, they had accepted the Carnegie offer. Within two years Homestead was producing thirty-six thousand tons of plate a month, and an experienced outsider considered its plate mill the finest of its kind in the United States.[34] Carnegie Steel had important outlets near at hand, but the company had already found it profitable to sell plate to British shipyards. Domestic shipbuilding, of which so large a part was concentrated in the near hinterland of Bethlehem, was at last starting to grow more rapidly.

Why then did Bethlehem fail where Carnegie Steel recognized and achieved success? Undoubtedly, it was not because of any deficiency in the plant, for as one Carnegie partner commented, "I have never seen mills not in active operation in as good condition as these appear to be." Nor does there seem to have been any inherent cause for the financial failure of the venture. As with rails and structurals, it seems undeniable that there had been a serious failure of nerve at Bethlehem. Fritz later noted simply that the plate mill had come too late and that the directors would not take it up fully, but his comment ignored the large outlay they had committed to it. There were two other considerations of some significance, one at least in part explaining Bethlehem's failure, the other helping explain why the company accepted it in an apparently rather offhand way. First, it seems that other mills could not then match the low price for basic open hearth steel available at Homestead. Second, having its fingers yet again burned in a new trade had Bethlehem directors convinced in their belief that special products would repay them better than the competitive hurly-burly of trade in commercial steels.[35] Much earlier, they had already moved more decisively in that direction. It took them into the large-scale manufacture of war materiel.

4

ARMAMENTS
AND ORES

By the 1880s, as Andrew Carnegie once proudly explained to Britain's Prime Minister William Gladstone, the United States had already pulled ahead of the United Kingdom as the world's leading economy. But although a pacesetter in the arts of peace, it lagged behind even many lesser European powers in its capacity to wage war on either land or sea, a very different situation from that during the Civil War, when it had the dubious distinction of pioneering modern, industrialized warfare. In heavy military hardware, its backwardness applied across the board—in guns, in ability to mount heavy ordnance in warships, and in protecting naval vessels from enemy fire. This situation—unsatisfactory if judged by the standards of worldly power—was summed up in one notorious instance, though retrospectively and by a deeply interested party: "When in 1882 the absolutely antiquated and helpless condition of the United States Navy, as compared with foreign fleets, began to be appreciated by the country, a first step was taken by Congress to provide ships protected with modern armor by authorizing the purchase of armor for the protection of the turrets and deck house of the double-turreted monitor *Miantonomah,* which vessel had been left in an uncompleted condition since the end of the civil war." The work was carried out in the New York Naval Yard, but as no armor manufacturing facilities existed in the United States, the armor had to be bought overseas at $550 a ton. The order for the compound armor was awarded to W. H. Wallace and Company of New York, representing two Sheffield manufacturers, John Brown and Son and Charles Cammell and Company.[1] A navy really worthy of a great nation would require new shipyards and an armaments industry very different from that which had withered and largely disappeared after 1865.

Reacting to this situation, in spring 1883, President Chester Arthur selected three army and three navy officers to constitute the Gun Foundry Board, which would be charged with considering which navy yards or arsenals should be adapted for manufacture of modern heavy guns. After visiting government and private arsenals, gun foundries, and factories in Britain, France, and Russia (Alfred Krupp would not give permission for a tour of his operations in Germany), the officers concluded that "while the rest of the world has advanced with the progress of the age, the artillery of the United States has made no step forwards. Its present condition of inferiority is only the natural result of such want of action." They returned home with licenses from Whitworth of Manchester and Schneider of Le Creusot for the exclusive use in the United States of their processes for making armor and guns. These rights were offered to the DeLamater Iron Works, located on the west side of New York City, but it was then being wound down and closed soon afterward. John Ericsson, renowned warship designer and builder, recommended the board should visit Fritz, and accordingly, during 1884, in pursuing their inquiries into possible sites for an ordnance works, the members of board came to Bethlehem. In the middle of that year, they recommended two government gun factories, one an army plant at Watervliet Arsenal, West Troy, New York, and one for the navy in the Washington Naval Yard. These two key machine shops would require dependable supplies of raw material, and it was vital that private steel makers should be encouraged to provide this material, for otherwise "virtually the United States is destitute of a source from which such an armament as the age demands can be supplied."[2]

At this point, the chronology of events is not completely clear. Fritz had already considered forge and armament work as a possible way of side-stepping

Bethlehem's disadvantages in commercial trades. Among his papers there is a translation of an article from *L'Illustration* of 20 January 1883 describing armor plate tests at Spezia, Italy, and a report of March 1883 on tests of solid and hollow shafting by Vickers of Sheffield. Although he presumably discussed possible changes with his directors, the vital initiative was taken by an outsider, the secretary of the Gun Foundry Board, a thirty-seven-year-old naval lieutenant, William Henry Jaques. At least as early as mid-1885, he contacted Bethlehem Iron about the supply of armaments or of materials for their manufacture. Jaques afterward claimed that Bethlehem embarked on production of both armor and ordnance "to carry out the writer's proposition." Exactly when and in what form this contact was made is unclear, but in conversations, especially with Fritz and Sayre, Jaques persuaded them that their company could make forgings of the necessary quality. Fritz, writing about these events many years later, seemed to imply that reluctance on the part of the directors had to be overcome, and there have been suggestions that it was the general manager, Garrett Linderman, who opposed plans to embark on the new trade.[3] Linderman, who was a son-in-law of Asa Packer, seems to have had a drinking problem, and he died in late September 1885. Early the next month, five representatives from Bethlehem Iron, including Fritz, Sayre, and Wharton, met Jaques in Philadelphia for more discussions, and shortly afterward the board referred "Captain Jaques's proposition" to an advisory committee.[4] Less than a month later, Bethlehem contacted the Whitworth firm about spending £85,000 (about $415,000) for a forging press and its necessary appurtenances. This short interval suggests that the scheme, with its inevitable complexities, must have been under consideration for many months, rather than the few weeks since Linderman's death. In short, despite Jaques's own claim, the plan may well have been contemplated considerably earlier than the reported receipt of his proposal. In any case, on 18 January 1886, a contract was drawn up with Whitworth. In March or early April 1886, after further correspondence with Whitworths, and through Lt. Commander Francis Barber of the U.S. Navy, representing the Schneider company, the Bethlehem board resolved "that Joseph Wharton be and hereby is appointed a committee to prosecute the negotiations thus commenced concerning the establishment of armor plate works in this country." Whitworth would supply the forging technology, and Schneider, the expertise in annealing, tempering, and other treatments for forgings. During April, Jaques spent some time in the Bethlehem offices and then sailed for England on 13 May. By early June, Fritz

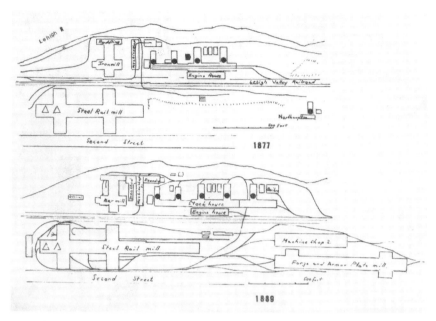

Map of the Bethlehem works in 1877 and 1889. Adapted from A. Holley and L. Smith, *Engineering* (UK), 1878; W. H. Jaques, "Description of Bethlehem Iron Company," 1889.

was also preparing to travel to the United Kingdom. In Europe, Fritz and Jaques closed both with Whitworth and with Schneider. On 18 June, Jaques submitted a long report on the Le Creusot method of making armor plate. By October, work was going well in laying the foundations for the new plant.[5]

Whatever the details of timing or the complications of decision making, the company's resolution to install what a key player of a later stage of the process spoke of as a forging plant "of the first order" was a turning point in the history of iron and steel manufacture at Bethlehem.[6] A good deal of early attention both in company reports and press notices focused on the possibilities it opened for manufacture of heavy shafting for marine and stationary engines. Stockholders were told in June 1886 that in recent years "the massive machinery used both on land and water" required a heavier class of forgings than American industry was capable of providing and, until then, necessary supplies had to be purchased abroad. In work on their rolling mills or in the construction of steamboats, unless they obtained shafting from overseas, they had to go without.

Fritz was abroad looking into this so that they could put their works "in condition to meet, in part at least, the requirements of this class of work."[7] An open hearth melting shop was commissioned in August 1888. That year, the company produced its first steel propeller shafts for U.S. warships, which until then were provided with shafts bought in Britain. Another early order from a quite different sector of the domestic economy was for shafting for the large engines being built to work the copper mines of the Calumet and Hecla Mining Company of Michigan. In the 1890s, it achieved success in making shafts for sternwheelers that plied the Mississippi and Ohio Rivers. Being hollow-forged, these were not only much stronger but lighter than the solid wrought iron shafts commonly used.[8] All this was important in terms of technical and commercial progress, but achievement in these fields was dwarfed by the possibilities opened up in the manufacture of war materiel.

In summer 1886, Secretary of the Navy William C. Whitney invited tenders for gun forgings and armor plate. Two companies made responses to his inquiry for armor and three for gun forgings: the Cleveland Rolling Mill Company and Bethlehem Iron for the former, and Cambria Iron, Midvale Steel, and Bethlehem for the latter.[9] Carnegie, Phipps, and Company soon let it be known that the open hearth furnaces and plate mill being installed at Homestead would be capable of producing the largest armor plates required by the government. Bethlehem submitted its bids for the armor and ordnance on 22 March 1887. The U.S. Navy had decided that preference should be given to a company able to supply both armor and gun forgings, and this—as well as the fact that its price was almost half a million dollars below that of its rivals—meant that three weeks after the deadline for the bids, Whitney accepted the tenders from Bethlehem Iron. The contracts were signed on 30 July 1887. Under their terms, the company undertook to supply 1,221 tons of steel for gun forgings and 6,700 tons of steel armor plate, the price to be $851,000 for the former and $3,611,000 for the latter. The armor, of varying specifications to suit the different parts of the vessels, ranged in price from $500 to $575 a ton. Armor deliveries were to begin before November 1889, amount to 300 tons a month, and be completed within two years.[10]

The development program at Bethlehem was upset by a serious delay in deliveries of plant and equipment, due in part to difficulties at the Whitworth firm in connection with the reorganization of its business. There were inevitable problems too in communications on a transatlantic scale. The delay and some evidence of tension comes out in the correspondence between the two companies. Things at first seemed to be going well. In October 1887, Jaques reported to Fritz that he had been assured by one of the Whitworth directors that "you will have everything within three months from the first of the year." Two months later, when Jack Gledhill wrote to Fritz from Manchester on behalf of his father, M. Gledhill, the managing director, he was optimistic: "We are pushing on as vigorously as possible with your work," which consisted of engines, pumps, and the hydraulic press itself. He would be handing to Jaques that week the particulars of their mixture for making Siemens steel. The arrangement of January 1886 had provided for completion of their work in two years, but the last press was not delivered until April 1889, and two months after that, some other units of plant had still not arrived. The secrecy endemic in armaments manufacture seems also to have been present in the relationship. A letter to Fritz following a visit to the Whitworth works in 1890 reported, "Mr. Gledhill showed me around the works himself but only gave me a very few minutes at each place."[11]

In addition to these inadequacies on the part of suppliers, it is clear that the Bethlehem management had underestimated the problems of operating the new plant. The learning process was difficult, and sufficient allowances for it had not been made. As well as providing capital for its new plant, management needed to recruit the expertise to run it. The Whitworth and Schneider contracts had provided for technical assistance in the form of temporary secondment of skilled men from Manchester and Le Creusot. Neither proved necessary, however, as Bethlehem chose to build up teams of its own men. Those attending the annual meeting of June 1889, were told about Whitworth's failings but also that, because much of the equipment was from abroad, the magnitude of the forging press, its tools, and appliances had not been fully appreciated. The annual meeting report also indicated that it should not "be forgotten that with the exception of our Chief Engineer and Superintendent and one of his assistants, no one of our employees had seen a forging press in operation," though now they were "turning out heavy forgings equal to the best made by any establishment in existence." Further delay resulted when they found that special tools were required for almost every order, a problem that would persist until they had built up a full set of tools to cover all their various types of work. In one year alone, $100,000 was spent on lathes, planers, drill presses, and the like. As a result, the first Bethlehem plate was not ready for testing at the Annapolis proving ground until the beginning of 1891.[12] The company had failed to make its first deliveries of armor by the target date, and consequently the secretary of the Navy negotiated with Carnegie, Phipps, and Company and, in November 1890, contracted for a tonnage of armor almost as large as that bought from Bethlehem, and under similar conditions. Thereafter, the two firms would compete for any armor required.

Its new interests in armaments changed the whole nature of the Bethlehem operation. Four open hearth furnaces were built, but the centerpieces of the extensions were the Whitworth hydraulic forging press and the associated heavy tools designed by Fritz and Gledhill. Even more impressive to contemporaries was the gigantic steam hammer, constructed to Schneider plans but engineered by Fritz. It was used to make gun forgings for the War Department for ten-inch and twelve-inch cannon, and it also forged the first Bethlehem armor plates. In building the new plant, the company made good use of its own manufacturing resources, as with a seventy-ton casting produced in 1890 that became the bedplate for the massive columns of this steam hammer. The new units of plant required important changes to the existing works. To accommodate them, land had to be reclaimed from the Lehigh River, which was realigned. Railroad tracks were relocated. Grounds for proving big guns were laid out at Redington between Bethlehem and Easton. The armor went to the government establishment at Indian Head near Washington for testing. In the course of all this activity costs spiraled upward; the original estimated expenditure on new facilities was about $2.5 million; by the mid-1890s, it amounted to more than $6 million.[13]

In November 1887, Jaques gave up his commission with the navy to join Bethlehem, undertaking to superintend the design, construction, or adaptation of machinery already there for ordnance and armor plate production. Three years later, he was offered an appointment as their ordnance engineer with "general consultative duties, but without independent or executive authority," at an annual salary of eight thousand dollars. The board minutes recorded that in relation to functions and remuneration, "Mr. Jaques replied, that although not satisfactory, he would accept." He served as ordnance engineer until summer 1894, when he was replaced by J. F. Meigs.[14] Even more important was Russell Wheeler Davenport, who after visiting many of the most important steel works in western Europe had joined Midvale Steel as a chemist in 1874. There he became a skilled metallurgist and, with no help from any foreign metallurgist, solved the problem of making material to the exact specifications of the Navy Board of Ordnance. While at Midvale, he visited Le Creusot and most of the

British works involved with heavy forgings, and he produced the first forgings made in the United States for six-inch guns. His employers failed to fully reward his achievements, and in September 1888, Davenport was induced to move to Bethlehem. There, not only was his experience vital but he continued to build on it. In 1890, he spent months at Le Creusot learning processes of armor plate manufacture and bringing back from there all the necessary information for its conduct at Bethlehem. Both the new trades and those who conducted them became of central importance to Bethlehem Iron. As early as January 1889, when business generally was bad, it was reported that the company had closed its bloom and rail mills and was planning to blow out two blast furnaces, but "work is about beginning on making 8 inch and 10 inch guns for the government."[15]

It was in this period of massive changes in plant and products and an unusual importation of talent from outside that Fritz's career at Bethlehem came to an end. He had urged the new trades on his directors and had participated in the design of the new plant, but in summer 1892, he passed his seventieth birthday and was nearing the end of a distinguished career. He resigned as general superintendent later that year. After another nine months, with expressions of appreciation and regret, the board accepted his resignation as consulting engineer. There were, however, other factors than age in his decision to leave. He resented the fact that, as he saw it, Robert Sayre's son had been allowed to encroach on his duties, whereas Davenport, recruited as assistant superintendent, had not been given the rapid advancement he had been promised. The outcome was a bitter row with Sayre, the man who had induced him to make the building up of Bethlehem Iron his life's greatest work. By early 1895, Fritz was planning to sell his Bethlehem Iron stock. Even more dramatically, he made serious moves in the direction of building up a major rival operation. He produced detailed plans for a forge plant to be located at Wilmington, Delaware —strangely enough for Joseph Wharton. It would be known as the Delaware Forge. The matter went so far as to involve him in making new inquiries about a Whitworth forging press.[16] Shortly thereafter he would become a thorn in the side of his old company in a different role.

Unfortunately, neither the technical achievement nor the output of new products saved Bethlehem from a number of serious and interrelated problems. At home, there was only one buyer. Naturally, the U.S. Navy wanted the best, and the manufacturer had to respond or else lose the business. But whereas costs increased as product and processes of manufacture became more sophisticated, the price the Navy Department was willing to pay did not. Technological change, especially in armor, was rapid and apparently unceasing, and the necessity to keep pace with this caused further increases in already high capital costs. In fact, at the very time of Bethlehem's entry into the business, the problem of a high rate of obsolescence was particularly serious in armaments because of an unprecedented rate of "progress" in technology. Armor plate of plain steel, oil tempered and annealed, which seemed the finest material when Bethlehem committed itself to use the Schneider "system," was quickly superseded first by nickel plate, then by face-hardened and reforged "Harveyized" plate, and after that by Krupp armor. In late 1896, the Bethlehem president was authorized to purchase an interest in the Krupp process on terms as favorable as those enjoyed by other leading armor makers, and two years later the company received its first order for it.[17] Plant could become rapidly outmoded, and initial high-capital investment followed by continuing large outlays resulted in heavier overheads than originally envisaged. As the company pointed out in what was effectively a plea for public support, their great steam hammer, "constructed at an extremely heavy expense"—and apparently at the insistence of the Navy Department— after an operating life of only three years, was supplanted by a 14,000-ton hydraulic forging press and had been standing idle ever since. Trying to make a virtue out of what was at the same time a problem, they described it as "a speaking instance of how rapidly in these days of progress costly machinery loses its value and is set aside by the onward march of improvement." Before the end of the decade, recognition that armor operations could be improved further in terms of machining and treatment facilities had pointed to a need for yet more expenditure.[18] Yet government requirements for armor varied greatly from year to year, and Carnegie Steel now competed keenly for any orders. In the first half of the decade, Bethlehem armor deliveries to the navy rose satisfactorily; in 1891–1892, it delivered 405 tons, and for the next three years, 2,379, 2,350, and 2,938 tons, respectively. But by 1 June 1896, the value of unfinished armor orders for the U.S. government was only $254,000. In 1896–1897, deliveries fell to 542 tons.[19]

Heavy outlays for plant, uncertain demand, and keen competition for business meant Bethlehem's new trades were not as reliably profitable as seemed likely in prospect. At the time it embarked on these new trades, it was expected that by 1895, it would have made more than $20 million worth of armor; in fact, by fall 1894, only about $6 million had been supplied. On the other hand, official estimates made in 1896 caused the government to claim that, after the initial outlay on plant, as much as 40 percent of what the company received on domestic deliveries of armor plate amounted to profit.[20] Early in 1897, Bethlehem Iron conveyed its strong reactions to this report in a letter to the secretary of the Navy: "We have taken enormous risks, have spent money lavishly, have established one of the finest plants in the world for the production of armor plate, have gathered and formed a corps of highly skilled men, and have spared no pains nor conscientious endeavor to meet all the severe demands of the Government to furnish armor equal, if not superior to any produced in the world. To have this magnificent plant lie idle, our highly trained corps of skilled workingmen scattered, and the success of an enterprise of such importance jeopardized would certainly be a national misfortune." In his "analysis" of the secretary of the Navy's report, Robert Packer Linderman (who had succeeded his father as a director) attempted to show how comparatively unprofitable the trade had turned out to be. In the process he indicated that, contrary to the general impression, it was a still a relatively minor part of their business: "In 1887, when we undertook the erection of a plant for Government work, our capital stock was $2,000,000, on which we were paying cash dividends at the rate of 12 per cent. per annum. We had no floating indebtedness, a bonded indebtedness of only $149,000, and we had a surplus of about $2,000,000." Since then the company had added $3,000,000 of new stock and $1,351,000 of bonds. During the eight years since 1889, average dividends had been less than in the years immediately before that date, while the increase in surplus, to which Navy Secretary Hilary Herbert had referred in his report, had gone into plant, materials, and working capital. Linderman concluded, "During the eight years from 1889 to 1896, both inclusive, the gross receipts of The Bethlehem Iron Company amounted to over $46,000,000, while during the same period the receipts from armor amounted to only $6,780,000, or about 14.7% of the total."[21] Whatever the balance of truth in its dispute with the government, in its predicament Bethlehem had already looked for help in three devices common in the rather esoteric world of armaments manufacture and trade.

First, collusion between producers might make it possible to push up, or at least maintain, prices. At home, this meant collaboration with the various Carnegie interests, which, from summer 1892, were consolidated into the Carnegie Steel Company. As early as September 1891, reporting to Andrew Carnegie on a meeting of rail makers, Henry Clay Frick added, "Mr. Linderman said to me, 'How about Armor? As between us we should not let the Govern-

Armaments in the 1890s: heavy guns for use in the war with Spain. *Courtesy of the National Canal Museum, Easton, Pennsylvania.*

ment get the best of it at our expense.' I told him we stood ready (as I had stated to him at the only interview we had on the subject) to work in harmony with them. I was glad he brought the matter up—and am sure there will be no trouble in working with them if we want to."[22] Over the next few years the two companies held numerous consultations and made visits to each other's armor operations. Details are unimportant, but there can be no doubt that they contributed to an improvement in "harmony," whatever that euphonious and innocent-looking word implied for the public purse. A logical extension was international consultation, which again usually resulted in some form of cooperative action also amounting to collusion. In March 1895, Linderman reported that Bethlehem Iron had been invited to send a representative to a "conference" of armor plate makers. He was chosen as their delegate. Two months later he reported on the Paris meeting of the main firms on 26 and 27 April and laid before his board a copy of the agreement they had reached.[23]

Second, an effort was made to increase demand by propaganda, essentially pump priming. This policy had indifferent results. In fall 1894, pointing out that its new plant was not adapted for ordinary commercial work and that to leave it idle would be injurious, Bethlehem put in a strong plea for additional congressional appropriations for naval orders. In fact, the directors had already realized these would not be approved.[24] Even so, over the next two years the company received a boost at home, in the form of large appropriations for coastal defense works and in expected orders for new battleships. Unfortunately, Congress also decided on a price ceiling of $300 a ton for the armor required. Only after a period of uncertainty, complicated by an ill-considered offer by Illinois Steel to enter armor manufacture, did the secretary of the Navy contract with Bethlehem and Carnegie at a price of $425 a ton. In March 1899, inviting bids for a new round of warship construction, the Navy Department made another effort to force prices down.[25]

A third way of securing a better loading for the plant was to widen the market, in other words, to enter the murky world of competition for overseas orders. Looking at the possibilities, Bethlehem found the Russian empire the most likely prospect. Carnegie Steel was already exploiting U.S. Navy contacts there, even seeking the help of Secretary of State James G. Blaine.[26] Bethlehem's relationship with the Russians illustrated the uncertainties and complications of this field of business as well as the opportunities of moderating them by collaboration. A directors' report in June 1895 described the circumstances in which contact began: "Over a year ago it became apparent that no appropriations were likely to be made by Congress in the near future for war vessels, and that, unless work could be obtained from foreign governments, it would not be long before our armor plate plant would be idle and our organization of specially trained workmen scattered."[27] The company approached the Russian Admiralty and in October 1894 received an official request through the Russian legation in Washington to tender for side armor for two battleships then under construction, the *Petropavlovsk* and the *Sevastopol*. The new engineer of ordnance, John F. Meigs, was sent to St. Petersburg to negotiate. On his arrival he found representatives of all the main European armor plate makers and of the Carnegie Steel Company in contention for the business. By mid-December, Bethlehem Iron had been chosen to supply armor. Chagrin at Carnegie Steel was increased when it became known that the price Bethlehem had quoted was considerably lower than their own.[28]

This Russian order amounted to 1,155 tons and was therefore of no more than marginal help to the armor department. In the course of the operating year 1894–1895, the company shipped 2,938 tons of armor to the account of the U.S. Navy and only 24 tons to Russia, but the price paid by the latter was less than half that for material supplied to the U.S. government. This pricing policy was justified as necessary to win the first overseas business rather than let it go, as in the past, to well-established European suppliers. Despite the small size of and low price for the order, Andrew Carnegie, as always hungry for business, wrote to Linderman some two months afterward, suggesting that the two companies should divide this order between them, for such an arrangement would look better "before the masses of the people" than Bethlehem standing out as a company that sold cheap abroad and dear at home.[29] Subsequent Russian orders were at prices comparable with those for domestic delivery, though some were for only small tonnages. In spring 1898, William Cramp contracted with the Russian government to build a battleship and a protected cruiser. Proof that there had been negotiations between the two armor makers was indicated by the fact that on this occasion Carnegie and Bethlehem quoted identical prices for the plate required.[30] Bethlehem was chosen to supply half the armor and all the engine forgings. There was also a prospect of furnishing guns, if the Russians allowed Cramp to supply them. Small contracts of armor for Japan were obtained in 1897–1898. Finally, although there were to be no early successes, from as early as 1894, Bethlehem had arranged to pay commissions to agents for orders secured in Brazil, China, and other countries.[31]

One important and indeed potentially ruinous outcome of the disagreements with the U.S. government about the price for armor was that the latter seriously considered entering production itself. The issue was contentious and was to be long drawn out. In March 1896, in hearings before the Senate Committee on Naval Affairs, Commodore Philip Hichborn, chief of the Bureau of Construction and Repairs of the Navy Department, advised against erection of a national plant near Washington, not far from Indian Head, the main government testing ground for armor. Hichborn reckoned that the cost of such a works, independent of site, would be about $2 million. He believed it would be impossible to keep it in full operation and that therefore it would be unable to retain the necessary regularly employed skilled work force.[32] Notwithstanding his recommendation, by July 1897, the decision was made to provide for a government plant unless the private firms lowered their prices. John Fritz, now seventy-five and alienated from his old company, agreed to design the works if the government went ahead. The expected cost was now put at more than

Armaments in the 1890s: armor plate for the U. S. battleship Alabama (launched in 1898) and the Russian battleship Retvizan (launched in 1900). *Courtesy of the National Canal Museum, Easton, Pennsylvania.*

$3 million for an annual capacity of about six thousand tons of armor.[33] When President McKinley's secretary of the Navy, John D. Long, advertised for proposals for construction of the armor plant, for sites, and for machinery and buildings, he received twenty-nine bids. Most were for sites only, but there were two bids for complete plants. The Huntington, West Virginia, chamber of commerce offered to follow the specifications of the board and to build a complete works, with site, buildings, and plant included, for $3.3 million. The other offer came from the John P. Holland Torpedo Boat Company of New York, whose president since 1897 had been William H. Jaques.[34] Eventually, a compromise price for armor was agreed upon between the government and the Bethlehem and Carnegie companies, and the government plant was not built; however, both the problem and suggested solution would recur.

One indisputable outcome of Bethlehem's large-scale entry to the trade in armaments and other heavy special steel products was that it won the company and the town wide recognition. Having declined to the status of a minor player in the rail business, it regained center stage in its new fields of production. As early as summer 1889, Bethlehem was visited by Secretary of the Navy Benjamin Tracey and the chief of the Navy Board of Ordnance, who inspected progress in forgings and castings for guns and preparations for making armor plate for new cruisers.[35] That autumn the Bethlehem display was hailed as "one of the most notable and remarkable" at the International Maritime Exhibition in Boston. Secretary Tracey made another visit in October 1891, this time to see 133-inch gun forgings and the forging of armor by the steam hammer. He lunched at Fritz's home before returning to Washington.[36] Interest in the plant extended into the international sphere. Some foreign visitors to Bethlehem during the American meeting of the Iron and Steel Institute in fall 1890 reckoned its open hearth plant the finest melting shop they had ever seen; the following year, Lt. Colonel W. Hope of the British army was reported as saying, "I consider the Bethlehem gun plant to be superior to any gun plant in the world."[37] Even more impressive by virtue of wide experience over many years was an accolade from the secretary of the British Iron Trade Association in 1902 at the end of his tour of American iron and steel districts: "One of the most striking of the many striking things that came under my notice in visiting American works was the engineering shop of the Bethlehem Steel Company. . . . This shop is altogether phenomenal—alike in its size, its equipment, its methods and the work on hand. Its equipment embraces some of the largest and finest tools in the world."[38]

Now firmly established in lines of business in which geographical position was of no account as either liability or asset, Bethlehem seemed by the late 1890s to have side-stepped the problems that had plagued its struggle to keep a place in commercial steels. As late as the 1895–1896 operating year, it produced 6,547 tons of forgings and 74,629 tons of Bessemer rails and bars; two years later it made 19,101 tons of forgings, but output of rail and bar steel was now negligible. By 1898, though the rated capacity of its open hearth furnaces was well under one-third that of its Bessemer converters, the latter section of the works was effectively redundant.[39] In late fall that year, the board went so far as to ask the new superintendent of manufacture to investigate the possibility of changing the Bessemer works into a steel foundry by putting into it open hearth capacity sufficient to meet the needs of its commercial operations, leaving the existing melting shop free to serve the armor plant.[40]

Over a few years at the end of the nineteenth century, Bethlehem Iron gained a high reputation for specialties. Were there also other, as yet unexplored, possibilities? Many concluded not. Most famous of these pessimistic assessments, by virtue both of the eminence of its author and of his specific reference to Bethlehem, was Andrew Carnegie's contribution to the Review of the Century number of the *New York Evening Post*. As he saw it, the decision by Lackawanna Steel to move from Scranton to Buffalo "and the splendid triumphs of the Bethlehem Steel Company in Pennsylvania in armor, guns and forgings as specialties, which give it a unique and commanding position, are proofs that, for the making of ordinary steel the East is not a favorable location."[41] This article appeared on 12 January 1901. By then the processes that would result in the formation of the United States Steel Corporation were already well under way. Largely as a derivative from that momentous development, the first steps would be taken a few months later toward another revolutionary change in the status and fortunes of steel making at Bethlehem.

In the late 1890s, a writer argued in *Iron Age* that calculations for deciding the best location for iron manufacture were at best inconclusive: "No one can sit down and figure out where I must haul so many tons of coal or coke, and so many tons of iron ore, at a minimum cost freight, so that, adding freight on product to market, I reach the lowest figure."[42] This sort of uncertainty also affected existing works, perhaps established many years before, but now reacting to new opportunities or challenges from rapidly changing patterns of mineral production and of markets. Companies and plants exist in time as well as in space. They cannot change the latter but must adjust as best they can. Their ability to do so depends on the quality of their top management. By the time of the *Iron Age* article, organization of iron ore supply in particular had long been a problem for Bethlehem Iron.

Before the mid-1880s, there were three main sources of ore supply for eastern Pennsylvanian works: the local area, including the mines of Morris County, New Jersey; the Great Lakes basin; or transatlantic ore fields. When first established, the blast furnaces scattered along the Lehigh valley had drawn on a mixture of eastern ores, found in or near the valley itself, on South Mountain, at the Cornwall ore banks, or from more distant supplies in New Jersey. Within a few years, those few of the old companies that switched from making iron for sale (known as merchant iron) or from using their own output in wrought iron manufacture to producing steel had to search for adequate sources of low-phosphorus ore. For a time in the 1870s and early 1880s, the question of securing a suitable mix of ores for steel making affected most of the national industry. In 1880, for instance, one of the blast furnaces recently built at the Edgar Thomson works in Pittsburgh was using a mixture of Lake Superior, Pilot Knob, and Spanish ores. Much of the overseas ore came as "ballast" cargo on returning grain-, cotton-, or petroleum-carrying ships and therefore at freight charges little more than those on a return journey in ordinary ballast.[43] Over the next few years further development in the upper Great Lakes ranges provided furnaces west of the Alleghenies with abundant supplies of "Bessemer" grade ores, but the ore problem persisted in the East. By 1884, when 488,000 tons of ore were imported from all sources, only 15 percent of the total was carried west of the Alleghenies.[44] Over the years, "western" ore continued to be brought to eastern furnaces in considerable tonnages. In 1888, 276,00 tons of Lake Superior ore was delivered to furnaces in eastern Pennsylvania and New York; two years later, iron works east of the Alleghenies used 680,000 tons. Even the small companies used some Great Lakes ore. For instance, the Warwick Iron and Steel Company of Pottstown, which in 1900 made about 54,000 tons of iron, had in January contracted for 50,000 tons of Lake Superior ore.[45]

Through the 1880s and 1890s, as ore production east of the Appalachians dwindled, Lake Superior established a dominance it never lost. Its share of national output was 23.6 percent in 1880 but 74.4 percent by 1900. Apart from need for low-phosphorus ores and the westward shift of production responding to the movement of the national economy, increased geological knowledge, and the application of enterprise and capital in the new orefields, there were two other general considerations affecting Bethlehem ore supply: the search for economies of scale, which led to concentration of output, and U.S. tariff policy. Concentration and associated changes in organization went ahead rapidly over the last years of the nineteenth century. As late as 1883–1884, the nine principal iron ore districts mined only a little over half the ore produced throughout the nation, and much of the old pattern of small producers serving local or not far distant furnaces remained in place. Over the next fifteen to twenty years, growth of long-distance bulk movements helped focus production in far fewer, much bigger workings, and smaller, even if nearby, mining and shipping operations became uneconomic.

In this field, tariff policy was the outcome of a long-running fight between eastern interests, in which the large firms at least favored low duties, and iron makers west of the Appalachians, who, having an increasingly important supply from the upper Great Lakes ranges, wished to ensure that eastern furnace companies were not helped by easier access to foreign ores. In 1883, the basis of the duty on imported ore was changed from 20 percent ad valorem to seventy-five cents per gross ton. Along with the general decline in the eastern iron trade, this tariff reduction caused a decrease in New Jersey ore output and the closure of many mines. Between 1864 and 1871, ore production in that state had doubled and the increase continued into the early 1880s, but within two more years New Jersey's share in ore production fell from 10.4 to 4.8 percent; by 1888, it was 3.7 percent. In 1897, Thomas Edison erected a magnetite ore concentration plant in the state, a project in which Bethlehem had interests, but it was not a great success.[46]

Though the majority of ore deposits in the East were small, there were some bigger ones, but even with these there was a general lack of purposeful development anywhere approaching that in the upper lakes. There were exceptions. The Cornwall magnetite ore deposit, which had attracted the critical comments of the Swedish expert Richard Ackerman, were after 1864 under the unified management of the Cornwall Ore Hills Company. Until the late 1880s, annual output was larger than that of any other mine in the United States, in 1888 amounting to 723,000 tons.[47] Farther away, in and around the Adirondacks, there were important masses of magnetite and local deposits of hematite. Worked since the late eighteenth century and important in the mid-nineteenth century, these deposits had not been systematically developed. A correspondent of *Iron Age* described their situation at the turn of the century:

> The whole region seems to be absolutely an unexplored section of our country so far as any definite and well digested plan of prospecting has been carried out, and even the largest of the companies now producing know but very little in regard to their properties, the fact being that the companies now producing ore have more ore in sight than they either have power to mine or have a market for, and it seems a mystery why a region that is so close to the market for iron in all its various shapes should remain so utterly ignored by the modern spirit of progress of this country.[48]

In fact, during the 1890s, ore production in New York fell more than in either Pennsylvania or New Jersey. By the early twentieth century, Howard M. Howe, professor of metallurgy at Columbia University, saw little prospect for eastern ores and was led to propound what he called a law to account for the new national geography of ore production: "The middle states, New York, New Jersey, and Pennsylvania, are known to have many great deposits of rich magnetite, which supplied a very large proportion of the American ores till the discovery of the very cheaply mined ores, of Lake Superior. In 1906 these latter formed 80% of the American production and the southern states supplied about 13% of it, while the rich deposits of the middle states are husbanded in accordance with the law that ore bodies are drawn on in the order of their apparent profitableness."[49]

Bethlehem Iron faced continuing difficulties in its search for supplies of Bessemer ore. Like other companies, it continued for many years to bring in considerable tonnages from Europe. Late in 1879, the company arranged to import twenty-five thousand tons of Elba ore of not less than 60 percent iron to be delivered on rail cars at six dollars a ton in either Perth Amboy, New York, or Philadelphia.[50] Year after year, Bethlehem's managers searched for ore throughout the Northeast, in 1880 contracting with the Chateaugay Iron and Ore Company in the northern Adirondacks for twenty-five thousand tons of Bessemer ore to be delivered either on boats or cars at Plattsburg, New York, in as nearly monthly quantities as possible through the 1880 lake and canal navigation season. They contracted with the Crown Point Iron Company on the southeastern side of the mountains for ten thousand tons delivered at Port Henry. In each case, the price at delivery was to be five dollars a ton.[51] Sometimes the company managers looked into prospects in inaccessible areas, as in summer 1881, when they joined Pennsylvania Steel and Cambria Iron in acquiring options on forty-two thousand acres in Jefferson County, New York, an area draining to the St. Lawrence River. After active prospecting, "ores were not found in either quantity or quality to justify further outlay of money and the option was surrendered." For a time there seemed a "reasonable" prospect of good Bessemer ore from a mine in Ontario, but it too failed to become an important supplier.[52] On a number of occasions there was failure to act decisively, and consequently a chance was lost to secure a major source of supply. Cornwall ore was used, but Bethlehem did not make long-term contracts for it at favorable prices, instead preferring to buy in dribs and drabs. By 1901, the Cornwall ore was controlled by Pennsylvania Steel. An opportunity was lost to develop the Tilly Foster mine, almost fifty miles north of New York on the eastern side of the Hudson valley from which Bethlehem had already obtained a small amount of good ore. In this case, the Lackawanna Iron and Coal Company showed greater initiative, by 1890 taking all Tilly Foster's seventy thousand tons' annual output of 50 percent iron ore, hauled by rail two hundred miles to Scranton. Looking back, Fritz summed up the situation his company had reached by the 1880s: "I could plainly see the end of the acid Bessemer process everywhere, and especially with us, as the company had let every ore property that was available for the Bessemer process pass beyond their control, and the end was in sight."[53] Bethlehem put off a day of reckoning by turning to new overseas sources of supply, but only as part owner.

At the annual meeting on 27 June 1882, the directors reported the failed search in Jefferson County, New York, recorded their hopes for Ontario, and referred to the disadvantages of dependence on Europe: "As a large portion of the ore that we use and of the pig iron that we buy comes from abroad—the Atlantic Ocean between us and our base of supply, with all the uncertainties of freight rates and ocean navigation—prudence and safety require us to carry large stocks of them." The following year, stockholders were told that, though expecting large amounts of good ore from what were called the Wilbur mines in Canada, the company would not be "pushed" because "we are led to believe that better ores in large supply and at a less cost are to be obtained from the Island of Cuba." Attention had been drawn to rich Bessemer ores in southeastern Cuba in 1881. In late June 1882, the directors decided to take an interest.[54] Company representatives visited Cuba in October, examined the mine, and canceled the contract. Then came a favorable report on the quantity, quality, and low cost of the ore available, findings on the labor situation, prospects for railroads and docks, and information on Spanish law as to title and so forth. Some skilled labor would be needed, among other things, for dock construction, but unskilled labor could be recruited from the black population close to the proposed mines, now described as Juragua East and Juragua West. The decision was made to organize a company to exploit the mines. Bethlehem and Pennsylvania Steel would each have a two-fifths interest.

On 26 March 1883, Garrett B. Linderman left Bethlehem to sail next day from New York to Santiago. A company press release explained that he would be accompanied not only by a number of "gentlemen" but also "a large force of engineers and mechanics, and will organize them into a working force for developing the extensive deposits of iron ore, building of railroads, and erecting docks, pockets, etc., on a very large scale." This marked the inauguration of the Juragua Iron Company. The mines were four miles from the Caribbean, although fifteen from Santiago, and it was planned that before a railroad was built, any ore produced would be carried by lighter from the nearest point on the coast to vessels off shore. (Interestingly, a press account of this arrangement noted that "with striking short-sightedness the Spanish government promptly proposed to put on an export duty of 40 cents a ton; but we understand that this has been abandoned." Not until three months later was the American import duty on ore *reduced* to seventy-five cents a ton.[55]) On 17 July 1884, Linderman and the superintendent of the ore company, Thomas H. Graham, officiated at an elaborate ceremony to inaugurate a 17.5-mile railroad from the open cut workings to a new ore dock in the port of Santiago, from which the first cargo of ore was shipped on 7 August. After receiving a "most favorable" report on the first year of operations from Professor James Kimball, the company decided to surrender leases on several mines in Lehigh County and, mainly because of the current low oceanic freight rates on Mediterranean ore, not to develop their Canadian ore properties. During the 1885–1886 operating year, Juragua monthly output was raised from 6,000 to 10,000 tons and the delivered cost for the ore in the United States was cut from $5.69 to $4.33 a ton. By June 1886, the ore company's capital was increased from $1 million to $1.5 million. Ocean freight rates rose in the late 1880s, but in 1889–1890, Juragua ore at Perth Amboy, Baltimore, or Philadelphia was only $4.45 a ton. That year Bethlehem took 100,000 tons of the 302,000 tons of ore produced.[56]

A total of 1 million tons of ore had been shipped from Juragua by August 1890. The next year that region accounted for 29 percent of all the iron ore imported into the United States. The quality was good, with samples from ten cargoes delivered before 1893 averaging 60.5 percent iron, 0.028 percent phosphorus, and 0.328 percent sulphur.[57] Having been first stimulated by reduction of the ore duty to seventy-five cents a ton from 1 July 1883, the inflow was boosted by a further cut in 1894 to forty cents. In 1895–1896, shipments were 327,000 tons, of which Bethlehem took 157,000 tons. By this time, the delivered cost had been reduced to $3.15 per ton. In August 1897, total shipments from Juragua passed 3 million tons.[58] Soon afterward, conditions in Cuba were disturbed, first by rebellion and then by the Spanish-American War.

The considerable mining operations in Cuba and the regular shipping arrangements for delivery to the mid-Atlantic seaboard of the United States were small-scale replicas of the mineral flows established on the Great Lakes. Recognizing this and the opportunities for coastwide and foreign deliveries of its products, Pennsylvania Steel, Bethlehem's equal partner in Juragua operations, made the logical decision that an excellent place to smelt some of the imported ore was the break of bulk point between ocean shipping and rail transport. Accordingly, in 1887, it acquired nearly one thousand acres of land six miles out of Baltimore on the estuary of the Patapsco River and Chesapeake Bay at Sparrow's Point (commonly spelled without an apostrophe in later years). Its initial plan was to build wharves and two blast furnaces, sending pig iron via a connection with the Northern Central Railroad into Pennsylvania and to the existing steel works at Steelton on the Susquehanna.[59] However, the decision was soon made to build steel capacity and rolling mills as well as blast furnaces, and a new subsidiary was formed, Maryland Steel. By 1896, Sparrows Point already had an annual capacity of 300,000 tons of Bessemer rails or two-thirds more than the parent plant. In 1901, its four blast furnaces produced 303,000 tons of iron; that year, the whole Lehigh valley made 481,000 tons of pig iron, an output involving twenty-nine furnaces.[60] Bethlehem's failure to follow Pennsylvania Steel's partial relocation of operations was largely to be explained by its preoccupation with its new role as leader in the heavy armaments trade.

II

FROM A

STRUGGLING PLANT

TO THE

SECOND RANK

IN STEEL

5

REORGANIZING AND REDIRECTING BETHLEHEM STEEL

ONE OF THE MOST DISTINCTIVE features of the Bethlehem Iron Company was the small, close-knit, localized nature of its controlling body. Of its nine-man board (excluding secretary and treasurer) in 1889, at least eight lived either in South Bethlehem or in the near neighborhood.[1] There was a good deal of intermarriage among the families of the principals, resulting in interlocking "dynasties." The best of those who entered the company employment stayed on, rising through its hierarchy to become members of top management or directors. Only rarely did men leave for key positions elsewhere in the industry. Similarly, few persons of renown in the industry were brought in from outside, although when this did happen, the individuals might prove to be of exceptional importance in changing the direction or tone of the business. Much was to change, but many of these features would also be characteristic of twentieth-century Bethlehem.

The first president, Alfred Hunt, and secretary, A. S. Schropp, remained with Bethlehem Iron until their deaths. More impressive still, Joseph Wharton was a director of Saucon Iron, Bethlehem Iron, and then of Bethlehem Steel from 1857 until he died fifty-two years later, though long before the end of his life he was also engaged in many other manufacturing activities. By the 1880s, he was the main Bethlehem stockholder. Although exceptional among the members of the board in that he lived in Philadelphia, he played a key role in various stages of Bethlehem's evolution, including its entry into armaments manufacture. Robert Heysham Sayre, born in 1820, had come to Saucon Iron two years after Wharton. At various times, he served as general manager and vice president. He lived in South Bethlehem near the plant and was associated with the company until his death in 1907. His son, Robert H. Sayre Jr., was made general manager in 1886; later, he was named superintendent, and he also was with the firm for the remainder of his life. As general manager, he succeeded the first occupant of that post, Garrett B. Linderman, who died in summer 1885. At the end of that year, Linderman's son Robert, only twenty-two, who had married the senior Sayre's daughter two years before, was appointed director in his father's place. The younger Linderman was a banker and coal operator as well as a manufacturer but became more closely involved in company affairs than his father had been. In spring 1888, he became vice president, and by spring 1890, he had succeeded W. W. Thurston, Wharton's nephew, as president. John Fritz was superintendent and engineer from 1860 and later a director, and, after retiring in 1892, he remained for a short time a director and consulting engineer, before he broke away completely.

Notwithstanding the "enclosed" nature of Bethlehem top management, the processes of aging and mortality inevitably brought changes. Another cause of change was the dramatic alteration in its product range from the mid-1880s, which meant that new individuals who could contribute special expertise had to be recruited. Two came from the quality steel producer Midvale Steel Works of Philadelphia. Before being dismissed in April 1901, Frederick W. Taylor not only introduced time and motion methods of production but also played an important part in Bethlehem's developing interest in tool steel technology. Russell Wheeler Davenport was appointed in 1888 and in 1891 became second vice president and general manager. He became general superintendent in 1899 and retained the post until August 1901.[2] A year after Davenport's arrival in Bethlehem, a twenty-four-year-old graduate of Lehigh University in mechanical

Archibald Johnston. *Courtesy of the National Canal Museum, Easton, Pennsylvania.*

engineering, Archibald Johnston, born in Phoenixville, joined the Physical Testing Department. Soon afterward, he was given charge of the building and operation of the gun and armor plate plants. His high quality was unmistakable; as early as January 1898, Robert Sayre wrote in his diary, "I think Johnston is the best man we have about the concern."[3] At the end of 1898, Johnston became assistant to the general superintendent, and by 1901–1902, he was superintendent. In June 1899, another Lehigh University graduate, this time in electrical engineering, started work at Bethlehem. At first, he seemed destined for a humble role in the company's future, for he joined as an electrical crane operator, but this twenty-two-year-old, probably then completely unknown to directors and senior managers, was Eugene Gifford Grace. Later, he would make his own mark.

As the new century began, the top personnel at Bethlehem at last underwent more rapid change. Sayre and Wharton were still alive, but they were too old and too detached to be of importance in the company's further development. In January 1903, Robert Linderman died at the early age of thirty-nine from blood poisoning, and by June that year, Davenport had left to join the William Cramp and Sons Ship and Engine Building Company, of which he became general manager. He busied himself with reorganization of their plant, but he died within nine months. Three weeks earlier, Robert Sayre Jr. had died in his fifty-fifth year, more than three years before his father. In this manner and in this short period, the way was unexpectedly opened for new blood and new thinking. Both were needed. By strange good fortune, they became available in the form of an exceptional injection of vitality at the very time, when, having reached a low ebb, the tide of fortune for the eastern steel industry was at last on the turn.

Well before the end of the century there was a wide consensus in the industry that the East was no longer a suitable location for mass production of ordinary commercial steels. Abram S. Hewitt, a former leading eastern iron manufacturer and once a prominent factor in the national trade, had for decades been convinced that the region was finished as a major player. In discussions about tariffs in 1893, he indicated that his company was proposing to give up making beams and girders at Trenton "because we are driven out of business by western competition and not by foreign products." Three years afterward, he pointed out that his "great works" was idle because of rivalry from firms using Lake Superior ores in the North and because of iron makers in Tennessee and Alabama. Later still, writing in the *New York Times,* he claimed the South could make pig iron for six dollars a ton whereas the North could not produce it for under ten dollars.[4] Others, nearer the heart of the contemporary industry than Hewitt, claimed to share his views, though the opinions they expressed often served their own best interests. Speaking to a naturally receptive audience at a banquet in Pittsburgh in 1898, Andrew Carnegie breezily assured his listeners, "In the East, Pittsburgh has nothing to fear. Steel cannot be manufactured on the Atlantic seaboard under any circumstances in competition with her."[5] A few months before, he wrote dismissively about Bethlehem Steel to his colleagues at Carnegie Steel: "except for Government work it would be just as Scranton and Pennsylvania." Eighteen months later, he tried to arouse them to the possibility of making a clean sweep of their eastern rivals: "My view is that, sooner or later, Harrisburg, Sparrows Point, and Scranton will cease to make rails, like Bethlehem. The autumn of last year seemed as good a time to force them out of business as any other. It did not prove so. The boom came and cost us a great deal of money."[6]

Outsiders generally concurred in thinking the great days of iron and steel making in the East had passed. Visiting the main steel districts of the United States in the immediate aftermath of the formation of the United States Steel

Corporation, the experienced secretary of the British Iron Trade Association, J. S. Jeans, subscribed to the view that Bethlehem had been forced to resort to high-grade products in order to survive in an area for which circumstances had worsened and in which, by extension, the auguries for commercial steels did not seem favorable.[7] However, some at least recognized flaws in these unfavorable assessments of eastern prospects in commercial steel. Reporting Hewitt's dismal comments early in 1898, *Iron Age* added that not all the *"younger* men" in the East would agree with him.[8] It was, however, someone only four years younger than Hewitt, and intimately involved with Bethlehem, who in 1900 demonstrated that the region need not be regarded as finished as a producer of competitively priced iron so long as mineral supply was efficiently organized and modern plant was installed, though he proved this only for merchant iron and not for blast furnaces associated with steel making. At this time, seventy-four-year-old Joseph Wharton built a modern blast furnace plant at Port Oram (later renamed Wharton) in Morris County, New Jersey, acquired coal mines, bought existing Connellsville coke ovens, and put up new beehive ovens in Indiana County, Pennsylvania. Before Wharton died in 1909, his four-furnace Port Oram works had become one of the nation's biggest merchant iron plants, with annual capacity of some 350,000 tons.[9] Others, too, began to sense that circumstances might be changing in favor of the East or at least were not worsening as quickly as many had assumed.

In the early 1890s, Henry Clay Frick had suggested that Carnegie Steel should consider buying the Sparrows Point operations only to be met with his senior partner's complete refusal to entertain the idea. A few days later, Frick was told by a recent visitor that, while it would not soon become a major factor in the trade, the Sparrows Point converting plant and rail mill were good. His informant was the general superintendent of the Edgar Thomson works, Charles M. Schwab.[10] Seven years later, and only a few weeks after Abram Hewitt's dirge for the East in the *New York Times,* the board of Carnegie Steel discussed their competitors' prospects. Turning to Lackawanna, their main rail making rival in the East, Frick argued that its raw material circumstances were not as adverse as some might conclude and that a better organization might work wonders with its prospects. Retrospectively, his remarks seem prophetic: "From all the information we have, they are in position to make very cheap pig iron, and could likely be made a formidable competitor if their company was well managed. If they had a man like Mr. Schwab, they would make things lively for us."[11]

Soon after this, although overshadowed in industry news and the public eye by the prospect of clashes between the newly formed product-based combinations and the big "western" integrated producers such as Illinois Steel and Carnegie Steel, Bethlehem Iron also caught the fever for profitable corporate reconstruction. In spring 1899, Wharton and Linderman, the two largest stockholders, decided to sell the Bethlehem Iron Company to a new company, to be called the Bethlehem Steel Company. The meeting in which the sale to the holding company was approved was held on 24 April 1899. Those present were Joseph Wharton, Elisha P. Wilbur, Robert H. Sayre, Beauvean Borie, Edward Stotesbury (a banker and member of J. P. Morgan), John Lowber-Welsh, and Robert Linderman, who was appointed president of the new Bethlehem Steel Company. Capital was increased from $5 million to $15 million, the directors of the Bethlehem Iron Company being offered two shares in the new holding company for every share they had in the old one. This extraordinary act of inflating the nominal value of their own investment was justified by a claim that the operations needed more capital: "The anticipated expansion of the business of the company will naturally require from time to time large expenditure for the acquisition of new property, for the purchase of machinery and for the general enlargement of facilities whereby the greatest production may be obtained at the lowest cost."[12]

The reorganization in 1899 proved to be only a first step. By early 1901, Wharton was discussing a possible sale of Bethlehem Steel to the leading British armaments group, Vickers Sons and Maxim Limited. Associated with Vickers in this bid was the Cramp shipbuilding group. At the end of negotiations, the Vickers group was unwilling to pay more than $22.50 a share and in addition wanted an extension of the time allowed for examination of the works before committing themselves. The latter requirement proved a decisive stumbling block. It was, as Robert Sayre wrote in his diary, "damn foolishness," for it lost the group their chance of acquiring Bethlehem Steel. Discussions were broken off, and instead, Robert Linderman negotiated with Charles M. Schwab, who offered $24 for each Bethlehem share. On 30 May, two days after the Vickers-Cramp bid failed, Linderman concluded the deal with Schwab, who bought eighty thousand shares from Wharton, sixty thousand from Linderman, and twenty thousand on the open market, thereby gaining a controlling interest in Bethlehem. On 15 August, the stockholders accepted Schwab's offer. The following day, the Bethlehem Steel Company purchased the properties of the Bethlehem Iron

Company, which then ceased to exist. On 27 August, at a director's meeting in which Schwab was represented by the lawyer Max Pam, there took place important changes in the board. Abraham Schropp resigned his long-held post as secretary and treasurer to be replaced by Henry Snyder. Edward McIlvain replaced E. P. Wilbur and took the post of president from Linderman, who for the time being remained a director. J. L. Welsh resigned and was replaced by Archibald Johnston. Russell Davenport also withdrew; as a memorial volume published a few years later summed him up, he was unlikely to find the new controllers of Bethlehem Steel congenial: "As a negotiator his success, by reason of his ingrained integrity, was naturally greatest in dealing with men of honor. He was not of the strategists of industry, whose sudden riches dazzle the vulgar."[13]

At the time he purchased Bethlehem Steel, Charles M. Schwab was president of the United States Steel Corporation, which had only begun trading on 1 April 1901. He tried to forestall any embarrassment that might result from his acquisition of the company by describing his venture as no more than "a flier," but in June, to avoid compromising his position at U.S. Steel, he assigned his interest in Bethlehem to a syndicate controlled by J. P. Morgan. It seems that at some point Morgan suggested that U.S. Steel should absorb Bethlehem, but the idea was not taken up. During the fall of 1901, E. H. Harriman is reported to have proposed that Bethlehem be merged with two or three other companies and to have asked Schwab to negotiate the deal. The plan failed. Remarkably, over no more than a few months, Bethlehem Steel had been saved from being absorbed into one of the biggest international armament groups, from being swept as a second-rank plant into the world's largest steel combine, and from becoming part of a new amalgamation. Given his U.S. Steel responsibilities, Schwab understandably had neither a place on the board nor an office in the company's operations. Even so, he was by no means inactive; he was providing considerable advice. Among the more active "new blood" in control of business were Edward McIlvain as president, Henry Snyder as secretary, and Archibald Johnston, who was made general superintendent.[14] The following year, Bethlehem Steel for the first time became directly involved with shipbuilding.

From the perspective of the late 1890s, it was difficult to believe that from 1800 to the late 1850s the United States had been the world's largest shipbuilder. After that, there had been a long drawn out decline. Western Europe and above all Great Britain were further advanced in the industrialization process, their concentrations of coal, iron, and engineering industries were generally closer together (though not more so than in the industrial district of southeastern Pennsylvania), and their mushrooming foreign commerce required huge merchant marines. By contrast, the United States was opening its vast interior regions with their varied resources, an exploitation process requiring first riverboats and then primarily trains and railroad companies, not steamships and shipping firms. New England maritime activity was not keeping pace with national economic growth, and water carriage between the eastern and western seaboards was eventually largely replaced by mainline railroad transport. This process of shrinkage in marine transport was taken even further because it did not take place insulated from the international economy. As the merchant marine dwindled, foreign shippers commanded more of the United States' overseas trade so that, by the middle of the 1890s, only about one-tenth of its foreign commerce was carried in American ships. This had a direct impact on what had once been a great national industry. In 1894, British yards built 850,000 tons of shipping for British-owned companies; only 16,000 tons of oceangoing shipping was constructed that year in the United States.[15]

In addition to these generally unfavorable national circumstances, American shipbuilding suffered from some serious operating handicaps. Other than under exceptional conditions, ships were custom built, designed for the special circumstances of various trades. There was much division of labor in the yards, but, as ships were not standardized items capable of being mass produced in any sense, they offered fewer opportunities for economies of scale than many other products. Reduced scope for mechanization meant labor quality and cost were more important considerations than in most other large-scale manufacturing processes. Inevitably, this situation penalized the United States. In 1902, a careful British student of the industrial scene reckoned that ships identical in type to those built in the United Kingdom cost 30 to 36 percent more to turn out in the United States. Once built, they had to compete in the same international arena.[16] Despite these handicaps, at the end of the nineteenth century, American shipbuilding once more began to grow.

Before the 1890s, only two yards on the Atlantic seaboard built vessels bigger than five thousand tons' displacement, but in the next decade there was a major revival in both mercantile and naval construction, though for the former—the only sector for which there are statistics—the recovery was for many years uncertain. Cramp in Philadelphia epitomized the situation. Between 1887, the beginning of a new naval reconstruction program, and 1894, it increased its capital from $500,000 to $5 million and its work force from sixteen hundred to almost six thousand. In the 1890s, it was equipped to build the largest cruisers and battleships.[17] More generally, this period of expansion involved not only reconstruction and extension of existing firms but also the founding of new companies and building of more shipyards. By 1908, eight Atlantic coast yards could undertake what was described as work of the heaviest kind. Six of those yards had already completed first-class battleships and cruisers, and four were considered to have the capacity and equipment to rival anything in Europe.[18]

In the new confidence about the prospects of shipbuilding in the late 1890s and early twentieth century, a number of attempts were made to connect this business, still obviously an "infant" industry, with steel, in which the United States was already supreme. The Cramp shipbuilding firm tried first to associate with Carnegie Steel and then, early in 1901, came the attempted merger involving Midvale Steel and Bethlehem Steel with the British armaments, steel, and shipbuilding group, Vickers. At more or less the same time, the New York Shipbuilding Company, erecting new works at Camden, New Jersey, tried first to link with the Carnegie Steel Company and then to make alternative arrangements with Carnegie's former chairman, Henry Clay Frick.[19] By far the biggest connection between the two industries involved Charles M. Schwab and Bethlehem Steel.

The United States Shipbuilding Company was formed to amalgamate a number of existing shipyards in anticipation of a boom in demand expected to follow proposed merchant marine legislation. Schwab agreed to buy back Bethlehem from J. P. Morgan and to merge it into this shipbuilding group, but only on terms that ensured that if things went badly, neither the steel company nor he would suffer serious loss. The failure of Congress to pass the hoped-for bill, a stock market panic during 1902, and the company's own inherent weaknesses meant that the U.S. Shipbuilding Company did fail. In part as a result of what was widely regarded as a scandalous situation in this shipbuilding group (though for many other reasons as well), in early August 1903, Schwab felt compelled to give up the presidency of U.S. Steel. Less than a year later, he resigned from the U.S. Steel board of directors. He was now free to devote his attention to the steel plant and shipyards he had acquired. By a strange inversion of arrangements, the remnants of the U. S. Shipbuilding Company were included in a new Bethlehem Steel Corporation, incorporated on 10 December 1904.

The capital stock and bonds of the Bethlehem Steel Corporation amounted to $33 million—only 46 percent as much as the value of the same properties under the U.S. Shipbuilding Company two years before. Employees numbered 9,461. Notwithstanding the recent controversy, the formation of the new firm received a strong vote of confidence, with more than 98 percent of the first mortgage holders of U.S. Shipbuilding Company bonds approving the reorganization plan. The Bethlehem steel works was far and away the most valuable property, representing more than three-quarters of the company's capital stock. A new nine-member board was selected in accordance with the reorganization plan for the whole business, shipbuilding as well as steel, but its composition pointed to Schwab's unquestioned dominance in its affairs. Two of the directors, George R. Sheldon and Charles W. Wetmore, were investors from the so-called Sheldon syndicate, which had gained control of U.S. Shipbuilding shortly before its collapse. Three of the directors were bankers: Thomas F. Ryan, John E. Borne, and a personal friend of Schwab's, Pliny Fisk. Two more were established Bethlehem men Archibald Johnston and Edward McIlvain, who had been among the seven directors on the board formed less than three and a half years earlier, when Schwab had first bought control of the steel company. The remaining two were Schwab and the secretary he had brought with him from his presidency of U.S. Steel, Oliver Wren. On 17 January 1905, an executive committee of four was elected at a meeting held in New York. Schwab was president and chairman—a significant combination of posts in view of his recent embattled position at U.S. Steel. McIlvain, president of the board in 1901, became vice president. Adolphe E. Borie, former vice president, was now second vice president, and Henry S. Snyder added the treasurer position to his role as secretary. Barry H. Jones took the new post of comptroller. It was decided that the main offices would remain in South Bethlehem.[20]

The charter of the new company authorized it to make iron and steel and to build and repair ships, marine engines, and so forth. To do so successfully, it would be necessary to undertake a considerable overhaul of the plant and organization in both the steel and shipbuilding sectors. Fortunately, the new company was headed by a man who possessed great energy and, though still in the prime of life, could draw on incomparable experience in the industry. He also had unusually wide contacts in the national and indeed the international economy. As early as October 1904, Schwab set himself and his colleagues a goal: "I intend to make Bethlehem the prize steel works of its class, not only in the United States, but in the entire world."[21] There would now follow years of resolute action to reach that target.

The reorganized Bethlehem Steel Corporation that began trading at the beginning of 1905 was an uneven agglomeration of industrial activities. Most of them were emphatically not state-of-the-art operations. From U. S. Shipbuilding, Bethlehem inherited a handful of yards, some in naval construction, others mainly in mercantile work, and most so inefficient that it was a high priority to close them and sell off what could bring in urgently needed funds for the modernization of the others. Bethlehem was the group's only steel works, and there, too, the situation was far from satisfactory. The Bessemer shop and rail mill were redundant, and a large part of the rest of the plant was concerned with war materiel for which demand was notoriously uncertain. A brochure produced in the previous year had listed the Bethlehem works's activities: forgings of all sizes for marine and stationary engines and for machine tools and so forth, steel castings, armor plate, finished guns of all calibers, carriages, mounts and ordnance material of all types, and also pig iron, muck bar, and the like. The works had eight open hearth furnaces and a fluid compression plant designed to deal with the high-quality steel used for shafting and guns. It made ammunition and projectiles.[22] This apparently wide competence was deceptive. Although a specialized and in some respects highly respected operator, Bethlehem Steel was small and not very profitable. In 1905 and 1906, the revenues of the new corporation averaged $16.1 million and net income was $1.6 million; for the same years, U.S. Steel's annual sales of products and services were $446.6 million, with income of $83.3 million. In fact, apart from its high standing and successes in armaments, Bethlehem was a backwater of a dynamic industry. It would not be easy to break out of this position. To his many friends and admirers, it must have seemed an act of miscalculated desperation on Schwab's part to have moved from U.S. Steel to stake his future on such an outfit. A decade of rationalization, economy, exercise of imagination, hard work by a dedicated team, risk taking, and good fortune would be required for the gamble to work out successfully.

From the start, Schwab was convinced of two things: that expansion was essential for success and that the form of control should be different from that he had experienced at the United States Steel Corporation. At the beginning of his presidency of U.S. Steel, he had outlined his prescription for steel in an article published in the *North American Review.*[23] In its emphasis on growth and method, this prescription reflected his experience at Carnegie Steel and was also a blueprint for future ambitions. In the article he wrote that "the large plant has an undoubted advantage over the small plant, and the advantage continues almost indefinitely as the process of enlargement continues." Under specialist managers, "nothing is left to chance. Every step of the process is carefully worked out in advance. All waste is cut off." A big company "can work on a narrower margin all around" but still manage to "develop its trade where a concern working under less scientific processes would be shut out." His other guiding principle was a reflection of painful experiences at U.S. Steel: "I was convinced that no great steel corporation can be managed from New York. . . . I was determined to reorganize the Bethlehem Steel Company and have it managed entirely on the grounds."[24] This policy was to be justified by results over the years, but building as it did on an already strong Lehigh valley tradition, it would ultimately have the effect of reinforcing Bethlehem Steel's dangerously inbred and inward-looking characteristics. Over the course of many decades, this insular character proved to bring with it some less than favorable consequences.

The effort to reorganize and expand Bethlehem Steel and make it a commercial success would involve imagination, sustained exertion over many years, and large capital outlays. It would depend on a talented team of men and an ability to convince the financial world that, in the end, the reorganized firm would repay the investment in it. In short, as the new owner, Schwab had to prove his ability to choose men who, like him, would have qualities and commitment similar to those who had made Carnegie Steel such a dominant force and to persuade the masters of capital of the possibilities. From an early stage, he showed he was willing to change management to obtain the ends he desired. An early casualty was the top management he had praised in January 1905, which seems to have resisted some elements of his plans for Bethlehem. On 18 June 1906, he was away, and in his absence a meeting of directors was chaired by the vice president, Edward McIlvain. In late June and through to the middle of July, there were no meetings of the executive committee because of the lack of a quorum, but on 17 July, Schwab attended a directors' meeting at which the resignations of McIlvain, second vice president Adolphe E. Borie, and Henry Snyder, secretary and treasurer, were accepted. Snyder was reappointed a director and financial vice president, a post he was to retain for another twenty years, until he retired. One of the places made available on the board by these resignations was taken by Archibald Johnston, who until then had been general superintendent at Bethlehem. The details of the conflict of opinions that led to this change have not come to light. Thus, it is necessary to be satisfied with the gloss given to the event by a later chairman who was a keen observer at the time: "certain cross-currents had developed."[25] Fortunately, in another important example of senior management changes from the same time, more insight is available.

In its early years, Bethlehem found that not only was some of the work in its shipyards unsatisfactory but also that a number of government contracts had to be worked off even though unprofitable, notably in the case of cruisers. This was especially the case at Union Iron Works in northern California, where, in 1907, six out of the seven ships completed resulted in a loss. There were various causes. The earthquake that struck the San Francisco Bay Area in 1906 had caused some damage at the shipyard, but human factors were more important than natural ones. To a considerable extent, problems there seem to have centered on labor conditions, with rising wages, decreasing hours, and poor workmanship, but there were also serious managerial deficiencies. In June 1906, a special meeting of the directors had considered the wish of Union Iron Works to bid for one of two new battleships for the U.S. government. Robert Forsyth, president of Union, had produced detailed figures for costs. It was "the sense of" managers gathered for a meeting in Bethlehem that they should submit no bid that did not show a safe margin for profit. Accordingly, it was decided to set the minimum for the bid at $4,250,000 to cover costs estimated at $4,090,000. A few weeks later Schwab reported to the board that the contracts had been awarded to the New York Shipbuilding Company and to William Cramp and Sons Ship and Engine Building Company, for $3,585,000 and $3,540,000, respectively. This news was followed up by dispatching John A. McGregor, who had been assistant treasurer at Bethlehem, to Union Iron Works. He reported that conditions there were unsatisfactory, and Schwab decided on a radical change in management, recommending to his fellow directors that McGregor should be made president in place of Forsyth, "whose resignation should be demanded." By 24 September, Forsyth and his vice president had resigned.[26]

The most important change in top management in the first nine years of the new company involved the rise of a man who went from crane operator to the presidency. After graduating from Lehigh University in 1899 with a degree in electrical engineering, twenty-three-year-old Eugene Gifford Grace immediately obtained a job in the steel works in the valley below as an electric crane driver. In 1902, he became superintendent of the yards and of transportation. Schwab seems to have first met him in 1904. From September 1905 to February

1906, Grace worked in Cuba as Schwab's chosen general superintendent of the Juragua Iron Company. On his return, he was made general superintendent of the Bethlehem works and given the responsibility of carrying through the construction of new plant on which the future of the whole company would depend. By 1908, he was general manager, responsible for manufacturing, purchasing, and sales, and being paid a salary of fifteen thousand dollars a year; as president, Schwab received fifty thousand dollars that year. In 1911, Grace became vice president and director and in April 1913, president.

Eugene Grace proved to be the perfect counterweight to Charles M. Schwab. The latter, only forty-two when he first met the twenty-seven- or twenty-eight-year-old Grace, had similarly risen from the most menial jobs and had had long experience as a plant manager before he became a company president. Except for not acknowledging Schwab's experience as plant superintendent, the authors of a short account of Grace's career make appropriate distinctions between the two men: "Schwab was the quintessential entrepreneur, the man of vision and financial acumen, with little interest in daily operations. Grace, on the other hand, was more remote and austere, the embodiment of the professional manager. It was Grace who oversaw the daily production, the man who hired, fired, and solved problems."[27] Over the years, Grace gained a reputation for aggressive defense of laissez-faire practices, championing capitalist business methods and opposing any interference with its freedom of action, whether by government or labor unions. He drove his colleagues and his workers hard, but he drove himself equally hard. The main distinction between him and them was that he would be rewarded on a princely scale. Not yet thirty-seven when he was chosen as president of Bethlehem Steel, he would dominate the company for more than forty years.

In large part, the remarkable success of Carnegie Steel had been the result of response to incentives. The awarding of partnerships and financial shares in the company secured the commitment of those who were chosen. Schwab introduced a variant of this to Bethlehem Steel. From the earliest days of his ownership of the company, he paid bonuses to those in top management to whom he believed much of their success was due. Thirty years later, in response to adverse publicity, he decided it was necessary to reveal something of the size of these distributions, which until then had been within his control. The first bonuses, paid in March 1902, covered five months from 1 September 1901 and amounted to a total of almost $10,758. By 1911, the bonus distribution had increased to $118,000 or, according to Schwab's assessment, 4.18 percent of net earnings for that year. In the prosperous year of 1913, bonuses amounted to $524,506, an amount equal to 7.31 percent of net income. Holders of common stock received nothing that year, and the distribution on the preferred stock was only $700,000.[28]

Some years later Eugene Grace reaffirmed the Bethlehem principles of looking after and providing incentives for key men and promoting them from within rather than bringing good men in from outside: "We believe that the sure way to kill initiative and throttle the enthusiasm of our faithful men is to fill our important positions with strangers from other companies. If a man isn't worth advancing, he isn't worth keeping." There was also a good deal of self-interested paternalism: "Every company should endeavor to so provide for its men ["important" men seems to have been implied] that they will not have to worry about financial affairs in their home. Once a man knows his family is provided for, he can give undivided, enthusiastic attention to his work. Worry more often than inability causes inefficiency." Like Schwab, he believed bonuses were effective in calling forth effort: "We pay our bonuses monthly, shortly after the salary checks are sent out. This causes each employee to be constantly keyed up to the highest possible pitch of efficiency."[29] As he later more pithily expressed it, he believed that nothing motivated men to work as much as money.

The whole prewar development program was so costly that it far exceeded income. Over the nine years through 1913, net income totaled $17.2 million; the net cost of additions, improvements, and acquisitions over those years amounted to $55.2 million. Shortages of funds, need for economy, and arrangements for borrowing, largely left in the hands of Schwab, frequently appeared as items of business. For instance, in June 1907, at a special meeting of the directors, "the financial situation as pertaining to this Corporation was gone over generally," and "after a free discussion, it was . . . resolved that the president be and hereby is authorized to borrow for this company such sums and on such terms as he considers necessary." Late in 1909, a special meeting of stockholders was informed of a plan to increase the indebtedness of the company from $22 million to $29.5 million; that year, net income was $800,000.[30] A few weeks later, Schwab exposed another problem with their financial situation. Though 1909 had resulted in a small surplus, they were then arranging to borrow considerable sums through the note brokers Hathaway, Smith, Folds, and Company, and he was personally required to endorse the notes. The brokers "were of the opinion that so long as the Company was borrowing as much money as at present, it would distinctly hurt the Company's credit if the payment of dividends were resumed." The directors voted against paying a dividend.[31] There were also cases of borrowing to support loans previously made, as in late summer 1912, when Schwab obtained a total of $936,000 in equal shares from the Mercantile Trust Company, the Equitable Trust Company, and Hallgarten and Company to enable him to continue his loan to Bethlehem Steel amounting to $1.5 million.[32] Four months before, he had hosted a grand occasion at Bethlehem for 150 of New York's leading "capitalists." Representing Kuhn and Loeb, William Saloman and Company, Harvey Fisk and Sons, and Hallgarten and Company, the syndicate that had underwritten the new first lien and refundable 5 percent $50-million bond issue of Bethlehem Steel Corporation as well as other prominent New York banking and brokerage houses, these leading men of finance were carried to South Bethlehem in a train made up of five Pullman cars and Schwab's own rail car, Loretto. As the press reported, the guests were shown the armor plate, structural, and rail departments "prior to being lunched by Mr. Schwab at his plant."[33]

In dramatic contrast with the wining and dining of those who helped provide the capital, conditions were far from congenial in this period for those who provided the labor for the processes of manufacture. Working conditions were hard and perilous and labor relations far from good. Men were engaged or dismissed to fit in with company convenience, but in times of high demand or financial pressure they could be driven to work harder. An example was provided by correspondence in July 1906 between Archibald Johnston as vice president and Eugene Grace, then general superintendent, on the question of armor production for the *South Carolina* and the *Michigan,* the first American dreadnoughts, which were to be laid down that autumn: "[I]t is my desire that you should push this work with the intention of making the armor in the least possible time, regardless of the fact that there is such a small quantity to manufacture. If this is not done the costs will run up considerably and this fact must be impressed upon the superintendent of the armor plate department. There must be no disposition to 'string it out' in order to take care of the men, as we cannot afford this."[34]

In 1909, 10 percent of those employed in the Bethlehem plant were injured, and twenty-one were killed. As seems to have widely been the case, men were laid off in times of trade difficulties. Average hourly earnings throughout Bethlehem Steel rose slowly through the prewar years, but not until 1913 did the rate rise above twenty-five cents an hour. Although, because of its expansion program, Bethlehem Steel produced more in 1908 than in 1907 (the tonnage of products shipped was up 62.1 percent, net income was one-quarter as large, and net income per dollar of total revenue only 38 percent), the average work force for the year was just over 80 percent as large and average hourly earnings were unchanged. The work force was not unionized, and the company was determined that this should remain so. On more than one occasion when the men asked for an advance in wages, the representatives who delivered their requests were dismissed. Men who were blacklisted could find that they could never again get a job in the industry.

The combination of long hours of toil, lack of freedom to organize, and pressure to produce led in early 1910 to a major strike, which lasted from 4 February to 18 May. There was some violence, most visibly by mounted state police, and one death. All in all, it was a relatively moderate dispute by the standards of the time, but the intractability and insensitivity of the company was blatant. In the end, it was ostensibly victorious, but the positions it adopted and those into which it forced the workers colored labor relations for the next thirty years.

6

WAR MATERIEL, SHIPS, AND COMMERCIAL PRODUCTS, 1904–1914

ALTHOUGH BETHLEHEM STEEL CONTROLLED A number of shipyards, Charles Schwab was sure from the start that the main asset and focus of attention must be the steel works. On 19 January 1905, a special meeting of the board of directors of the Bethlehem Steel Company was held to consider the offer of the plants of the United States Shipbuilding Company. Invited to comment, Schwab did not completely write off the shipyards but made unmistakably clear where the strength lay:

> Gentlemen, I can speak more specifically of the Bethlehem Steel Company, than I can of the others; and I can only say that I consider the value of the property has been many times enhanced in the past three years by the system and methods of business now in existence there. The company is in a most prosperous condition, with some four millions of dollars in the bank, no debts (except current bills), a very good business and altogether perhaps in the soundest condition it has ever been in during its existence. It has been most

ably managed during the past three years, and the business in hand is in excellent shape.

The Bethlehem plant had a valuation of $9 million and did annual business of $10 million to $11 million. In fact, Schwab was putting a favorable gloss on the situation of what was a rather minor and not particularly successful operation. During 1905, Bethlehem Steel would have a net income of $2.4 million; in the same year, U.S. Steel, whose board he had left only in the previous summer, made $68.6 million. Even so, the new company was setting out purposefully to develop its facilities. A day after Schwab had summarized their position, a $3.34-million program of spending on work in progress or contemplated was announced. The largest single items were $500,000 for a new gun shop and $500,000 for improvement at the Juragua iron ore operations.[1]

Bethlehem was exceptional among American steel firms in its inclusion of capacity for shipbuilding, and this would remain an important element in its structure. Over the long term, this sector was to be involved in extended periods of low levels of activity, short bursts of higher peacetime output, and frenetic work in wartime. In his 19 January 1905 assessment of their operations, Schwab was much more somber about shipbuilding than about steel: "The shipbuilding companies I cannot make such a favorable report upon, excepting that they are capable of development at least into a considerable asset. I think it is going to be best to sell these properties, and I think at a sum beyond which most of us have been figuring upon." Apart from Hyde Windlass, the shipbuilding division had sustained a considerable loss. The next day he recommended to his fellow directors the sale of their Hyde Windlass, Bath Iron Works, and Eastern Shipbuilding properties. By spring, Bethlehem had already disposed of the Bath Iron Works in Maine and of the Hyde Windlass Company, turning over the proceeds of their sales to the Bethlehem Steel treasury, to be used for the steel works improvements begun immediately by the new company. Within another year, much of the New London, Connecticut, works of Eastern Shipbuilding had been dismantled, with only three big cranes remaining to mark its former activity. By September 1907, Schwab had made arrangements to sell this yard for fifty thousand dollars.[2] From now on, the main Bethlehem marine operations were Harlan and Hollingsworth in Wilmington, Delaware, Samuel L. Moore in Elizabethport, New Jersey, and the Union Iron Works in San Francisco.

Despite its early problems and the fact that its main attention was given to steel, Bethlehem Steel interested itself in expansion in shipbuilding. In considerable part, this policy was related to the armaments capacity of the Bethlehem works, for, as in a number of the bigger European groups, it was seen that major advantages could be gained from being able to build, armor, and arm a warship in one organization. Having closed a good deal of its original building capacity, Bethlehem was willing to acquire more if this pursuit promised advantages. Late in 1908, it bought the San Francisco Dry Docks Company and merged it with Union Iron Works. Two years later, it was reported, in error, that it had acquired a large interest in the Cramp shipbuilding firm. In fact, for its biggest new departure, Bethlehem turned to New England.

The Fore River shipyard at Quincy, Massachusetts, had been established in 1884. At the beginning of the twentieth century, the company underwent a major expansion, including construction of a new yard. By 1902, it had eleven vessels, valued at more than $20 million, under construction. The following year, its top direction was changed, with Rear Admiral Francis T. Bowles being brought in as president. Further developments included, from 1903, the development of the Curtis turbine and, the following year, a start on submarine construction for the Electric Boat Company. Bigger triumphs lay ahead. In 1910, Fore River won a contract for one of the two battleships ordered by Argentina from United States yards, the *Rivadavia*. At the same time, Bethlehem Steel was awarded the $10-million contract for armor and ordnance for the Argentine naval program, including both the *Rivadavia* and her sister ship, the *Moreno*, which was to be built by the New York Shipbuilding Company at Camden, New Jersey. Over the next few years, the financial standing of the Fore River company was weakened by the burden of the construction costs for the *Rivadavia*, and it was eventually faced with the prospect of large losses. Seizing the opportunity this crisis presented, Bethlehem Steel Corporation took over the faltering shipbuilding company in 1913. The purchase price was $700,000, but by introducing an incentive scheme, apparently inspired by Schwab, Bethlehem succeeded in turning the Fore River operations from loss to profit so quickly that the cost of the acquisition was recouped out of operating profits there within a year. More important, as Bethlehem's annual report for 1913 recognized, "The control of the Fore River plant gives to your Corporation facilities for building . . . complete battleships fully armed and equipped."[3] The timing of such an acquisition could scarcely have been better.

Like shipbuilding, the manufacture of armaments was an uncertain business, for government orders varied greatly from year to year and foreign orders for war materiel had to be won in keen contest with a number of major and well-entrenched European groups. As early as spring 1905, Schwab returned from Russia with a reported $1-million order for armor, but his charm and the supporting skills of the Bethlehem negotiating team might not always be so successful. The following year provided an object lesson in the uncertainties of this field of business. Armor plate and ordnance makers received a boost at the end of 1906 when Secretary of the Navy Charles Bonaparte recommended that the new construction program include four battleships rather than the two expected, but a few months earlier his department had shown how dangerous it could be to rely on such orders. Midvale Steel, though the lowest bidder, had received only part of a government order for armor plate, the remainder being divided between Bethlehem and U.S. Steel's Carnegie Steel Company—on the condition that they accept the price Midvale had quoted. Bonaparte justified his decision on the grounds that if he proceeded otherwise, one or the other, perhaps both, of the two established makers might turn their armor capacity over to other purposes, leaving the government dependent on a single supplier. He recommended that, so as to avoid combination or collusion on prices, his department be authorized to seek bids from overseas manufacturers. In addition, reviving old issues, he recommended that the U.S. government equip itself to make at least some of the armor it would need in a federally owned plant.[4]

Although both shipbuilding and the manufacture of armor and guns were important parts of Bethlehem Steel, Schwab, as effective owner and director of its fortunes, recognized from the start that it was essential to build a firm base in commercial products. His convictions were reinforced by the company's experiences during the first few years of its existence. Until 1905, work for the U.S. government was Bethlehem's main source of income, but then for a number of years this business declined. Work in hand for the government amounted to $4.4 million at the end of 1905, $4.0 million a year later, and $2.6 million by the end of 1907.[5] Fortunately, various circumstances were changing in ways that improved the prospects for an eastern manufacturer of bulk steel. They were especially relevant to a company headed by a man with the experience, reputation, and ambitions of Charles M. Schwab.

One important new consideration was the rapid advance of steel making in the open hearth furnace at the expense of the Bessemer converter. In 1890, 500,000 tons of steel were made in open hearth furnaces and 3.7 million tons by Bessemer converters. Their respective tonnages in 1900 were 3.4 million and

6.7 million and, by 1910, 16.5 million and 9.4 million tons. Open hearth practice made possible much closer quality control than in Bessemer operations. Steel could be made for a wider range of specifications, and a wider range of ores could be smelted in the blast furnaces that supplied the melting shops. Economy in fuel consumption and large reductions in outlays for labor when the Wellman mechanical charger was introduced ensured that costs for open hearth steel could compete better with those for Bessemer steel. As discussed previously, one of the long-term liabilities of the Bethlehem Iron Company had been the difficulty in obtaining Bessemer grade ores at a time when large-scale, efficient acid Bessemer practice had formed the essential basis for success in the rail trade. Now rails made from open hearth steel were becoming more competitive with Bessemer rails, but, even more important, the share of rails in the total production of finished rolled steel was declining, and open hearth furnaces could better supply material for a number of other finished products for which Bessemer steel was increasingly recognized as less suitable. Although some firms continued to use Bessemer steel for structurals, during the 1890s, consumers increasingly preferred open hearth steel and in some cases engineers already specified that it be used. Finally, open hearth furnaces could use a much higher proportion of scrap, which, relative to demand, was more abundant and usually, though not invariably, cheaper in the East than in Pittsburgh. In 1904, the average price of heavy melting scrap was $12.78 per gross ton in Pittsburgh and $12.94 delivered in eastern Pennsylvania, but in 1910, the respective figures were $15.34 and $14.76 and, by 1914, $11.50 and $10.38.[6] Early Bethlehem extensions would be in open hearth steel, largely in basic furnaces, so that between 1901–1902 and 1906 the proportion of Bethlehem open hearth production that was made by the acid process fell from 71 to 51 percent of the total. After that, the switch to basic practice took place even more rapidly.[7] In 1910, the company contracted for the installation of two new acid Bessemer converters, but these were designed to be used in "duplexing," that is, in part purifying the hot metal from the blast furnaces before it was sent on to be finished in the open hearth. Duplexing increased tonnages while maintaining the quality of the final product.[8]

Market prospects in the East improved in this period. Most seagoing shipbuilding capacity in the United States was on the mid-Atlantic seaboard, and its expansion provided a concentrated outlet for plate and angles. Here, too, there were important centers of railroad equipment manufacturing that required tires and axles (most famously in the Baldwin Locomotive Works) and, as with marine engineering, outlets for boiler plate. Most of the multi-story building construction using structural steel was in the region, as was a significant share of that used in bridgework. For rails, consumption was now concentrated in the West, but as Sparrows Point had shown, the eastern seaboard was a good area from which to supply coastal zones along the Gulf of Mexico or on the Pacific coast. The eastern seaboard was also the most favored of all locations for foreign business. Moreover, the balance of advantage in supplying these outlets was shifting more in favor of plants within this region. At this time, railroad freight charges were increasing more quickly than rail prices. Testimony at the congressional tariff hearings of 1908–1909 suggested that, roughly speaking, 1908–1909 freight rates were three times the level of 1899, whereas prices for billets or rails had fallen, the former from $31.12 at Pittsburgh in 1899 to an average for 1908–1909 of $25.46 and, for rails, from $28.12 to a steady, administered, price of $28.00[9] The more complete adoption of "Pittsburgh plus" pricing penalized eastern consumers but gave producers there a fillip in the form of "phantom" freight—the amount added to mill cost to represent a supposed rail haul on the product from Pittsburgh. Finally, there was the general live-and-let-live policy adopted by U.S. Steel, the effects of which were far wider than the avoidance of more active government intervention against itself. In 1906, five years after the corporation was established, Judge Elbert H. Gary commented, "We are on friendly terms with all our competitors. We have been the most effective influence in maintaining stability—in preventing extremely low or extremely high prices."[10] No growing medium could have been more congenial than this for new rivals. When one of these rivals was headed by the man Gary had ousted from his prime position at U.S. Steel, there existed a prescription for an exceptional success.

Modernization and extension in existing lines of commercial production received immediate attention at the new Bethlehem company. Within seven weeks of incorporation, an improvement program had been outlined. It was costed at $3.3 million in the first instance and $5 million in the longer term. The investment was to be partly in extensions in war materiel, including a new gun shop, and in spending on gun carriage production and projectile manufacture, but it would also involve quality commercial products, including crucible steel for tires, springs, and so on. Already there were signs of a new, larger scale of thinking, for example, with $600,000 being allocated for Juragua, including improvements at mines, another railroad, and new ore docks. A few weeks later, there were rumors that Bethlehem had moved in another direction, acquiring Tidewater Steel of Chester, Pennsylvania, and with it "a good plate plant."[11] This proved a false trail, but widening of interests was not long in coming to light, a shift encouraged by a decrease in government orders during 1905. The annual report for 1905, and Schwab's annual statement in April 1906, gave him opportunity to explain the changes, though for some time they had already been followed in the trade press. He referred to the $3 million already spent to improve old plants and to expand in such new lines as crucible steel, staybolts, and drop forgings, the latter within about a year including products for the automobile industry. He then went on to sketch out much bigger things: "A careful study of the situation at this plant convinced the officers and directors that a still further development was desirable, and it was determined to continue the increase of the old plant, particularly in blast furnace capacity, as well as to establish a new plant to be devoted to the manufacture of open hearth steel, structural shapes, rails, and billets." When this was completed, they would have an annual capacity of up to 500,000 tons of rails and structurals. To accommodate this expansion, they had purchased 250 acres of land extending from the edge of the existing works toward Freemansburg. The sum of $12 million would be spent on new facilities, of which $3 million had been awarded in contracts by mid-March 1906.[12] The project for what would be called the Saucon works marked the start of a development process that would soon transform the Bethlehem Steel Corporation.

By the end of 1907, $4.6 million had been spent on improvements and additions to old plant and $8.3 million on new facilities. Shortly afterward, a new blast furnace and a melting shop of ten 60-ton open hearth furnaces, the basic unit of the Saucon works, were commissioned. Naturally, the new plant was superior to the capacity it supplemented. For instance, blast furnace E, which began production in December 1907, within three months was producing more than twice the output of the individual existing furnaces.[13] The capacity for iron in 1908 was 60 percent and for steel, more than double that of the previous year. A new blooming mill, a twenty-eight-inch rail mill, and two structural mills were installed. One of those structural mills was a forty-eight-inch finishing mill (a Grey mill) for both standard beams and wide flange beams, and the other was a standard twenty-eight-inch mill. The new rail mill came into production in early September 1907, and by the year's end, it had rolled 33,754 tons of open hearth rails. An economic recession that began in early fall delayed the

PART II. From a Struggling Plant

commissioning of the Grey mill by about two months, to 8 January 1908, and of the twenty-eight-inch mill by five or six months, to the summer of 1908. For both units the company reported that "these mills began operations with an unusual absence of the difficulties customarily encountered in starting up a new plant."[14] In 1908, $1.5 million was spent, mainly at the Saucon mill. Operations were affected by the decline in trade, but though rail output fell sharply, that of structurals increased. Financially, 1908 was unsatisfactory, total revenues being $16.8 million compared with $28.4 million in 1907. Net income fell even more, from $1.6 million to $400,000, and employment was down by 20 percent. Bethlehem remained a minor actor, but it was visibly making headway.

The early years of the century were ones of rapid change in the rail business. In 1905, when the decision to make open hearth rails was made, only 180,000 tons were produced nationally as compared with 3.19 million tons of Bessemer rails. Basic open hearth rails had been made in Alabama in 1899. The Ensley works in Birmingham completed an open hearth rail plant in 1902 but made no significant tonnage before 1904, when it began duplexing steel. In 1906, U.S. Steel decided to make open hearth rails in the new works it was starting to build at Gary, Indiana, and in 1907, it began to build open hearth furnaces to feed its Edgar Thomson mill. National capacity for open hearth rails increased rapidly, by 1910 being estimated at 1.5 million tons, of which the Gary and Ensley works accounted for 900,000 tons and Bethlehem for only 200,000 tons. In 1911, production of open hearth rails pulled ahead of Bessemer rails.[15] Having returned to the ranks of producers, Bethlehem Steel was to remain an important rail maker for the rest of the twentieth century, though later most production did not take place at the Bethlehem works. The year 1906, in which the new Bethlehem rail mill was under construction, would prove to be a year whose national output for that product would never again be reached. The situation was very different for the other new product, structural steel.

Business revived in 1910, and by the year's end the Bethlehem directors recognized a need to embark on more extensions. The main encouragement for this came from the success of their structurals business, for which, though management had expected it would take "some years" for the advantages of the new shapes to be fully recognized by builders, they could now claim that "even in dull times we receive a most satisfactory share of such contracts as are placed." Their new mills operated to the fullest extent of the steel tonnage available.[16] When they chose duplexing to increase steel output, there were further conse-

Table 6.1 Bethlehem Steel Corporation activity, 1906, 1910, and 1913						
Year	Capacity (thousand tons)		Output/shipments (thousand tons)		Total revenue ($millions)	Net income per dollar revenue (cents)
	Iron	Steel	Steel	Steel products		
1906	224	213	136	112	17.5	4.4
1910	364	571	538	403	26.3	7.6
1913	840	1,109	670	460	47.7	11.7

Source: Bethlehem Steel Corp., annual reports, 1906, 1910, 1913.

quences. To service the increased steel capacity, three more blast furnaces were planned, and this expansion required better and more secure supplies of iron ore and guaranteed delivery of coke. Late in 1910, the Pennsylvania Engineering Works of New Castle was awarded a contract for two twenty-ton converters. They were at work by February 1911. Work was also under way on two blast furnaces.[17]

The years 1912 and 1913 were record-setting ones for the industry, each year's steel output being more than 5.5 million tons above the previous highest and more than twice the level of the first four years of the century. Because of its expansion programs, Bethlehem's achievement was even more striking. In 1902, the first full year following U.S. Steel's formation, it produced 10.9 million tons of raw steel; output had doubled by 1912 and 1913. In 1905, Bethlehem Steel's first year, it made 115,428 tons of steel; its average in 1912 and 1913 was 783,619 tons. In products shipped, its record was even better, a ninefold increase. It had been particularly successful in three fields: as a world-ranking armaments manufacturer, in carving out a new commercial sector, and in reorganizing raw material supply.

Now and again over the early years of Bethlehem Steel, Schwab proclaimed his intention of making the company a supplier of armaments at least equal in stature to Krupp. By 1912, this goal, too, was being reached. Each month, Bethlehem could finish up to one thousand tons of armor plate.[18] In winning $10 million in contracts for guns and armor for Argentina, it had triumphed over its major European rivals. It was contending with the same companies for major orders from the Ottoman Empire, and it was seeking work in China. Already owning important naval building capacity on the Atlantic seaboard as well as Union Iron Works in San Francisco, Bethlehem had rounded out its facilities before the great European war began by acquiring Fore River, a first-class warship yard capable of building the largest vessels on the East Coast. The full significance of expansion and success in these departments of business, some of which had seemed to be encumbrances when the company was formed, would become clear over the next few years.

Above all, Bethlehem had now made a large-scale and successful return to commercial steels. In giving evidence before the Tariff Commission of 1908–1909, Schwab reckoned the Bethlehem plant could make 500 tons of rails and 1,000 tons of structurals a day, though not until 1911 were shipments at that level.[19] Its rail manufacture was symbolic of Bethlehem's revival as a power to be reckoned with, but its outstanding achievement was unquestionably in structurals. It claimed, and experience of rivals confirmed, that it was turning out a superior product by a newer, more efficient process while also enjoying unrivaled market access. At Carnegie Steel, Schwab had been closely associated since the mid-1880s with the Homestead structural mills, and he was general superintendent there when what one press report referred to as "the great beam mill" was installed in the mid-1890s.[20] Much structural steel was used for other purposes than in building, but use of fabricated structural steel was reckoned to have increased from about 250,000 tons in 1892 to about 1,222,000 tons nineteen years later.[21] When Schwab moved to Bethlehem, he recognized that the growing vogue of skyscraper construction, above all in mid-Atlantic cities, presented an opportunity for production of heavy structurals on a much larger scale than then undertaken in that region at the Pencoyd steel works and Passaic mills. To these market opportunities was added a much more effective production technology.

This opportunity had come in the form of an approach from Henry Grey, who in 1897 had designed the first really effective universal beam mill, about which he had been in correspondence at that time with John Fritz. The Grey mill was equipped with both horizontal and vertical rolls, which enabled it to roll H-beams direct from bloom "blanks," thus avoiding all the elaborate and labor-intensive fabrication that until then had been needed to produce the largest beams. From 1902, a Grey beam mill was at work at Differdange, Luxembourg, and Grey made efforts to interest American firms to take up his process. He was in contact with Bethlehem as early as November 1904; on 15 December 1905, a contract was signed for a mill designed by him.[22] During 1906 and more particularly in 1907, inquiries were already coming in from engineers about the new structural shapes. Well before his contract with Bethlehem, Henry Grey had claimed that, even after allowing constructional engineers a generous re-duction in price to encourage their custom, his process might double the nor-mal profit on beams.[23] The Bethlehem Grey mill was projected to cost about $4 million, but as construction went on, it became clear that the real cost would be some three times that estimate. At the same time, the company was hit by the economic panic of 1907–1908. Most of Schwab's colleagues were skeptical as to the wisdom of going on with the mill, and for a time he seemed ready to agree. However, the decision was made to complete the installation. Schwab raised more loans, the Philadelphia and Reading and the Lehigh Valley Rail-roads accepted freight on credit, and some of the contractors were willing to continue work for deferred payments.[24]

As a result of these acts of faith, the first Bethlehem Grey beams were rolled on 9 January 1908. Experience vindicated Grey's claims about profits, and ship-ments mounted quickly. In May, only four months after it came into operation, the Grey mill shipped twenty-one hundred tons, in July, thirty-one hundred, and by September, fifty-eight hundred tons. Its wide flanged beams were more quickly accepted than Bethlehem had expected. A splendid public demonstra-tion of the beam's advantages was provided by its use in the new Gimbels de-partment store at Thirty-second Street and Fifth Avenue In New York City. The contract to supply the twelve thousand tons or so of beams at thirty-two dollars a ton was signed in March 1909, the fabricating work to be done by the receivers of Milliken Brothers, a firm whose own new open hearth steel plant and struc-tural mills on Staten Island had failed in rather confused circumstances two years before. It was said that the forty-six-pound Bethlehem sections used at Gimbels were equivalent in strength to standard sections of fifty to fifty-five pounds. Generally, the costs of producing the Grey beam were so competitive that, though prices in 1909 were at their lowest in ten years, Bethlehem Steel was able to claim "we are making a satisfactory profit on every ton produced." Experience quickly proved the advisability of greatly increasing capacity for the new products. A year later, Bethlehem reported that "the rails and structural shapes produced at Bethlehem are in the nature of a specialty, in that the rails are rolled of open hearth steel and the structural shapes are of a patented, spe-cial economical section not produced elsewhere in the United States."[25]

From 57.9 percent of the national total in 1902, the share of U.S. Steel in pro-duction of structural shapes of all types had already fallen to 54.9 percent in 1907, before the new Bethlehem mills were at work. Over the next three years,

The construction of the Gimbel store in New York, 1909: the first major project using Grey beams. *Courtesy Bethlehem Steel Corporation.*

the decline was more rapid, dropping to a 51.3 percent share by 1910. Discussions among the board members of Carnegie Steel made clear that Bethlehem competition was a major factor in this decline. By January 1907, with its Grey mill still in an early stage of construction, Bethlehem was already reported to be trying to attract some Carnegie Steel men from its eastern offices. By fall 1908, when the industry generally was depressed, the worst affected section of Carnegie Steel was in structurals. There was considerable business, but its board was told "we are getting practically nothing of what is being placed." In sharp contrast, Bethlehem Steel was running all its structural mills full and had six months' work in hand. Indeed, as one Carnegie Steel director ruefully remarked, "I do not believe they are in position now to take business offered to them." By early

1910, it was said at Carnegie Steel that "Bethlehem is cutting quite a swath in the east at present on their 'H' sections, and taking some business from us." In one week at the end of that year Carnegie had lost fifteen hundred tons worth of orders for structurals in five jobs in New England; for four of those, specifications had called for the use of Bethlehem sections.[26]

New finished steel lines, and expansion in both iron and steel capacity to support the successes of the rolling mills, increased the urgency of breaking through Bethlehem's traditional weaknesses in raw material supplies. Within three years the problems with both fuel and iron ore supply seemed to be solved, but the solution in coke proved premature and in ore, though sound, the fruits of success were deferred by circumstances beyond company control. In using Connellsville coke or, indeed, coke from other Appalachian districts, Bethlehem, like other eastern iron producers, was naturally disadvantaged because of distance. Late in 1899, the breakup of the old management team at Carnegie Steel Company, which involved the ejection of Frick, was associated with a bitter debate about establishing a permanent price for Connellsville coke supplies at $1.35 a ton. At almost the same time, the annual coke contract with Bethlehem Steel provided for its full requirements at the rate of $4.75 a ton delivered at South Bethlehem, a price that would net the H. C. Frick Coke Company $2.95 at the ovens.[27] This sort of problem persisted. In addition, there were accusations of discriminatory pricing by railroad companies. In spring 1914, for instance, five eastern iron and steel companies protested to the Interstate Commerce Commission about increases in coke rates from Connellsville and from the Latrobe and mountain districts of Pennsylvania and the Fairmont region of West Virginia to the Lehigh and Schuylkill iron districts. Their complaint was that "the rates are already in and of themselves unjust and that the existing rates on coke when compared with the rates on coke to the Pittsburgh district are so high as to constitute an unjust discrimination against the eastern furnaces and in favor of Pittsburgh."[28] A way out of some of these difficulties that would provide other advantages was to build by-product coke ovens. By 1909, Bethlehem Steel was preparing to move in this direction.

During autumn 1909, it was announced that Schwab had contracted with the Didier-March Company to build a coke plant on a four-hundred-acre site. Didier-March would finance, build, and own the ovens but be supplied with coal for the ovens by Bethlehem—forty thousand tons a week in stage one and fifty thousand in the second stage. In turn, the independently owned battery would

PART II. From a Struggling Plant

supply coke to Bethlehem without charge and sell it gas at a fixed price, to be used in part in the Bethlehem furnaces and in part for illumination and fuel throughout the Lehigh valley. A little later, Schwab negotiated to supply gas to cement makers in this area, which was then a national leader in that industry.[29] At the end of 1913, what were expected to be the last shipments of Connellsville coke to Bethlehem were made before it became dependent on locally made by-product coke. There followed an unexpected and sharp setback. By April 1914, because of its unsuitability for the type of coal supplied, the coke plant had degenerated so badly that it was decided that the 300 ovens already installed at a cost of $4.5 million must be demolished. A new Lehigh Coke Company, or-ganized by Schwab, planned to build 424 Koppers ovens to replace what were now described as "the worthless" Didier-March ovens.[30] This was an embar-rassing but exceptional setback for a company that for a decade had recorded one success after another. With vague echoes of the United States Shipbuilding Company, it was either good fortune or remarkable prescience that had induced Schwab to draw up the agreement in a form that meant his own firm suffered little financial penalty.

For decades, iron ore supply had been an even more serious problem. Like his predecessors, Schwab searched for regional ore supplies, buying ores in the Boyertown area and from Sanford, in the Adirondacks, for instance. For a time there were even hopes of tapping the low-grade ores of eastern Texas, from which some shipments were made in 1913, before it was decided the investment of time and money would not turn out well. In looking overseas for supplies, the company was helped by a progressive reduction in import duties. The forty cents a ton tariff of 1894 was cut to fifteen cents in 1909 and in the case of Cuba, to twelve cents. From 1913 on, ore imports were duty free.[31] Returning briefly to the practices of the Bethlehem Iron Company, the new corporation looked once again to Europe, in 1911–1912 contracting for some 3 million tons of Swedish ore over the next nine years.[32] But more and more attention shifted to Latin America. The first major achievement of Eugene Grace had been to reorganize the Juragua ore operations. Output increased and ocean freight arrangements were improved, but it was obvious to those in charge at Bethlehem that supplies from Cuba could not support the essential large increase in iron making.[33] The focus of the search moved to South America. Millions of tons of high-grade ore (up to 66.8 percent iron) had long been known to exist in the Imataca Moun-tains of Venezuela, and it was suggested they could be mined and shipped at

Charles M. Schwab and Eugene G. Grace c. 1912. *Courtesy of the National Canal Museum, Easton, Pennsylvania.*

low cost. Bethlehem examined these ores in 1909 but went no further.[34] In the years immediately before World War I, the company was still making do with a variety of sources of supply. In fall 1913, C. A. Buck told Congress's Stanley Committee, investigating the organization of U.S. Steel, that Bethlehem used 1.25 to 1.50 million tons of iron ore a year. Cuba and Kiruna, in northern Sweden, each supplied about 400,000 tons; the remainder was procured from Lake Superior or mines in the Adirondacks.[35] By that time, a new situation was already taking shape.

Construction of the Panama Canal not only promised improved facilities for supplying West Coast markets both within the United States and in the Pacific states of South America but also made the mineral resources of the latter area more accessible. Although no ore was then mined except for small quantities used in smelting silver ore, by the 1890s, a string of iron ore deposits was known to exist in Chile. In 1909, a blast furnace plant was under construction on Corral Bay south of Valdivia. This was financed by Schneider and Company of Le Creusot. From 1905 on, the promoters of the Corral furnace, initially designed to use local ores, also owned the large and rich ore deposits of El Tofo much farther north, and in 1910, some of this ore was shipped to the new furnace at Corral Bay. The latter worked well below capacity, operating only four months in 1911. Meanwhile, Bethlehem examined the El Tofo property. The ore was of high grade, in part running at 67 percent iron, was at the surface, and required little in the way of stripping of overburden. In addition, the deposit was so near the coast that ores were transportable by wire rope tramway. After almost a year of negotiations, on 3 January 1913, Schwab signed a contract for control of El Tofo on highly favorable terms. In such circumstances it was not surprising that the next annual report concluded its account with the statement, "The officers and engineers of your Corporation consider the acquisition of this ore one of the most important developments in its history."[36]

Both outsiders and its own controllers recognized that Bethlehem fortunes had been revived, but so far the success had been limited. The large outlays had been very inadequately covered by earnings. The contrast with the United States Steel Corporation was a stark one. Over the nine years through 1913, U.S. Steel reinvested almost $295 million in its business; over the same period at Bethlehem Steel Corporation, the net cost of additions, improvements, and acquisitions was $55.2 million. But whereas in this period net income at U.S. Steel amounted to $674.1 million, the figure at Bethlehem was only $17.2 mil-

Bethlehem Steel from the New Street Bridge looking east, 1910.
Courtesy of the Historic Bethlehem Partnership.

lion. Time and again Schwab and his colleagues had to struggle to finance their investment programs. As early as January 1905, Bethlehem Steel had announced that it would spend $3.3 million in the first instance and that later construction would raise this to $5 million. Early in 1906, the company committed to spend another $12 million on a new plant for new products. In 1908, when continuation of their large expenditure program coincided with a sharp recession, efforts had to be made to sell products for which they had not already found an outlet. As Schwab then wrote to one of his most trusted colleagues, "We are endeavoring, for monetary reasons, to turn everything we can into cash." Work on a blast furnace had to be deferred indefinitely.[37]

Even so, by overcoming imbalances in plant and pursuing a purposeful and imaginative development policy, the management of Bethlehem Steel had achieved a great deal by the boom of 1913. National output of rolled iron and steel was just double that of 1901, the year of Schwab's first involvement with Bethlehem. Since 1902 (its own first full year), U.S. Steel, of which he had then been president, had increased its shipments of finished products from 8,913,000 to 13,387,000 tons. Another long-established rival, Cambria Steel, made 467,000 tons of finished steel in 1901 and 1,193,000 in 1913. For Bethlehem, the respective figures were 18,000 and 700,000 tons.[38] Circumstances seemed set for even greater success in the future. Promise of major improvements in the fuel situation had suffered a setback in the Didier-March fiasco, but with the Koppers ovens, improvement in that area was again foreseeable. Solution of the age-old ore difficulty was in hand. Writing in 1913 in his annual report for 1912, Schwab told the owners of Bethlehem Steel that taking advantages of opportunities "may require the entrance of your Corporation into fields not heretofore contemplated." Little more than a year later, the situation was transformed in another unexpected way. In August 1914, the outbreak of war in Europe disrupted established patterns of trade and postponed a breakthrough in ore supply. Much more important, it gave an unprecedented boost to and new directions for Bethlehem Steel.

7

WARTIME ACTIVITY,
EXPANSION,
AND MERGERS,
1914–1923

THE HEADWAY MADE BY THE Bethlehem Steel Corporation during the first nine years of its existence was impressive. Schwab had earlier announced that one of his ambitions was to build a company to rival Krupp. He was well on the way to achieving this; in the 1914 edition of the world authority on naval power, *Jane's Fighting Ships,* the full-page Bethlehem Steel Corporation advertisement appeared sandwiched between ads for Whitworth and Krupp AG as well as for Cammell Laird and for Vickers. Capacity for steel had been extended more than fourfold, from 210,000 tons to 1.11 million tons; for pig iron rather less, from 220,000 to 840,000 tons. In 1905, shipments of steel products were under 55,000 tons; by 1913, they were 606,000 tons. Yet, though it was clear to commentators and competitors alike that a formidable new eastern steel company was taking shape, Bethlehem was still not particularly profitable. Net income over the whole of this nine-year period amounted to $17.2 million, equal to no more than a third of the profit made by the United States Steel Corporation in the depression year of 1908. Dividend payments at Bethlehem seemed derisory, nothing being paid on common stock and only $2.2 million on preferred. A total of $55.5 million had been spent for additions, improvements, and acquisitions, but much of this had been borrowed. For all his remarkable achievements, Schwab's claim that he had made not a penny out of Bethlehem was scarcely an exaggeration.

By this time, his once dominant position as an owner of its capital stock had been very much reduced. At the annual meeting of stockholders on 7 April 1914, it was reported that there were 297,700 shares in the corporation's capital stock. Schwab held 51,823 of these; Grace had only 108 shares.[1] Schwab had already spoken of further expansion and of possible entry into new lines of production, but there seems to have been little promise for any radical change of pace or degree of success ahead. Yet over its second nine years, Bethlehem Steel was to be transformed from a successful, growing, but small and rather indigent concern into a major company, second only to U.S. Steel. The motivating force in its early growth had been the combined drive and imagination of its top management. Both qualities continued to be required and were forthcoming, but now opportunism would also be a prominent feature. The catalyst for these fundamental changes in Bethlehem's circumstances and fortunes was provided by the Great War, which broke out in Europe in early August 1914.

For the steel industry, 1912 and 1913 had been banner years, with raw steel production averaging more than 31 million net tons, or 5 million more than in the previous best year, 1910. In sharp contrast, 1914 was a year of recession, with national steel output falling 25 percent. At U.S. Steel, sales were 26.5 percent and income 71 percent lower than in 1913. Bethlehem did not escape the setback. Early in 1914, activity in its armament shops was boosted by work on big guns to be supplied for ships being built for the Greek navy in German shipyards, but by late spring, operations generally were slowing down. In late May, Schwab even went so far as to write to Judge Gary to suggest their two companies should build a first-class battleship for sale upon completion. The summer was slack, and successive Bethlehem directors' meetings scheduled for 28 June and 25 July were not held because of a lack of a quorum. By August, while taking advantage of the opportunity provided by the depressed state of business to spend $2 million on another Grey beam mill, Bethlehem was operating at about 60 percent of capacity. Workers were on reduced hours, and some men were being laid off.[2]

On Tuesday, 4 August, a stated meeting of the Bethlehem Steel executive committee was to be held at the office of the chairman, 111 Broadway. It was canceled because there was no quorum. Also on that day, Great Britain declared war on the German empire. Over the next few months, the company's wholesale response (especially Schwab's) to the opportunities provided by Europe in self-inflicted torment quickly turned decline and retrenchment at Bethlehem into high activity. War materiel orders of unprecedented size soon came in from Britain, France, and Russia. In fall 1914, Lord Kitchener, the British minister of war, asked Bethlehem Steel to supply a million shells in the course of a year. Although Schwab reckoned that at that time all the armament works in the United States together made only 100,000 shells a year, he accepted the order. The company filled the order in ten months.[3] Installation of the new beam mill was shelved for a time as the company embarked on a feverish regimen of producing war materiel. Most firms were continuing to suffer from the effects of depression, but at Bethlehem this unexpected autumnal boom meant that for the whole operating year of 1914, Bethlehem's performance was even better than in 1913. Revenues rose 7.2 percent, income by 9.8 percent. When the war began, the value of unfilled orders on the company books was under $25 million; by the end of January 1915, that figure had reached $100 million. By then, money was being spent to expand capacity for war materiel. Speaking at the annual meeting on 6 April 1915, Schwab neatly summed up their favorable circumstances: "While the year so far has been very bad for the general steel business, the Bethlehem Company has been fortunate in being engaged in the manufacture of lines which are in strong demand."[4]

In spite of some recovery in 1915, output, sales, and income at U.S. Steel continued to lag behind the 1913 figures; at Bethlehem, the tonnages shipped were lower than two years before, but, war materiel being more valuable than commercial steels, revenues were 232 percent and net income almost 250 percent higher. Cambria Steel provided another benchmark for measuring Bethlehem's changed fortunes. It, too, had been modernizing. Around the time of the peak levels of national production in 1912–1913, Cambria hired expert advice and spent some $500,000 to remodel its blast furnaces and thereby cut iron costs by about $3 a ton, making it a low-cost producer by northern standards. Yet, whereas Cambria's net income in 1913 was 21 percent higher than Bethlehem's, over the next two years it earned $5.7 million, compared with the $23.4 million Bethlehem earned.[5]

For four years, sales to the Allied powers and to the U.S. government remained at high levels. When Schwab spoke at the annual dinner of the American Iron and Steel Institute at the Waldorf-Astoria in May 1916, he was in a euphoric mood and seems to have let down his guard about the foundations on which the general prosperity depended: "Boys, we are in a period of great prosperity. I wonder if any of us ever expected, anticipated or dreamed that we should ever see any such state of affairs as we see today. . . . Boys, may this prosperity continue."[6] For more than two years it did continue, accompanied by an unprecedented orgy of destruction, killing, and maiming a comfortable three thousand miles away. By late 1917, 90 percent of Bethlehem orders were from government agencies. (For the steel industry as a whole, in the second half of 1917, it was estimated that 75 percent of output was absorbed by the war effort.) At the end of that year, orders on hand at Bethlehem Steel were twenty times as great as at the end of 1913. By the time the war ended, in the course of the more than four years of the fighting in Europe, Bethlehem Steel had turned out 60 percent of the finished guns and 65 percent of the gun forgings made by all American firms.[7]

One line of Bethlehem business that seemed surprisingly slow for much of the war was the manufacture of armor plate. By the end of 1915, all other departments were fully extended, but the armor plant had practically completed its contracts for the U.S. government. Yet it was at this time, to the company's distress and outrage, that yet another bill was introduced into Congress providing for the construction of a government-owned armor plate plant. The company protested that, if built, the proposed plant's capacity to produce twenty thousand tons a year would effectively wipe out the $7 million that Bethlehem reckoned was by now the value of its own investment in this line of manufacture.

In addition to munitions of war, Bethlehem also expanded in commercial steels. By as early as January 1915, it had resumed work on the plant extensions that had been under way when war began and that had been temporarily halted. These extensions were now projected to cost between $20 million and $30 million. Before the end of December that year, new construction had cost $12.5 million. Steel capacity had been 1.1 million tons, but a further 600,000 tons of steel capacity had now been completed or was under construction. By now, the company was also highly regarded in the world of finance. In 1913 and 1914, its common stock usually sold for about $30, but in the new feverish times, standards of assessing company worth were quite different. In the course of 1915,

Table 7.1 Bethlehem Steel Corporation business data, 1913–1918				
	Steel products shipped (thousand net tons)	Orders on hand at year's end ($thousands)	Net earnings from operations ($thousands)	Average number of employees
1913	605.9	24,865	8,753	15,052
1914	460.5	46,513	9,650	15,586
1915	579.9	175,433	24,821	22,064
1916	1,300.8	193,374	61,717	47,013
1917	1,900.0	453,809	53,979	64,782
1918	1,816.7	328,946	57,189	93,964

Source: Bethlehem Steel Corp. annual report for 1918.

the stock price advanced to as much as $600.[8] By early 1916, not only the munitions plant but also the structural, rail, and bar mills were all running at capacity.

In shipbuilding, too, Bethlehem was at full capacity. By the end of March 1916, 38 percent of all the shipping under construction in the United States was in Bethlehem yards.[9] At the close of 1917, Bethlehem's orders in hand for naval and merchant ships amounted to $273 million out of a total order book of $454 million. It ranked high even during the feverish national construction activity associated with the Emergency Fleet Corporation, which Schwab headed for a critical period in 1918. Between the time the United States entered the war and the end of 1918, Bethlehem yards delivered 625,000 tons of merchant shipping, which was 22 percent of the output of the entire country in this period. (In the years 1912 and 1913, the entire tonnage built in the nation, including what was constructed in the Great Lakes region, had been 579,000 tons.) In the course of the war, the company built more destroyers at Quincy than were constructed in all other yards in the United States combined. By summer 1918, Bethlehem Steel Corporation employed 120,000 persons, of whom 65,000 worked in its shipyards. At that time, it was anticipated that the work force in these yards would increase by another 5,000 by October.[10]

One consequence of the activity of these years was the grinding, unrelenting pressure of work; its beneficial counterpart was a transformation of the Bethlehem Steel performance indicators. Over the five years in which there was fighting in Europe, the company's net income amounted to $110 million or well over six times the total of the previous nine years. Dividends paid to stockholders took $24.5 million of this net income, leaving most of the wartime profits to finance extensions and acquisitions. Its high profile, obvious successes, and powerful momentum enabled the company to raise further capital far more easily than before, when it was concentrating on expansion in commercial steels. Furthermore, the departments of the army and navy assisted in financing operations necessary to meet their demands. Most important of all, in the war and its early aftermath, those in command at Bethlehem took such effective advantage of the opportunities made available by these exceptional conditions that by the end of 1923, the capacity they controlled for iron and crude steel had been raised to 7.4 million and 8.5 million net tons, respectively. For nearly sixty years, Bethlehem Iron and then Bethlehem Steel had been a one-plant company; now it owned six fully integrated works, distributed over an area extending 100 miles inland from the Atlantic and 280 miles from the shores of Chesapeake Bay to Lake Erie.

It had achieved this extraordinary change in its position by absorbing firms whose size was comparable to or even in excess of its own. The first move in this process was taken not by Bethlehem Steel but by one of Schwab's former colleagues. After many years at the Carnegie Steel Company, William Ellis Corey succeeded Schwab as president of the United States Steel Corporation in 1903 but resigned in 1911. As he was by then only forty-five he was unwilling to retire from business. For a time he became interested in copper, but the new conditions and opportunities of wartime persuaded him to follow Schwab into the eastern steel and armaments complex. In September 1915, leading a group of friends who had also been at U.S. Steel and with help from New York bankers, financiers, and local business leaders, Corey purchased the Midvale Steel Company of Nicetown, in northern Philadelphia, for $22 million. Founded half a century earlier to make alloy and special steels and steel products, Midvale also produced ordnance, and in the last decade before the war, it had joined Bethlehem and Carnegie as a supplier of armor plate. However, in contrast to Bethlehem, the former Midvale management had refused to produce war materiel for sale to those engaged in the fighting in Europe. Corey's new firm, incorporated on 15 October 1915 as the Midvale Steel and Ordnance Company, issued $75 million of stock and set out, like Bethlehem Steel, to win orders from the combatants. In addition to its Nicetown operation, Midvale included a plant for small arms manufacture at Eddystone, Pennsylvania, and the medium-sized steel and plate operations of Worth Brothers at Coatesville some forty miles west of Nicetown. Following Midvale Steel and Ordnance's incorporation, there were four months of reports and rumors about further mergers in the East.[11]

The next step in reorganization was related to the long-term effects of the Hepburn Act of 1906. One of its provisions was to limit railroads' ownership of subsidiaries whose products they carried. This act induced the Pennsylvania Railroad to begin looking for others to take over its part ownership of the Pennsylvania Steel Company, which controlled the plants at Steelton and Sparrows Point. Steelton had begun to make Bessemer steel in 1867. By 1882, capacity there was 250,000 tons, but in the later years of that decade it began to feel the same competitive pressures from works farther west that burdened Bethlehem Iron. As previously discussed, in 1887 it chose its own distinctive reaction to these pressures by purchasing a site on Chesapeake Bay as a location for blast furnaces. By 1892, it had expanded this new plant with a Bessemer steel works and rail mill, under the title of the Maryland Steel Company. It was at this early stage that Henry Clay Frick asked Andrew Carnegie "if we could purchase Sparrows Points [sic] works on about the same basis of Duquesne, and pay in 20 year bonds, would it not be a good thing to have?" He thought it might be a good place to build ships, and as Pennsylvania Steel did not seem comfortable financially, "a time might come when we could pick it [Sparrows Point] up cheap."[12] In fact, in the face of harsh competition in the 1890s, both the Steelton and Sparrows Point works suffered badly, were underutilized, and lost money. Pennsylvania Steel was in receivership in 1893 partly because of its failure to provide enough capital to complete the coastal works of its subsidiary; a little later, Sparrows Point was idle for three years. Early in the new century, the Pennsylvania Steel Company revealed how relatively inefficiently it had been operated. If it had controlled sufficient ore and coking coal, it could have saved $2.9 million over the cost of the open-market purchases it had to make in 1900. Recognizing a need for more capital to keep up with technological improvements and to acquire more mineral resources, it was reorganized in April 1901. Steelton then had a steel capacity of 500,000 and Sparrows Point, 400,000 tons. Over the next few years there was further expansion and modernization, but operations remained ill balanced and were not viewed by others as highly competitive. An interesting insight into comparative costs of production is available. From 1902 onward into World War I, the price of Bessemer rails at mills in Pennsylvania was held steady by the United States Steel Corporation at $28.00 per gross ton. In 1907, the cost of rail production at U.S. Steel mills averaged $22.81 a ton; at Maryland Steel, they cost $25.37. Over the seven years to and including 1908, net income per ton of ingots produced by U.S. Steel was

$12.18, but at Pennsylvania Steel it was only $5.25.[13] The lack of balance in the Pennsylvania/Maryland plants was well illustrated by the operating experience of the shipyard built at Sparrows Point in 1890. When the yard started, some hailed it as destined to become the greatest shipbuilding operation in the United States, if not in the world. A main reason for this hope was the expectation that all its steel would be made on the spot in plate and shape mills. This did not happen, with rails remaining Sparrows Point's only product. In 1912, two-thirds of the plate used in the shipyard was brought from Steelton, and the rest had to be purchased in the open market, from Worth, Lukens, or the United States Steel Corporation.[14] The Pennsylvania and Maryland operations continued to perform poorly.

A week before the formation of Midvale Steel and Ordnance, there were rumors that Schwab was planning to amalgamate Pennsylvania Steel and Bethlehem Steel and that Cambria Steel might even be included. A day after the Midvale incorporation, there were other reports of a Bethlehem Steel–Pennsylvania Steel link. The situation then became even more confused. First, there was talk of a successful takeover of Pennsylvania Steel by a party headed by W. H. Donner and Henry Clay Frick and then rumor of a possible Bethlehem-Pennsylvania-Midvale link. December brought a strongly diverging account of an amalgamation of Lackawanna, Cambria, and Youngstown Sheet and Tube.[15] The state of uncertainty lasted into the new year. Then, on 7 February 1916, Midvale announced it had paid $72 million for Cambria Steel. This gave it an integrated works with a capacity of 1.4 million tons of iron, 1.5 million gross tons of raw steel, and 1 million tons of finished steel, as well as Cambria's estimated fifty-year supply of Lake Superior ore.[16] The raw steel capacity of the new group was about 2.5 million tons, ranking it second only to U.S. Steel. However, it retained this high rank for only a few days, for on 16 February, Bethlehem purchased Pennsylvania Steel and the Maryland operations. The price paid was $31.9 million, but, though it was now well provided with funds (as recently as 20 January it had made the striking announcement that it would pay a 30 percent dividend on its common stock), Bethlehem chose to pay in 5 percent improvement bonds secured by mortgages on the plants acquired. Along with the two steel works, it obtained a 54.2 percent share in the Cornwall ore banks (recovering the interest Bethlehem had sold years before), control of the Mayari ores of northern Cuba, and coal mines in central Pennsylvania producing more than a half million tons a year.[17] Steelton was an important acquisition, including as it did a new combination structurals and rail mill, but it was soon clear that the prime material gained was Sparrows Point.

Although contemporaries recognized the importance of the Sparrows Point shipyard, by now able to build vessels up to six hundred feet in length, the real prize was the steel works and, above all, its potential. Bethlehem Steel now had new opportunities for a diversification program that it had already seen as essential but which, without the acquisitions, would have had to be at Bethlehem. Many years after the war, Schwab explained to stockholders that their directors had known that the end of the war would bring an end to high activity and might "annihilate" their principal business, its main plants becoming "worthless." To meet the challenge they had planned a well-rounded, thoroughly integrated steel operation, producing a full line of commercial products. At a directors meeting on 17 February 1916, the day after the merger, he filled out details of the course of action they had until then been contemplating for the Bethlehem works. They had planned more blast furnace capacity, a new Bessemer plant, and mills to make bars, tinplate, and possibly wire. On the other hand, for a long time they had wanted a seaboard plant for the export trades. Sparrows Point was a superior location and would enable the company to achieve the expansion and diversification it sought; its existing Bessemer plant could easily be extended.[18]

With the Sparrows Point facility, they could provide direct access for imports of Cuban iron ore or the new Chilean ore and also ship finished steel to foreign or coastal markets. At the time, a rough estimate was that Sparrows Point might have an edge of $1.50 a ton on overseas sales over all competitors. Even for its rail mill, this was a significant advantage because Bessemer standard rails for fifteen years had been priced at $28 a ton and open hearth rails at $2 or so more than that. Within a few months, plans were revealed for long-term outlay on new facilities. About $30 million would be spent at Bethlehem and $40 million to $42 million at Pennsylvania Steel. Between $10 million and $12 million was to be spent at Steelton, but $30 million would go into Sparrows Point. There, another one thousand acres were acquired to accommodate the new plant, and before the end of the year there were contracts for four new blast furnaces, an open hearth plant, and blooming and plate mills. By August 1918, more than $22 million had been spent there and it was reckoned that another $20 million would be needed to complete the construction program.[19] Within eight years, Sparrows Point was almost three-quarters bigger than Steelton.

There were other Bethlehem acquisitions during the war years, less spectacular than that of Pennsylvania Steel, but important in rounding out operations. The Baltimore Sheet and Tin Plate Company, bought in 1916, was a small operation but marked Bethlehem's first involvement in thin flat-rolled steels. During 1917, the nearby Lehigh Coke Company and the Lebanon properties of the Lackawanna Iron and Steel Company were bought. That year it also took in the American Iron and Steel Manufacturing Company, which had a small steel works and nut and bolt manufacturing facility at Lebanon and Reading, Pennsylvania. By 1916, Bethlehem shipbuilding plants used about twelve thousand tons of rivets a year, and it had contemplated building a works to make them. It was reckoned that acquisition of the Lebanon and Reading works would save them two years that would have been involved in constructing a new plant.[20]

As expected, the Armistice was followed by a sharp decline in activity and government cancellation of unfilled contracts. The annual report for 1918, dated 1 April 1919, made reference to "the war now happily ended," but the new peacetime situation would inevitably be more difficult.[21] Hoping to find new outlets, Bethlehem joined nine other companies in late December 1918 in a new concern, the Consolidated Steel Corporation, to foster the export trade in steel products. In fact, the industry passed on into a peacetime boom in 1920 and only during the year after that into severe depression.

Throughout the early postwar period, Bethlehem was rounding out and consolidating its expanded steel operations. The process was eased by government payments for munitions supplied during the fighting, and the direct connection between those payments and company improvements was recognized. For instance, early in 1917, the company had received $37.6 million in British treasury notes as payment for munitions Bethlehem supplied to Russia. Two years later, the annual report mentioned that the maturing of these notes "provides for the entire present construction program as stated below and for additional working capital. This places the finances of your company in good condition." The main expenditure in 1919 was at Sparrows Point, where the increased output was to be largely devoted to sheet and plate manufacture.

In 1919 and 1920, a good deal of attention was given to raw material supply, stockholders being informed that enlargement and development of the steel works had now largely been completed. A major part of the program concerned delivery of El Tofo ore. Development work had continued at the mines;

now it was time to build the ore carriers. It was announced first that the Bethlehem Shipbuilding Company would construct two 20,000-ton ore/oil carriers, then that the Ore Steamship Company, which already carried supplies from Cuba, would operate five new 20,000-ton vessels bringing Chilean ore northward and taking oil, coal, or coke on the return journey. It was hoped these carriers would be in operation by April 1922. In fact, construction work was partially stopped in 1921 because low ocean freight rates during depressed trade conditions made it commercially advantageous to use independent carriers. The first vessel in the new ore fleet was completed in February 1922, and it delivered its first cargo from El Tofo to New York on 6 June. An agreement in that year with Swedish operators provided for them to build and operate on Bethlehem's behalf two more carriers of comparable size. By 1924, El Tofo could supply 1.5 million tons of ore annually.[22]

Improving the supply chain for fuel also required action. With the completion of the new by-product ovens at Bethlehem and the addition of the batteries at Sparrows Point and Steelton, it was essential to control more coal. In 1919, Bethlehem Steel purchased the Elkins Coal and Coke Company, which owned forty-six thousand acres of coal lands in West Virginia. The following year, it took over a neighboring producer, the Jamison Coal and Coke Company, whose annual capacity was 1 million tons of low-sulphur coal.[23]

As the national economy pulled out of the depression of 1921, a new round of mergers began in the steel industry. Bethlehem Steel was the leading player, a role for which its wartime earnings were still an important asset. In the seven years to the end of 1921, it had earned almost $150 million but had distributed less than $45 million to its stockholders. Much had been plowed back into the business, but it still had ample resources for further acquisitions. As usual, the scope of the links considered or rumored extended far beyond what was achieved. Late in 1921, there was discussion of a merging of seven important integrated firms. If that merger had occurred, it would have produced a new company almost half the size of U.S. Steel and more than three times the size of Bethlehem. The discussions were long and difficult. Then, in a new turn of events, Bethlehem focused on Lackawanna Steel. After production had finally ended in Scranton in March 1902, the company had begun making steel on the new site of Lackawanna near Buffalo. Its promoters (largely local or banking interests; the Scranton family had quickly pulled out) had ample resources and built what was in many ways a magnificent plant. But they also made some poor choices, such as installing Bessemer converters and continuing to specialize in rails, with a new rail mill having the largest capacity of any in operation at a time when both the steel process and the product were being superseded. There was serious disagreement as to development policy between the local management and the New York financial interests that controlled the company, the most prominent among them being Moses Taylor. Labor problems and worker militancy increased. (In 1910, half the workers were of Slavic origin, but during World War I there was a large influx of black laborers from the South.) Poor financial performance resulted from this combination of difficulties. In 1907, for instance, nationally a good trade year, net income at Lackawanna per ton of ingots produced was only $4.92, as compared with $5.25 at Pennsylvania Steel and a remarkable $13.47 at U.S. Steel. Later, it was claimed that rail rate increases on coke penalized the Buffalo area as compared with Pittsburgh and Gary, Indiana. Lackawanna was profitable during the war, but it was especially hard hit by the depression in 1921; its earnings that year were 180 percent below those of 1920 as compared with a drop of only 29 percent at Bethlehem. Its steel capacity was 1.8 million tons, whereas Bethlehem now accounted for 3 million tons. By the following year, Lackawanna Steel's debt was $22 million, equal to half its capital value.[24] It was at this time that Lackawanna lost its independence. The circumstances were unusual.

During spring 1922, negotiations were under way for the seven-company merger. Lackawanna was one of the principal parties to these plans. A tour of inspection of the various plants to be included in the amalgamation was arranged, beginning and ending in New York. President George F. Downs of Lackawanna Steel was a member of the inspection party, which returned from its travels on 11 May. On the same day, Grace announced that Bethlehem Steel was to acquire Lackawanna, "a distinct surprise" to its top management, as *Iron Age* put it. The negotiations had been with Moses Taylor, chairman of the board, and with other directors who held a majority of the stock. On 16 May, the agreement was ratified by the two boards.[25] Although challenged on antitrust grounds, eventually the merger was allowed to go ahead. Bethlehem paid $35 million and also assumed some $21 million of Lackawanna debts. The annual raw steel capacity of the Bethlehem Steel Corporation increased to 5.5 million tons. With the plant, there also came important raw material properties, notably upper Great Lakes ore.

The purchase of Lackawanna was quickly followed by another, even bigger addition. In late November 1922, an agreement was reached for Bethlehem Steel to purchase the properties of the Midvale Steel and Ordnance Company. The

Nicetown plant, Midvale's main war materiel plant, was excluded. The acquisition was carried through in 1923. Bethlehem paid $95 million and assumed Midvale's considerable debt. The largest addition to Bethlehem Steel Corporation capacity from the Midvale takeover was at Cambria Steel. Founded in 1852, its Johnstown plant had made Bessemer steel since 1871, had widened its product range, had, like Bethlehem, reconstructed its finances and organization at the end of the 1890s, and had expanded after that. Cambria net income in 1913 had been $6.2 million as compared with $5.1 million at Bethlehem Steel, but whereas the latter made profits of $23.4 million over the following two years, Cambria income had been only $8.4 million.[26] From early 1916, the Cambria Steel Company had been controlled by Midvale, and Cambria was now brought into the combination with Midvale. Yet again, important coal and ore properties were involved, including 100 million tons of Lake Superior ore. Grace assured his board that Bethlehem was getting all this at a very reasonable cost. He told them they would pay $97.8 million for Midvale and Cambria, even though the valuation committee that had recently been assessing them for the proposed seven-company group had valued the same properties, but this time *including* Nicetown, at $258.7 million. The Mahoning ore mine in the Mesabi Range, which came with Cambria, was carried in the Cambria books at as little as $210,000, but the seven-party committee had valued it at $45 million.[27]

During the five years from 1917 through 1921, average annual earnings at Lackawanna had been $5.14 million and at Midvale and Cambria, $15.51 million, compared with $16.68 million at Bethlehem Steel.[28] Together, the Lackawanna and Midvale mergers had boosted Bethlehem's steel capacity by more than 150 percent in less than three months. It was now able to make all important commercial products except for pipes and tubes, although in some lines its involvement was small. Naturally, the company hoped for substantial gains from the new grouping. Looking back early in 1923, the annual report summarized these expectations. The statements made were general, though specific remarks seem to refer to Midvale. The report first drew attention to the newly acquired mineral resources: "Their operation in conjunction with properties now owned by your Corporation will permit of more economical assembling and better mixture of raw materials, while the unifying of the operations of the manufacturing properties will permit of a more advantageous allocation of orders. Through these important advantages as well as by a reduction of overhead expense and the elimination of duplications in distributing costs, the position of your Corporation in competition with other commercial steel producers will be materially improved."[29] Such aims were the common justification for all major mergers, but, as was also generally the case, their realization proved difficult and costly. In fact, much of the effort of the Bethlehem Steel Corporation through and beyond the 1920s would be devoted to that task.

8

BETHLEHEM STEEL
IN THE
1920S BOOM

IN EVERY AGE, AND IN any field, it is dangerous to assume that things will continue as they have in the recent past. By the early 1920s, the activities that had provided Bethlehem Steel with large profits over the previous few years were already becoming of minor significance. The company was in the difficult position of being the largest maker of heavy armaments at a time when it seemed that munitions of war would no longer be needed. This was apparently confirmed by the international agreements on limitation of navies that followed the so-called Washington Conference held in fall 1921. At this time, Midvale had a capacity of 90,000 tons of forged products, the Homestead works of U.S. Steel could make 22,500 tons of armor and heavy forgings a year, and Bethlehem's capacity for armor was 12,000 tons and, for heavy forgings, as much as 125,000 tons.[1] The Bethlehem Steel board was forced to conclude that for the foreseeable future, the success of their operations must depend on commercial products.

Shipbuilding of all kinds, so important a part of company operations during World War I, shrank back to levels comparable with those of prewar days. In the third quarter of 1921, ship production was worth $14.67 million and steel and other products, $15.37 million, but in 1922, the sales made in the year amounted to $7.61 million for ships and $141.6 million for steel and other products. By 1924, apart from Fore River, which was "fairly well occupied," most of the shipbuilding plants were mainly concerned with repair work. No important new shipbuilding contracts were received during the year. There were still occasional highlights, such as the Fore River launching of the first American aircraft carrier, the USS *Lexington,* in 1925, but generally shipbuilding was a burden rather than an asset. This would be the pattern throughout the decade. In the first half of 1929, manufacturing profits from the steel plants amounted to $39 million, but for shipbuilding and repair they were only $1.75 million. Strangely, in the third quarter of 1929, an improvement over the second quarter in terms of orders in hand was attributed to additional shipbuilding business. Because of this, Fore River was operating at practically full capacity and was profitable.[2]

For steel, the 1920s constituted a watershed of more than average significance. In that decade, there occurred a revolution in the size and structure of the national economy, as America began to lead the world into the age of mass consumption. Between 1919 and 1925, there was an increase of 29 percent in the quantity of goods produced in the whole industrial sector, but the relative strengths of various parts of industry underwent important changes, many of which affected demand for steel. Ship and boat building activity fell by 93 percent, but wartime demand had of course caused a tremendous surge in that activity. Output of railroad cars and locomotives decreased 27 and 62 percent, respectively. Automobile production went up by an amazing 204 percent. Except for 1918, the annual output of passenger cars had exceeded 1 million after 1915; after 1923, it was more than 3 million.[3] In this decade, the closed-top car and the emerging domestic appliance industry as well as rapidly increasing use of canned goods provided major impetus for the production of thin flat-rolled steel products.

Through the 1920s, Bethlehem Steel grew spectacularly, but in the early years of the decade, most of this growth was due to acquisitions. Later, it was preoccupied with restructuring the huge but rather rambling structure created as a result of the three great mergers that took place from 1916 to 1922. Meanwhile, other companies, some newly or fairly recently established, were prospering in new steel growth lines and pioneering technologies that within a few years would transform the industry. When the merger with Midvale was agreed to in November 1922 and Bethlehem became the second largest steel company, its new capacity seemed a triumph. Of its total of 6.4 million tons' finished product capacity, structural shapes accounted for 870,000 tons and rails for 1.26 million tons, whereas capacity for tinplate was only 100,000 tons and for sheets, a mere 70,000 tons. Although it seemed a triumph at the time, it was in fact an augury of problems.[4] Over the next few years, the company handled problems of growth and rationalization well, but diversification in response to the new patterns of demand was less vigorously pursued.

At the end of 1924, as the Bethlehem Steel Corporation completed its first twenty years, its controllers celebrated what they had achieved. Steel capacity had increased fortyfold, as compared with a national rise of less than 150 percent and an increase of 98 percent at U.S. Steel. At the beginning, it had operated a single and ailing plant; now it possessed six integrated works. Then, it ranked low among steel companies; it was now second only to U.S. Steel. It was also second worldwide, its size being more or less equal to that which Vereinigte Stahlwerke would command at its formation in 1926, when it brought together half the steel capacity of Germany. In 1904, Bethlehem owned only two mineral properties: the Juragua ores in Cuba and the McAfee limestone quarry in New Jersey. Now Bethlehem had widespread interests in nearly all the minerals it required. Having closed or disposed of most of its original shipyards, it had again expanded in this field and now owned ten building or repair yards. When Eugene Grace remarked in the course of the twentieth anniversary celebrations, "We have reached one turning point in our history, yet I am sure we stand on the threshold of a new progress which will rival that made since 1904," it seemed a reasonable claim.[5] Over the remaining six years of the 1920s, national steel capacity increased by 7 million tons or almost one-ninth and that at Bethlehem Steel by 800,000 tons or one-tenth. U.S. raw steel production in 1929 was a record 63 million tons, of which Bethlehem turned out almost 9 million tons. Yet during these few generally favorable years, there were a number of problems. They may be summarized under the categories of material supply, of the expansion, modernization, and rationalization of process plant, and of responses to significant changes in the market situation.

By the 1920s, Bethlehem operated batteries of by-product coke ovens at most of its integrated works. To supply them, by 1924 it had acquired by amalgamation or direct purchase 150,000 acres of coal land in Pennsylvania and West Virginia, together containing some 800 million tons of fuel suitable for iron and steel making. The once tight iron ore situation seemed at last to have been made secure. The mergers had brought in large holdings of Lake Superior ore, and the company now controlled both the Cornwall ore banks and an estimated two-thirds of the ore in Cuba. Above all, it was at last able to complete the organization of production and deliveries from Chile. By the 1920s, El Tofo was estimated to contain about 200 million tons of 60 to 65 percent ore. During World War I, development work had continued at the Bethlehem Chile Iron Mines Company even though a shortage of shipping had meant that deliveries to the United States in 1916 were only about 50,000 tons. The following year, the capital of this mining subsidiary was increased from $4 million to $10 million. The first large importation of 260,000 gross tons of Chilean ore was in 1922; by 1929, 1.7 million tons came in. Chilean ore was increasingly attractive compared with Great Lakes ores. Between the first years of the century and the late 1920s, the average price of Lake Superior ore doubled and iron content fell four percentage points, to 51.15 percent. Schwab could take legitimate pride in the way his Chilean purchase was working out. Hauled forty-four hundred miles, El Tofo ore could be laid down at Sparrows Point for $6 per ton of pig iron. He claimed iron could now be made there more cheaply than anywhere in the Midwest.[6]

Before the mergers, the Bethlehem board had to decide on the pace and type of expansion for one plant; from 1923, it had to plan rational development for six plants as well as for important non-steel operations. A pressing problem was that the condition of the works acquired left much to be desired. The report to stockholders on operations in 1922 had listed the gains to be derived from amalgamation: "more economical assembling and better mixture of raw materials, while the unifying of the manufacturing operations will permit of a more advantageous allocation of orders. Through these important advantages as well as by a reduction of overhead expenses and the elimination of duplications in distributing costs, the position of your Corporation in competition with other commercial steel producers will be materially improved." Real though the benefits might be, they could be won only at the cost of great efforts in welding together formerly separate management teams, each with its own often very different ethos, and by revamping procurement patterns for raw materials, plant product lines, and the composition and direction of efforts of the various sales organizations. In short, it was a task of considerable magnitude, one that the only similarly sized amalgamation, that of U.S. Steel, had to some extent side-stepped by acting as a holding company, leaving for a later date the difficult job of thorough-going rationalization. By early 1924, when Bethlehem's report on 1923 operations was written, the scale of what needed to be done was being recognized. Hope of the advantages was still there, but it was now known that Herculean effort was necessary to secure them:

> The outstanding problems of your Corporation during the year have been the coordination of the raw material properties, transportation facilities, and producing units acquired from the Lackawanna, Midvale, and Cambria companies with other Bethlehem properties and the realignment of administrative and operative organizations, together with the formulation and execution of commercial policies to meet the new conditions created. Much has been accomplished but it will naturally require some time before the full benefits can be realized from the consolidation of the properties. The work of modernizing and rounding out the new properties is being carried out as rapidly as conditions permit.

The next report referred back to their acknowledgment at the time of the acquisitions in 1922 and 1923 that "considerable" expenditure was needed to "improve, enlarge, and coordinate them with the other properties of your Corporation." Something of the financial costs can be deduced from the fact that capital outlay was at a fairly high level through the mid-1920s and, at the same time, net income in relation to capital stock was lower than in both the early and last years of the decade. In 1925, 1926, and 1927, production and shipment levels were good, but no dividends were paid on common stock; in contrast, preferred stock was well rewarded. In November 1927, as the newly elected president of the American Iron and Steel Institute, Schwab revealed that over the last four years his company had spent $167 million on development of its plants.[7]

Apart from organizational change, there were the questions of expansion for some of the mills and concentration or relocation of particular lines of production. In fact, though the pattern of extensions indicated some aspects of the long-term thinking in the development strategy, there were a number of complicating factors. These factors included the type of product (was demand for it increasing?), the possible duplication of facilities within the expanded company, and which plants in the new group were best able to make the product. One consideration was the type and quality of the process plant; another

Table 8.1 Raw steel capacity of Bethlehem Steel plants, 1904, 1916, 1924, and 1930 (thousand net tons)

	1904	1916	1924	1930
Bethlehem	215	1264	1625	1900
Steelton	-	(1697)	860	760
Sparrows Point	-	(786)	1495	1965
Lackawanna	-	(1792)	1830	2220
Johnstown	-	(1994)	1905	2045
Coatesville	-	(476)	795	380
Total	215	1264	8510	9270
		(6745)		

Note: Parentheses indicate plants acquired between 1916 and 1923.

Source: Bethlehem Steel Corp. annual reports for 1904, 1916, 1924, and 1930.

had to be its location. Rationalization was proving a complex business, and in some cases it was not finished until well into the 1930s. Unfortunately, by then many circumstances had changed yet again.

Since 1917, when it acquired the American Iron and Steel Company plant in Lebanon, Bethlehem had controlled an important center of nut and bolt production. Over eight years, this plant was practically rebuilt. In 1926, operations there were combined with those of the special plant at Reading that made rivets, bolts, and spikes.[8] Over the next decade, the rolling of billets was discontinued at Lebanon; thereafter, its nut and bolt operations depended on semi-finished steel from Steelton and Sparrows Point. One small steel making plant is not listed above because it disappeared so quickly. The Wilmington Steel Company, when taken over by Midvale, had a steel capacity of 90,000 tons and made blooms, billets, merchant bars, and castings. By 1922, it had been extended to a raw steel capacity of 160,000 tons, but, lacking supporting iron plant and replicating capacity found elsewhere in the group, it was soon closed. Steelton and the Coatesville works, the smallest plants after the mergers, were both landlocked but had blast furnaces. The main product at Coatesville was plate. After a period of slowdowns, iron and steel making was abandoned there in 1931. The Coatesville plate mill, whose capacity when acquired had been half as big again as that at Sparrows Point, was moved to the latter, whose iron and steel making costs were so much more favorable and where at least some of the output could be used in the local shipyard.[9] After this, Coatesville was confined to one of its old specialties, the manufacture of boiler tubes.

Postwar hopes of a major new boost for the rail trade were dashed. Bethlehem had reentered this business in 1907, when rails amounted to 20.6 percent of all finished rolled steel; by 1929, their share was 6.6 percent. In 1920, having absorbed Pennsylvania and Maryland Steel, Bethlehem Steel accounted for 6.75 percent of the national rail output and Lackawanna Steel, for 15 percent. The inclusion of Lackawanna and shortly afterward of Cambria meant that from 1923, Bethlehem had five rail plants. By the end of the decade, it controlled more than one-fifth of U.S. rail making capacity, and rails accounted for a higher proportion of its mill tonnages than was the case at any company except Colorado Fuel and Iron. Gradually, it concentrated its rail production. Steelton had a combination structurals and rail mill with a capacity of up to forty thousand tons a month. This plant had been installed only in 1915, but counterbalancing this advantage was the fact that its location made iron making costs there relatively high. Consequently, during the 1920s, much of Steelton's rail business was transferred to Sparrows Point or Lackawanna. The heavy and light shape mills at Bethlehem and Lackawanna took over its other main product, thus confining Steelton largely to rolling billets, though it could produce rails if required. Rail production at the Bethlehem works was also ended in favor of the more recently acquired mills at tidewater and on Lake Erie, freeing it for larger involvement in the expanding structurals trade. A new rail mill was completed at Lackawanna in early fall 1928. There was to be an interesting sequel to this rail rationalization program. When rail demand fell even more sharply, Lackawanna, like U.S. Steel's Gary works, moved over to rolling semi-finished products on its rail mills. Then, as calls from newly installed finishing mills were made on Lackawanna's steel capacity, a larger share of rail making was again focused at Steelton.[10]

Between 1909 and 1928, fabricated structural steel capacity in the United States increased from about 180,000 to 385,000 tons a month. By 1922, the national capacity for the structural shapes on which this fabricating industry depended was 3.6 million tons, with Bethlehem and U.S. Steel dominating the supply of heavier shapes.[11] In the mid-1920s, U.S. Steel scrapped its old-style structural mills at Homestead, and from January 1927, it offered a new range of wide flange beams. It called them "Carnegie beams," but they were rolled on what was effectively a Grey mill. In December 1928, after a bitter dispute, Bethlehem sued the U.S. Steel Corporation for infringing on the Grey patents. Almost a year later, the case was settled when the complainant agreed to grant U.S. Steel a license to use the process.[12]

Table 8.2 Bethlehem annual rail capacity, 1922 and 1935 (thousand gross tons)		
	1922	1935
Bethlehem	250	-
Steelton	420	360
Sparrows Point	350	200
Johnstown	240	-
Lackawanna	500	275
Bethlehem Steel	1,760	835

Source: *Iron Age* and Ford, Bacon, and Davis. "Reports on the Operations of the United States Steel Corporation." 200 vols. (Unpublished, 1936–1938).

Two of the newly acquired plants presented particularly serious problems. Their previous owners had not followed the highly effective prescription that Schwab had learned at Carnegie Steel: the unceasing necessity to modernize. In the late 1930s, comparing his own company with U.S. Steel, Schwab told the reporter Sidney Whipple that "the Corporation never tore down a plant, never scrapped obsolete equipment, because it didn't have the men with vision enough to dare to do it. When we took over Lackawanna and Cambria we found run-down, useless mills. We tore them down and built new ones." Both the initial problem and the Bethlehem remedy were as he stated, but as the longer term would show, non-material problems were more difficult to deal with and deficiencies in location were more intractable still. Nearer the time, Grace had spoken of the need for "considerable expenditures . . . to improve, enlarge, and coordinate" the Lackawanna, Cambria, and Midvale properties with Bethlehem's existing plants and "after careful analysis of the manufacturing problems and commercial possibilities . . . a construction program has been formulated which contemplates not only the modernization of portions of the plants to effect important economies in operations but also the addition of finishing capacities."[13]

Lackawanna had not been well maintained by its previous owners. Bethlehem acquired it for about $60 million, and during the remainder of the 1920s, it spent $40 million on the plant. In the middle of the decade, at 1.6 million tons of steel capacity, it was second in size only to Johnstown in the expanded Bethlehem Steel Corporation and it was 300,000 tons bigger than Sparrows Point. Even so, a Bethlehem-produced (but unpublished) "History of the Lackawanna Plant" recognized some years later that, when acquired, it was "antiquated and in such rundown condition that it was only a matter of time before the Lackawanna Steel Company would have been forced out of business." In short, it had not been kept up to date and production costs were high. Bethlehem reconstructed the coke ovens, shifted from hydraulic power to electricity in the rolling mill drives, and the No. 1 melting shop, blooming mill, and structural and plate mills were rebuilt. The independent Lackawanna had turned out lighter structurals but had been only a small producer; in a nine-month period of 1919, it had shipped 9,515 tons, and Cambria works, 8,695 tons, whereas Bethlehem shipments were 59,105 tons. During 1924, Bethlehem Steel revealed plans to build a twenty-eight-inch and a thirty-five-inch structural mill, enabling Lackawanna to enter the heavy structural business on a considerable scale. It shipped its first Grey beams late in April 1927.[14]

When a special meeting of directors was held in November 1922 to discuss the acquisition of Midvale and Cambria, Grace had talked up the advantages of Johnstown. Because of its local coal and its interest in the Mahoning open pit on the Mesabi Range, "it is felt that the Cambria plant should be able to produce steel for as low a cost as any other steel plant in the country." In addition, as he pointed out, that plant would widen their product range, adding wire rod, wire, and wire products, steel freight and mine cars, large plates, and quality plate for boiler construction, flanged plate products, boiler tubes, car axles and wheels, and a large range of products used in agricultural machinery manufacture. Cambria would also give them a facility that, as Grace put it, "is practically in the Pittsburgh district" and had good access to midwestern markets. In fact, although the Johnstown works widened Bethlehem's product capacity, most of what it added was not in rapid growth fields. Also, in terms of its geographical position, it was landlocked and uncomfortably placed between the eastern centers of production and the great agglomerations of competing capacity in Pittsburgh, the Valley district, and along the shores of the Great Lakes. It had already suffered because of its geographic position. Like Lackawanna, it was allocated a good deal of expenditure for improvements, about $35 million by 1926 and another $10 million announced in spring 1929. However, it was clear from an early date that, notwithstanding Grace's claims regarding both product range and location, it was not marked out to be a leading growth point. The group's biggest plant at the time of the Midvale merger, Cambria by 1930 was already trailing Lackawanna.[15]

At Sparrows Point, the scale of expansion undertaken in the 1920s confirmed what had been said frequently since 1916—that it was a highly favored location, both in terms of iron and steel making costs and for access to the large markets of the mid-Atlantic region, the Caribbean, and the West Coast. In May 1921, a $25-million spending program was announced. In 1922, plans were revealed to start wire manufacture, and though acquisition of Johnstown brought with it capacity for wire rod and wire, late in 1924, a new Sparrows Point wire mill was announced. Tinplate capacity was then being increased by 50 percent. Four years later, a 216,000-ton-per-year pipe mill was completed. In 1916, Sparrows Point had accounted for 9.8 percent of the steel capacity at the six integrated works, which, through merger, Bethlehem would control by 1923. By 1922, its share was 17.6 percent and in 1930, 21.2 percent. Late in 1923, there was even a rumor that the company was thinking of moving its headquarters there from Bethlehem.[16]

With its massive investment program in the mid-1920s, Bethlehem Steel set itself well on the way to completion of the modernization and reconstruction of its largely extended operations. Even so, it was difficult to keep up with increasing competition. Between 1923 and 1925, operating costs were reduced by $5.12 a ton, but over those two years the average price it received for its steel products fell $5.85; in spite of all its efforts, net operating profit per ton fell by seventy-three cents.[17] Moreover, although it had achieved a great deal, there remained two outstanding issues: its product range and, even more intractable, the distribution of its plants in relation to the national market. They were not unrelated problems because the contemporary switch of emphasis in the industry to lighter products was linked to a new distribution of steel consumption. For one major product not in that lighter category, effective action was taken to improve the market situation by greater involvement in further processing.

Between 1922 and 1930, national capacity to produce structural shapes increased 45 percent.[18] For heavy structurals, the competition to secure dominance in this expanding trade was above all between U.S. Steel and Bethlehem Steel. The mills at Bethlehem were well situated to hold their place in the eastern seaboard markets, and in the open season, the new Lackawanna mills could ship by water throughout the Great Lakes region. Some years later, the rail freight rate per long ton of steel from Buffalo to Chicago was $8.74, but the water rate was only $1.79. As a result, though the Illinois Steel division of U.S. Steel largely increased its structural capacity in these years, the Lackawanna mills managed to compete in this major market area. In 1928, Lackawanna ran a weekly boat to Chicago and Milwaukee, and it shipped 45,000 tons direct to a site on the Chicago River for the massive new Merchandise Mart. At the same time, however, U.S. Steel penetrated eastern markets that were obviously tributary to

Bethlehem. The Empire State Building, completed in 1931, required 58,000 tons of steel. The U.S. Steel subsidiary, American Bridge, split the contract with its keenest competitor, McClintic-Marshall, and the steel shapes used were rolled by U.S. Steel.[19] With the onset of depression, construction and, consequently, demand for structural steel, fell off. U.S. Steel had its own important fabricating outlet, and Bethlehem now took decisive action to command its own.

Early in 1928, Bethlehem Steel acquired the Danville Structural Steel Company. Three years later, it made much bigger steps in this direction. The McClintic-Marshall Company had been organized in 1900 by two Lehigh University trained engineers, with financial involvement from Andrew Mellon. Beginning in an old steel plant in Pottstown, Pennsylvania, it had at first been dwarfed by American Bridge but then had expanded rapidly in part at the latter's expense. It fabricated 52,000 tons of steel in 1902 but within eight years was dealing with an output of 133,000 tons. Over the next two decades, it became the world's largest fabricator and erector of structural steel; by the end of 1924, it was operating ten fabricating shops, including Pottstown and Baltimore in the East; Leetsdale, Rankin, and Carnegie near Pittsburgh; two Chicago-area plants; and a bridge works in Buffalo. Its annual fabricating capacity in 1924 was about 400,000 tons of shapes and plates, and through an affiliate in Leetsdale, it could consume another 150,000 tons of plate. In 1925, McClintic-Marshall opened a fabrication shop in Los Angeles, and by the end of the decade, it also had a base in San Francisco. Its business for 1929 totaled more than $50 million. At that time, its Pittsburgh-area operations accounted for about 240,000 tons of its 600,000 tons' annual capacity, and much of their structural steel and plate was drawn from nearby U.S. Steel plants.[20]

Such circumstances made it a considerable coup when, four months after a visit from Eugene Grace in early December 1930, it was announced that McClintic-Marshall had become a subsidiary of the Bethlehem Steel Corporation. Its annual fabricating capacity was reported as about 700,000 tons.[21] The Mellon interests that had a controlling interest in McClintic-Marshall in turn became large holders of Bethlehem stock. G. H. Blakeley, already associated with Bethlehem for twenty-five years and manager of their plate and structural sales, was appointed president of McClintic-Marshall. There were other moves in the same direction. During 1931, Bethlehem took control of three smaller construction engineering firms in the New York area as well as the Kalman Steel Company, which fabricated and distributed products such as concrete bars and had

Bethlehem beams in New York construction in the interwar years. *Courtesy Bethlehem Steel Corporation.*

warehouses in the East and the Midwest. An even more conclusive way to reduce competition was to close rival capacity. There was an interesting example
of this strategy in 1931. In the 1920s, the Eastern Steel Company of Pottsville had
a rated structural steel capacity of 150,000 tons. By spring 1931, it was idle when
Bethlehem bought it from Luria Brothers, a scrap firm. The purpose of the acquisition was satisfied by dismantling the plant, the new owners explaining that
the company could not operate the plant profitably in such a location.[22]

Even after the reconstruction of its plants, Bethlehem Steel remained heavily
biased to production of heavy products, and its operations were confined to
the eastern part of the manufacturing belt. In this period, and especially toward
the end of it, efforts were made to break out of both limitations. Having achieved
so much in bidding for rivals at the beginning of the decade, Bethlehem Steel
now had one further important success but failed in two other attempts. In
1922, Bethlehem was reported to be planning to open up two new lines of business by installing a wire making plant at Sparrows Point and tube manufacturing facilities at Steelton.[23] An opportunity to avoid expenditure on either seemed
to open with the prospect of purchasing the Pittsburgh Steel Company. From
a small rolling mill operation started in 1901 at Glassport, on the southern edge
of the Pittsburgh industrial district, Pittsburgh Steel the following year began
a much bigger rod, wire, and nail plant on a virgin site at Monessen, further up
the Monongahela River. In 1907, it installed open hearth furnaces and a bloom-

ing mill and bar mills, and six years later it added two blast furnaces. Coal and coke properties were acquired and steel capacity extended in 1917. Eight years later, a manufacturer of seamless tubes with operations at Monessen and at nearby Allenport was purchased, by which time Pittsburgh Steel had an annual finished steel capacity of 600,000 tons. Coke came by barge along the Monongahela, and in the mid-1920s, the company also developed barge transport for products destined for southwestern markets, establishing large warehouses in St. Louis, Memphis, and Houston.[24] This company was relatively small for an ordinary carbon steel maker, and its size made it vulnerable to corporate predators in an industry of many much larger operators. Its products and its river access to markets that Bethlehem could not easily reach made it an attractive target for acquisition by the giant. Negotiations for the purchase of Pittsburgh Steel were held but abandoned in 1922 after a difference over the value of its shares. Two years later, the Pittsburgh Steel president denied that another bid was being made, though by then the rationale for such a takeover had been reduced as Bethlehem had obtained its own rod and wire capacity at Cambria Steel. In 1931, there were renewed negotiations, which at one stage almost resulted in an agreement, but Pittsburgh Steel never was absorbed into the Bethlehem group.[25]

It is said that over many years Bethlehem Steel had a tacit understanding with the United States Steel Corporation that it would not move into the Midwest, presumably in return for a commitment that the latter would not attempt major incursions into Bethlehem's own heartland.[26] At the end of the 1920s, relations between the two companies were at a low ebb, in part because of the discovery that U.S. Steel was secretly building a Grey-type beam mill at Homestead without obtaining a license. One sign of the tension was the fact that within a month, Bethlehem followed U.S. Steel's acquisition of Columbia Steel by its own purchase of steel capacity on the Pacific coast. The far western industry into which it bought its way had a history that had been fairly long but scarcely distinguished.[27] As long ago as 1901, Schwab, as chairman of U.S. Steel, had pointed to the unsuitability of the West Coast for integrated works because of the long hauls required to assemble raw materials. Fourteen years later, addressing the San Francisco Commercial Club, he reckoned the coast now consumed about 600,000 tons of steel products a year. Rail freight charges from the East were about fifteen dollars a ton, but via Panama, the sea rate from the East Coast was on the order of five dollars a ton. The following year, Schwab's own company acquired Sparrows Point, the eastern mill best situated to serve this sizable but scattered market.[28] Evidence given in 1923 to the Federal Trade Commission showed that no more than 4 to 5 percent of Bethlehem shipments of plate and structurals were then going to the Pacific coast.[29] Expansion and diversification at Sparrows Point, especially of two products of particular importance in western markets (tinplate and tubes) capitalized on the advantages it possessed there, and by 1925, when increasing rail charges were penalizing eastern interior operations trying to serve the Pacific, Bethlehem decided to consolidate its position by establishing large warehouses in the four main foci of commercial activity: Los Angeles, San Francisco, Portland, and Seattle. Several new freighters were to be built to supply them from East Coast mills. By 1927–1928, the rail freight charge on semi-finished steel from Chicago to the West Coast was around twenty dollars per net ton; by sea from the eastern seaboard, the freight charge was then about eight dollars.[30]

Expansion of the indigenous steel industry in the Far West made considerable inroads into markets there during the 1920s. Installed capacity scarcely grew at all in the Pacific Northwest but was doubled to 850,000 tons in California. One substantial company there was the Columbia Steel Corporation, which by the end of the decade had a steel plant at Pittsburg on San Francisco Bay and at Torrance, near Los Angeles, as well as small iron ore and coal mining and coke and iron making operations in Utah. Another important group was the Pacific Coast Steel Company, whose operations in San Francisco had begun as a local business initiative to rebuild the city after the earthquake in 1906 and which by the 1920s also had a steel works in Seattle. Although at various times there was rumor of a possible association with small blast furnace operations at Irondale or Bellingham, Washington, and even of a blast furnace plant near Long Beach, in 1924, Pacific Coast Steel used 84 percent scrap in its furnaces.[31] A third important West Coast enterprise was that of the Californian Industrial Company, later known as the Southern California Iron and Steel Company, which in 1914 built its first open hearth furnace. The company hand-charged its Los Angeles furnace with Chinese pig iron, old horseshoes, and other scrap. Two years before, this company was said to have entertained the idea of an integrated works at Wilmington, in Los Angeles County, smelting ore from Southern California or Mexico, and, through a patent device, using crude oil as its furnace fuel.[32] Following several months of rumor, in November 1929, U.S. Steel acquired control of Columbia Steel. Even before this acquisition was completed, on 24 October 1929 the board of Bethlehem Steel approved the purchase of the Pacific Coast Steel Company and the Southern California Iron and Steel Company. Four days later, Grace and a party of fellow directors left Bethlehem on a tour of inspection of their northeastern works. Then on 27 November, Grace set out on the private rail car "Bethlehem" to visit their new plants in the Far West. In January 1930, the Pacific Coast Steel Corporation was organized to control the 380,000 tons of steel capacity that a company until then confined to the eastern part of the manufacturing belt now controlled along the Pacific rim.

Within two months of these purchases in the Far West, Bethlehem was negotiating a much bigger incursion into the core area of the American steel and steel consuming economy—the area lying between the upper Ohio River and Lake Michigan. In 1922, there had been extensive negotiations for a large amalgamation of steel interests—a second billion-dollar merger as it seemed to contemporaries—extending across the whole length of the manufacturing belt and including at its broadest eight companies: Republic, Midvale, Lackawanna, Inland, Youngstown Sheet and Tube (YS&T), Brier Hill, Trumbull, and the Steel and Tube Company of America. In addition to the usual difficulties about valuations, there had been objections from the Federal Trade Commission. Then came the withdrawal of first Lackawanna and then Midvale because of their acquisition by Bethlehem. By early 1923, Youngstown Sheet and Tube had absorbed both Brier Hill and Steel and Tube of America. For some three years from 1925, there followed desultory talks about a possible link between Inland and YS&T, but these broke down early in 1928 over disagreements about directorate control. A few months later, in evidence to the Interstate Commerce Commission concerning a proposed railroad extension in the Youngstown area, Frank Purnell, the YS&T assistant president, revealed that, but for its Chicago-area operations, which in raw steel capacity accounted for only one-third of the whole, his company would scarcely have been profitable in 1927. His advocacy was no doubt colored to some extent by a desire to foster the railroad improvement, but Purnell indicated that it was likely that his company's future growth would be in Chicago, investment in the Valley district being only as much as was needed to lower the costs of production.[33]

Notwithstanding Bethlehem's alleged understanding with U.S. Steel, there had long been stories of Bethlehem interest in Chicago-area development. Immediately after the acquisition of Midvale, it was rumored to be planning a large tube mill, and some reckoned this plant would be near Chicago. Three years later, there were reports of a possible Bethlehem plant in Indiana.[34] Then, in January 1930, the seventy-five-year-old James Campbell, the leading factor in the creation of YS&T thirty years earlier, retired from its presidency to be succeeded by Frank Purnell, who for a year in the early 1920s had been vice president in charge of sales for Bethlehem Steel. That month, negotiations began for a combination of Bethlehem and Youngstown Sheet and Tube. The Youngstown board gave its approval by a 6-to-1 vote, and on 12 March 1930, an agreement was entered into for Bethlehem to acquire its rival for $87 million. By early April, this agreement had been endorsed by 70 percent of Youngstown stockholders. From the point of view of YS&T, a merger would provide access both to new markets and to Bethlehem's greater source of investment funds. Bethlehem would gain Youngstown's pipe and wire capacity, which, like that of Pittsburgh Steel, was well situated for shipments down the Ohio. Above all, it could provide for the first time the advantages of direct involvement in the Chicago area in the form of YS&T's Indiana Harbor plant, whose potential had not been fully developed. Moreover, whereas Bethlehem remained mainly a "heavy" product company, the product range at YS&T was primarily in lighter categories. Grace estimated at this time that his company was 78 percent "heavy" and 22 percent "light"; YS&T was 31 percent "heavy," 69 percent "light." Because Bethlehem Steel was so much the bigger party, a combined company would still have a strong bias to the heavy end, the respective ratios becoming 66 and 34 percent.[35] Unfortunately for further progress, at Youngstown Sheet and Tube a minority of stockholders opposed the merger and lodged suits against it. After hearings and long deliberation, the courts rejected the merger. There was an appeal, however, and the link was at last given court approval in August 1931. However, the impact of severely depressed trading conditions and distress at Youngstown Sheet and Tube caused Bethlehem to exercise its option to cancel the agreement to buy.[36] It was recognized as more urgent for Bethlehem Steel to settle into the less exciting task of weathering the deepening storms of the Great Depression.

9

RETRENCHMENT,
RECONSTRUCTION,
AND WAR,
1930–1945

IN 1931, EXPLAINING TO STOCKHOLDERS the controversial bonus system he had introduced more than a quarter century before and had controlled ever since, Bethlehem's life-long chairman, Charles M. Schwab, made special reference to their president, Eugene Gifford Grace, recipient of by far the largest sums. He stressed that Grace's "genius, good judgment and untiring energy" had been the principal factor in the company's success. Over the twenty-three years to 1941, Grace would receive on average $600,000 a year, all but an insignificant part of this sum being his bonus. He lived in what was called at the time a "regal structure," which was guarded by company police, situated in the higher, quieter part of the borough, the exclusive executive quarter, an area known locally at the time as "bonus hill." He also had a holiday retreat in the health resort of Aiken, South Carolina, a town laid out amid gardens of jasmine and orange trees and where the mean winter temperature was 50°F. Grace paid a high price for his wealth and fine homes. He had always worked hard and drove others to do the same. On the third of each month, he and his main managers received a report from the head of each section itemizing the previous month's amount, costs, and profits of production. He was punctilious in his yearly visits to each plant to meet the negotiators in the employee representation scheme, but he seems to have kept his distance from their workers. Frances Perkins noted with distaste that when, as U.S. secretary of labor, she tried to bring representatives of capital and labor together, the only prominent leader of the former group to respond to the opportunity of direct contact with the men was William Irvin, president of U.S. Steel. Grace was among the majority who continued to shun those who led organized labor. Other leaders from early years had now gone, Archibald Johnston and Henry Snyder both retiring in 1925. Quincy Bent, who had joined Bethlehem in 1916 as part of its first great acquisition—Schwab once referred to him as "the biggest asset we bought in Pennsylvania Steel"—was now vice president in charge of steel operations at all the Bethlehem plants and therefore prominent in this period as a key senior colleague.

Throughout most of the 1930s, Bethlehem Steel struggled, like the rest of the industry, to weather the worst storm that had ever affected the national economy. At 59.4 million net tons, U.S. consumption of steel in 1929 had been just short of half as large again as in the prosperous year of 1920. Within another three years, it had fallen by almost three-quarters. In 1929, average national steel consumption per capita was 978 pounds; the figure for 1932 was a mere 236 pounds. Demand began to rise after 1932, but as late as 1937, a good year by the standards of this decade, the nation used only 53 million tons of steel.[1] In this setting of near prostration, followed by a struggling and long drawn out recovery, Bethlehem Steel was at first content to hold on and survive, but then it made heroic efforts to reconstruct and diversify.

Like its competitors, Bethlehem had ended the 1920s on a high note. Revenues in 1929 were above those of any year since 1918; 1929's net income of $42.2 million had been exceeded only in 1916. Over the six years to and including 1929, annual capital outlays for extensions, improvements, and acquisitions had averaged $26.7 million. U.S. Steel was almost three times as big, but in some respects, Bethlehem had been managing to narrow the gap; in those same six years, its total revenues increased from 26.7 to 31.9 percent, and even more impressively, net income rose from 10.46 to 21.37 percent that of the larger business concern. In 1927, Bethlehem Steel operated 73.6 percent of its crude steel capacity, in 1928, 82 percent, and through 1929, it averaged a 91.8 percent utilization rate. Understandable pride in such results was checked and then shattered by the sudden onset of depression. There was a short period of reviving hopes before a plunge to previously unimagined depths.

In late 1929 and the early months of 1930, it was not at all clear whether what was being experienced would turn out to be more severe and protracted than previous sharp but short setbacks to trade. During the first half of 1929, the various Bethlehem steel plants had made a total of $39 million in manufacturing profits. Contributions to this result from individual plants varied widely: $10.39 million from Bethlehem, $6.90 million from Sparrows Point, $7.73 million from Johnstown, $6.49 million from Lackawanna, $4.50 from Steelton, and from Lebanon, $800,000. By late July, the operating rate for the company as a whole was approximately 99 percent, and in the whole of the third quarter, Bethlehem operated at 97.8 percent of its rated steel capacity. By late October, the rate was about 82 percent, the decline being attributed to a slowing in the automobile business. The last quarter registered a sharp drop to 76.8 percent, and by early January 1930, they were down to 74 percent. Grace was then reported as expecting that requirements from the construction industry in 1930 would exceed those of the previous year. For a time, indicators did improve; the first quarter operating rate in 1930 was back to 80.8 percent, and at the end of this period, Grace figured 85 percent might be anticipated for April.[2] But instead of showing an upward trend, things worsened, so that for the whole of 1930 Bethlehem's utilization rate was only 61.7 percent; in the third and fourth quarters, it was 54.6 and 42.5 percent, respectively. Bethlehem's net income fell much more sharply than that of U.S. Steel. In 1931, the latter managed a net income of $13 million. A rapidly expanding newcomer, National Steel, earned $4.4 million, but Bethlehem was by now hovering on the border between profit and loss with a positive margin of no more than $100,000. That September, it reported a quarterly deficit for the first time since 1909. (It should be recorded, however, that other major companies were also registering huge shortfalls. That year, losses at Republic, Youngstown Sheet and Tube, and Wheeling together amounted to $19.3 million.) By April 1932, Grace had to report to his stockholders that operations were using as little as 20 to 21 percent of their capacity and that they needed at least a 50 to 55 percent rate to make even a reasonable profit. At the same meeting, Schwab, who had celebrated his seventieth birthday a few weeks before, admitted the outlook had never been so depressing and unpromising. During 1932, no more than about 110,000 tons was added to national steel capacity and nothing at all in pig iron.[3]

Bethlehem Steel lost $19.4 million in 1932, but the scale of its loss was now dwarfed by a U.S. Steel deficit of $71.2 million. Even so, as stock market prices showed, in the estimation of the investing public Bethlehem had fallen further. The deep depression year of 1932 turned out to be the worst for the industry and for Bethlehem. There was another deficit in 1933, but it was smaller, and by December, after nine quarters and a total loss of more than $30 million, operations once more resulted in a quarterly profit, though only of $300,000. Unquestionably, the main cause of Bethlehem's terrible operating and financial record in the early 1930s was the general depression in business, whose effects no company could side-step, but there were also particular factors. One, at first glance of seemingly small significance, burdened its balance sheets. Bethlehem Steel had a relatively high level of funded debt. At U.S. Steel, in the course of two years before the depression, Myron Taylor, as chairman of the finance committee, had "retired" $265 million of its $400 million in funded debt, as a result of which the corporation's annual interest payments were cut from $24 million in 1928 to between $5 million and $5.5 million a year from 1930 onward. Over a longer period, there had been important reductions in funded debt at Bethlehem, but proportionately less than at U.S. Steel—from $237 million in 1924 to $117.5 million by the end of 1930. As a result, when adverse trading conditions arrived and operating rates fell, the burden of interest payments on each ton of product was particularly high. In 1928, interest payments per ton of Bethlehem steel shipments had been $2.22, in 1931 they were $2.62, and in 1932, $4.61.[4]

Bethlehem also had problems associated with organization and business structure. It was now a huge, fully integrated company, with large coal and ore holdings. By the early 1930s its annual coal producing capacity was 12.7 million net tons as compared with 1.44 million tons for Inland and 600,000 tons for National Steel. However, control of large-scale mineral reserves, which in times of high activity were advantageous, in periods of depression became a financial burden. At such times a less widely extended company could buy ore, fuel, and fluxes cheaply on the open market. On the other hand, as compared with U.S. Steel, Bethlehem's higher dependence on scrap was beneficial when trade was bad. In 1928, U.S. Steel made three times as much steel as Bethlehem but consumed only half as much scrap. Scrap was normally one to two dollars a ton cheaper than pig iron, but in periods of depression the differential was wider.

	1930	1931	1932	1933	1934	1935

Table 9.1 Profits and losses of Bethlehem Steel and other leading steel companies, 1930–1935 ($millions)

	1930	1931	1932	1933	1934	1935
Bethlehem	23.8	0.1	(19.4)	(8.7)	0.5	4.3
U.S. Steel	104.4	13.0	(71.2)	(36.5)	(21.7)	1.1
Republic	(3.5)	(9.0)	(11.3)	(4.0)	(3.5)	4.4
Jones and Laughlin	9.1	(2.3)	(7.9)	(5.8)	(3.7)	(0.4)
National	8.4	4.4	1.7	2.8	6.0	11.1
Inland	6.5	1.0	(3.0)	0.2	3.7	9.4
YS&T	7.0	(7.0)	(13.3)	(8.3)	(2.7)	1.6
Armco	0.1	(3.1)	(2.0)	(0.7)	1.0	4.3

Source: Based on W. T. Hogan, *An Economic History of the American Iron and Steel Industry,* 5 vols. (Lexington, MA: Lexington Books, 1971), passim.
Note: Parentheses indicate losses.

As late as March 1936, when recovery was well under way, scrap was five to seven dollars a ton cheaper than iron. Bethlehem plants were well situated in the eastern scrap market and had a particular advantage in having no major rival purchaser in the region.[5]

Other considerations important in a comparison of Bethlehem and other major companies under depression conditions were product mix and location. Inland Steel, still a largely "heavy" product company with the advantage of a single plant and a Chicago location, in 1929 earned profits of $11.7 million as compared with Bethlehem's $42.2 million; over the years 1931–1935, it recorded a net loss only in 1932. Its net income for these years totaled $11.3 million, whereas Bethlehem lost $23.1 million. This differential throws light on the fact that for a short period after the failure of its planned merger with Youngstown Sheet and Tube, Bethlehem negotiated for association with Inland. For Armco, which had a decidedly "light" product emphasis, the net loss in these years was only $500,000, and National Steel, with unrivaled advantages of location and product range, was exceptional in making profits throughout the depression; its net earnings over the five years amounted to $26 million.

Bethlehem responded to the hard times with not only short-term emergency measures but also actions geared to the longer run, such as the revamping of product lines and major alterations to the technology and ranking of its plants. To hold the line and weather the worst of the economic storm meant a temporary shelving of plans for expansion. For example, although in fall 1929 Bethlehem had purchased a considerable interest in West Coast steel making, for the next few years it undertook no important expansion there. There was a general cutback on spending for additions, improvements, and acquisitions. Absorbing steel fabricators was of more immediate help, and it was primarily this sort of activity that caused this category of spending to rise from $22.2 million in 1929 to an annual average of $55.4 million over the next two years. Then, as the depression took deeper hold, capital spending almost stopped, the net costs of additions and the like falling to $3.5 million in 1932 and averaging $2.5 million over the next two years. After that, as signs of revival became more pronounced, larger outlays returned. Average annual net capital spending rose to $28.7 million for 1935, 1936, and 1937.

Another approach to economy was through employment costs. To a large extent, this goal was achieved by spreading the work available. Such a policy meant that reductions in the work force and in hourly earnings were kept to relatively low levels, but as employees worked fewer hours, their average take-home pay was reduced considerably. Between 1929 and 1932, there were decreases of more than 74 percent in the tonnage of products shipped and of 78 percent in raw steel output, but the recorded number of employees was down by only 21 percent and hourly earnings decreased by only 12.6 percent. On the other hand, the total payroll fell 67 percent. An important key to interpreting this situation was provided by a change in the way employee numbers were recorded. For years prior to 1932, the company's annual report listed the average daily work force; from 1932 on, the figure for average number of employees was based on the number of those receiving pay. Because its figures were still listed on the old basis, the annual report for 1932 (dated 6 March 1933) revealed a much larger drop in employment, from a daily average of 64,316 in 1929 to 30,364 on the same basis of computation during 1932.[6]

Another way to adjust to difficult times was to spread the operations of the company to new areas and to gain increased security of outlets, though such moves might involve substantial spending in the short term. As the Wall Street crash occurred, Bethlehem bought its way into West Coast steel making, attempted to merge with Youngstown Sheet and Tube the following year, and in 1931 again tried to take over Pittsburgh Steel. Defeated in each of the last two of these attempts to spread production facilities, it gained greater control of outlets during 1931 by acquiring McClintic-Marshall and other steel fabricators. After these successes and failures in the early part of the decade, there was a lull for a few years while industry and firm struggled through the depths of depression. Then, in the late 1930s, the company made three more significant if not major purchases that provided outlets for some of its smaller product divisions. The Williamsport Wire Rope Company in north-central Pennsylvania was bought in 1937. With the opening of the Sparrows Point pipe mills in 1928, Bethlehem had extended into tubular products for the first time. In 1936, purchase of the retail chain of Taubman Supply and two years later of the International Supply Company of Tulsa, Oklahoma, brought in outlets for tubular products in the oil well supply business.

Other changes in demand made possible some important economies. One instance linked the company's old staple of heavy structural shapes and a new and rapidly increasing interest in light flat-rolled steels. Capacity in the structurals business had expanded rapidly in the 1920s, partly because of the competition between Bethlehem Steel and U.S. Steel. With the onset of depression, there was a steep drop in demand. A few years later, when Bethlehem built a hot strip mill at Lackawanna, it decided that it should obtain its supply of slabs from the primary mill built to supply blooms to the beam mill, a unit that had for years been heavily underutilized.[7] This switch toward the production of lighter grades of steel and especially to thin flat-rolled products was the outstanding new departure for Bethlehem during this decade.

Within the industry, though not at Bethlehem, there had been a strong trend in the 1920s toward lighter products. It had resulted in particularly impressive growth for companies largely involved in these lines, such as the American Rolling Mill Company, Weirton Steel, and, at the end of the decade, National Steel. Into the next decade, Bethlehem had little involvement in lighter products. In 1930, commenting on advantages from a link with Youngstown Sheet and Tube, Grace had estimated that Bethlehem Steel was utilizing only 22 percent of its capacity in light products of all kinds. In the depression years, demand for heavy products fell the most, and when recovery began, demand for them grew very slowly. Between 1929 and 1932, national rail output fell from 3.05 million to 450,000 tons. One-seventh of Bethlehem capacity was in rails. The decline in structural shapes was even greater, from 5.35 million tons to 1.05 million tons. For light flat-rolled products, the decrease in demand during the depression was serious but proportionally much less than for heavy products, going from 11.8 million net tons in 1929 to 4.3 million tons in 1932. Over these years, this sector of the industry increased its share of all steel shipments from 25.1 to 39.7 percent.[8] More impressive than this relatively small shrinkage was the rapid recovery that followed. In 1935, rail output was little more than one-quarter the 1929 level, structural production not much over one-third, but tinplate consumption was greater than six years before and output of all thin flat-rolled products was back to 94.5 percent of the level in 1929. They now made up 43 percent of all shipments. It was high time for Bethlehem to begin to move into this product range.

When the 1930s began, Bethlehem's only involvement in thin flat-rolled steels were the tinplate mills it had installed at Sparrows Point and the 125,000 tons of black sheet capacity that supplied their requirements. At U.S. Steel, the situation was much more favorable, for, though it too was overrepresented in heavy lines, its subsidiary, the American Sheet and Tin Plate Company, controlled major capacity in flat-rolled product growth lines. In fall 1932, Bethlehem took a first, very modest step into sheet manufacture, acquiring the Seneca Iron and Steel Company of Blasdell, near Buffalo, which bought its sheet bars from Lackawanna. Annual capacity for sheet at Blasdell was 150,000 tons, largely material for the automobile and furniture trades. Soon after the purchase, it was announced that K. L. Griffith, former Seneca president, had been placed in charge of all sheet products made by Bethlehem. The corporate total of 275,000 tons of sheet was still small, however, and the whole of it was made on old-style sheet mills. In contrast, many competitors were already operating wide continuous hot strip mills, units that turned out larger tonnages of a superior product with much less labor and at lower cost. As soon as a revival of business seemed firmly established, Bethlehem Steel set out to make good its lack of such plant. It decided to graft the radical new technology onto what it judged its most suitable existing mills. This in turn meant that these operations would become the focus for still further expansion, because, after belatedly entering this trade, the company would not build another hot strip mill for thirty years.

The biggest single consumer of sheet steel was the automobile industry. Demand for this product was concentrated primarily in an area stretching from western Ohio into Indiana and especially in southern Michigan. As evidenced by the weekly trip of a vessel that carried structural steel to Chicago and Milwaukee to supply outlets in the western part of the Great Lakes basin, Bethlehem's most conveniently located mill for access to this industrial region was Lackawanna. On the eastern seaboard, the Baltimore area, once the center of canning, was still important. As all other major sheet producing companies were west of the Appalachians, it could be expected that many of the outlets for sheet and tinplate in the whole region might be secured by Bethlehem. Moreover, although the cannery industry had shifted its concentration to the Pacific coast, that area was more easily reached from eastern tidewater mills than from any other major existing plant. Sparrows Point had already made a start in tinplate and was the ideal coastal growth point for a bigger Bethlehem venture into these trades. Fortunately, Lackawanna and Sparrows Point were already its largest and, in other respects, its most favored plants. Johnstown was ruled out because of its landlocked location. Its general unsuitability was highlighted by the fact that 60 percent of its capacity was in merchant bars, 15 percent in plate, and 10 percent each in wire and wheels that were products in which primary steel costs were not the most important cost consideration.

Although from 1931 to 1934 Bethlehem annual reports made almost no mention of development, in 1935, two major projects were begun. One was a continuous wide strip mill for sheet and light plate at Lackawanna; the other involved large-scale expansion at the Sparrows Point tinplate works to enable it to produce and use cold rolled strip. In the short term, the Sparrows Point plant would work on hot rolled coils from the new Lackawanna mill. After the project was announced at the beginning of February 1935, ground for the Lackawanna strip mill was broken the next month and it was ready for production by 2 January 1936. By 1938, hot rolled strip made up almost 37 percent of the finishing capacity at that plant. About three-quarters of the output was sent to the Detroit area. The annual report for 1936 referred to small additions to rod and wire operations at Johnstown, but far and away the most important capital project announced that year was for Sparrows Point, where $35 million was to be spent by the end of 1937, partly for additions to the rod and wire departments and the plate mill but mostly to build a 600,000-ton hot strip mill. Over the three years from 1932 through 1934, the net cost of additions, improvements, and acquisitions had totaled $8.5 million; over the next three years it was $86.2 million. In June 1938, when the pricing system for steel was changed, Bethlehem made both Lackawanna and Sparrows Point into new basing points for hot rolled, cold rolled, and galvanized sheets, further increasing their regional market advantages.[9]

The two strip mills were oriented to different markets, and they differed in other respects as well. The Lackawanna mill, which had output of 600,000 tons per year, was seventy-nine inches in width and designed mainly to supply auto body sheet to the press shops in the industrial heartland of the Midwest. The Sparrows Point mill was fifty-six inches wide, its strip being intended for the tinplate trade or to be marketed as narrower sheets than much of what was being used in automobile manufacture. It soon proved that the decision to build the two mills had been made at an opportune time because, as Grace informed those attending the annual general meeting on 13 April 1937, the tonnage of structural steel used by the construction industry in 1936 had been less than the tonnage of steel used in the manufacture of tinplate.[10] Despite large outlays for the strip mills, to the extent that they accounted for almost half the company's mill capacity, Bethlehem remained primarily a "heavy" product producer. The share of heavy products in its total output had been reduced in eight years from 78 to 47 percent, but compared with, for instance, Inland, Bethlehem still had a long way to go. By 1938, 23 percent of Bethlehem Steel capacity was in sheet, strip, or tinplate; at Inland Steel, that share was 44 percent.

Given trade conditions and changing patterns of consumption, it was natural that during the 1930s, slow growth characterized the older or heavy product plants—Bethlehem, Johnstown, and Steelton. In addition, after the Pacific coast plants were acquired as the depression began, there was no further increase in capacity there. Between 1930 and 1938, steel capacity at Lackawanna and Sparrows Point increased by 2.04 million net tons; at the other three works in the Northeast, it fell by 100,000 tons. Lackawanna was better placed for access to the biggest and most rapidly growing markets in the nation, but in that setting it also faced competition from other major works, some considerably better situated to serve their requirements. Demand on the Atlantic seaboard was smaller, but Sparrows Point was unequaled in its commanding position there. For assembly of materials for iron manufacture, it was superior to any of their other operations. At the end of the 1930s, Chilean ore cost about three dollars a ton delivered at Sparrows Point as compared with about four dollars a ton for Lake Superior ore at Lackawanna; an independent assessment three years later put the cost of 58 percent iron El Tofo ore delivered to Sparrows Point at about 9 percent less than that of 51.5 percent iron Mesabi non-Bessemer grade ore delivered to Lake Erie ports.[11] The richer grade of Chilean ore meant that blast furnaces smelting it required less coke per ton of iron than with Great Lakes ores. In 1916, Sparrows Point had made only rails; twenty-two years later it retained rail capacity, but this was now dwarfed by a hot strip mill considered capable of 780,000 tons of annual output. It also had two cold reduction tinplate units, a tinplate works of traditional type, three plate mills, steel pipe mills, and a high speed mill capable of producing 240,000 tons a year of rod and bar.[12] As late as 1930, Lackawanna had been Bethlehem's largest plant, with 2.22 million net tons of annual steel capacity as compared with 1.96 million tons at Sparrows Point, which was then slightly smaller than the Johnstown plant. Over the next eight years, expansion at Sparrows Point was roughly twice the level of that at Lackawanna, and Johnstown registered a substantial decrease. The trends were more striking when considered over the span of the interwar period. From 1920 to 1938, Johnstown capacity fell almost 16 percent, Lackawanna grew 41 percent, and at Sparrows Point the increase was 153 percent.[13]

After improving only slowly until 1935, Bethlehem Steel operations rebounded rapidly, in 1937 reaching a level three-quarters as high as in the record year of 1929. The next year depressed conditions returned, cutting operations to 43.3 percent of capacity and reducing profits by more than 80 percent, but from then on, revival of trade and the impetus derived from the approach of the war in Europe brought the company back to solid profit in 1939 and to a new high in 1940. Having slipped slightly in the middle years of the 1930s, Bethlehem had come back strongly to improve its relative standing in the industry in the last four years of the decade. In terms of capacity, it added 1.6 million tons for raw steel or an increase of 16.7 percent in the seven years from the beginning of 1931, which compared favorably with the 5.1 percent rise at U.S. Steel and 7.9 percent at Jones and Laughlin, though it was much lower than the increases at Armco, Inland, and especially National. In net income terms, Bethlehem was in a good place as the decade ended. Income in 1939 was 3.4 percent more than in 1930, whereas at U.S. Steel it was 60 percent lower; even at National, net income in 1939 was only a little more than two-thirds as high as in 1930. Utilization of steel capacity in 1939 was at 70.8 percent. During that year, twenty-five thousand additional workers were hired. By November 1939, the operating rate in Bethlehem's steel plants was 103.9 percent of rated capacity, the first time the company had exceeded a 100 percent rate since May 1929. So elated was Grace with "that splendid performance" that he hosted a dinner at his Bethlehem home to which he invited the heads of the various sections of the corporation.[14]

By the time the 1930s ended, Bethlehem Steel had emerged from the depression, partially transformed itself into a diversified steel company, and consolidated its position as the world's second leading producer. Over the years from its founding through 1940, it had earned $431 million, distributed $245 million in dividends, but spent about $1.9 billion—an average of $1 million a week—on repairs, improvements, and additions.[15] As this period ended, there was one more major change, a decisive break with the company's past. Effective control of its destinies had long ago passed to Grace, and Schwab had "half-retired" in the early 1920s and declared himself fully retired ten years later. But he had remained chairman of the company he had saved and transformed in the first years of the century. He last attended a meeting of the board of directors on Wednesday, 21 June 1939. Sometime after that, he left for Europe, where he became seriously ill. As war broke out in Europe at the beginning of September 1939, he lay dying in his New York apartment.

A running caddie is said to have brought news of the outbreak of war in Europe to Eugene Grace as he played golf with a group of his vice presidents at the Saucon Valley Country Club. After reading the note he was handed, Grace turned to his colleagues and remarked, "Gentlemen, we are going to make a lot of money."[16] In fact, as in 1914, there would soon be immense orders from the Allies ($300 million from Britain alone for guns, warships, and ammunition), but for Bethlehem Steel, the approach to World War II and its experiences as the war ran its course were in many respects very different from those of the earlier war. Then, the fighting had come suddenly and after a long period of company growth; this time, it came on the heels of depression, during the course of which there had been many indications of the approach of another war. During and shortly after World War I, Bethlehem Steel had grown massively by acquiring its rivals; World War II would bring no major new amalgamations. Expansion in the industry during World War I had been privately financed; as the 1940s began, the government played a much larger role, both in providing funds and in determining what should be installed and where it should be located. In the earlier war, growth of Bethlehem's operations had been one of the outstanding features; this time, expansion elsewhere was on a much bigger scale. During the five years to January 1945, there was an increase of almost 14 million tons or 17.0 percent in national steel ingot capacity; at Bethlehem, the increase was only 12.5 percent. Over the years from 1936 to 1939, the average utilization rate at Bethlehem Steel was 63.7 percent; for the six years from 1940 through 1945, it was 98.1 percent. Finally, notwithstanding Grace's golf course expectations, because of large increases in taxes, Bethlehem net income during wartime went up only slightly. Between 1940 and 1944, the years of both maximum steel output and the largest shipments of steel products, total revenue increased from $603 million to $1.75 billion, but net income actually fell, from $48.7 million to $36.2 million. Compared with company figures from

World War I, the ratio of net income to tax payments during the whole of the World War II years was highly unfavorable. From 1914 to 1919 inclusive, taxes had totaled $35.4 million and net income $120.6 million; for the six years from 1940 through 1945, taxes were $550.5 million and net income, $211.8 million.[17]

Through the interwar period, steel had dominated Bethlehem's activities. During these years, the shipbuilding division had accounted for about 20 percent of revenues and of profits. By 1940, this section of the business was more active, and of total billings that year of $602 million, about $165 million came from shipbuilding. Over the next few years, though steel production reached new peaks, Bethlehem's greater glory was in its shipyards, its most vital contribution to the war effort. The corporation's overall monthly average employment increased from 95,029 to a peak in 1943 of 289,232; in shipbuilding alone, employment rose from 7,000 to 182,000. There was another striking difference from steel. In its wartime steel expansion, Bethlehem contributed many times as much as the government, but it provided only about 10 percent of the money spent on shipbuilding expansion, with the government financing the rest.[18]

As early as February 1939, the Fore River yard was said to have an order book sufficiently large to keep its sixty-seven hundred employees at work for five years.[19] By December, all Bethlehem yards were operating at full capacity. Fore River was then working on a thirty-five-thousand-ton battleship, had an aircraft carrier almost ready for trials, and was building two cruisers and two destroyers, as well as being active with mercantile work. Sparrows Point was working on a merchant ship; the Staten Island yard, acquired a year before, had cargo vessels and navy tugs under way; and the Union Yard in San Francisco, newly reconditioned, was starting on five cargo vessels.[20] As the war years passed, there were additions to the tally of Bethlehem yards and also the odd disposal. In 1941, the company leased a former shipyard at Baltimore with four building ways, to which it added another nine. By 1943, at Fairfield Yard on Baltimore Harbor, there were almost forty-five thousand workers. That year, the company sold its yard at Wilmington, Delaware. There was a good deal of specialization among the fifteen company yards. Baltimore and Fairfield, located in the same area, concentrated on Liberty ships, Sparrows Point, on tankers; Staten Island and San Pedro mainly turned out destroyers, and a new yard at Hingham, Massachusetts, as well as the San Francisco operations, built destroyer escorts. Fore River remained the centerpiece of Bethlehem's shipbuilding operations, and during hostilities, it constructed four aircraft carriers, a battleship, and thirty-one cruisers.

Although it built both mercantile and naval tonnage, the company made its most important contributions to the war effort in the latter category, producing one-third of the naval vessels built in private yards. This emphasis led to a rather unseemly controversy over productivity. To August 1945, Bethlehem had 545 merchant vessels to its credit as compared with 1,109 for the mushrooming Kaiser shipbuilding operations. But much of the standardized tonnage from Kaiser yards was completely welded, whereas a large part of the mercantile shipping launched by Bethlehem was both riveted and welded. Naval building in turn required far more work per vessel and as a result registered what seemed to be lower productivity in terms of labor hours and costs. In a speech at the Staten Island yard at the beginning of 1944, Grace pointed out that the hours of work required to build a battleship were equal to those involved in constructing 40 Liberty ships. The hours required to build one heavy cruiser equaled the hours needed to build 18 standard merchant vessels of the same class. That being so, Grace estimated that in 1943, in terms of work done, his company had built the equivalent of more than 1,000 Liberty ships. Though its management was prickly on this score, even in relation to the latter class of vessel, Bethlehem had made remarkable progress in productivity. In 1941, its first Liberty ship took 244 days to complete; two years later, construction time had fallen to 41 days. Given such achievements, it is less surprising that, whereas in 1935 a little under one-eighth of Bethlehem's gross business consisted of shipbuilding, by 1943 the proportion was well over half. Altogether, in the course of the war Bethlehem Shipbuilding constructed 1,127 vessels and repaired or overhauled to varying extents an astounding total of some 37,000 other ships.[21]

The immediate impact of the war on steel production was less immediate and dramatic than in 1914. Indeed, in March 1940, reviewing their marked recovery in net income from the depressed conditions of the previous year, Grace maintained that "the increase was due almost entirely to commercial steel orders. The war in Europe has not resulted in any important amount of munitions business for your Corporation."[22] To a considerable extent, the distinction was meaningless, for commercial orders fed an economy that would more and more turn to preparations for war. The pace of recoil from the lows of 1938 was increasing. In the whole of 1939, the company's steel operating rate was 70.8 percent, but in the last quarter, it reached 98.6 percent. For 1940, the operating rate fell back to 93.3 percent, but over the next four years it averaged 100.8 percent, implying an almost intolerable pace of work for the employees and a great strain on both equipment and organization. Over six wartime years, the company produced 73.3 million tons of steel, or 14.8 percent of the national total. In some areas, its contribution was much more significant; for instance, it delivered one-third of the U.S. Navy's requirements of armor plate and gun forgings.

In April 1941, *Fortune* magazine ran a long feature on the Bethlehem Steel Corporation. In the course of it, overseas ore supply was considered and the comment made that "if the Panama Canal were badly damaged or the company's ships were permanently detained at the bottom of the ocean, Bethlehem might find itself in the more expensive position of shipping Minnesota ore to Sparrows Point."[23] Eight months later, when the United States was plunged into the Pacific struggle with Japan, a declaration of war from Germany meant it also had to fight on the Atlantic front. As *Fortune* had anticipated, an early casualty in this theater of operations was the delivery system for Chilean ore. The route for Bethlehem ore carriers through the Florida Straits proved a highly productive hunting ground for German U-boats. After five of its seven vessels had been lost, the company withdrew the remaining boats from service. By summer 1943, no ore was being received from Chile, though two-thirds of the work force there was still digging and stockpiling it. The company was hurrying ahead with the development of ore concessions it had owned for more than twenty years in Venezuela, but it recognized that supplies from there—equally vulnerable—could not be expected until late 1944 at the earliest. They would in fact be delayed until long after that.[24] Meanwhile, Bethlehem's blast furnaces had to depend on domestic ore supplies. Looking ahead to better times, the company began work on eight new ore carriers of twenty-five thousand tons' capacity with a speed of 16 knots as compared with twenty thousand tons and 8 to 10 knots for the older vessels, hoping they might be available promptly when the fighting ended.[25]

In the three years from January 1940, Bethlehem's capacity for raw steel was expanded by almost 1.5 million tons, or one-eighth. After that, there were no further increases for five years. As it had for so long, Sparrows Point remained the prime focus of company attention, receiving 538,000 tons of the 1.1 million tons' expansion Bethlehem made in open hearth capacity. In iron making, the biggest expansion was at Lackawanna. To a much greater extent than in the industry as a whole, wartime steel expansion at Bethlehem was company financed. This practice was closely linked with another striking feature of its steel situation during the war; in contrast to a number of other leading companies, Bethlehem did not become involved in construction or operation of any major new plants built on behalf of the government. It lost out on two projects for which it would have seemed suitable. Well before the United States entered the war, it had been realized that there would have to be major expansions of national capacity for plate, mainly for shipbuilding. Plans were drawn up for 3 million tons of new plate capacity, mostly at four existing mills, but with some of it at two of the new works, located in Houston, Texas, and Fontana, California. At the first of these, construction began in spring 1941, as the first plans were being submitted for the second plant. At this time, a new 700,000-ton plate mill was projected for Sparrows Point, but this was canceled in favor of locating the capacity at Geneva, Utah. U.S. Steel was responsible for building and running the Geneva works for the government, Armco was to handle the integrated works at Houston. The newly formed Kaiser Steel Corporation would run the mill at Fontana, and Republic would operate a large electric furnace plant in the Chicago area.

There were other signs that the government did not favor Bethlehem. During the war, the Charleston Naval Ordnance Plant in West Virginia, idled since the early 1920s, was reactivated. It was placed under the management of U.S. Steel's Homestead works. Then, when the U.S. Navy wanted major extensions to sheared plate production backed by additional steel making, it insisted that this too should be at Homestead. The armor plant at Bethlehem, despite its long-established reputation, underwent much smaller extensions. Even so, the extraordinarily high level of wartime activity at the Bethlehem works involved an increase in its work force from 13,055 at the outbreak of war in 1939 to a 1943 peak of 31,523.[26]

A further indication of Bethlehem Steel's relatively low profile in wartime steel expansion may be seen in the West, the area that recorded by far the biggest relative expansion in the whole industry. At the beginning of 1940, Colorado, Utah, and the three Pacific coast states contained a steel capacity amounting to 2.2 million tons. Over the next four years, an additional total of 2.7 million tons was installed. Although, uniquely among important steel companies, Bethlehem already operated mills in each of the three main coastal complexes of population and economic activity, it accounted for only 92,000 tons of this expansion: 50,000 tons in its California operations and 42,000 in Washington. As with the plate program, in the West too it had seemed for a time that Bethlehem's part in the overall expansion would be much larger. Thinking along the same lines, which a few months before had caused *Fortune* magazine to question the wartime viability of the Panama Canal, government steel consultant W. A. Hauck in early autumn 1941 suggested that for strategic reasons the Pacific coast should be made largely independent of supplies from eastern mills. Accordingly, he had proposed a western steel expansion of 1.86 million tons. Of this total, it was at that time anticipated that 981,000 tons would be controlled by U.S. Steel and 708,000 tons by Bethlehem Steel. Bethlehem apparently made a proposal to build a new integrated plant near Los Angeles that would contain two blast furnaces and mills for billets and bars as well as for structural products and rails—perhaps the wrong product mix to attract strong government support. At that time, Kaiser was thinking of blast furnaces in Utah, a steel works near Los Angeles, and electric furnaces in the area of the Bonneville Power Administration in the Pacific Northwest, but his scheme had not been given final consideration.[27] Two months after Hauck's plan was unveiled, the attack on Pearl Harbor occurred, and for a time the Pacific coast seemed vulnerable. Bethlehem thus drew back from the idea of a major new integrated works. Kaiser went on to build a complete works at Fontana and U.S. Steel constructed the Geneva plant.

Before the war, Bethlehem used very large tonnages of scrap in steel making. In 1940, for instance, its output was as much as 48 percent dependent on scrap charges; half these were its own arisings, half purchased. The corollary had been a relatively low pig iron and coke capacity in relation to steel tonnage, representing a saving in capital outlay. Much of the steel used in the war could not be expected to return rapidly if at all to the production cycle as scrap, and so during this period, despite losing its main overseas sources of ore, Bethlehem had to make urgent efforts to expand iron production and output from various departments supporting blast furnace operations. The company was sometimes so short of coke that in 1941, for example, when its own ovens were operating at capacity and despite all the terrible uncertainties of Atlantic transport, it even imported some from Britain. Overall, between 1940 and the end of 1945, its extensions in coke and blast furnaces relative to those in steel were far above the national average, in raw steel increasing 1.43 million tons but in iron capacity by 2.19 million tons.

Although all in all it received relatively little government money for wartime investment, Bethlehem was the first company to purchase government-financed iron and steel plant from the Defense Plant Corporation. Early in 1944, it paid between $22 million and $23 million for the coke ovens and blast furnaces it had built on government account at Bethlehem, Steelton, Sparrows Point, and Lackawanna (table 9.2).[28]

Table 9.2 Company-financed and government-financed wartime expansion at Bethlehem Steel and other integrated companies, 1940–1945 (thousand net tons)

	Coke		Pig iron		Open hearth steel		Electric furnace steel	
	Company	Govt.	Company	Govt.	Company	Govt.	Company	Govt.
Bethlehem Steel	1578	-	1889	-	858	300	120	-
U.S. Steel[1]	3689	400	2422	1419	2889	1700	204	165
Other integrated[2]	2032	3709	3645	4467	2451	2774	638	799
Total	7299	4109	7956	5886	6198	4774	962	964

Source: Based on Hauck, "Steel Expansion for War," reprinted in Steel, June 1945, 63, 64, 66, 68.

[1] Excludes the Geneva plant.

[2] Includes the Geneva plant.

By the end of the war, the Bethlehem Steel Corporation was the nation's seventh largest industrial company. As the fighting drew to an end, the company's state of exceptional activity was reduced. In 1945, shipments of steel products were 900,000 tons less than in 1944, crude steel production was down by almost 1.5 million tons, and the steel operating rate, which was 102.8 percent in 1944, the next year averaged only 91.7 percent; by November 1945, it was down to 79.0 percent. By fall of that year, the shipbuilding division was already closing two of its wartime shipyards: Fairfield-Baltimore and Hingham, Massachusetts.[29] As 1945 ended, a change in organization reflected the prominence and successes of the shipbuilding division. In the six years since Schwab's death, his position as chairman had remained vacant. Now Grace was elected to fill it. At the same time, he chose the man who had headed wartime shipbuilding to be his own successor as president. Arthur Homer had been vice president in charge of shipbuilding since 1940. His initial response to the suggestion that he should now take the presidency was to say that he was a shipbuilder and the world of steel was relatively unfamiliar to him. To this Grace replied, "That doesn't make any difference; you can acquire that experience." By this time, Grace was sixty-nine and the new president was forty-nine. It seemed reasonable to expect that Homer might succeed to the chairmanship in a year or so. In fact, Grace remained firmly in control for another twelve years. In that time, he would continue to make special use of his close circle of steel colleagues in the Bethlehem headquarters. Homer was thus kept at arm's length until he rather suddenly had to take over as effective leader. Sidelined in this way, Homer and his wartime achievements were turned into something counterproductive in terms of Bethlehem's longer term health.[30]

10

MATERIAL SUPPLIES,
GROWTH, AND COMPETITION
IN THE EAST,
1945–1957

IN AUGUST 1945, AS THE WAR in the Pacific came to an end, Eugene Grace entered his seventieth year. A few days before he reached that milestone, he received a letter from Archibald Johnston, who thirty years before had supported his appointment as president of Bethlehem. Johnston had been retired for twenty years, and the shakiness of his handwriting bore witness to his age. His sentiments were warm, and he made clear his conviction that the company's future depended heavily on the near septuagenarian: "My Dear E.G., It is a pleasure to wish you another happy birthday and *many more* to come, with the same *strength* and *energy* and *ability* to *serve* you and the Bethlehem Steel Company for many years to come. For the future will surely require these qualities to meet the times and win out. As ever, Arch Johnston."[1] His fears of difficult days ahead were widely shared, but in fact, the period from 1945 to the end of 1957, which marked the last stage of Grace's career, was in many respects the most successful and least troubled in Bethlehem Steel's history.

Table 10.1 Shares of national steel capacity held by major companies in the postwar period (percent)

	1945	1948	1954	1958
Bethlehem	13.5	14.6	14.9	16.3
U.S. Steel	33.8	33.1	31.1	28.6
Republic	10.2	9.1	8.2	8.7
Jones and Laughlin	5.2	5.0	5.0	5.3
National	4.1	4.3	4.8	4.8
Youngstown Sheet and Tube	4.3	4.2	4.4	4.6
Armco	3.4	3.6	3.9	4.5
Inland	3.6	3.6	3.8	4.1

Source: *Steel*, 16 August 1954, 53, and AISI, *Directory of the Iron and Steel Works of the United States and Canada*, for each of the years indicated.
Note: Data are as of 1 January in each of the years indicated.

Over these twelve early postwar years, Bethlehem steel capacity increased from 12.9 million to 20.5 million tons, and the company improved its relative standing in the industry by a greater degree than any of its major rivals. Operations were often at a high level of capacity. As had been the case under the insistent pressures of wartime, such extremely high rates were not always convenient or even efficient in the fullest sense. At this time, an 85 to 90 percent steel utilization rate was considered most desirable, but for long periods Bethlehem operated at more than 100 percent of its rated capacity. In 1937, net income had reached a peacetime record of $31.8 million; twenty years later, net income was $191.0 million. Plant and equipment were modernized, much of the expansion being obtained by upgrading existing installations. For nine years beginning in January 1946, steel capacity rose by 6.2 million tons, but only 1.6 million tons of this involved new furnaces; the other 4.6 million tons came from improved practices and design in existing furnaces as they were periodically rebuilt. This method of expansion reduced operating costs as well as the amount of capital that had to be found. Similar improvements were made in coke ovens, blast furnaces, and rolling mills. As a result, the 6.2 million tons' steel expansion was estimated to have required capital outlay of about $600 million, or $100 a ton. In the same period, largely because it built a completely new works, U.S. Steel's expansion work cost $270 per ton of steel. In fact, between 1946 and 1953, the Bethlehem Steel Corporation costs for expanded capacity were lower than that at any major company except Youngstown Sheet and Tube.[2]

Although the postwar era was a period of major growth and financial success, important difficulties had to be tackled and elements that would prove to be weaknesses in the future began to surface. A continuing problem was the distribution of the Bethlehem plants in relation to raw material supplies and markets. An important new problem was that for the first time since the early 1920s, Bethlehem Steel had to face up to the challenge of large-scale competition from a well-placed operator of integrated iron and steel operations within its northeastern heartland.

In the early postwar years, the shift in emphasis from heavy to lighter steel products that began in the 1930s was continued. Between 1930 and 1946, shipments of lighter products increased from 31 to 52 percent of the total; by 1955, they reached 67 percent. (These were slightly higher figures than the changes in capacity, thus showing that the company operated a higher percentage in its lighter lines for more of the time.) In tonnages delivered, lighter products had increased more than threefold over a twenty-five-year period; heavy products increased by about one-tenth.

In spite of important wartime expansion, Bethlehem, when compared with most, though not all of its competitors, was still operating with a pig iron capacity that was small in relation to that for crude steel. In fact, the ratio of its pig iron capacity to that in crude steel fell slightly, from 65.6 and 65.8 percent in 1938 and in 1950, respectively, to 62.6 percent by 1957. (In 1957, the figure for the whole industry was 65.0 percent, for U.S. Steel it was 74.2 percent, for Republic, 70.0 percent, National, 81.8 percent, J&L, 69.8 percent, and for YS&T, 66.3 percent. Among the majors, only Inland, with 54.7 percent, and Armco, at 42.4 percent, were well below Bethlehem.) A corollary of underprovision in iron making was a continuing dependence on scrap. Purchased scrap usually made up about half the tonnage used and remained cheaper than in some of the steel producing areas west of the Appalachians, notably Pittsburgh. In addition, as always, high scrap usage provided a useful counterweight to the effects of recession, for at such times purchases could be reduced so as to keep blast furnaces as fully employed as possible. The sharp recession of 1954 illustrated this well. Crude steel production was 21.8 percent less than in 1953, but Bethlehem's purchased scrap tonnages fell 41.2 percent.[3] Even so, by this time, two-thirds of the company's steel output was backed up by iron making plant. A leading feature of this period was the effort put into increasing and widening the iron ore supplies on which the blast furnaces drew.

It had long been recognized as a weakness that Bethlehem iron ore reserves were small. In spring 1941, they had been computed as about 139 million tons—

57.5 million in the upper Great Lakes region, 52 million in the Cornwall ore banks, and the rest in Chile. All told, this was sufficient for only about twelve years at the rate of usage in 1940.[4] Since then, the company had increased iron production to meet wartime needs. Throughout its history, both as a single plant and as a multi-plant operation, the distance of the majority of Bethlehem's capacity from the main flows of Lake Superior ore had been a serious disadvantage. By the early 1950s, Lackawanna and Johnstown were operating mainly on Lake Superior ore, but their combined pig iron capacity in 1954 was less than 40 percent of the group total in the Northeast. Some Great Lakes ore was used at Steelton, Bethlehem, and even at Sparrows Point, though at the last this was mainly in order to produce a mixture of the desired character. Foreign ore was smelted at Sparrows Point and Bethlehem, and, as in the nineteenth century, the latter also used some New Jersey ore. At Steelton, sinter from the Cornwall ore banks was important in the furnace burden. Some New York state ore was used at Steelton, Bethlehem, and Sparrows Point.[5] This pattern of ore procurement began to change as the industry was forced to acknowledge that the direct-shipping Lake Superior ores were nearing exhaustion. Like other leading companies, Bethlehem Steel had to search for adequate alternatives.

Investment in both mining and mechanical processes to concentrate what were effectively low-grade iron ores in the strata surrounding the Iron Range of the upper Great Lakes region was one way of ensuring long-term supplies. However, to turn out a usable product from these "taconite" deposits required investment on a scale far greater than in the old-style open pit quarries. In the mid-1950s, it was estimated that, whereas open pit mining had required investment of about four dollars for every ton of ore output, the mining, crushing, and concentrating necessary to make pellets from taconite involved outlay of between thirty and forty dollars per annual ton. In short, the change to concentrated ore introduced a new inflexibility into the Lake Superior ore industry. As early as 1947, Bethlehem, which held ore deposits on all the main ranges, had collaborated with Youngstown Sheet and Tube to gain control of large acreages of taconite lands in the Mesabi district.[6] By the mid-1950s, it owned a 45 percent interest in the Erie Mining Company, which was building a processing plant near Aurora at the eastern end of the Mesabi Range. It was designed to produce 7.5 million tons of pellets each year, from which Bethlehem would receive an amount proportionate to its investment. A railroad was built to a new shipping point to be known as Taconite Harbor, well north of the existing ore docks on

Lake Superior. Trial pellet shipments were made in fall 1957, and full-scale production began the next summer. By the early 1960s, Erie Mining had invested $300 million.[7]

Taconite development mainly benefited plants already using Great Lakes ore. The opening of the iron orefields in Quebec/Labrador could be of importance to tidewater and eastern interior locations. When the proposed St. Lawrence Seaway was opened, ore from those areas could also be delivered to mills on the Great Lakes. The Quebec/Labrador ore had been discovered in 1929, and seven years later a Montreal mining interest secured a concession of twenty thousand square miles. Mapping and survey work began in 1942, and, after another seven years, the Iron Ore Company (IOC) of Canada was formed to open mines and build a railroad to link them to Sept-Îles on the St. Lawrence estuary. The IOC was owned by the Hollinger and Hanna companies and by five American steel companies: U.S. Steel, Republic, National, Youngstown Sheet and Tube, and Wheeling. Bethlehem had no early financial interest, but by the mid-1950s, it had entered into long-term contracts ensuring substantial supplies. Canadian ore production was 2.7 million tons in 1948, but ten years later that figure had reached 14 million tons. The St. Lawrence Seaway opened for navigation in April 1959. In the previous year, Bethlehem Steel at last acquired interests in the Iron Ore Company of Canada.[8]

In addition to these major reserves, each of which was 900 to 1,000 miles from the Bethlehem plant, the company invested in much smaller, nearer sources of ore. Two projects seemed to point to a measure of desperation about future supplies. Canadian geologists proved the existence of ore at Marmora, 130 miles northeast of Toronto, in 1949. Bethlehem undertook diamond-bit drilling there, followed by five years of exploration and mine construction in which 20 million tons of limestone had to be stripped away before the ore beneath could be worked. In April 1955, Marmora was brought into production as a "low-grade, open pit" operation. Its ore was highly variable, contained pockets high in sulphur, and averaged only 37 percent iron content. After extraction, the ore was crushed and beneficiated to produce pellets of 65 to 67 percent iron content. These pellets were then railed 64 miles to Picton on the northern shore of Lake Ontario and shipped across the lake and through the Welland Ship Canal to Lackawanna. In 1958, Marmora supplied more than 500,000 tons of pellets. The other source was much nearer blast furnaces. In the late 1940s, airborne geophysical surveys proved ore bodies near Morgantown in Berks County, Penn-

The Grace Mine, end of the 1950s. *Courtesy Bethlehem Steel Corporation.*

sylvania, well below workings of iron ore abandoned seventy or more years earlier. After an outlay of $60 million, the new "Grace Mine" there began deliveries to Bethlehem works, little more than 40 miles to the north. It was soon producing 1,000 tons of concentrates daily and was expected eventually to ship up to 3.5 million tons a year.[9]

After World War II, Bethlehem Steel for the first time looked to Africa for ore, and by 1959, it had a 25 percent interest in a Liberian project whose initial output was expected to be 4 million to 6 million tons of ore and to rise to as much as 10 million. By 1963, facilities for the Nimba mine were completed. A few years later, Bethlehem, with others, explored the possibilities of a major orefield just across the border in Guinea, but by then the trend of trade was such as to deter such a risky venture.[10] Latin America remained, as it had since the 1880s, Bethlehem's main overseas supplier, but the chief sources within that continent changed. Having produced more than 48 million tons of iron ore between 1921 and 1957, El Tofo was producing smaller yields by the mid-1950s. In 1936, the company had acquired another important ore body, El Romeral, twenty-five kilometers north of La Serena, but did not begin to develop it as a partial replacement for El Tofo until 1948. After constructing a railroad and a new port at Guayaca, by 1955, Bethlehem was ready to ship Romeral ore. A year later, the new orefield was in full operation and production at El Tofo ceased except for the gathering of ore by contractors.[11] But though its ore was 63 percent iron, Romeral held only 20 million tons of ore. Because requirements were rising, it could not fully replace El Tofo. Fortunately, the company had already turned elsewhere in Latin America for its main supplier.

As early as 1890, iron ore was known to exist at Mina El Pao, thirty miles from the Orinoco River port of San Felix, but the real scale of Venezuelan ore reserves was not realized for another half century. In 1933, Bethlehem obtained exploitation rights to twenty thousand acres of land, and by mid-1944, it had begun work on a mine projected to yield 2 million tons of ore a year. Late in 1945, the work was reported to be nearing completion, but the next few years witnessed political upheaval in Venezuela. There were other causes of delay as well, including the difficulties of working in a virgin tropical environment and the necessity for major investment in infrastructure, including a road, a thirty-six-mile railroad to the river, and a new river port near San Felix. Additionally, six four-thousand-ton ton barges had to be provided to operate on the Orinoco, where water levels varied seasonally by up to forty feet. Also, a new transshipment port was required on the Gulf of Paria, where navigation was imperiled by shifting sandbanks. By the end of 1949, $60 million had been invested in the project, though it was now overshadowed by U.S. Steel's opening of the Cerro Bolivar deposit, fifty miles farther from the Atlantic, where reserves were estimated to be almost eight times those at El Pao, enabling capital outlay there to be covered by ore deliveries spread over a much longer period. The first token shipment from El Pao was made at the end of 1949; regular production began in 1950. By the early 1950s, Venezuela was the largest overseas source of ore for Bethlehem Steel, with Chile and Canada accounting for half its total supply.[12]

In the course of the first postwar decade in which Bethlehem Steel was reshaping its ore supplies, the situation of its major plants in the Northeast changed in other important respects. Between the wars, the introduction of a multiple basing point system and, in 1938, the removal of many of the price differentials between these basing points had helped to compartmentalize the steel markets of the nation. Ten years later, in response to signs that all forms of basing point pricing might soon be declared illegal, the industry took the process to its logical conclusion and introduced a free-on-board-at-mill or FOB

Saucon works, Bethlehem, early 1950s. *Courtesy Bethlehem Steel Corporation.*

pricing system. At this time, postwar increases in rail freight rates made long distance movements of steel even more difficult, thus reinforcing the division of the nation into regional or "natural" market areas.[13] It was still possible for any mill to "absorb" freight, that is, to accept a lower net return on an order so as to sell more, improve the loading of its mills, and cut unit costs of production, but the new pricing policy, rising freight rates, and a steady increase in truck rather than rail deliveries of steel seemed to confirm Bethlehem's dominance in eastern markets. One result was summed up in 1950 by the chairman of the House Subcommittee on the Study of Monopoly Power: "You cannot get an ounce of steel in the City of Washington unless you buy it from the Bethlehem Steel Corporation."[14] But regional monopolies were not only attractive to established producers and anathema to customers or governments; they also constituted targets for potential competitors, especially at a time when the drift of ore supply and changes in the distribution of economic growth seemed to promise a great future for steel making in coastal districts.

In its northeastern heartland, Bethlehem Steel now had to face a major challenge to its dominating position. Encouraged by the changing raw material and marketing situation, a number of companies were reported to be planning new works on the Atlantic coast at the end of the 1940s. The process was helped along by pressure from government for increases in steel capacity in the interests of national security and by rather vague intimations of help through tax concessions or by other means. Things were brought to a head by the general expansion of the industry during the Korean War. In January 1951, the President's Economic Report to Congress recommended that over three years, or sooner if possible, steel capacity should be increased from 104 to 120 million tons; at that time, the industry was thinking of a 22-million-ton expansion. Of this total, 2.6 million tons would be undertaken by Bethlehem Steel, and all but 60,000 tons of it would be in the Northeast. When, on 22 January 1951, Arthur Homer submitted fifty construction schemes to the Bethlehem board, the outlay involved totaled $89.7 million, of which far and away the biggest items were $51 million for Lackawanna and $19 million for Sparrows Point.[15] Expansion schemes for existing integrated works of other companies were of relatively slight importance in the overall scheme, but 5.6 million tons of new steel capacity were scheduled for four new eastern projects. Three of them were never built. They included a 1.3-million-ton plant proposed by Barium Steel (for a short time the new name of the old Phoenix Steel Company) for a site on the Delaware River between Burlington and Florence, New Jersey, and farther downriver, at Paulsboro, a 1.5-million-ton National Steel mill. By early 1951, along with half a dozen or so other companies, Bethlehem had been invited to consider building a 1-million-ton-a-year integrated works at New London, Connecticut. After studying the economics of this scheme, Bethlehem, like the others invited, declined to become involved. The only new works to materialize was a U.S. Steel operation on the Pennsylvania side of the Delaware River just south of Trenton, New Jersey, named after the corporation president, Ben Fairless.[16]

The Fairless works began production in December 1952. Soon afterward, it was rated at 1.2 million tons of crude steel. Expanded to 2.2 million tons' capacity by 1954, it had by then cost about $400 million or $182 per ingot ton. Between 1945 and 1953, Bethlehem Steel had extended capacity at Sparrows Point by almost exactly the same tonnage. Although assessments made in the early 1950s seemed to indicate that the new U.S. Steel plant would be able to command considerable freight cost advantages over Sparrows Point for deliveries into New York and Boston, the latter's lower overheads, slightly lower costs for fuel, greater economies of scale, and advantages from established customer contacts enabled it to meet the challenge from this powerful newcomer. After announcing a $100 million program in 1955, Bethlehem then revealed in 1956 its plans for

Sparrows Point works, mid-1950s. *Courtesy Bethlehem Steel Corporation.*

a 3-million ton, $300 million expansion of its plants over the next two years—an expenditure per ton roughly half that represented by the Fairless works. Of this expansion, 1 million tons would be divided between Lackawanna and Bethlehem and 2 million tons would be at Sparrows Point, whose finishing mills now had 1.5 million tons more capacity than its melting shops could support.[17] An even more important development program was being contemplated. By this time, Bethlehem Steel was shaping up to invade the industry's Chicago heartland, in which up to this point it had not had any iron or steel making operations.

Both the big expansion programs carried out in the mid-1950s and Bethlehem's scheme for the Midwest were made possible by the company's remarkable success in the early postwar years. It made large profits, with net income going from under $42 million in 1945 to $191 million in 1957. During that period, it increased its share of the national output from 13.5 to 16.3 percent. In the last

	Table 10.2 Bethlehem Steel data, 1950–1957			
	Raw steel capacity (thousand net tons)	Raw steel production (thousand net tons)	Operating rate (%)	Net income as a percentage of sales
1950	15,000	15,116	100.8	8.5
1951	16,000	16,406	102.5	5.9
1952	16,800	14,116	84.0	5.3
1953	17,600	17,663	100.4	6.4
1954	18,500	13,810	74.6	8.0
1955	19,100	18,800	98.5	8.5
1956	20,000	18,300	91.6	6.9
1957	20,500	19,100	93.2	7.3

Source: *Iron Age*, 5 January 1956; Bethlehem Steel Corp. annual reports for the years indicated.

seven years of this period, raw steel capacity increased by one-third. It was at this high point, what in retrospect may be seen as the very peak of its achievements, that the corporation had a change in its top direction. The cause of change was necessity, not choice. The process revealed much about the man involved and also about the extraordinary ethos of the company he had led.

Eugene Grace had joined the newly formed Bethlehem Steel Company as a graduate electrical engineer in summer 1899. At the beginning of 1957, in his eighty-first year, he was Bethlehem Steel Corporation chairman, having been its effective leader for more than forty years. In 1913, when he was appointed head of steel operations, Bethlehem's capacity for raw steel had been 950,000 tons; by early 1957, that figure was 20.5 million tons. Grace had been unwavering in his pursuit of company success, always pushing himself, his officers, and their employees. At one point, he sent out photographs of himself, autographed and bearing the exhortation "Always more production." But he was good at more than just hard driving; he could also inspire subordinates. In the 1950s, an individual entering Bethlehem's famed "Loop" training course gathered with the other new trainees. He recalled almost sixty years later that Grace came into the hall where the new trainees were gathered, sat on the edge of the stage, welcomed them, and spoke impressively of the role they might play over the years and the fact that the future of a great company would now depend on them.[18] Over the years, he had become one of the outstanding figures in the industry. In March 1957, this unrelenting but rapidly aging colossus suffered the first of

PART II. From a Struggling Plant

a series of strokes. The last regular quarterly meeting of directors he attended was on 25 April, but he remained chairman. At last, in October, he gave up the chairmanship and his role as chief executive officer. The former position was eliminated, as it had been for six years after Schwab's death almost twenty years before. Arthur Homer remained president but also took over as chief executive. Both Homer's private remarks and public statements made clear how introverted Bethlehem's top management had become. To the board meeting on 31 October at which these changes were announced, he said,

> Mr. Grace, on the advice of his physicians, has requested that he be relieved of the responsibilities of his office as chairman and chief executive of the Corporation. He would, of course, remain a director of the corporation and continue to participate in the councils of management. I think that we must comply with the request which Mr. Grace has made. I am sure, however, that it will be some time before any of us will be able to think of anyone other than Mr. Grace as Chairman of the Corporation. I therefore suggest that, as a tribute to his incomparable services to Bethlehem over more than half a century, the Board at this meeting amend the by-laws of the Corporation so as to eliminate the office of Chairman, and further, that it adopt a resolution making Mr. Grace Honorary Chairman of the Corporation.[19]

His public explanation of the delay in taking action was even more revealing of the manner in which the control of one of the nation's greatest industrial companies had become intermingled with personality: "We had to wait to see how Mr. Grace felt, and if he wanted to relinquish his position as chief executive officer. He didn't want to announce this because he felt he would be all right. The company was the greatest thing in his life, and to change that is a pretty big thing for any man to do." He described Grace as "a great and wonderful man, with complete integrity."[20]

For some time as honorary chairman, Grace seems to have tried to retain a degree of control. Edmund Martin, who was elected a member of the Bethlehem board on 30 January 1958, recalled that at some early meetings he attended, Grace took the chair. The conditions, though so much more benign, were reminiscent in some ways of the frightful situation faced by Stalin's entourage when it was feared that he had died but no one was brave enough to burst into his room and confirm the fact. Martin indicated that "sometimes he [Grace] would nod off to sleep, and everybody wouldn't dare do anything until he woke up. We didn't leave. We didn't continue with whatever business was being discussed.

Eugene G. Grace in the last years
of his chairmanship.
Courtesy Bethlehem Steel Corporation.

We just waited in silence until he woke up and resumed the meeting as if nothing had happened." In the mills, Grace had for decades been recognized as the
authoritative figure, "a man you knew was in charge," as one fairly senior employee of the time recalled. As Homer took his place, it was soon realized even
at the shop floor level that things were not managed as firmly or as well.[21] Grace
eventually became bedridden, and at a special meeting of the board on 31 August
1959, his resignation as a director was presented and accepted. On 25 July 1960,
he died. Homer expressed deep regret in the loss of "a friend, a fellow member
of this Board, and adviser to the Corporation." The minutes of the board meeting described him as "an inspiring leader of the Corporation . . . primarily responsible for its great development." Their late chairman's "energy and keen
intellect, the warmth of his personality, and his enthusiasm made him a great
leader not only of Bethlehem but in the steel industry. The Corporation, the
industry, and the country have lost a great man and his directors a loyal friend
and adviser."[22]

Homer's succession to the chief director's role in the company took place
under difficult circumstances. Grace had chosen him as his heir in 1945.[23] But as
late as the mid-1950s, though he had been president since 1945, Homer was often
bypassed by Grace and by his close steel associates. Now that he was CEO, for ex-

Arthur Homer and Edmund F. Martin, 1960. *Courtesy Bethlehem Steel Corporation.*

pertise in the steel sector he largely depended on the experience of Ed Martin. Another problem caused by the long delayed succession was that Homer was sixty-one when he became chief executive, and therefore, in view of his own wish to lower the retirement age for executives, he had at most only a few years of control ahead. Even so, he began to force through the withdrawal of some of the now aged men who had been Grace's vice presidents. In this respect, Bethlehem's experience over the next few years would be strikingly different from that of its leading rivals. Roger Blough became chairman at U.S. Steel in 1955. Of the eleven leading officers at the helm of U.S. Steel in 1957, six were still there by 1964. At Republic Steel in 1960, Charles White was succeeded in the chairmanship by Thomas Patton, but half of the company's ten leading officers in 1957 were still in office seven years later. By contrast, in 1957, the boards of the Bethlehem Steel Corporation and of its subsidiary, the Bethlehem Steel Company, comprised sixteen men. Only two of these individuals were still in place by 1964. There was an even more immediate problem for Homer to face than the composition of the board and of top management. As he recognized as early as March 1958, for Bethlehem and for the industry in general, "the past several months have been difficult ones in steel." His first full year in control was also that of the first major postwar setback to steel expansion. Not until after Grace had died did Homer take the title of chairman.[24] Over the next few years, many more of the traditional certainties of the steel world would dissolve. Each company had to look for new directions. In some respects, none of them did so more dramatically than Bethlehem Steel.

11

STEEL MAKING
IN THE FAR WEST
AND MIDWEST

AT THE END OF THE 1930s, Bethlehem controlled 46 percent of the steel capacity that it and U.S. Steel owned in the West. During World War II, the Kaiser corporation built the Fontana works. U.S. Steel, having constructed and operated the Geneva works for the government, purchased the plant shortly after the war ended. In spite of considerable extensions, particularly in Seattle, Bethlehem's share of western capacity fell to 20 percent. After falling for a time, western consumption of steel revived at the end of the war and then grew strongly, yet in the postwar years, Bethlehem's share in the regional steel economy declined further. In 1940, the seven western states had consumed 2.25 million tons of rolled steel; by 1955, they used 6.3 million tons but could supply only half what they consumed. By 1957, when the area was consuming almost 7 million tons a year, projections pointed to 8 million tons by 1960 and perhaps 10 million a decade later. In fact, however, growth was to level off in the 1960s, reaching 7.5 million tons in 1964, touching a high of 9.5 million in 1968, and falling to 8.7 million tons by 1970. More important still, by the early 1960s, competition in supplying this region was becoming keener as imports grew rapidly—more so than in the nation as a whole. By mid-1962, foreign steel was being delivered on the West Coast for twenty-five to thirty dollars a ton less than the price of domestic material.[1]

Imports were 800,000 tons in 1959 but 1.0 million tons 1963 and 2.4 million in 1970. In 1962, Kaiser Steel tried to preserve its position by removing the differentials over East Coast prices, extras that had more or less reflected costs of transport from there. In a less dramatic move, Bethlehem acted to protect its eastern plants and above all Sparrows Point by replacing its old fleet of ten ships with six new ones to provide better service. As the protection of distance from competitors was removed, production costs for West Coast steel making were also changing. Scrap differentials remained favorable but narrowed; No. 1 heavy melting scrap in Los Angeles was 80.0 percent of the Chicago price in March 1945, 82.3 percent in December 1955, and six years after that it was 93.0 percent. Inevitably, rolling mill costs remained higher than in similar eastern mills because of generally smaller runs of particular specifications. Whereas its main competitors throughout the West—U.S. Steel, Kaiser, and Colorado Fuel and Iron—all possessed big integrated works with ore and coal mines in the region, Bethlehem remained dependent on cold metal practice and also faced the operating cost disadvantages (counterbalanced in part, however, by gains in delivery costs) of having plants in each of the three main Pacific coast industrial regions. In summer 1945, telling reporters his company would not bid to acquire the Geneva or Fontana works, Eugene Grace claimed, "Our prices meet competition on the Pacific Coast. We can produce and deliver plates, tinplates, sheets, wire products, and bars made at Sparrows Point and structural items made at Bethlehem, Los Angeles, San Francisco, Portland, and Seattle at a cheaper cost than steel can be made locally." In October, steps were taken to consolidate the situation in the West by forming the Bethlehem Pacific Coast Steel Corporation to run the properties of the former Pacific Coast Division. Its West Coast executives were to be given more initiative in operating the plants under their control. Then, announcing new steel and bar mill capacity at Los Angeles, H. H. Fuller, vice president on the West Coast, adopted a fighting posture: "This is the beginning of a definite, long-range program of expansion. We are in this market, we're going to stay in it, and we're going to grow with it."[2] If the continuing involvement of Sparrows Point in the West Coast steel business helped inhibit larger scale company development there, it was estimated in 1947 that the cost of carriage from Geneva to Los Angeles was only 14.5 cents less than the water rate from Sparrows Point.[3] Even so, in the late 1940s and 1950s Bethlehem did expand its western capacity and reduce its production costs. By 1947, it planned to double capacity at the Los Angeles works, and over the years, more of its capacity was concentrated at this mill, so that its share of Bethlehem steel capacity in the West rose from one-fifth in 1945 to almost 48 percent by 1958.

After 1950, Bethlehem replaced the open hearth furnaces at the Southern California plant with three large electric arc furnaces whose production costs were estimated to be about 10 percent lower. In 1955, a new fabricating plant was opened at Torrance to replace a thirty-year-old unit in Los Angeles. Most of its steel came by the company's Calmar line from Bethlehem and Sparrows Point, but some of it was drawn from the West Coast works. By the 1960s, Bethlehem's Los Angeles works had reached a raw steel capacity of 600,000 tons.[4] Although disappointed in hopes of help from government tax concessions, the company closed the 246,000-ton Seattle open hearth melting shop in 1958 and replaced it with electric furnaces that increased its capacity 70 percent. A blooming mill, modern bar mill, and thirty-inch universal plate mill were also added.[5]

Bethlehem made two moves that seemed to promise much bigger West Coast development, but in each case the initiative fizzled out. At the Los Angeles works in 1959, the company seemed ready to side-step at least some of its raw material deficiencies in the West while at the same time providing more effective support for its extended steel capacity there. Work began on an H-iron plant, that is, an operation in which ore is reduced to a crude metal in a hydrogen atmosphere at high pressure but relatively low temperature. Production of an iron suitable for use in the electric steel furnaces was expected by mid-1960.[6] Within a short time, trade circumstances had changed, and having briefly attracted attention, the Los Angeles H-iron plant disappeared from reports of Bethlehem Steel facilities.

The South San Francisco works was a casualty of the policy that concentrated investment at the other two western works. In 1962, its 280,000-ton open hearth capacity was closed, a process helped on by pressure from the Bay Area Air Pollution Control Board. The billet mills also closed, and remaining rolling operations there were subsequently supplied from the modernized blooming and billet mills in Los Angeles. But, late in 1963, the company took a step that seemed to indicate a much stronger confidence in its long-term prospects in Pacific coast markets. It recognized that it could not make further large-scale developments in the area of the existing South San Francisco works because it was hemmed in by the site of U.S. Steel's Consolidated Western Steel Division, which could not be expected to be accommodating. Instead, Bethlehem Steel acquired a large site almost twenty-five miles away at Pinole Point, seven miles from Richmond on the southern shore of San Pablo Bay. It intended to build a major works. The project would start with finishing operations and gradually integrate backward. It was planned that when backward integration reached the point of iron making, the Calmar line, which had commonly carried lumber eastward and steel westward, would bring coal required for the new mills from Atlantic coast ports. It is not clear where the ore would have come from, and both the Venezuelan and El Romeral orefields were farther from Pinole Point than from Sparrows Point. As far as markets are concerned, it should be remembered that at this time there were lively expectations that the already rapidly growing western markets would before long receive a further major boost from the establishment of Pacific coast automobile assembly lines and body shops. Walter Williams, who had been in charge of coke ovens and blast furnaces at Lackawanna before being involved with the Burns Harbor project, was also project engineer for the planned Pinole Point works. The questions of whether the company had the technical or the financial resources to carry through the two major projects at the same time seem not to have been aired, at least publicly.

The first stages of the Pinole Point development were duly completed. Steel fabricating facilities, some transferred from the older works, were installed on the site. A 160,000 tons per year continuous galvanizing line was announced, to be supplied with coil from Sparrows Point, and this unit completed its first full year of operations in 1969. Things seemed to be following much the same pattern as at Burns Harbor on Lake Michigan, but at a slower pace. For a time Bethlehem did nothing to dampen public speculation that the process would go on and that it would in the end produce a fully integrated West Coast mill. In 1965, it was even reported to have shown a plan for long-term development to business leaders in nearby Richmond, California. This plan included coke ovens and blast furnaces (one report indicated as many as five furnaces with room for three more), basic oxygen converters, and a crude steel capacity of 6 million tons. It was pointed out that there was no firm construction schedule.[7]

The Pinole Point fabricating works and plant site, 1964. *Courtesy Bethlehem Steel Corporation.*

A prerequisite for going ahead with the full scheme for Pinole Point was a further expansion of western outlets for flat-rolled products, and any hope for the arrival of automotive manufacturing plants was dashed by increasing car imports from Japan. At the same time, the expanding flood of imported steel had an especially severe impact on the West Coast market. Construction of further finishing plants and backward integration of processes were stopped. By 1972, Bethlehem had decided to sell off the Pinole Point site except for those parts with already operating finishing plants. By 1975, it had also sold the fabricating shops as part of its program to withdraw from that field nationwide. Soon after, contraction was under way in all its Pacific Coast operations.

Arguably, the 1960s was the decade in which decline in the traditional iron and steel industry, including the Bethlehem Steel Corporation, began to appear amid all its wealth and outward show of confidence. Yet, paradoxically, this was to be the period in which, for the first time since the construction of the iron and Bessemer steel plant at Bethlehem in the 1860s and early 1870s, the company built a major new works on a virgin site. It chose this line of development as a second-best option.

World War II had temporarily distorted the structure and trends of national steel consumption and production. Plate and structurals for merchant ship-building became of central importance along with the more obvious munitions of war, but afterward there was a sharp return to consumer goods. The struggle to satisfy the demand coming from consumer durable industries and above all from the automobile manufacturers again became the chief engine for growth in steel. In supplying this market, the Bethlehem Steel Corporation was doubly disadvantaged. It remained to a greater extent than most rivals a "heavy" product company, and its operations were peripheral to the core area of national consumption. In the 1950s, the company made another attempt to solve both problems along lines it had followed more than twenty years earlier. When it failed, it struck out on a new line of attack.

In a report issued to the company's employees in March 1955, Grace pointed out that, in 1930, only one-third of their finished steel capacity had been in light products but that soon two-thirds of it would fall into that category. But in the key sector of thin flat-rolled products, they still lagged. In 1954, 46.8 percent of the finished rolled capacity at U.S. Steel, 52.5 percent at YS&T, 59.2 percent at Inland, and 94.9 percent at National Steel was for hot rolled sheet and coil; the Bethlehem figure was 42.9 percent. The western parts of the manufacturing belt, above all in southern Michigan, northwestern Ohio, and the greater Chicago industrial area, were the outstanding growth centers for metal working. Demand for steel was now spreading rapidly to the South and the West and more widely throughout the United States, but even so, this long-established core area of manufacturing more or less held its share of national consumption. The eastern seaboard, after making early postwar gains in its share of consumption, began to fall away. One calculation of the pattern of demand at this time showed how important the industrial Midwest was for steel fabricators—and therefore for steel makers. Estimates based on figures for receipts of 28 million of the total output of 51 million tons of hot rolled steel in 1946—almost half of which was delivered to metal working plants—indicated that consumption in the mid-Atlantic states (New York, New Jersey, Maryland, and most of New England) was 19.9 percent of the national total. (This figure does not include three states: Pennsylvania, whose markets were partly east and partly west of the Appalachians, and New Hampshire and Delaware, for which no figures were produced.) Ohio alone consumed 14.3 percent of the national total, and the four states clustered around Chicago—Michigan, Indiana, Illinois, and Wisconsin—consumed 36.2 percent.[8] Over the next few years, this last area more or less held its relative share, and, in absolute terms, greatly increased its consumption.

According to one calculation, between 1946 and 1955, 935 new metal working firms employing 155,000 workers moved into the Chicago metropolitan area. By October 1955, metal working jobs in that area were estimated to total 587,000

Table 11.1 Share of national consumption of steel mill products by metal fabricators by location in the manufacturing belt, 1947, 1954, and 1963 (percentage)

	1947	1954	1963
Eastern region[1]	11.8	12.6	10.5
Central region[2]	27.1	25.2	23.5
Western region[3]	40.3	38.1	39.0

Source: Based on Economic Review of Federal Reserve Bank of Cleveland, October 1969, 10.

[1]New England, New York, and New Jersey.
[2]Pennsylvania and Ohio.
[3]Michigan, Indiana, Illinois, and Wisconsin.

as compared with 534,000 in the Detroit metropolitan area and 252,000 in and around Pittsburgh. Over eight years to 1956, steel consumption in the Chicago area increased from 4.2 million to 5.6 million tons.[9] Bethlehem Steel plants were not well placed for access to this core area or even to other key markets. It is true that in the mid- and late 1950s, Lackawanna was shipping about 1 million tons of steel a year to Detroit-area automobile plants. During the lake navigation season, deliveries could be made overnight, but for four months a year it was necessary to dispatch products by rail or road. This required absorption of freight charges of about 1.5 cents per ton mile.[10] The Chicago area was even more difficult to penetrate, yet projections by the Bethlehem commercial research department suggested that by 1970, national steel capacity would need to rise by 44 million tons and the Chicago area would require some 13 million tons of that amount.[11]

Continuing imbalance in product lines and less than ideal access to the most rapidly growing markets seemed of little concern in 1953, when Bethlehem output exceeded that of all previous years and the company plants were operating at full capacity. But the next year was one of recession, with Bethlehem's steel output falling by almost 4 million tons and the operating rate of 74.6 percent being the lowest since 1939. The sharp shock of 1954 reactivated the idea of a merger with Youngstown Sheet and Tube. A newer element also figured into the idea for a merger, and that was U.S. Steel's recent construction of its Fairless works. Referring to Bethlehem's revived interest in YS&T, Edmund Martin linked the two events: "It was in many ways a reciprocal move. Up until the Fairless plant was built, there had been a sort of understanding that U.S. Steel and Bethlehem wouldn't invade each other's territory. But, when U.S. Steel built at Morrisville, Bethlehem deemed it imperative to establish a presence in the Midwest."[12] Bethlehem Steel and YS&T had remained independent operations since their earlier efforts to merge had failed, but there had been a measure of joint planning in the development of both raw material resources and new facilities with a possible eventual merger in mind.[13] New thoughts of amalgamation during 1954 did not become public knowledge until mid-1955, when testimony was given to the Senate Subcommittee on Antitrust and Monopoly by Arthur Homer, president of Bethlehem Steel, and George McCuskey, vice president of YS&T. Taking up points made twenty-five years earlier, Homer stressed the two companies' complementary range of products and the fact that they largely operated in different market areas. It was argued that higher freight charges meant that competition in steel was now regional rather than national and that, as a result, the two companies were not effective rivals. Consequently, if they merged, competition would not really be reduced. Indeed, the claim was even made that the creation of a bigger company, capable of competing with other majors in more areas, would in effect increase competitiveness in the national steel market. Homer indicated that if a merger went ahead, Bethlehem would spend some $350 million on improvements to YS&T plants. Later, Grace stressed that this could be done more rapidly and at one-third the cost of building comparable capacity in a new plant. It was made clear that most of the expenditure and expansion would be concentrated at the East Chicago works. For its part, YS&T supported the argument that the two companies were complementary, emphasizing that a merger would reduce wasteful cross hauling. It stressed that alone it could not afford investments on the scale Bethlehem proposed.[14]

Gradually, more details emerged. If the merger went ahead, $90 million would be invested at the Youngstown district plants for an additional 600,000 tons of crude steel capacity and expansion of hot and cold rolled sheet capacity. Outlay at East Chicago would be $268 million, boosting capacity by 2 million tons and adding new plate and structural mills, products until then of minor importance at YS&T. Compared with this total bill for $358 million, construction costs for the same facilities in a wholly new works were estimated at $750 million. Although the improvements to be made to the YS&T plants would cost $135 per ingot ton, a high figure as compared with an average of about $70 per ton for existing works across the nation, this figure was very attractive in comparison to the $250 or $300 or more in an operation developed on a "greenfield" site. Savings in outlay would result in much lower overheads per ton of product. The high costs involved in building a wholly new plant cited by the two companies were challenged in evidence by other steelmakers.[15]

When Bethlehem had begun "extended negotiations" with YS&T in 1954, the plan had been submitted to the Department of Justice. It advised the companies that it believed their scheme violated antitrust law and that if they went ahead, it would seek an injunction to stop them. On 11 December 1956, a decisive step was taken in the form of a "Reorganization Plan and Agreement between the Youngstown Sheet and Tube Company and the Bethlehem Steel Corporation." Under the terms of this plan Bethlehem agreed to acquire YS&T in exchange for shares in the common stock of Bethlehem Steel. It would also assume YS&T's debt, including funded debt of $100 million. Grace had asked counsel to prepare the reorganization plan, but, at the same time, he informed his fellow directors that the Justice Department would bring a suit against them, enjoining the merger. One of his successors has suggested that Grace was prepared to fight for the merger all the way to the Supreme Court, but in spring 1957, he suffered his first stroke and by fall that year had given way as chief executive to Homer.[16] In December 1958, an order was issued enjoining the acquisition on the grounds that it would violate section 7 of the Clayton Antitrust Act, a section that had been strengthened by Congress as recently as 1950. Because it was advised by counsel that an appeal could not be heard before 1960, on 29 January 1959, the Bethlehem directors decided to withdraw. The two companies for the second time formally announced the end of their plan to merge.[17]

In marked contrast to the situation in 1930–1931, Bethlehem Steel was now unwilling to accept the status quo, although there was no immediate announcement of an alternative. However, notwithstanding statements it had made in recent years, it resolved to build a new mill on a greenfield site. There would be some important compensating advantages in using a virgin site, though these had understandably not been fully aired when the merger was under consideration. They were vividly laid out in retrospect by Martin: "Most of our plants have been rebuilt several times over, at a cost of hundreds of millions of dollars. The equipment may be state-of-the-art, but you're still squirming, gerrymandering, and leap-frogging around on a cramped site that was selected in an age that predated computers, telecommunications, global competition, the environmental movement, labor relations, the automobile, and even electricity." In short, highly efficient layout and linkages between the various units of plant could cancel out at least some part of the impact of extra capital investment in terms of annual overheads.[18]

As early as 1930, the chamber of commerce in Valparaiso, Indiana, had promoted a site known as Burns Ditch on the shore of Lake Michigan as being well suited for industrial development. In 1950, after plans for the U.S. Steel East Coast works were revealed that January, Bethlehem representatives began a search for a possible works site in the Chicago area. After rejecting a potential location on the western side of Lake Michigan, they opted for Burns Ditch. In 1956, the company began to buy land there, and by summer 1957, it had assembled and surveyed a tract of thirty-five hundred acres comprising poor farmland, swamp, and dunes. Before the merger was ruled out, the $6 million paid for this land was said to be for expansion of the "nearby" YS&T facilities. In any event, as Grace put it, they had not made the purchase to provide a bird sanctuary.[19]

On 3 October 1962, Homer "informed" the Bethlehem Steel management committee that the company would build at what would be known as Burns Harbor. He envisaged that in the future it might possibly be their biggest plant. On 3 December 1962, Bethlehem Steel made a public announcement of the new mill. The president, Edmund Martin, with career-long experience in steel works operations, was put in charge of the project. The delay of four years since rejection of the merger, and of more than eight years since it had first been mooted, proved extremely fortunate in one major respect. The new works would not be provided with obsolete steel technology. During the 1950s, the industry had built new or had expanded existing open hearth furnaces to the extent of about 40 million tons' annual capacity. By the early 1960s, scaled-up versions of a new steel making process, the oxygen converter developed in Europe during the previous decade, were recognized to cut capital costs for new capacity by twenty-five to thirty dollars per annual ton and to reduce operating costs by five dollars a ton of output, as compared with open hearth furnaces. Bethlehem planned a gradual process of backward integration, from rolling mills into the making of steel in oxygen converters. The practicality of large-scale continuous casting had not yet been proved, and it was therefore decided that the works would be equipped with the traditional, well-proved, but costlier slabbing mills.[20]

Although it was to act on a bigger scale and with a broader process of development, Bethlehem was not the only outsider responding at this time to the attractions of a Chicago-area location. Having contemplated development in the area for thirty years, like Bethlehem Steel, National Steel had been given approval in 1960 by the Army Corps of Engineers for land reclamation at Portage, Indiana. On this site, it would install more than $100 million worth of finishing operations, and it projected a progressive backward integration sometime in the future when the rolling mills had already secured major outlets.[21] Within a year of Bethlehem's decision to go ahead at Burns Harbor, Jones and Laughlin had announced it would build finishing mills at Hennepin on the Illinois River, again with an intention of later integrating backward to produce a major iron, steel, and rolling mill complex.[22] Like National Steel and J&L, Bethlehem planned for a phased development over a number of years so as to spread the heavy capital costs, but more definitely than either of them, it was committed to a program of providing upstream facilities. A 160-inch plate mill was brought into production in December 1964, followed the next year by a cold rolled sheet and tin mill operation. In September 1966, an 80-inch hot strip mill was commissioned. Expenditure to this point had amounted to $400 million, half as much again as had been planned for investing in YS&T's East Chicago works. Phase 2 began in 1966 with construction of a harbor by the state of Indiana and a start on the iron and steel making plant. By late 1969, a large blast furnace and coke ovens were at work. In the latter instance, the company overreached itself. The dimensions of the individual ovens of the coke batteries were made bigger than normal, and for years this caused serious operating difficulties. Coking coal, amounting to some 1.3 million tons even at the relatively low level of operations in 1970, came by rail from Bethlehem's own or shared mines at Ellsworth and in Cambria County, Pennsylvania, and from Itmann, Sewell, and Kayford, in West Virginia. Pelleted iron ore was obtained through Bethlehem's involvement in Erie Mining, and up to one-third of the total tonnage used at that time came from the new Pea Ridge mine near Sullivan, Missouri. Two 250-ton basic oxygen furnace (BOF) converters and a slabbing mill were brought into use in 1970. By this time, Burns Harbor was a fully integrated works with 2 million tons of finished product capacity, and it had cost $1 billion. Further expansion toward a capacity of 4 million tons of steel and large increases in hot rolled steel products were expected to reduce unit production costs. Reports at the time indicated that the layout of the works provided for an ultimate capacity of up to 10 million tons.[23]

This major new mill was a direct challenge to the other major integrated works in the Chicago area: the Gary and South Works of U.S. Steel as well as

Burns Harbor, 1965. *Courtesy Bethlehem Steel Corporation.*

those belonging to Inland and to Youngstown Sheet and Tube. U.S. Steel was sufficiently alarmed that it held a meeting in May 1963 "for the express purpose of reviewing the current situation in Indiana, as it affects political and community attitudes to U.S. Steel, particularly in the light of aggressive efforts by competitors who have established plants in the area." It resolved to set up a group to meet regularly. There was good reason to feel a need for positive response, for there was always a danger that expansion of capacity would outrun that of the market. Between 1960 and 1974, the steel capacity of the U.S. Steel plants in the area was expanded by 1.6 million tons. By 1974, Burns Harbor was rated at 4.3 million tons. As well as affecting local competitors, its construction had important implications for other Bethlehem plants.

It was ironic that many of the key members of the team that designed and built Burns Harbor, from Edmund Martin downward, were drawn from Lackawanna, for it was that mill that Burns Harbor mortally wounded in the long run.[24] During the few years before its upstream units of plant were brought into production, Burns Harbor drew above all on Lackawanna for semi-finished steel, first as slabs for the plate mill, later for the hot strip mill. For a time, it also drew on Lackawanna's hot rolled coil for its cold strip mill. Smaller contributions of steel were drawn from Sparrows Point. At the time, much was made of the fact that the New York Central Railroad, which ran across the site of the new works, would act "essentially as a conveyor belt" for semi-finished steel. The shuttle service employed five hundred special railroad cars marked for that purpose, which was anticipated to cost $5.25 per gross ton in freight charges. By the end of 1965, six thousand tons of slabs were being brought in weekly, the railroad boasting that when the slabs arrived they were still warm.[25] By early 1969, when Burns Harbor employed about 4,000, Bethlehem still had more than 16,500 workers in the Buffalo area alone. Yet, when it became fully integrated, it was essential to operate the new Chicago area works as near to full capacity as possible because of its high capital cost. As it was also only thirty miles from Chicago and less than half as far as its rival from the press shops of southern Michigan, it constituted a clear potential threat to Lackawanna's future.[26]

For the inauguration of the first units at Burns Harbor in late summer 1965, Bethlehem Steel decided to hold a great celebration. In the course of a two-day "open house," three thousand persons, only one-tenth of whom were affiliated with the company, toured the mill and were feted. Their host, Ed Martin, now company chairman, recorded the event: "The grand opening of Burns Harbor, a week-long extravaganza in September 1965, was a feat of showmanship that would have made Charles Schwab and Eugene Grace very proud. We spent a million dollars on that grand opening. . . . In a unique but appropriate way, the greatness of Bethlehem Steel had been displayed to an important national audience."[27] His recollections were written a quarter century after the event. By that time, million-dollar plant openings had long ceased to be appropriate.

III

TRIUMPH,

CRISIS,

AND

COLLAPSE

12

SHIPBUILDING,
STEEL, AND LABOR
IN BETHLEHEM'S
PEAK YEARS

COMPARED WITH EUGENE GRACE's forty-four years' leadership of Bethlehem Steel, Arthur Homer's tenure as head of Bethlehem was brief, lasting only seven years from fall 1957. In April 1964, he was succeeded by Edmund Martin, who retired in 1970. In contrast to Grace, who retired at eighty-one years of age, each of his immediate successors retired at sixty-eight. Grace's last decade in command had been one of spectacular growth and solid financial success; during the leadership of his successors, the operating environment was less favorable. After recovery from the 1954 recession, for the three operating years from 1955 through 1957 Bethlehem's annual shipments of steel had averaged 13.43 million tons and net income was 7.6 percent of total revenues. From 1958 through 1960, annual shipments averaged 10.46 million tons and income per dollar of revenue was six cents. Not until 1965–1969 were annual shipments well above the levels of a decade earlier, and even then, profit margins were a good

Table 12.1 Key indicators for steel companies, 1963 as percentage of 1957			
	Sales	Operating income	Earnings per share
Bethlehem	-19.5	-26.0	-48.9
U.S. Steel	-17.8	-37.0	-55.0
Republic	-9.2	-26.6	-35.4
Armco	-13.1	-9.6	-12.5
National	+32.1	+38.7	+34.2
Jones and Laughlin	-0.02	+11.2	-3.5
Inland	+5.8	+16.1	-9.9
Youngstown Sheet and Tube	-7.8	-11.1	-10.2

Source: *Forbes*, 1 August 1964, 20, 21.

deal lower. National expansion was slower: between 1950 and 1959, steel capacity had increased 46 million tons; over a period twice as long, from 1960 to 1977, it expanded by only 10 million tons.[1] Bethlehem's rated capacity in its operations in the Northeast over the fourteen years to 1960 went up from 10.4 million to 22.0 million net tons; for the next fourteen years, the net increase was 2.1 million tons. Despite the change of pace, it was a distinction of Homer's chairmanship to have made the decision to build the company's only completely new integrated works since Bethlehem Iron had begun operations a century earlier.

In retrospect, it can be seen that the Homer chairmanship and the later years of the 1960s marked a turning point in company history. It is an inherent defect (or perhaps "limitation," to avoid any suggestion of culpable negligence) of capitalist corporate enterprise that it lacks long-term forward perspective. Because of preoccupation with immediate issues such as profits and short-term planning, those in charge usually cannot foresee the consequences of trends that begin in modest fashion. During the 1960s, the rather dark hues of the signs of the times were sufficiently muted that it was easy for top management to conclude that things might soon improve. It would have required leadership of exceptional discernment to recognize that a watershed was being crossed. New circumstances in international trade, in technology, and in the trends and structure of demand henceforward would provide a less satisfactory business environment. Most other major integrated firms were in the same state, still expanding, performing reasonably well, but certainly not pushing ahead as they had previously. In fact, among the biggest firms, Bethlehem's record ranked it somewhere in the middle. Between 1960 and 1968, national steel production increased 32.2 percent, and that figure for Bethlehem was 27.8 percent, comparable with Republic (26.6 percent), far ahead of U.S. Steel (18.6 percent), but well behind Inland's 37.2 percent and National's 47.1 percent.

Two important considerations were that demand grew less than in the early postwar years and a considerably higher proportion of consumption was met by imports. Between 1953 and 1957, annual per capita consumption of steel averaged 1,274 pounds; over the next five years it was down to 1,058 pounds. Before the 1960s, there had been decades of loudly expressed concern about foreign competition, dumping, the need for tariffs, and so on, but in fact, for eighty years supplies of rolled steel from overseas had not been a major factor in the American steel market. Now the situation suddenly changed, and from this time onward the question of steel imports would not be only a matter of theory and rhetoric but of hard practical concern, affecting company fortunes and scores of thousands of jobs. Until 1959, the United States was a net exporter of steel, with a peak favorable balance of trade of 5.15 million tons in 1957. With hindsight, it can be seen that the recession of 1958 provided ominous pointers to what was to come, for in that year, with every incentive for hard-pressed companies to look for outlets wherever they might be found, net exports fell to 1.33 million tons. The following year witnessed strikes; workers were out for 116 days and returned with substantially increased wages. Some have attributed a good deal of subsequent difficulties to that wage increase, but an even clearer effect of the dispute was that the balance of trade in steel moved against the United States so much that in that year there were net imports of 3.39 million tons.

In terms of costs of production, the balance of advantage was moving against American firms as compared with leading rivals overseas. Most commonly referred to, for obvious reasons, was the fact that unit labor costs were high in the United States and generally rising while those of major overseas steel makers were not only much lower but also fairly stable or falling. It was easy to overlook the fact that these differing trends were in part the result of the installation of newer equipment overseas. Having been led to believe foreign steel was inferior, consumers compelled to use it in 1959 while domestic mills were strikebound generally found that such was not the case. This discovery helped ensure that what might have been no more than a short-term anomaly in international trade figures was only partly corrected the next year, with net imports amounting to 620,000 tons. After that, imports increased rapidly, by 1968 reaching an extraordinary 16.78 million tons or equal to nearly 2.5 million tons more than all the steel products shipped that year by Bethlehem Steel. In the same year, a German periodical, after quoting testimony given to the Senate Finance Committee that the problem of the U.S. steel industry was "not the high wages it pays but its loss of technical superiority" made the knowing comment, "Faced by overseas developments such as the vast new oxygen plants of the German giants now under construction , and a Japanese steel industry which predicts a total output of 80 to 85 million tons against this year's figure of 62 million, the American steel makers' campaign for import quotas is easily understood."[2] Already, many American firms were complaining bitterly of this unfavorable balance of trade and its impact on their production. It was just as well they could not foresee that over the next thirty years these highs would be often, even regularly, exceeded by considerable degrees.

The difficulties of the times were complicated by fundamental changes in technology. Early in the century, Bethlehem had benefited substantially from the rapid advance of steel produced in basic open hearth furnaces at the expense of Bessemer converter output. Now, like most other major firms, it was slow in moving into a new generation of steel making processes. Only 230,000 tons of its production in 1957 of 19.5 million tons of steel outside its Pacific coast plants was made by the electric furnace. In its small involvement in electric steel making, it was by no means alone. U.S. Steel electric furnace capacity was then 387,000 out of 39.6 million tons, and National Steel and Inland Steel had no electric melting capacity at all. Indeed, the progress then being made by Bethlehem in West Coast operations made it something of a pioneer, the share of electric steel in its capacity there increasing from 44.7 percent in 1954 to 72.4 percent five years later. In the field of oxygen steel making, it was definitely among the laggards.

The basic oxygen converter, pioneered in small units in Austria in the early 1950s, had within a few years proved capable of being transformed into a bulk steel making process. As such, it required substantially less capital outlay and had lower operating costs than open hearth furnaces, yet it turned out a high quality product. Although it advanced only slowly in the United States in its early years, in the 1960s it made remarkable headway. As late as 1960, only 3.4 percent of American steel was made in oxygen converters; by 1965, the figure was 17.4 percent and two years later, about one-third. Having first passed the output of the open hearth melting shops in August 1969, its share of total steel output through 1970 averaged 48.1 percent. Given this rapid advance from a very low level, a critical consideration for any steel company was when to make large increases in its steel capacity. It thus had to consider whether to install what had proved to be the up-and-coming process or commit itself to older methods by investing in plant that would take many years to fully amortize, and which would either block or make especially costly the introduction of oxygen converters. In some respects, Bethlehem was particularly unfortunate. In 1956, the share of oxygen steel in national production was minimal, and its suitability for American mass production had not been proved. The new process was being adopted only by companies operating under special circumstances, such as McLouth in Detroit. It was at this time that Bethlehem Steel decided to make the major improvements at Sparrows Point, which within two years brought capacity there to more than 8 million tons. The company concluded that the oxygen steel process was at an early stage of development, and consequently the decision was made to build more open hearth furnaces at Sparrows Point. It was when Bethlehem was in the middle of this 2-million-ton expansion program that the Aliquippa works of Jones and Laughlin proved that the new process could be used for high outputs. In short, Bethlehem's decision may be seen to have been understandable, even reasonable, but why did Bethlehem, unlike McLouth, Kaiser, and J&L, not see the signs of the times and, notwithstanding all the uncertainties that would have been involved, play a lead role in assessing and upgrading the new process? Was the company (and others, too, notably U.S. Steel) guilty of entrepreneurial failure? Although it by no means followed that there was a lack of insight and initiative within the whole company, the fact that Grace, as a very dominating chairman, celebrated his eightieth birthday in August 1956 must surely have some relevance in relation to his company's choice of a well-tried rather than a pioneering role. As things turned out, having been built at higher capital cost, the new Sparrows Point melting shop was already becoming less than the most efficient of steel producing units by the time it had passed its teething troubles; by 1961, 7.5 million tons of oxygen capacity was in operation in the United States. Five companies now had oxygen steel plants, but neither Bethlehem nor U.S. Steel was among them. Within another two years, the economic advantages of the new process were obvious for all to see. The capital outlay required per ton of oxygen steel annual capacity was now put at some twenty-five dollars less than in open hearths, and the basic oxygen converter could process molten iron to steel for eight to nine dollars a ton as compared with ten to fifteen dollars a ton for most conventional open hearths.[3] In 1962, Bethlehem authorized its first two basic oxygen converters.

In the late 1950s, its massed banks of open hearth furnaces made Sparrows Point, in Eugene Grace's colorful phrase, "the greatest show on earth." The plant had contained 39.0 percent of Bethlehem capacity outside the Pacific coast in 1946, but though by 1960 its share was down to 37.3 percent, at 8.2 million tons it had edged past Gary to become the nation's largest works. In mid-1964, Bethlehem Steel announced that it would spend $27.6 million for two BOFs at Sparrows Point to replace the No. 1 open hearth shop, built between 1910 and 1916. On 22 June 1966, the Bethlehem directors held a special inspection meeting at Sparrows Point, a visit timed to celebrate the fifty years during which that plant had been owned by Bethlehem Steel. It was noted that when the plant was acquired, its raw steel capacity was 700,000 tons and it made only rails and billets. Now, twenty-eight thousand persons were employed on a three-thousand-acre site, steel capacity was over 8 million tons, and the mills rolled a wide range of products.[4]

On 26 October 1965, the directors toured the Burns Harbor works. The next day, they approved Edmund Martin's suggestion that Crowdus Baker, a leading Chicago-area businessman, should be appointed as an additional member of their board in view of the increasing importance to the company of the Midwest. It was yet another indicator of the changing priorities in company thinking. Over the next few years, a series of major new units were added to the new plant. As this happened, it became clear that the company had taken full advantage of the opportunity to design and build the best plant from scratch on a virgin site. The finest equipment that could be bought was installed. Care was taken to ensure that the layout was the most efficient possible to minimize movement and handling. Self-unloading ships would deliver the ore to the stockyards from which the blast furnaces were fed by conveyor belt rather than the usual hoists. The result of all this careful planning and generous outlay was that a new standard of excellence was attained in terms of efficiency, and when further extended and operated at its capacity, Burns Harbor proved itself capable of reaching new lows in terms of production costs.[5]

Lackawanna, then America's fourth ranking plant by size, was expanded in the mid-1960s more than any other of the company operations. In October 1964, Bethlehem Steel's first oxygen converter capacity, 2.5 million tons in all, was commissioned there. It replaced fourteen open hearth furnaces and caused a net increase of 300,000 tons a year in Lackawanna steel capacity.[6] In 1966, a third converter raised capacity to 5 million tons, enabling the company to claim it as the largest basic oxygen furnace unit in the world. Between 1960 and 1967, extensions in steel at Lackawanna were twice as big as at Sparrows Point. Yet in the midst of this high tide of expansion, even before all its new capacity was installed, one can trace with rare precision the beginning of the end for this major plant: the date on which the company announced its plan for a new works near Chicago.

As the years would show, the more capacity was brought on stream at Burns Harbor, the more Lackawanna would be edged out of markets in which it had long been favored as the company's western outpost. From now on, it would be awkwardly placed between Bethlehem's main foci for plate and sheet products at Sparrows Point and Chicago and would have unquestioned market dominance in only a relatively small Niagara frontier region. Within a few years of the commissioning of Burns Harbor, *Iron Age* entitled one of its articles "Lackawanna: To be or not to be?" Although the circumstances were very different, Bethlehem's decision to build in Chicago had, in principle, replicated what Gary or, earlier still, Illinois Steel had done for the viability of eastern mills. After its brief period of glory as a key player, Lackawanna would become a corporate liability.

For other Bethlehem plants, construction of a Chicago mill had much less momentous short- or medium-term consequences. At the Bethlehem works, which was busy with structural steel, the company completed its third oxygen steel plant in 1968. It could produce 2.5 million to 3 million tons, but retirement of open hearth furnaces meant that capacity there was no bigger than a decade earlier. Steelton, with rail and railroad products, was a special case. It was now also an important producer of line pipe, drawing supplies of plate for its pipe mills from either Johnstown or Sparrows Point.[7] Although a new coke oven battery had been installed in the mid-1950s, a decision was now made to discontinue iron making. In 1968, Steelton was provided with the first of three 150-ton electric furnaces, an alternative way of displacing the open hearth process and one that could use the scrap supplies no longer required for the melting shops. Steelton remained the company's smallest unit in the East. At the remaining major facility, Johnstown, open hearth shops were not replaced, a situation that spoke volumes about the company's assessment of its prospects.

As suggested above, for Bethlehem and other major companies, the 1960s were years of transition not only in growth rates and technology but also in

Table 12.2 Raw steel production of the United States, Bethlehem Steel, and other major centers of world capacity, 1953, 1957, 1965, and 1975 (million net tons)

	1953	1957	1965	1975
United States	111.6	112.7	131.5	116.6
Bethlehem	17.7	19.1	21.0	17.5
Japan	8.4	13.8	45.4	112.8
European core economies*	54.5	78.1	106.4	114.2

Source: AISI, annual reports for the years indicated.

*West Germany, France, Italy, and the United Kingdom.

international competitiveness. For many years, steel expansion had been more rapid in the other main world centers of the industry. In spite of this, until 1967 Bethlehem was the second biggest steel maker not only in the United States but also in the noncommunist world. That year almost all the bigger firms in the United Kingdom were united as the British Steel Corporation, which for a time took over the second place. In 1970, the merger of Fuji and Yawata Steel to form Nippon Steel created a group that at last surpassed even U.S. Steel. In contrast to the airy indifference of domestic producers toward foreign steel industries that was characteristic of the 1950s, overseas producers were now, and from this time onward, regarded with suspicion. Edmund Martin provided an extreme example of this new attitude many years later in his memoirs: "I remember going to Japan when I was head of the American Iron and Steel Institute. [He was president in 1968.] They'd rebuilt their war-decimated steel industry and they were already shipping a lot of steel to America. I made a lot of speeches to them, and they smiled and printed all the speeches, but they kept right on doing what they were doing. You couldn't trust them when they smiled. You still can't."[8]

All in all, for Bethlehem the indices from the 1960s were mixed. It performed less well than most other majors between 1957 and 1963 but ended the decade on an upbeat. Yet it was clear that it faced more changes and many difficult issues. What was to happen to Johnstown, which, though a major plant, still had no oxygen steel capacity? Equally ominous and even more pressing were the question marks about the future of Lackawanna. For many years there had been even more grounds for concern about another major sector of Bethlehem's business, shipbuilding.

In the mid-1950s Bethlehem was the nation's leading shipbuilder; some thirty years later it could already be classed as a "second-rank" supplier. On one occasion during the 1960s, when a senior member of the Sun Shipbuilding and Dry Dock Company asked a Bethlehem representative why a leading steel maker should be involved in shipbuilding, the reply was that it was because there would always be wars.[9] In fact, there were no more conflicts on the all-out scale of the world wars that might have justified that simple reply to a ship-builder's question. In any case, even though naval vessels would continue to be needed, from now on the conduct of warfare primarily employed the more so-phisticated products of industries other than shipbuilding.

In World War II, shipbuilding had been Bethlehem's most important divi-sion, accounting for more than half its business and, at its peak in 1943, much more than half the work force. In steel and even more in war materiel, the cor-poration had been of great significance; in shipbuilding, it had been the leading company. It was for his successes in organizing this vital part of the company that Homer had been chosen as president of Bethlehem Steel Corporation in 1945 and marked out as Grace's eventual successor. Yet, almost as soon as the fighting ended, the international economics of the shipbuilding industry began to revert to traditional patterns, as they had after World War I. This meant that, though Bethlehem had again proved preeminent in wartime, under peacetime conditions U.S. yards would find it difficult or impossible to compete in the building of merchant ships in such a labor-intensive activity, whose product was usually a one-off, unique design of ship. However, there was to be no straightforward decline to near extinction, as between the wars, but rather sharp oscillations of activity superimposed on a long-term decline.

The Hingham, Massachusetts, and Fairfield-Baltimore yards were quickly closed. The Harlan and Hollingsworth yard, partly reactivated in the war to build landing craft, was shut down again after the fighting ended. In the postwar world, shipbuilding was revived by the boom in oil tanker construction. In 1949, launchings from all American yards totaled more than 600,000 gross registered tons, but this was already a dramatic falling away from wartime levels of pro-duction. Whereas in 1943 the United States had launched an amazing 11.58 mil-lion gross registered tons of shipping compared with 1.14 millions from United Kingdom yards, their respective annual averages from 1947 to 1950 were 340,000 tons and 1.24 million tons. As in the aftermath of World War I, the economy had turned inward. Growth focused on quite different sectors so that, despite short-term bursts of activity, shipbuilding shrank over the longer run.

After good years in 1949 and 1950, merchant shipbuilding was at a low ebb in 1951, completely outclassed in tonnage terms by the revived traditional European front-runners and soon afterward by a reconstructed and rapidly expanding Japanese industry. Within this severely shrunken industry, Bethlehem did better than most of its competitors. Except for the launching by the Newport News Company of the 51,500-ton liner *United States* in 1951, Bethlehem yards turned out a bigger tonnage; in orders in hand, it accounted for half the national business. Sharp variations followed. The national tonnage in 1955 was 73,000 gross registered tons, but three years later, boosted by the need for more large tankers after the closing of the Suez Canal in 1956, the tonnage launched was ten times that level. Bethlehem shipbuilding, too, followed an uneven course. In 1953, the Sparrows Point yard led the world, launching 216,000 deadweight tons, and in 1954, with 430,000 tons of merchant ships turned out, Bethlehem was the world's biggest shipbuilder, Quincy and Sparrows Point being the most productive of its six building yards. The next year it accounted for only 77,000 tons, but for the following four years, it increased output annually, to 150,000, 340,000, 400,000 and, in 1959, to 503,000 tons. That year, it was again the world's leading shipbuilder.

The shipbuilding division was separate from the rest of the company's top administration, which was concentrated in its Bethlehem headquarters. The general offices for Bethlehem shipbuilding were in New York, and the Central Technical Department, which handled research, design, and engineering, was at Quincy.

In the early 1960s, there were eleven yards. Quincy and Sparrows Point were exclusively builders, San Francisco and Beaumont, Texas, were in both construction and repair work, and there were seven yards involved with repair and conversion—two in Brooklyn, two in Baltimore, and one each in Hoboken, New Jersey, Boston, and San Pedro, California. On Staten Island, there was a propeller plant and foundry. At this time, 12 to 15 percent of Bethlehem's dollar billings were represented by shipbuilding as compared with 60 to 65 percent for steel and 23 to 25 percent for all other activities.[10]

Soon afterward, as orders began to dwindle, a pruning of this large and scattered operation had to be undertaken. It was ironic that in 1962 Homer had to write what was in effect an advance notice of the impending demise of the division in which he had spent the larger part of his working life: "Our Shipbuilding Division has had a long and distinguished history and has contributed substantially to the development of ship design, both naval and merchant, in times of war and peace. We must, however, reluctantly accept the fact that it is difficult to envisage enough private shipbuilding in this country or a sufficient amount of Navy or other government-financed ship construction to enable our

Quincy, Massachusetts, shipyard, 1958. *Courtesy Bethlehem Steel Corporation.*

shipyards to operate at a satisfactory level. Our shipbuilding operations are being adjusted to meet these conditions."[11] An early casualty was the largest unit, the former Fore River yard at Quincy. Although it was the center of the division, Quincy had generally not done well in the postwar years, even when the company's other yards had been successful. The work force in 1959 was thirteen thousand, but by the end of 1962 the yard had only fifteen hundred workers, and at this point it was closed. Two years later Fore River was sold to General Dynamics, which continued to run it during the next few decades. Three yards on New York Harbor were closed in 1962–1963: the Twenty-seventh and Fifty-sixth Street yards in Brooklyn and the Staten Island yard, activities in that area being concentrated in Hoboken. Reference to shipbuilding now disappeared from the annual report until activity picked up again in 1967. By the late 1960s and into the 1970s, money was being invested in an attempt to improve efficiency in both building and repair work, including a new basin at Sparrows Point to take vessels of more than 300,000 tons and a major new dry dock at the San Francisco yard.

Such efforts proved incapable of stopping the decline. A decrease in the corporation's net income in 1972 was largely attributed to losses in its marine division, due to the completion of contracts entered into years before, when costs were much lower. Reacting to this situation, the company resolved that from then on, contracts should be made only if they allowed for cost inflation.[12] An even more serious blow to this section of the business resulted from the world energy crisis that began in fall 1973. Over a number of years, this situation depressed demand for new tankers, and through its adverse impact on both the national and the global economy, it helped reduce the general level of demand for steel. The effect was so gradual that even in the most exposed sectors there continued to be important successes, for instance, in the mid-1970s, when the Sparrows Point yard delivered the first of five 265,000-ton oil tankers. By this time, Sparrows Point was the shipbuilding division's leading operation, and it was considered able to build vessels of up to 350,000 deadweight tonnage.[13]

The general emphasis in Bethlehem yards shifted over the years from new construction to repair work and, in so far as any new building work was still undertaken, from ships to oil and gas platforms. By 1980, the company still operated six yards around the coasts, but Sparrows Point was now its only shipbuilding yard. San Francisco and Beaumont had facilities for repair work and the construction of marine equipment, including offshore drilling platforms. At Baltimore, Hoboken, and East Boston there were repair operations. In addition to its home yards, Bethlehem also had a 70 percent share in a Singapore yard building mobile oil platforms. Unfortunately, the marine division suffered a serious blow to its reputation in 1980, when a federal court found Bethlehem guilty of billing foreign ship owners for illegal commissions on repair work and imposed a fine of $325,000.

Bit by bit all of these marine operations were pared back. In 1983, the company disposed of its San Francisco yard the old Union Iron Works, which had pioneered Pacific coast shipbuilding in the nineteenth century and had caused Schwab much annoyance in the first decade of the twentieth century. It was sold to local port officials for the token sum of one dollar. The repair yards in Baltimore, Boston, and Hoboken were closed. The U.S. defense budget for 1985 allegedly included a sum of $173 million for the navy to order two survey ships, which would enable Bethlehem to keep Sparrows Point open longer for new construction. A few years later, during Operation Desert Storm in Kuwait and Iraq, the U.S. government pressed the company to build roll-on/roll-off ships for army and navy use. It made clear that it was prepared to pay a very liberal price for these vessels. Having decided by 1986 that Sparrows Point would undertake only repair work, Bethlehem Steel rejected this extremely favorable offer.[14]

Strangely, in the midst of all its difficulties, Bethlehem embarked on a new endeavor in marine work. It opened a yard at Sabine Pass, near Port Arthur, Texas, in 1985. This yard was claimed to be capable of dry-docking the largest oil drilling rigs. Within two years, however, the company decided to sell this yard as well as those at Beaumont and Singapore. By 1995, the only operation still open was that for repair work at Sparrows Point. It, too, was proving un-competitive, and in 1996, Bethlehem Steel announced it had decided to "exit" the business. The company followed through on this decision by the third quar-ter of 1997, after which Bethlehem Shipbuilding was sold to the Veritas Capital Fund, marking the end of a sector which had been an integral and sometimes vitally important part of the company since before its formal organization in December 1904.

The 1970s and 1980s were remarkable decades in Bethlehem Steel history, occupying the transition from an age of growth to one of contraction. At the beginning of this period, Bethlehem was one of America's leading businesses. In 1970, it ranked fourteenth among industrial companies, made 20.6 million tons of steel (15.7 percent of the national total), and employed 130,000 persons. By 1990, it produced only 10.5 million tons of steel (11.0 percent of the total) and employment was below 25,000. Yet through this period, it operated what was the nation's lowest cost integrated steel plant. Clearly, much of the rest of the company's operations were not competitive. The broad context for these changes was provided by major shifts in the national economy and the position of the major steel companies within these shifts.

Between 1950 and 1970, national steel consumption increased almost 37 per-cent; consumption in 1990 was 5.4 percent lower than in 1970. In fact, the situ-ation was even worse. Domestic shipments fell by 6.4 percent, and imports increased their share of the market. These are, of course, only marker points. Consumption and domestic shipments varied considerably from year to year, but shipments in 1990 were in fact the highest for nine years. Suffering from the effects of a markedly less buoyant domestic market and from a massive ad-verse balance of trade in steel, Bethlehem also had to manage a wholesale and costly transition from dependence on the open hearth furnace to use of the basic oxygen converter, while at the same time meeting increasingly serious competition from steel makers who replaced the complicated processes based on blast furnace iron (and on all ancillary processes) with a much simpler se-quence in which scrap was melted in electric furnaces. One index of the headway of the latter is that whereas in 1970 the tonnage of steel made in electric furnaces was 31.8 percent as great as that made in converters, by 1990, it was 63.2 percent as large. In short, there was three-way pressure on the major steel companies in this period: slower, less certain growth in steel consumption and increasing competition from both overseas mills and domestic electric arc furnace operators. The changing position of any company within this broad setting was determined by the nature and quality of its whole organization and its individual plants, inherited from earlier years, and by the wisdom of the choices made by its top management in response to the situation as it changed from year to year.

Bethlehem Steel remained inward looking, preserving much of the parochialism that had ruled during Eugene Grace's long leadership. The traditional close-knit character and very comfortable life-style of its top officers and staff continued. A headquarters lunch remained a "four-star dining experience": "silver water pitchers and silver coffee ports adorned beautiful wooden tables covered with expensive linen." (In the middle of the first decade of the twenty-first century, some of these artifacts from a now vanished age would be sold to the public from a local bookstore.) Much more significant as a factor in the company's long-term survival, its top management continued to be promoted from within rather than recruited from the industry.[15] On the other hand, there were now some major changes in the nature of the organization. In the sixty-six years prior to 1970, only four men held the top post at Bethlehem Steel. With the exception only of Arthur Homer's seven-year leadership, the company was headed by practical steel men. Over the next twenty-two years, it would have four more heads, of whom only one, who occupied the chair for only six years, could be described as a steel man, though two others had long been involved in steel sales. During the same period, the balance of power in the selection of the chair and chief officers also shifted. This in turn reflected the changed composition of the board of directors. In 1963, when Lewis Foy joined the board, all fifteen of his fellow directors were employed by Bethlehem Steel, and all but one of them were, like him, a "principal officer." The following year, when Edmund Martin succeeded Homer, the board was increased to nineteen members, with the addition of four "outside" directors: the president of the Stevens Institute of Technology and the chairmen of three prominent companies—the First National Bank of Maryland, the Chemical Bank, and Standard Oil of New Jersey. In 1965, so as to reflect Bethlehem's new presence in the Chicago area,

Crowdus Baker, retired chairman of Sears Roebuck, was added. By 1970, the number of directors had been reduced to twelve, but five of them were outsiders. Eleven years later, at the time Reginald H. Jones, former chairman of the General Electric Corporation (GEC), and a man well known to the public for changing the relations between government and business, was elected, half the directors had not worked for Bethlehem. By 1985, eight of ten directors were in this category. This change in the balance of the board was accompanied by an increase in its power in selecting the chief officers. This was demonstrated in the succession to Foy. He had appointed Richard Schubert as president to succeed Frederic West, but when Foy retired, both he and the board recognized that Donald Trautlein was a superior candidate for the chairmanship. Schubert was thus passed over, and he retired from the company two years later. Through the 1980s, Reginald H. Jones in particular assumed an important role in representing the power and views of the board of directors. Even so, through this generally difficult period the different predilections and policies of the chairmen continued to play a key role in shaping the company's response to the challenges and opportunities of the times. They affected the balance between steel and other activities, the configuration of plants, and relations with competitors and labor interests.

From the end of the 1960s into the early years of the new decade, Bethlehem seemed likely to continue in a secure position as the industry's second ranking company. Outsiders generally concluded that the auguries were good. A widely respected student of the industry summed it up:

> With almost seventy years of existence behind it, the present Bethlehem Steel Corporation, with its nationwide operations and worldwide raw material resources, faces the 1970s with abundant high quality raw materials and good modern facilities. Almost half of its steel is produced by the basic oxygen converter [in 1971, the year in which this account was published, the national share for oxygen steel was 53 percent; in Japan it was 80 percent] and it has added three of the newest, most modern electric furnaces. In addition, the company's blast furnaces are among the most modern in the industry and its rolling mill facilities are modern, with the exception of some of those at the Johnstown plant, which will need replacement. . . . As with all the other steel companies, Bethlehem faces problems in the decade ahead; however, its assets and potential should allow it to cope with them in a successful and profitable manner.[16]

For a time, events seemed to justify this assessment, but soon after, both the evaluation of Bethlehem's plants and the upbeat conclusion to which this had led would be seen to have been far too optimistic.

Through the early 1970s, there were many indicators of success and suggestions of further expansion. A high point came in 1973, with production and shipments at record figures. Two years later, capital spending was at a level not previously reached (at least in current dollar terms). On the other hand, the force and effects of competition from various quarters were increasing, margins were narrowing, and the ability of the company to control the situation was decreasing. The major integrated companies that had for so long dominated the steel sector were being challenged by forces beyond their control, including shifts in markets, technologies, and the pattern of production both on a national and a global scale. Within a few years, these giants of the steel world would all be responding to worsening conditions and darker outlooks, with major closures of plant and disposals of raw materials. Bethlehem Steel would suffer with the rest.

The trend of net income, though it followed an uneven course year to year, was downward overall. Stewart Cort was fortunate to be chairman at the apparent peak of Bethlehem's fortunes, but in February 1974, in his last annual report, he recognized the adverse trend. He looked back on "the best year in the history of Bethlehem in terms of steel production, shipments, sales and net income . . . [but] our profit margins remained disappointingly low."[17] In fact, a number of indicators had already become unfavorable. The company had shipped about 3 million tons more than in 1957, their banner year, but the return on revenue had been only 4.9 percent compared with 7.3 percent at the earlier date. Even more striking, in terms of constant dollars (i.e., with the effects of inflation discounted), earnings in 1973 were about 30 percent lower than in 1957. In that year, imports of steel had amounted to 1.5 percent of apparent national consumption; by 1973, they were 12.4 percent. Employment costs in 1957 had been $1.0 billion in relation to total revenues of $2.6 billion; sixteen years later, they were $1.76 billion and total revenues were $4.17 billion; at the two dates, the cost of labor was, respectively, 38.1 and 42.1 percent of revenues. Higher costs and lower returns provided an incentive to raise prices, but doing so helped make the U.S. market increasingly rewarding for foreign suppliers and steel from overseas even more attractive to major consumers. Rising prices were also seen as undesirable by presidential administrations keenly concerned with minimizing inflationary pressures. Bethlehem already had direct experience in how difficult it was to force prices up to cover increasing costs. Early in January 1971, it announced increases for plates and structurals. The government made clear its opposition, another major producer announced smaller advances, and Bethlehem gave in, adopting the lower increase beginning on 1 March 1971. In 1973, federal price controls were in place for domestic steel; imported steel commanded premiums above these prices.

In the relative euphoria following its excellent performance in 1973, Bethlehem announced an important expansion program and intimated it would embark on something much more ambitious if external circumstances improved. After what it described as the first stage of a strategic planning study, it would spend $500 million for a 1.6 million ton increase in steel capacity by 1977. There would be a new blast furnace at Sparrows Point, an additional million tons of steel capacity and more finishing capacity at Burns Harbor, and a 600,000-ton addition to the recently depleted steel capacity at Lackawanna. At the same time, Cort indicated that during the next ten years his company was willing to spend a total (including the 1.6 million ton expansion by 1977) of more than $2 billion to increase its crude steel capacity by more than 25 percent or 6.6 million net tons, to a total of some 30 million tons. However, this larger program would be conditional on both government willingness to release the industry from price controls and a 10 percent across the board price increase.[18] By 1975, results were worse than expected, and the expansion program to be completed by 1977 was stretched out by one or two years. Some parts of it were not implemented. The bigger scheme running through to 1985 never materialized. In fact, contraction was already under way in some fields.

With the full commissioning of Burns Harbor, which made its first coke, iron, and crude steel in 1969, Bethlehem owned five fully integrated works. At Steelton, it had a million-ton mill using cold metal. On the Pacific coast, there was another million tons of steel capacity, well located in the main centers of population and economic activity. But penetration by imports, troublesome enough on the national scale, were proportionately much greater in the West, and withdrawal was soon under way there. The first full year of operations for the new galvanizing line at Pinole Point was in 1969, but the influx of foreign steel over the next two years caused the abandonment of plans for a major integrated works. The fourteen-hundred-acre tidewater site was offered for sale. By 1976–1977, the South San Francisco works was closed and Pacific coast operations were confined to Los Angeles and Seattle. The Los Angeles–area mill ceased operations in 1981–1982, and Seattle followed during 1984.

There were already serious difficulties in what were later to be designated "non-core" activities, though these sectors had previously been important. In some cases, their closure would result in important losses of outlet for the "core" steel making operations. Shipbuilding had faded as a major profitable sector, and, as seen elsewhere, closures were soon under way. In the 1950s, Grace had encouraged those seeking evidence of his company's importance to look at the skyline of Manhattan. Through the 1960s, the company's position in this respect seemed very much as it had in the past, with Bethlehem fabricating as well as rolling the structural steel for leading building projects across the nation, such as major developments at Madison Square Garden and construction of the second Delaware Memorial Bridge. Some were to see, perhaps mostly in retrospect, an ominous symbolism in the fact that when the World Trade Center took shape as the new dominant feature of the New York landscape between 1971 and 1973, most of its structural steel was rolled in foreign mills. By this time, Bethlehem was tackling competition more resolutely, as when it introduced a new pricing system for structurals in 1972, quoting a delivered price no higher than the FOB mill price at the nearest structural mill—its own or that of a rival plus freight.[19] But problems persisted, and four years later the company took the dramatic step of closing the six surviving plants of its Fabricated Steel Construction Division. As late as 1962, there had been eleven plants; by 1976, six had closed and an additional one had been opened at Pinole Point. The decision in 1976 to give up fabricating meant that from this time on, the Bethlehem structural mills had to compete in the open market for the custom work of the independent structural engineering industry. Between 1970 and 1979, the share of structural shapes and piling in Bethlehem net sales fell from 11.4 to 8.9 percent. The process was to be long drawn out, but withdrawal from the company's most distinctive product area had begun. On the other hand, some lines of business were still expanding. An interesting example was the fabrication of reinforcing bars. In 1956, Bethlehem had seven plants engaged in this business, thirteen years later it had fifteen, and by 1979 it had nineteen. But here, too, cost structures proved unfavorable for retention of the trade. Reinforcing bar was a low value mill product, and its manufacture was soon being largely lost to either importers or to operators of mini mills. In the 1980s, Bethlehem withdrew from this field too; by 1986, it had sold its fabricated reinforcing bar division.

Lewis Foy, mid-1970s. *Courtesy Bethlehem Steel Corporation.*

In 1974, when Stewart Cort handed the chairmanship over to Lewis Foy, business was at a high point. The previous year, Bethlehem had achieved records: 23.7 million tons of raw steel and 16.6 million tons of steel products shipped. Net income in 1974 was an unprecedented $342 million; the work force numbered 122,000. That August, Foy remarked, "The job we have to do now is expand the industry as rapidly as possible so we don't get into a [shortage]. I think we are in a new day. I really do."[20] What then seemed likely to be the start of an advance, however, was to prove the beginning of a long rearguard action.

Bethlehem Steel reached a turning point in 1977, a year in which the momentum for expansion ran out and after which retrenchment and closure became dominant. As the year began, the outlook was deemed promising. Early in February, after reviewing the disappointments of trade in 1976, Lewis Foy told the stockholders, "We believe that steady and more balanced economic growth is likely in 1977." His optimism proved ill founded. Operations that year produced a deficit, the first since 1933, and the loss overall totaled $448 million. This was largely due to a $750 million pre-tax charge for closing steel and related facilities, an action that was itself the outcome of the board's recognition that not only could it no longer expand but that marginal plants must be closed. The

Shipbuilding, Steel, and Labor   199 operating rate fell while national imports of 17.5 million metric tons amounted to 17.8 percent of domestic steel supply.

By the end of the decade, steel production was less than two-thirds as high as the 1973–1974 peak of 23 million tons. There had been sharp reductions in at least some departments of all the works, with the exception of Steelton and Burns Harbor, the company's oldest and newest plants. Indeed, whatever happened elsewhere, expansion continued at Burns Harbor. By 1972, it had a capacity of 2 million tons; the following year, capacity was increased to 4.3 million tons. However, difficult trading conditions caused some delay in implementing plans even there, as in October 1975, when the company abruptly stopped work for a time on a new $150 million rolling mill, after already spending about half that sum.[21] In 1975, the company's first continuous slab caster was brought into operation at Burns Harbor, and by 1978, it had a 110-inch plate mill. With a third oxygen converter, it was capable of producing 5.2 million tons of steel a year. Fortunately for its future, the large bar mill that had been planned was never installed but was put in at Lackawanna instead, even though, in mid-1974, it was decided that steel capacity there should be cut to 2.8 million tons. This reduction, as well as a smaller cutback at Johnstown and the closure of other, less important, marginal facilities, involved plants on which the company had put a price of $750 million. It was estimated that production costs in the steel making units involved were some 30 to 40 percent higher than at Burns Harbor.[22] By 1978, though still short of its tenth year in steel making, this works accounted for at least one-quarter of Bethlehem steel capacity. It had become the largest plate maker in the United States.

In other ways, mind-sets still in place in the 1970s were starting to shift before the decade ended. The annual report for 1974 contained this sentence: "Bethlehem is continuing to seek opportunities to enhance and diversify its iron ore and coal reserves." That year, $63 million had been spent on raw material–related projects, and at the year's end, planned capital expenditure in that field amounted to $257 million, a fifth of all the authorized outlay at that time.[23] However, here, too, there were important changes, some involving closures. Early in 1972, it was announced that the Cornwall ore banks, worked since colonial times, would cease production because of depletion. In fact, the flooding of the nearby Lebanon plant by Hurricane Agnes precipitated the end, for old electrical power transmission facilities were ruined and would have been impossibly expensive to repair. Pellet production there ended five years later. Much more dramatic were the ore closures announced in 1977. The company's puzzling mining venture at Marmora, Ontario, was to go out of production two years ahead of its expected life expectancy, and Bethlehem was to pay almost $23 million to the St. Joseph Lead Company to sever its connection with the Pea Ridge, Missouri, iron ore mining operation. Most surprisingly of all, it decided to close the Grace Mine and the 1.9 million tons per year pellet plant in Berks County, Pennsylvania. This decision seems to have been a serious commercial miscalculation. Bethlehem had several long-term ore purchase contracts with Venezuela, Chile, and, on a much smaller scale, with the Mount Hope mines in New Jersey. Now that an expected shortage of ore was turning into a glut, the company decided to close its own mine even though it had large reserves and splendid equipment. The general superintendent at Grace Mine was so convinced of the folly of his superior's decision that he held on to the hope that they might realize they had made a mistake and kept the pumps going to prevent flooding for another four years.[24]

Late in the twentieth century it was common to attribute some of the persistent problems of the major steel companies to the inflexibility and intransigence of organized labor. Although there was much evidence to support this opinion, there seems to have been a lack of recognition that the roots of the problem lay deep in the history of the industry and that, in fact, much of the reason for it was to be found in the inflexibility, intransigence, and lack of imagination on the part of management teams in the past. Much of what happened at individual companies was part of a national pattern, as the whole industry negotiated with workers, but each firm represented a variant on the general pattern. The whole postwar history of labor and of company relations with the United Steelworkers of America (USWA) made up an unhappy tale. Because of these considerations, although this is a company history and not a labor history, this aspect of operations must receive some attention.

One important effect on Bethlehem of the outbreak of World War II had been to belatedly force it to recognize the rights of its employees to unionize. Like other steel companies between the wars, it had operated plant unions, its Employees Representation Plan (ERP) dating from 1919. Each spring in the 1930s, Grace had visited their main plants in turn, usually only for a day, in order to make the necessary arrangements with their workers for the next year. The event was punctiliously registered in his engagement diary. Things began to change late in the decade. In March 1937, the United States Steel Corporation at last recognized the rights of its labor force to unionize by signing an agreement with the Steel Workers Organizing Committee (SWOC), which was supported by the Congress of Industrial Organizations (CIO). That May, after a short strike, Jones and Laughlin also admitted the SWOC. In the summer, along with Republic, Inland, and Youngstown Sheet and Tube, Bethlehem refused to recognize the right to unionize and a strike occurred. There were violent episodes, particularly at Republic's East Chicago works, at which ten strikers were killed and forty wounded. For Bethlehem Steel, the most serious confrontation was at Johnstown. In summer 1939, the National Labor Relations Board, which Grace had violently denounced ever since it was set up in 1935, instructed Bethlehem to disband its ERP because it was not a union. Two years later, the CIO, which had been working away in Bethlehem for some years, called a strike. The state police were brought in, and for a time there seemed to be signs of a repetition of the violent events of the strike in 1910. However, at this time the government was about to offer important contracts for war work, and rather than lose a chance of winning them, the company decided to recognize the union. By 1942, the successor of the SWOC, the United Steelworkers of America, had negotiated the first union contracts with Bethlehem.

Though the figure would vary considerably from year to year, there was a long-term decline in the size of the company work force. In the frenzied activity of wartime, average employment in all the varied activities of Bethlehem Steel Corporation reached an all-time peak in 1943 at slightly more than 289,000. In 1944, the last complete year of the conflict, the number employed averaged 260,000, but by 1946, that figure was already under 144,000, a level more or less maintained over the following few years. By 1957, the year Grace retired from active management, it was at a peacetime record of almost 165,000. During the mid-1970s, when the highest ever levels of steel production were reached and net sales peaked, there were 120,000 jobs. Within another twenty years, employment would be below 20,000 and falling further.

In the immediate aftermath of war, as the inflated work force was necessarily sharply reduced, there were serious labor problems. There were important strikes in 1946 in a number of major industries. In January and February, the biggest national steel strike in history occurred, involving some 800,000 workers. After four weeks, the strikers returned to work with an 18.5-cent increase, average steel wages thus rising to $1.09 an hour. The strike at the Lackawanna works began ten days before the national strike. Then, in April and November, there were important strikes in the coal industry, lasting in all for more than ten weeks. Inevitably, these other strikes affected steel production. In 1945, operations had been at 91.7 percent of capacity; the operating rate in 1946 was only 77.6 percent. The next year it was back to 99.3 percent. Bethlehem Steel average earnings per hour in 1946 were 7.1 percent above those of 1945; company net income was 19.5 percent greater. Bethlehem more than compensated for the extra cost of wages by increasing prices to its customers. Generally, its steel prices went up by $5.00 a ton.[25]

In December 1951, the union asked for a national wage increase of thirty-five cents an hour, and when the companies refused to even discuss the claim, the union threatened that 650,000 workers would leave their jobs at the end of that month. The dispute was referred to the Wage Stabilization Board, and the union agreed to postpone a strike until April 1952. Eventually, the board suggested a compromise increase of twenty-six cents an hour, and this was accepted by the union. The companies also agreed, but only on the condition that they were allowed to increase steel prices by an average of twelve dollars a ton. President Truman opposed such an increase, and the union prepared to strike. As the Korean War was still not settled, Truman nationalized the mills, citing national necessity. His action was declared illegal by the Supreme Court in June, and a seven-week strike began. The industry claimed that it lost 21 million tons of production as a result of the strike. In fact, national output of raw steel in 1952 was 12 million net tons or 11.4 percent less than in 1951; at Bethlehem, the decrease was larger than average, amounting to 2.3 million tons or 14.0 percent.

There was a sharp steel recession in 1954, a year during which average employment throughout Bethlehem Steel Corporation was reduced almost 14 percent. Business revived in 1955, and then in 1956 there was another and, as it turned out, vital strike. After being out for thirty-five days, steelworkers throughout the nation were given a three-year contract that included provision for a cost of living escalator. Even more significantly, with its union locals, Bethlehem agreed to an additional clause, one that was not in the national agreement. This section, numbered 2B, was a so-called "past practices" clause. Designed to allay worker fears that machines would replace jobs, it provided that staffing levels for particular tasks could not be altered, whatever the changes in technology. Why the company agreed to such a restriction of its future freedom of action is at first puzzling. Two considerations must have been important. First, at that time there seemed little likelihood of revolutionary change in the main processes and methods in the industry. Even so, in the light of subsequent events—and of numerous earlier experiences—the adoption of such a position must appear surprising, but it must be remembered that Bethlehem had just committed itself to its largest ever expansion of established methods of production in the form of 2 million tons of open hearth capacity for Sparrows Point. Second, there was an urgency to get back into production. In 1956, raw steel production nationwide was down by 1.8 million tons from the level in 1955. Bethlehem output fell from 18.82 million tons in 1955 to 18.32 million the next year. Its works at Bethlehem alone had lost $43 million during the strike. Imports of all iron and steel products increased by more than a third, to 533,000 tons, though the balance of trade was still "favorable," there being a net export amounting to 3.2 million tons.

After reaching a peak of postwar prosperity in 1957, the next year the industry and the company passed into a sharp recession. Raw steel output by Bethlehem was down by 5.7 million tons or 30 percent. Net income fell from $191 million in 1957 to under $138 million, and the work force was pruned by more than twenty-four thousand. Employment costs fell 14.3 percent. But distributions to stockholders increased marginally and, giving substance to the suspicion that the burden of the less than great performance was unequally borne, six of the company's leading men were ranked that year in the top ten of *Fortune's* list of the highest paid executives.[26] Yet, at the beginning of 1959, when Arthur Homer looked ahead to a better year, he stressed the need to reduce costs. He chose, in a brief and rather simplistic statement, to label the employees as the prime obstacle to reaching that goal:

> Reducing costs and improving quality are not the responsibility of management alone, but call for continuous effort all along the line. . . . For each dollar of earnings in 1957, Bethlehem had to sell about fourteen dollars worth of its products. Under the reduced volume of business available last year, we had to sell about eighteen dollars worth of products to make a dollar of earnings. To put it another way, every dollar we can save today in the performance of our jobs is equivalent to increasing our sales by eighteen dollars. Every dollar we can save through lower costs is a dollar that can be used to provide new and improved equipment, more research and development, and better material resources. Thus each dollar saved will be helping Bethlehem to grow and to be more competitive, to produce better steels, and to attract investors' capital to our business.[27]

Two months later he was both more specific and more dramatic. He still thought 1959 could be "a very good year for everyone," but

> the fact remains that we are approaching a fork in the road. One route, leading to greater efficiency with resulting lower costs, means a wider demand for steel and products made of steel, without the threat of further inflation. It also means fuller employment and a stable economy. The other route leads deeper into inflation, with the disastrous consequences of falling employment and further rises in living costs. . . . Wages in the steel industry are now at an all-time high, at the very top level among all manufacturing industries. It is in the best interests of everyone to avoid another brutal round of inflation that would hurt us all. It is time to apply the brakes to any trend that would surely set in motion another senseless inflationary spiral and thus undermine employment by pricing goods and services out of the market. How much better to follow the second course—and not fall for the specious argument that constantly rising wages for one group are good for everyone no matter how they affect cost. How much better if we take full advantage of the favorable prospects ahead and build on economic truths rather than economic fallacies.

His case crystallized into a proposal that the Bethlehem workers accept a one-year pay freeze.[28]

Although Homer had only once mentioned wages, and his statement centered above all on the rather vaguer question of inflation, he had managed to convey the impression that all would suffer, including employment. The contention that wage restraint might keep down steel prices and thereby widen the market ignored the fact that, for most users, a little more or a little less on the price of their steel purchases was of small significance in relation to their overall costs and certainly was of negligible account in the cost structures of, for instance, the automobile industry. What neither Homer, his company, nor indeed the rest of the industry recognized was that the decision to fight the USWA in 1959 on the question of wages, an issue that might over the long term affect market prospects for the companies, would also let in foreign steel. Over the years, this import activity would prove a far more dangerous threat to future prospects—to utilization rates, to profits, dividends, jobs, and eventually even to the survival of major firms. In this sense, at least, it would eventually be possible to look back on the labor conflict of 1959 as a great divide in the history of the industry and of the Bethlehem Steel Corporation.

A nationwide strike began on 16 July 1959. The issues in dispute were wages, incentives, pensions, and paid holidays. At Bethlehem there was an additional important item, clause 2B, which had been agreed to three years before and which had undoubtedly been abused by some workers who had, for instance, insisted on maintaining existing demarcation of jobs. The Eisenhower administration obtained an injunction forcing workers back to work for 80 days, and they returned on 8 November, after being out for 116. At the end of December, under the guidance of Vice President Richard Nixon, negotiations were resumed, and within a few days, the dispute was settled, the workers receiving increases in pay, pensions, insurance, and other benefits. Remarkably, clause 2B remained in force at Bethlehem. Because of high activity in the first half of 1959 in anticipation of this confrontation, both in the industry generally and at Bethlehem, production was higher than in 1958, despite the strike. Even so, Bethlehem Steel's net income fell by $20 million, or one-seventh. Far more ominous, a net export of 1.3 million tons of iron and steel in 1958 was next year converted into a net import of almost 3.4 million tons. Consumers who bought foreign steel discovered it was not inferior to that bought from domestic suppliers, and it was also less costly.

In 1962, under pressure from the Kennedy administration to check increases in wages and prices and guided in their negotiations by Secretary of Labor Arthur Goldberg, once a general counsel for the USWA, the industry and union agreed to a three-year settlement. Lyndon Johnson acted decisively during summer 1965 to prevent another strike, and as a result, a new three-year agreement gave workers an additional sixteen cents an hour, twice what company negotiators had planned to concede to them. The next three-year deal, in 1968, granted workers a forty-four-cent an hour increase, improved pensions, and other benefits. Three days after this settlement, Bethlehem Steel raised its prices by 5 percent to cover the increased labor costs. The wage and price increases were to prove another small step in making their operations—and those of other major companies —a little less able to meet the gradually rising competition from foreign steel and from a new sector of domestic production. The new sector consisted of the "mini-mills," which were already increasing in number, though as yet seeming almost insignificant in a world dominated by giants.

In the 1970s, when prosperity was at a high level, arrangements were made with labor that later on would further hamstring the industry and the company as they moved into more difficult times. A strike in 1971 gained workers considerable advances in benefits and wages. More significant was the clumsily named Experimental Negotiating Agreement (ENA) of 1973. This was an attempt to avoid the old pattern of triennial periods of difficult wage negotiations and resulting disruption to production schedules. Instead, strikes for pay increases would be ruled out in return for a guaranteed 3 percent annual wage increase and automatic cost of living adjustments. The ENA arrangement lasted until 1982. In this period, wages for steel workers almost tripled. Average employment costs per hour throughout Bethlehem Steel were $7.26 in 1972 and $22.52 ten years later. With provisions for health care, pensions, and vacations, the real cost of labor per hour reached more than $26.00 by 1980. This increase also burdened the company's efforts in the further processing of steel. Those working in the steel fabricating plants and workers in the reinforcing bar fabricating shops had steel union contracts. The union refused to make concessions on wages or rules to allow these Bethlehem operations to meet competition from operators of either nonunion or non-USWA plants. (In retrospect, management was willing to admit that even if their workers had been more flexible, the company still would not have been able to tackle the competition.) In 1976, this situation led to the abandonment of the Bethlehem fabricating business; a decade later, it caused the sale of its rebar fabricating operations. Profitability and employment declined together. Having reached a peak in the early 1970s, the cost of labor, in relation to all operating charges or to net sales, began a long-term decline.

The strength and the potential effects of competition from foreign steel producers were already a key concern. Cort had once addressed the question of whether or not the American steel industry could survive. He noted that, in the last decade, the industry had invested $16.5 billion in new plant and equipment, but he figured that capital development projects in Japan cost only about a third as much as in the United States for comparable plant. Firms there could afford to scrap and replace a mill that was only seven or eight years old, whereas at home it was impracticable to re-equip a facility so rapidly; their industry could scarcely avoid lagging in the most modern technology. An important instance was continuous casting. By 1978, 46.2 percent of Japanese steel was continuously cast (or "concast") in some form or other. In the United States, only 15.2 percent of steel was concast; for integrated works, the figure was as little as 11 percent.[29]

Sometime before Cort retired as chair of the company, he and Foy, then president, visited Japan. Their guide in one of the works they toured was a plant manager trained at Sparrows Point in the 1950s, a time in which it would have been laughable to suggest that Japanese firms could ever trouble their American

Table 12.3 Selected performance indicators at Bethlehem Steel, 1970–1980			
	1970	1973–1974 average	1980
Raw steel production (million net tons)	20.59	23.00	15.00
Steel products shipped (million net tons)	13.84	16.45	11.08
Net income ($millions)	90.1	548.6	121.0
Net income per dollar of net sales (cents)	3.1	5.8	1.8
Number of employees (thousands)	130.0	120.0	89.2
Capital spending on property, plant, and equipment ($millions)	320.9	386.5	466.1
Capital spending as percentage of net sales	10.9%	8.1%	6.9%
Dividends ($millions)	78.9	86.3	69.8
Dividends as percentage of net income	87.5%	31.4%	57.7%

Source: Bethlehem Steel Corp. annual reports for the years indicated.

counterparts. Now things were radically different. Japanese steel companies had built a number of major new tidewater plants. By 1974, raw steel production in Japan was almost 89 percent as large as that of the United States. Whereas American output was 41.7 percent more than in 1960, in Japan the increase had been 437.6 percent. Even more important was the increase in Japanese efficiency and the competitiveness of its costs. As Foy later recalled, during their return flight he had remarked to Cort, "They're going to kill us; we don't stand a chance."[30] Unfortunately, time proved his prediction correct; the process would be protracted and painful.

In December 1979, the Bethlehem Steel Corporation had its seventy-fifth anniversary. A short film was made celebrating its many achievements and describing its present eminence. It ended on a rather somber note, acknowledging that a good deal of the great company's facilities had already been closed.[31] On 10 December, which was the very date on which the company was organized in 1904, Foy, only its sixth head, hosted a celebration dinner in the Homer Research Laboratory high above the Lehigh valley. From there, one looked across the wooded hillside to the broad valley beyond, where still here and there a plume of smoke marked the surviving units of what had once been the national focus of cement manufacture. In the middle distance, the slope was covered by the roofs of the city of Bethlehem, and stretching along the Lehigh River in its midst were the furnaces, chimneys, and mill buildings of the Bethlehem works on which the whole vast corporation had been built. A few weeks later as he looked forward to his forthcoming retirement from the chairmanship, Foy made clear that he did see difficulties ahead: "Bethlehem's earnings, like those of most domestic steel producers, have been well below the average earned by all manufacturers. It is virtually impossible to raise sufficient capital on an ongoing basis without adequate profitability. In fact, our capital spending for the past 20 years has been more than double our earnings. Unless we can improve our profitability and cash flow, our capital spending will necessarily have to remain below the levels that are needed for adequate replacement and modernization of our production facilities." Yet he ended this "chairman's letter" on an upbeat note: "I have every confidence in Bethlehem and will retire with great pride in the management team that will succeed me. I wish them every success as they guide Bethlehem in the years ahead."[32] No one who listened to Foy's speech on that winter's evening or who read his last remarks as chairman could have imagined that before its centenary, the company in which they took so much pride would have ceased to exist. Perhaps it was fortunate that it could not then be foreseen that, rather than being a short period of difficulty from which there would soon be a return to normality, the decline experienced in the previous few years marked the onset of something more serious, indeed a critical stage both for it and the whole of the traditional iron and steel industry.

13

RESPONDING

TO CRISES

IN THE 1980S

THE 1980S PROVED EVEN MORE traumatic than the 1970s for Bethlehem Steel. In the early part of the decade, the company faced its problems with leadership from a very different background than in prior years. Lewis Foy retired in spring 1980 and was succeeded by Donald Trautlein, who, after a career at Price Water-house, had joined Bethlehem as comptroller only three years earlier. It has been suggested that the sixty-five-year-old Foy believed that Trautlein, because of his lack of experience in steel, might find some consultancy role for him. This did not happen, and Foy remained a director for only two more years. In other senses, the company parochialism continued; it was a matter for remark that top management did not include anyone with work experience outside the United States. On the other hand, it was true that the effectiveness of the hand-ful of vice presidents who had been brought in from outside proved disappoint-ing.[1] Trautlein was not liked in most quarters of the company, but he provided

Donald Trautlein c. 1982. *Courtesy Bethlehem Steel Corporation.*

it with a vital service that managers raised in the Bethlehem tradition would have found and later did find much more difficult. He pushed through a wholesale rationalization program.

Like other major integrated companies, Bethlehem Steel now operated in an industry whose output and profitability varied widely from year to year but in which the long-term trends indicated that radical reconstruction was a precondition for long-term survival. Unfortunately, constraints on successful action in this direction were greater than in any period since the Great Depression, and there was another striking contrast with that time in that there now seemed no real prospect of an end to the difficulties. Yet, though intractable, and in many respects complicated, the nature of the main problems of these years may be easily summarized. Demand grew more slowly and less certainly than in the past, there was large overcapacity both at home and abroad, and, helped by a strong dollar, foreign suppliers now took a share of the American market unequaled for more than a century. Through the 1970s, America's dependence on imports had averaged 15.5 percent; for seven years starting in 1982, this figure was 22.6 percent. In understandable frustration at the size of net imports, Bethlehem found it tempting to exaggerate. A short history of Bethlehem later referred to the situation in the 1970s as "the tide of *illegal* imports."[2] Within the

United States, steel making was now divided between the "majors," operating fully integrated plants whose output grew slowly at best and more generally declined, and unintegrated "mini mills," a group whose diminutive title increasingly belied their rising status. For a time, the major companies supplied the more sophisticated segments of the market, whose needs mini mill technology could not meet, but it was ominous that bit by bit the latter moved into higher category products. In short, struggling in an uncertain market, long-established operators such as Bethlehem were beleaguered on one side by foreign competitors and on the other by new, cost-efficient producers at home. Adding to their woes, the environmental impact of the mining, blast furnace, and bulk steel making operations, traditionally viewed as the necessary price to be paid for the services of an essential industry, was now increasingly unacceptable to the public. Legislators were busy establishing new, more stringent anti-pollution standards.

In spite of uncertain signals in the late 1970s, the next decade began with renewed public expressions of optimism about the long-term future of the industry. The American Iron and Steel Institute suggested a need for expansion from a capacity of 158 million to 168 million tons within eight years. To achieve this goal, industry-wide capital spending would have to increase from $2 billion to $5 billion a year. The predictions proved wide of the mark, and large-scale expenditure became necessary not for expansion but for retrenchment. Domestic demand, on whose growth any rational case for extension depended, was soon flagging. In 1981, steel consumption amounted to 131.4 million net tons, and during the next two years, apparent steel consumption fell, averaging only 91.2 million tons; for the following three years, it was 101.7 million.[3] Imports held up, the annual net inflow being 18.9 million tons in 1981, 16.8 million over the next two years, and for the next three, 25.6 million tons. Various government attempts to check the inflow were, as these figures proved, relatively ineffective. At the beginning of the 1980s, a "trigger price mechanism" was in place, setting a price floor based on Japanese costs (then considered the world's lowest) and allowing for an 8 percent profit margin above this figure. Steel products entering at lower prices were theoretically liable to trigger an anti-dumping investigation. Discontent with this system led to its failure in 1982 and to wider complaints about dumping. From the mid-1980s, "voluntary restraint agreements" (VRAs) were negotiated with the main foreign suppliers. The system was based on an assumption that a five-year respite from the full force of foreign competition would allow domestic producers time to reconstruct their operations. Imports were limited to about 20 percent of the market, but this did not solve the problem to the satisfaction of steel makers, whereas steel consumers were seriously affected. In the mid-1980s, the Institute for International Economics estimated that VRAs cost users of steel about $7 billion a year; the protection saved perhaps nine thousand jobs in the steel industry but caused the loss of an indeterminate but certainly far greater number in steel fabricating and other metal-using industries.[4] In 1988, the industry asked for more time to rebuild its competitiveness, and that autumn, visiting Pennsylvania three days before the presidential election, Vice President George H. W. Bush committed the administration he was soon to form to extend the period under which VERs (voluntary export restraints, for foreign suppliers) would operate. They survived to 1992.

An important loophole in attempts to stop foreign penetration of the American markets became apparent in the 1980s. If defeated by import controls, competitors could buy their way into production inside the barriers erected against them. Asian firms were prominent among those who employed this strategy. After being frustrated in an attempt to buy the Ford River Rouge steel operations in Michigan, the Japanese firm NKK in 1984 pioneered acquisition of interests in U.S. integrated steel making by paying $290 million for a half share of National Steel. Kawasaki Steel, CVRD of Brazil, and some American investors were then preparing to try to rescue part of Kaiser Steel's Fontana operation. Two years later, U.S. Steel entered into a joint arrangement with the Korean company, Pohang Iron and Steel, to reconstruct its Pittsburg, California, plant.[5] All this was disturbing, but a potentially far more deadly enemy was already inside the walls.

The mini mill, or Electric Arc Furnace (EAF), section of the industry had begun in a small way in the early postwar years with electric furnaces, primary mills, and finishing mills. It was then preoccupied with higher value products, in which by definition bulk steel makers had little part. After this, a more important expansion of this sector began, involving a linking of larger electric melting furnaces with continuous casting plant and rolling mills, and a striking switch to products offering bigger outlets, such as lower grades of bars and rods. These mills began to tap the large supplies of bulk scrap widely available through the nation. Many firms were to be involved, but a symbolic point of departure for mini mills as a serious irritant for the large-scale steel firms was the formation in 1966 of a new re-rolling operation, Nucor, reconstructed from a failed instruments and electronics company. Three years later, Nucor built its first electric furnace. Sales that year were $46 million as compared with $2.93

billion for Bethlehem Steel. Yet it soon became clear that mini mills possessed a number of major advantages over integrated mills.

The capital outlay required for a major greenfield integrated works could be so high as to render such an operation uncompetitive. Proof of this was to be found in the fact that only two such units had been constructed in the United States after World War II: the Burns Harbor complex and the Fairless works of U.S. Steel. In striking contrast, as it involved less upstream plant and substituted continuous casting (concasting) for primary rolling mills, building a mini mill required much smaller investment. It also had lower operating costs than integrated works. Of almost equal importance, most companies in this sector were new, relatively small, and nonunionized. Many of them opted for sites that could be served by water transport. They usually located in rural areas, well placed for access to both scrap and regional markets. In these areas labor rates were relatively low, but the operators sometimes secured solid commitment from their work force by means of profit-sharing schemes. In the integrated industry, the dire trading conditions of the early 1980s and the stark contrast of lower labor costs in the mini mills at last forced unions to make concessions, in the hope of saving jobs. In February 1983, when Bethlehem and other major companies were facing grave financial forecasts, it and six other major companies entered into a new forty-one-month agreement with the USWA. The companies made certain concessions, but from the point of view of their costs, the favorable change was that the workers accepted a wage reduction of $1.25 an hour and other changes in benefits that together cut labor costs by almost $3.00. The disadvantage compared with the mini mill was reduced but by no means eliminated. At the end of the decade, the CEO of Nucor, Ken Iverson, estimated his company's labor costs per ton were under half those of the average integrated firm.[6]

Mini mills had other important, if unquantifiable, advantages. Even in the 1960s, when they were not very important in terms of tonnages, it had been recognized that they were generally commercially more nimble than their bigger integrated rivals. As the president of one of them had put it, "We're shipping while they're still writing the order."[7] Expansion in this new sector of the industry went on at an increasing pace. Although as late as 1980, one estimate put the share of steel shipments coming from mini mills at only 11 percent, taken along with the drop in demand and high level of imports, this growth meant that there was now excess capacity at home as well as worldwide, rather than the shortages that had been predicted. Publicly, major companies said little about mini mills. This silence was understandable since the mini mills were home-grown competition, the product of free enterprise. Even privately, the large firms seem not to have been greatly disturbed at this time. There were two main reasons for their complacency: the nature and the size of the competition. During the 1970s, an internal report was submitted to the Bethlehem vice president for planning. He indicated his agreement with its conclusion that the mini mills would make inroads, but he was not greatly disturbed because he believed that this competition meant only a nibbling around the edges of their bulk products. For him and his colleagues, high volume, high grade products were the focus of attention. Author John Strohmeyer neatly summarized the attitude of Bethlehem top executives: "If some guy comes on stream with 60,000 tons of raw steel a year, let's not worry about that."[8]

In the course of the 1980s, the mini mills increased their output and their share of national steel production and, in addition, improved the grades of steel they were able to make. By the end of the decade, they were starting their assault in a sector previously beyond their capability: the manufacture of thin flat-rolled products. In 1988, Ken Iverson of Nucor referred to a Bethlehem report on the strip mill his company was then building at Crawfordsville, Indiana, which purported to show that the new plant would not work. As Iverson put it, "It is now apparent to them that the American mini mills are at least as much a threat to them as imported steel. It's taken them about 20 years to realize it." It was expected that the Nucor mill would make sheet steel for about 20 percent or sixty-five dollars or so less per ton than most of the integrated firms could. Under such circumstances, Burns Harbor might still be competitive, but Sparrows Point might be only marginally so, if at all. Iverson aggressively summed up the situation: "Foreign steel came in in the back door and we came in the front door of their snug little house." Even then, they did not publicly admit they had an intruder. Yet it was beginning to be recognized that, having already established the basic cost structures for bar, rod, and wire, the mini mills might eventually do the same for ordinary grades of strip mill products, costs that long established firms with their integrated operations and USW contracts would be unable to meet. Within Bethlehem Steel, top management now recognized the changing situation and regularly debated the options, only to come to the conclusion that ultimately their older facilities would not be able to compete with the newer, lower cost operations.[9]

Like other long established major companies, Bethlehem had to tackle problems associated with new technology as well as those represented by the mini mills. The establishment of its Homer Research Laboratory in 1959 had been intended to facilitate innovation in making, shaping, and finishing steel, but in practice success was often elusive. Eventually, referring to "Homer research" seems to have become a company joke, in some quarters at least. The existence of so much commitment in well-proved processes was one barrier against change, but this understandable material inertia was matched by that from established structures of work. Firmly set habits of thought and attitude compounded the problem. It was easier for a relative newcomer to steel than for a long established leader to be open minded. The resistance to change was firmly entrenched. When Arthur Homer had once remarked that the future steel industry would come from the laboratories, someone suggested that European technology was ahead of what was common in the United States. His response is said to have been, "I don't believe it." Three-quarters of a century before, British steel makers, when shown superior American practice, had said similar things, and they had subsequently paid the price for their short-sightedness.[10] Bit by bit, Bethlehem did or rather had to change its technology, but there were a number of setbacks to the process, and it could never start over again.

During the slump of the early 1980s, the company shut down the last of its Sparrows Point open hearth furnaces, to rely after that on oxygen converters. It temporarily reactivated two of the old furnaces there in 1988–1989, when demand was high and the domestic market was sheltered from foreign competition by tariff protection and a devalued dollar. (Others did the same, and in 1988, nationwide open hearth steel output was not far short of double that of 1987.[11]) Another new technology that cost older firms like Bethlehem much trouble was large-scale continuous casting, which, by removing the need for primary rolling mills (which established producers had to write off) reduced capital and operating costs and at the same time improved yield and quality. As early as 1966, with the collaboration of the Republic, Inland, and Youngstown Sheet and Tube companies, the Homer Research Laboratory began to test a concasting machine for slabs at the Bethlehem works. Partly because the plant was made up of pieces from a variety of different sources, it ran into difficulties, and the project was abandoned in 1969 on the grounds that the process probably could not turn out the high volumes required. Soaking pits and primary mills continued to be installed, and the initiative in slab casting passed to others.[12]

Burns Harbor was initially provided with a 3.4-million-ton slabbing mill, but when it commissioned its first continuous slab caster in spring 1975, the annual report celebrated the economy in time and efficiency it represented: it could convert three hundred tons of molten steel into solid slabs in forty-five minutes, as compared with at least twelve hours for rolling ingots. By 1980, a little more than 12 percent of Bethlehem's steel was concast, about average for the American industry, but in Japan the figure was more than 50 percent. After 1980, the major firms made rapid progress. By 1983, Bethlehem Steel had concasting at Steelton and was planning further units for Burns Harbor and Sparrows Point, which were commissioned in 1985–1986. The company now side-stepped the problem of finding the financing to cover their high costs by leasing the units from their builder, the Austrian firm Voest-Alpine International. With commissioning of the new 2-million-ton unit at Burns Harbor in mid-1986, about two-thirds of the company's steel was concast. In the key sectors of sheet product and plate production at Burns Harbor and Sparrows Point, only 24 percent of slabs were continuously cast in 1982, but five years later the proportion was 80 percent.[13]

Donald Trautlein's term of office began in 1980. There were early successes. In 1981, sales were a record $7.3 billion. Although shipments of steel were up only 4.4 percent, net income was 74 percent greater than in 1980. But in 1982, net sales were down by 28 percent and there was a deficit on a previously unequaled scale: nearly $1.5 billion. Two-thirds of the total was due to the closure of the iron, steel, primary mill, hot strip, and cold sheet mill operations at Lackawanna. This deficit proved to be the first of five years of losses, the worst in company history to that time. Over the six years to the end of 1987, capital expenditure was $2.2 billion, yet, even excluding the $1 billion provided for restructuring in 1982, net losses in this period amounted to $870 million. The work force was cut by more than half. Together, this outlay, great efforts to rationalize production, and a recovery in national consumption succeeded in bringing a return to profitability in 1987, 1988, and 1989. Cutting back time and again, though painful, had seemed to yield positive results.

Fears of shortfalls of capacity in relation to demand had by now been replaced by threats to viability posed by chronic overcapacity. At the beginning of 1986, Bethlehem managers estimated that domestic steel capacity was 15 million to 20 million tons in excess of requirements; in the rest of the non-communist world, excess capacity might be ten times as much. Not surprisingly, international trade problems persisted. An interesting if minor instance of their impact on Bethlehem involved steel specialties. This example also highlights the fact that the issues were often complex. Into the mid-1970s, Bethlehem operated four small bar mills at Lebanon, in eastern Pennsylvania, with a combined annual capacity of 200,000 tons. The Lebanon facility made industrial fasteners. Ten years later, by which time its work force was down to six hundred (it had once been twenty-four hundred), Lebanon was closed. Bethlehem blamed the necessity to end its bolt production there on continuing weak demand and stiff import competition. It failed to point out that, during the same year, Nucor was opening a new bolt plant. (In this case, there was an unexpected but interesting sequel; a small, family-owned Canadian operator of an obsolete bolt making plant for a time drastically undercut even the new Nucor bolt plant.[14]) Trautlein claimed in 1984 that during a four-year period, Bethlehem Steel had lost almost $2 billion in revenue to steel dumped on the market at prices below cost from 1981 to 1984; the company's revenues totaled $23.3 billion.[15] Given such circumstances, it was understandable that Bethlehem should play a prominent part in the fight against imported steel. Cort recalled in 1979 that he had once heard Grace say that the only way he would go to Washington was if he received a subpoena to appear there. Now, the chairs of steel companies eagerly campaigned for government action to protect them from overseas producers. Generally, they argued that "unfairly traded" steel was subsidized by foreign governments, which did not require producers to bear the heavy costs of environmental protection and restrictive labor contracts that U.S. steel makers had to pay. Foy had made Richard Schubert president of Bethlehem Steel on the grounds that, having served in the Labor Department of the federal government, he would be "well known in Washington." Now Donald Trautlein took up the struggle. In summer 1983, he testified twice on trade issues, first to the Senate Judiciary Committee, later to the House Subcommittee on International Economic Policy and Trade. He made clear that he believed that unfairness in the steel import trade was a major cause of their difficulties, and he repeated the time-worn conviction that the United States was uniquely well endowed to be the world's most favored steel producer. Other countries might have good ore or coal reserves or ample markets, but "unlike America, however, none of them has all the necessary components for a dynamic and healthy steel industry." The Japanese were "efficient and disciplined," but its government artificially promoted low-cost raw materials and helped the steel companies in other ways, including protecting their domestic markets. Europe was much worse; it was indeed "a microcosm of all the things that can go wrong in the steel business," with government-owned or part-owned companies, carefully controlled domestic markets, and so on. In fact, Trautlein testified, "it is deeply troublesome to realize that the financial viability of U.S. producers is being undermined to accommodate the type of irresponsible performance exemplified by many government-subsidized European steel producers."[16] When, in 1984, net imports accounted for 23 percent of U.S. steel consumption, Bethlehem went so far as to ally itself with the United Steelworkers of America in lodging an action with the International Trade Commission. The Reagan administration agreed to pursue voluntary restriction deals with foreign countries. Seven years later, Trautlein's successor again emphasized the connection between excess capacity and trading problems and maintained that for both situations, the focus of the problem lay outside the United States: "World steel markets are still burdened with international overcapacity and trade problems related to decades of subsidies, closed borders, and other market disturbing devices."[17]

During the last two decades of the twentieth century, a leading theme at Bethlehem and at most other major steel firms was concentration. In other words, producers were focusing on fewer plants, a narrower product range, and, against the trends of the previous century, a reduction in the amount of integration between various stages of manufacture. There would also be less complete control over raw materials and a decrease in further processing. Emphasis was moving from production to economy, from tonnage to efficiency. The latter required cuts in capacity. Foy, who had worked for so long in steel and had been conditioned to think in terms of expansion, was reluctant to cut deep, but even so, between 1975 and 1980, raw steel capacity was reduced from 22.7 million to 21.5 million tons. In five years under Trautlein, it fell more dramatically, to 17.6 million tons. The Seattle and Los Angeles operations were closed. On the other hand, Steelton, an old location where steel making was no longer supported by iron making, proved to be stubbornly tenacious of life. However, closures at Lackawanna and Johnstown, examined elsewhere, highlighted the new geography of production and some of the uncertainties involved in company strategy.

The Trautlein years were critical for modernization. It was thought that decisive action at that point might save the company, as was happening at United States Steel under the chairmanship of David Roderick and the presidency of Tom Graham. On the face of things, Bethlehem achieved a great deal. Over four years, between the first quarter of 1982 and the first quarter of 1986, it was profitable in only two quarters and altogether lost $2 billion, but it managed to reduce costs sharply. Operating charges per net ton of product shipped were $611 in 1981 and $516 in 1986. During 1982, for each employee, output of finished steel was 220 tons but 410 tons in 1987. Did rationalization go far enough? Subsequent events would suggest it had not, but were the policy decisions of the time rational within the necessarily limited knowledge of those who had to make them?

During Trautlein's chairmanship, it became clear that, like all other major integrated producers, Bethlehem Steel faced a long uphill struggle to survive. For those companies that were multi-plant operations, there would be particularly difficult choices. At Bethlehem, it now also became obvious that the existing top management was not fully up to the job of overhauling the company. Being himself an unusual choice as CEO, Trautlein determined to take radical action. He already had an experienced steel man as president and chief operating officer. Walter Williams had joined Bethlehem Steel in 1951 and had served at Lackawanna before being prominently involved in the construction of Burns Harbor. In 1982, Trautlein formed a new four-man steel group under Williams. Two of the men, appointed to be in charge of sales and of services, were already vice presidents; the third, Edward H. Kottcamp, age forty-eight, was brought in from steel research. He was put in charge of steel production and given a mandate to reduce costs.

It soon became apparent that most of the plants were in a bad way, that a majority of managers were set in old ways, and that not all new projects had been carefully evaluated. Over the next few years, a number of separate studies revealed the dimensions of the problem. Over the same period, it became clear that any solution to these problems would involve some hard policy choices and possibly a combination of approaches: closing plants and concentrating spending for modernization on the few operations that could give promise of long-term viability and/or cooperating, combining with, or selling out to others. In retrospect, it may be seen that the 1980s were the last years in which it would be possible to produce a reshaped Bethlehem with the ability to survive. If such an opportunity was missed, it would be only a matter of time before the company failed. Some, but not all, of the top management of the time were willing to acknowledge this crisis.

Early in 1984, an internal report identified some of the "strategically inappropriate" investments made in the recent past. Included were some low or no-

The "steel group" executives, 1982. W. Williams (president) is seated; standing left to right are D. Sheldon Arnot, Paul A. Henschen, and Edward H. Kottcamp.
Courtesy Bethlehem Steel Corporation.

return projects at almost every one of the major works. The report mentioned the 110-inch plate mill at Burns Harbor, the expansion of the rod mill at Sparrows Point, spending on both basic oxygen and electric furnace shops at Johnstown, and, at Lackawanna, the large outlays in the 1970s on a scrap melter and the 13-inch bar mill. Approved in 1972, the last of these projects had not been completed until 1978, by which time its original estimated cost of $60 million had rocketed to in excess of $200 million. Another example of not fully appropriate investment was at Steelton. There, between 1968 and 1970, three large electric furnaces had been built to replace open hearth capacity. In 1983, a continuous casting unit was installed. It was well suited to produce the blooms needed for the plant's rail mill but was also expected to serve large bar mill operations, for which it was far less suited than the billet casters used in mini mills. Having dissipated capital in these various ways, Bethlehem was now short of funds for such essentials as large-scale slab casting. There had been a failure indeed, a lack of strategic thinking. As the report recognized, financial analysis, faulty though it had proved, should be treated as "a framework for debate, not as a mechanistic criterion for decisions."[18]

By spring 1986, analysis had moved on from the bad decision making of the past to a consideration of its possible result in the failure of the company and of possible ways to avoid this. Reports were received from the renowned strategy consultants of Booz Allen and from the New York investment bank First Boston Corporation. Both were brutally frank in ways that shook both the board and its chief officers. First Boston highlighted the ways in which, despite its large capital outlays, Bethlehem Steel's position in the industry had deteriorated in the first half of the 1980s. Noting that the company had already taken a number of steps symptomatic of an impending liquidity crisis, First Boston's assessment contained a deeply disturbing conclusion: "It could be argued that the company is already in a state of slow liquidation, consuming its short- and long-term assets to fund operating losses." Though not optimistic that Bethlehem could earn enough in the future to cover its liabilities, the bank recommended a number of steps that might ease the situation. The last of these was that Bethlehem should seriously consider Chapter 11 bankruptcy as a way of helping it to overhaul its cost structure and remain competitive.[19] The delivery of this report came as a bombshell to the Bethlehem board. It helped precipitate the departure of Trautlein. He had recognized the seriousness of their problems and had struggled to tackle them, but, being an outsider, he had also had to spend time at the beginning of his chairmanship learning the full measure of the company. Consequently, he had not been able to carry through as extensive a change as he would have wished. As a Bethlehem Steel man for thirty-five years, his successor, Walt Williams, was infinitely better equipped to understand steel making, but he was less trained to pursue cost economy and, most dangerous of all, was also emotionally committed to preserve as much as possible of the old Bethlehem Steel Corporation. This emotional attachment was particularly unfortunate when a second major report by outside consultants made clear that survival might depend on a radical shake-up.

Booz Allen pointed out that, despite all efforts to date, the Bethlehem Steel Corporation in 1986 was essentially only a slightly smaller version of what it had been a decade earlier, maintaining most of its manufacturing plant and operating a full product line. The consulting firm concluded that external circumstances would not improve and that major restructuring would have to take place if the company was to survive. This would concentrate it on a core business in which it could have a competitive advantage. There were some facilities that were able to compete well, including the Burns Harbor works, the primary end of Sparrows Point, and possibly the rolling and finishing section of the Bethlehem works. The consultants indicated that it would be best to close not only Johnstown but also those parts of the ongoing plants that they had not singled out as worthy of preservation. In addition to closure, there might be possibilities of progress through sale, cooperation, and joint ventures.[20] Various suggestions for exploring such avenues were made. In each case, circumstances prevented a favorable or straightforward outcome.

Consultants identified Johnstown as a clear case for closure. The manner in which, over many years, company policy for this plant followed an uncertain course is considered in detail elsewhere. In the mid-1980s, Bethlehem Steel received an offer to buy its Bethlehem works. The offer came from the Wesray Corporation, a leveraged buyout concern created and, until 1984, controlled by William Simon, who had received his college education in the lower Lehigh valley, had been secretary of the treasury under Presidents Nixon and Ford, and was a strong advocate of laissez-faire capitalism. This bid came to nothing, and the Bethlehem works continued into the mid-1990s. The company did no better with schemes for cooperation with other steel makers, at home or abroad.

During the meetings of the International Iron and Steel Institute in Tokyo in 1982, there were high-level but ultimately fruitless talks between Trautlein and other leading Bethlehem representatives and leading Japanese and Korean steel companies about possible joint ventures. (A few years later the *Economist* suggested that every big steel company, with the exception of Bethlehem, had "some sort of agreement" with a Japanese producer.[21]) The discussions with domestic companies were more numerous and produced some results but failed to bring about radical solutions. During the 1980s, there were meetings about possible cooperation or collaboration with other producers of strip and plate mill products, including Armco, Inland, National (half of which from mid-1984 was owned by the Japanese company NKK), and the United States Steel Corporation. For Bethlehem, the focal point of consideration was the future of Sparrows Point.

In 1986, consultants showed that the cost of producing hot band at Burns Harbor was $29 a ton or 10 percent lower than at Sparrows Point. (Compared with at least six hot strip mills, its costs were less by more than $40 a ton.) In further processing the hot band, too, there was a marked contrast between these two key Bethlehem plants. At Sparrows Point, five cold strip mills had a combined capacity of 4 million tons. Burns Harbor had one mill and an annual capacity of 1.8 million tons. But the Sparrows Point mills had been installed in 1937, in 1947, and between 1951 and 1957, a period in which three were installed. By 1989, the average power per mill was 12,320 h.p. The Burns Harbor mill dated from 1965 and was supported by 33,000 h.p.[22] The consultants pointed out that though rolling mill costs were high at Sparrows Point, it was competitive at its primary end, that is, in iron and steel making. Why then should it not concentrate on producing semi-finished steel to be sent to other works for further processing? There was one possible outlet within Bethlehem Steel, the works at Bethlehem, where primary costs were high. An outside possibility was to sell slabs to Armco, but its works were relatively far away, in the Ohio valley. A much more practical proposition seemed to be to link Sparrows Point and the U.S. Steel Fairless works at Morrisville on the lower Delaware, 110 miles to the northeast. At Fairless, steel costs were high (it still depended on open hearth furnaces) and, in 1983, U.S. Steel had seriously considered a link that would have supplied it with slabs from a Scottish mill. To close much or all of the finishing operations at Sparrows Point and the primary end of Fairless would cut overall costs at both plants, even after taking into account extra expenses for transportation and energy. A top-level team from Bethlehem visited Tom Graham in Pittsburgh to explore the possibilities. In the course of discussions, Graham made clear he would entertain no association. The only Bethlehem plant for which he had a high regard was Burns Harbor, and he did not think there was any possibility of progress on that front because he was convinced that the government would not allow any one company to control both it and the Gary works. Bethlehem was left to pursue its own rescue program, apparently to the relief of those who were convinced of the need to preserve the company's independence. From the mid-1980s on, Bethlehem Steel began a partial modernization of the finishing operations at Sparrows Point, including its 160-inch plate mill and its sheet and tin mill operations. In 1988, it authorized a $200 million modernization of the 68-inch hot strip mill.

Bethlehem now took part in important joint ventures, which reduced capital outlay and spread its production more widely than if the company had tried to

Table 13.1 Bethlehem Steel indicators, 1979–1992

	1979	1981	1984	1987	1992
Employment (thousands)	97.7	83.8	51.4	34.4	24.9
TONNAGE (MILLION TONS)					
Steel capacity	22.4	22.1	18.0	16.0	16.0
Steel production	19.4	16.7	12.2	11.5	10.5
Steel shipments	13.4	11.6	8.9	9.4	9.1
FINANCIAL RESULTS					
Net sales ($millions)	7,137	7,298	5,392	4,620	4,008
Net income/(loss) ($millions)	276	211	(112)	174	(449)
Net income/(loss) per ton shipped ($)	20.54	18.23	(12.60)	18.59	(49.55)

Source: Bethlehem Steel Corp. annual reports for the years indicated.

Note: The period from 1979 to 1992 corresponds to the interim between the end of the chairmanship of Lewis Foy (1979) and that of Walter Williams (1992).

undertake developments alone. It joined Inland Steel and the Pre-Finish Metals Company in 1984 to build an $80 million, 400,000-ton electric galvanizing plant at Walbridge, Ohio, near Toledo. A few years later it increased its share in this operation. By the mid-1990s, 75 percent of the coil used there would be procured from Burns Harbor.[23] Even more important was restructuring in the wider Bethlehem group that involved increased emphasis on "core" activities and the discarding of "peripheral" lines. In fact, this policy meant the end of some activities that for a long time had seemed almost as central as steel manufacture. Compared with its leading rivals, Bethlehem was more completely dependent on steel. In 1980, steel and related products accounted for 88 percent of all sales as compared with 62 percent at U.S. Steel and 49 percent at Armco, but steel made up 100 percent of sales at Republic and Wheeling-Pittsburgh.[24] In the 1980s, again in contrast to others, Bethlehem set its face against further diversification, successive chairmen making clear that they did not expect to find salvation by spreading into other manufacturing areas or into service industries but would do so by resolutely tackling modernization in their "core" sector. In fact, having already gone some way in this direction, it drew back, further increasing its dependency on steel. Most existing downstream manufacturing activities were sold. The most dramatic instance was the long-term decline and eventual elimination of shipbuilding. Trautlein had been greatly impressed by the success of Chrysler's Lee Iacocca, who was born in Allentown, and he followed the car maker's prescription of cutting off those subsidiaries that were not core businesses. In February 1982, after two quarters of contracting sales and rapidly falling net income, Trautlein promised stockholders "the largest plant modernization program ever undertaken by Bethlehem," and he also outlined board thinking about other activities. Immediate prospects did not seem favorable to a major overhaul, but he seemed to leave the way open for revisiting the possibility: "Our present intention is not to undertake any major new program of diversification outside steel. Near-term investments in non-steel businesses will be limited to those in which we are now engaged. Our plan is to consider other diversification after we have modernized those steel facilities whose profit potential warrants further investment." The following year, he was more explicit: "I am frequently asked why Bethlehem remains in the steel business. Why don't we diversify? The answer is twofold. First, we believe that Bethlehem can generate acceptable earnings in steel with an improved economy, restructured operations, more competitive employment costs and continuing reductions of other costs. . . . Second, we have already diversified, through participation in other businesses such as raw materials, marine construction, building products, and plastics."[25]

When, in 1982, U.S. Steel made the major investment that married its steel operations to Marathon Oil, there was deep skepticism at Bethlehem as to their rival's wisdom in taking this step. In fact, for a number of years it was hugely beneficial to U.S. Steel, the oil operation's major cash flows helping to cover the huge costs of closure and rationalization in steel, including funding U.S. Steel's pension liabilities. In contrast, Bethlehem divested itself of non-steel activities. In 1970, it had bought control of Kusan, a maker of plastic and other building products, which was a yearly contributor to group profits until 1980. During the second quarter of 1985, Bethlehem took over a company having closer connections with its own business and that seemed to promise openings in areas of the country in which Bethlehem was not at all directly represented by steel manufacturing. The company paid $96 million to acquire Tull Industries, a distributor and processor of steel and of other metals, with service centers throughout the Southeast and in Texas. Then, with surprising speed, Bethlehem withdrew. Tull was sold, passing to the control of Inland Steel, a company Bethlehem had outbid in its purchase of Tull only a year before. By the end of 1985, the Bethlehem Steel Corporation had suffered five consecutive years of net losses, and as the annual report for that year explained, "Early in 1986, we concluded that Bethlehem's financial condition would preclude further diversification away from our steel business in the foreseeable future. Accordingly, since we could not afford to support the desired growth of our existing diversified businesses, we decided to sell them."[26] In the same year, it disposed of its long-established rebar division. As with mineral reserves, proceeds from these sales contributed to further investment in steel. In retrospect, it is perhaps too easy to conclude that Bethlehem was short-sighted in selling the diversified businesses it already had and in refusing to go further in that direction. Marathon Oil was more or less as big as U.S. Steel and for years was more profitable. Through troubled times, it was a considerable help to its partner company. In contrast, Bethlehem's non-steel ventures were much smaller, and the attention they demanded—as well as the capital they required for expansion—was judged not to be a priority when the core sector was so much in need of cash.

Although he had only served for six years and was only sixty, by early 1986, Trautlein had been badly worn by the struggle to keep Bethlehem Steel viable. His last annual report was exceptional, though not unique, in not containing a photograph of the chairman. By spring of that year, he had handed day-to-day control of the company to his president, Walter Williams. For a time, he did not reveal what his plans were, but in fact he chose to retire. He had been widely reviled for the harsh human impact of his rationalization program. However, as was later recognized by the man he elevated in 1985 to become his vice president for the steel related group of their business, Gary Millenbruch, "he did what had to be done, what should have been done much sooner."[27] Now the chairmanship passed to a man who, unlike Trautlein but like most of his predecessors, had the valuable twin credentials of long-term Bethlehem service and plant-level experience. At all levels of the company down to the shop floor, Walter Williams's appointment was warmly welcomed. Unfortunately, in a short time it became clear that by now the power of any top executive to steer an independent and successful course was limited.

Williams began his chairmanship with five important plants, including Johnstown. Three of the works were integrated operations. The radical restructuring advised by consultants had not been carried out. Some within the company's top management shared their conviction that large-scale spending should be confined to Burns Harbor and Sparrows Point, that Steelton and Bethlehem should receive only very restricted investment, and that non-core plants should be rationalized or sold.

Yet, in 1984, it had been decided to spend $68 million on modernizing the old Grey mill at Bethlehem and to install a new long-rail facility at Steelton. A year after Trautlein's retirement, disagreement about the best way to proceed caused another change in top management. Edward Kottcamp, though only fifty-two, retired from the company "to pursue other opportunities," and he was replaced as senior vice president of steel operations by Roger Penny, who for the previous six years had managed Burns Harbor.[28]

It is interesting to compare Bethlehem's fortunes in this difficult decade with those of U.S. Steel (which at this time was the steel division of USX). U.S. Steel suffered its first annual net loss in 1979, and from 1980 through the end of 1989, there were three more years in which operations resulted in large losses, including 1986, when the company had a long fight against labor. Over those ten years, its net income was $424 million. Bethlehem was profitable in five of these years, but for the whole decade, its losses exceeded profits by $939 million. At U.S. Steel, rationalization cut deeper than at Bethlehem. Between 1983 and 1991, it was under the control of Tom Graham, an experienced steel man, ruthless in cutting out what he judged could not be made viable. Under Trautlein and Williams, Bethlehem reconstructed and modernized, but their cutbacks were less radical.

In 1973, Bethlehem Steel accounted for slightly less than one-sixth of national steel output. Ten years later, with the industry already in severe recession, it made 10.7 million tons of crude steel and shipped 8.7 millions tons of products. After 1983, things seemed for a time to have stabilized, so that by 1990 the figures for steel produced and products shipped were 10.9 million and 8.9 million tons, respectively. In 1987–1989, net income totaled 40 percent as much as the losses of the previous five years. Slowdowns and eventual closure at Lackawanna and Johnstown and maintaining a simple status quo for the situation through modest investments at Steelton and Bethlehem meant that capacity and still more profitable operations were concentrated at either Sparrows Point or Burns Harbor. The latter was, by the 1980s, not only a lower cost steel producer than the former by a significant margin but could produce at lower costs than any integrated works in the United States. Major concasting units were brought into production at both plants in 1986, at an overall cost of some $500 million. By the end of the 1980s, work was under way on hot dip galvanizing lines and, at Sparrows Point, the hot strip mill was being modernized. Future success depended on these two works. The fate of the remainder of Bethlehem Steel Corporation would be at the mercy of the tides of commercial fortune.

14

PARING AWAY
THE UNVIABLE

ON ONE OCCASION DURING THE 1980s, a senior executive at Bethlehem Steel suggested that the company should close down all its steel operations except for Burns Harbor and Sparrows Point.[1] The idea was greeted as outrageous and unacceptable. In fact, in fifteen years to 1992, Bethlehem closed five of its nine plants with a capacity of well over 8 million tons of raw steel. Still, there often seemed to be an uncertain sense of direction. There is some evidence that the chairman's work background may have been an important factor when plant closure decisions were being made.

Bethlehem's output of 23.7 million net tons of steel in 1973 proved to be its highest ever output. Annual rated capacity was then 27 million to 28 million tons. Almost 11 million tons of it was in open hearth furnaces, whose costs were increasingly seen as too high to be competitive. This capacity included all of Johnstown and more than two-thirds of Sparrows Point, which then accounted for more than one-third of the company's steel capability. These units would soon have to be closed, thereby reducing plant capacity, or would have to be replaced by either basic oxygen furnaces (BOF) or electric furnaces. From the mid-1970s forward, production varied much more than in the previous decade. This variability made for a difficult context in which to make decisions about slowdowns, closures, or spending on the installation of new facilities. Even so, it must be concluded that uncertainty, hesitation, and backtracking would be appropriate labels under which to group many of the choices made about plant development over the years. A more critical commentator might even conclude that the top management of Bethlehem Steel dithered. This was particularly the case in planning the future for Lackawanna and Johnstown.

In the 1960s, Lackawanna had expanded and seemed to prosper, in part by supplying semi-finished steel to the rolling mills at Burns Harbor; during the same period, the industrial economy of the Niagara frontier region was shrinking rapidly and Buffalo suffered a severe population decline. Early in 1970, a new coke oven battery was nearing completion. Lackawanna was now a 6-million-ton plant, ranking it sixth among the nation's steel works. It had 4.8 million tons of BOF steel capacity or one-third of Bethlehem's total. On the other hand, it contained a great deal of old technology, had grown piecemeal, and was much less well placed to serve premium markets than the new, superbly equipped, and well laid out Burns Harbor plant. By the 1970s, the lake shipments that had served Lackawanna well for many decades were declining. There were various reasons for this, including a large loss of the Detroit automobile steel market to other domestic producers and to imports, the increasing preference of major consumers for truck deliveries direct to their own warehouses, and growing competition from within the company involving supplying these outlets from Burns Harbor. No reasonably informed observer could escape the conclusion that success and expansion at Bethlehem's Chicago plant implied a crisis for the older plant. Bethlehem Steel claimed that the viability of Lackawanna was undermined by unreasonably high local taxes, tightening environmental regulations, and falling labor productivity. At one stage, the company pointed out that whereas Burns Harbor employed sixty-four hundred persons to operate its 4.3 million tons of capacity, the 4.8-million-ton capacity at Lackawanna had twelve thousand workers. This highly unfavorable comparison was unfair. Burns Harbor was a product of the previous ten years or so; Lackawanna was a plant that, however modified, had roots going back three-quarters of a century. Apart from primary mills, there were five rolling mills at Burns Harbor in 1974, with a combined rated capacity of 7.2 million tons. Burns Harbor made only plate, sheet, and strip. Lackawanna at the same time rolled sheet and strip, structurals, bars, billets, and rails and contained twelve finishing mills in all, with a combined rated capacity of 10.7 million tons.[2] Labor relations at Lackawanna continued to be bad, but they were not good at Burns Harbor either. As early as the good years of the early 1970s, the question of Lackawanna's future began to come to a head.

In June 1970, Edmund Martin, the Bethlehem chairman who had served at Lackawanna as assistant general manager and general manager between 1946 and 1957, toured the Lackawanna works. During the visit, he was reported to have said that it was "the damned best steel plant in the country" and to have promised to keep it that way.[3] Given the circumstances, it was an extraordinary remark. On 1 December 1970, Martin retired and was replaced by Stewart S. Cort, who had spent most of his working life in the Pacific coast division; Lewis Foy became president. On Monday, 30 November 1970, the day before Cort took over, it was announced that raw steel capacity at Lackawanna would be cut from 6.0 million to 4.8 million tons. Half of the work force of eighteen thousand was to be laid off. Foy blamed "oppressive taxes," "unrealistic environmental laws," and most of all, "an uncooperative labor force." Whatever the reason, this blow proved to be the first in a long but uncertain process of slowdown.

Three years after the first reduction, at the end of the record year of 1973, Cort indicated that the large expansion program for the next four years might include a 600,000-ton increase in Lackawanna steel capacity. But after peaking in 1973 and 1974, output and net income fell sharply. In 1977, national steel production was 2.1 percent lower than in 1976, but at Bethlehem Steel, the decline was 12 percent. The proposed expansion at Lackawanna never occurred. Early in 1977, the plant's operating situation and commercial standing were worsened by a period of severe winter weather that closed it for a time and cost some $10 million. On 17 August, as hopeful expressions for the company's year proved misplaced, it was announced that Lackawanna capacity would be cut a second time, this time from 4.8 million to 2.8 million tons. The estimated cost of closure of "steel making and related facilities" in 1977 amounted to $750 million, or not far short of one-seventh of net sales. The reductions at Lackawanna accounted for the largest part of this cost.

Remarkably, despite the uncertainty over prospects, the company continued to entertain ideas of expansion and, in some instances, to spend large sums of money at Lackawanna. There was a lack of purposeful sense of direction. For instance, the works contained a rolling mill with an annual capacity in 1974 of 715,000 tons of rails or billets. On the day before it was decided that this unit should be permanently closed, the company was discussing the purchase of new equipment for it.[4] In the mid-1970s, the decision was made to invest in a new thirteen-inch bar mill, claimed by Foy to be "the world's most technologically advanced." This "highly sophisticated installation" began test rolling steel early in 1976, but construction and installation of computers and finishing facilities continued through 1977 and were completed in 1978. The improvements were originally estimated to cost $30 million, but the decisions made during those years to equip the plant with more and more elaborate facilities, including new dimension controls, pushed the cost up to $200 million. A new scrap melter was installed in 1977, and investments continued into the early 1980s. In 1981, a galvanizing line was expanded and an improved heating system was put into the coke ovens. Looking ahead in the early months of 1982, managers expected that a sinter plant pollution control system costing $17 million would be completed that year.[5]

Yet, as these developments occurred, the company was moving toward the closure of Lackawanna operations. As Foy put it in his annual report for 1977, when Lackawanna employed eighty-five hundred people, "We concluded that the decline in our profit margins had permanently undermined the economic viability of certain of our marginal facilities and that additional capital investment to modernize and add pollution controls to these facilities could no longer be justified." The following year, the warning was repeated.[6] Operating conditions improved markedly in 1978 and 1979, but after that there was a sharp downturn. By 1982, Lackawanna already had little more than a skeleton crew. For the last quarter of that year, when the steel industry nationally lost an estimated $2.0 billion, well over half of this total, $1.15 billion, was recorded by Bethlehem. This extraordinary situation resulted from an allowance of more than $900 million for shutting down Lackawanna.

The announcement of the closure was handled clumsily as well as insensitively by the company. On Monday, 27 December 1982, the first working day after Christmas, workers were informed that their plant would cease production in the course of the following year. In mid-March, Walter Williams, as Bethlehem president, rejected the cost-cutting plan put forward by the USWA.[7] The plant closed in October 1983. Bethlehem Steel Corporation capacity was thus reduced by more than 3 million tons. The surviving Lackawanna galvanizing operations were transferred to the control of Burns Harbor, and its bar mill facilities were grouped with those at Johnstown in a new, separate business organization. Coke ovens and by-product recovery also continued at Lackawanna. Although thirteen hundred jobs remained, seventy-three hundred had been lost. About two-thirds of the "restructuring cost" involved the "employment costs" of the closure, largely the huge bill for mandated benefits.

Johnstown had even more obvious weaknesses than Lackawanna. It was now by far the smallest of Bethlehem's integrated mills, and by the mid-1970s, it was alone among them in being wholly dependent on open hearth furnaces. It then contained three billet mills, seven bar mills (with a combined capacity of 1 million tons), and a rod mill. There were also two plate mills with a combined capacity of 500,000 tons facilities—much smaller and less sophisticated than those at Burns Harbor or Sparrows Point. It was not plagued with persistent labor problems such as those that had dogged the management at Lackawanna for so long. At Johnstown, the main concerns were outmoded technology, the high costs of correcting that situation, and unviable product lines, which had persisted over the years because the plant was obviously not well placed in the array of Bethlehem operations for either market access or raw material supply. For years, the company's response to the situation of this plant showed amazingly little sense of direction. In mitigation, it must be remembered that it is easier to identify failings in retrospect than it is to make the right choice at the time when partial knowledge acts as a heavy drag.

The decision to build a continuous caster at Johnstown was made in 1969, but after millions had been spent on site work and foundation laying, the project was abandoned. From then onward for almost twenty years, various methods were tried to make this works viable. Retrospectively, at least some of those who occupied top positions in Bethlehem Steel recognized that the company committed too much money to these efforts. By midsummer 1973, when long-term development plans were announced, Johnstown contained four blast furnaces and eight 180-ton open hearth furnaces. Despite the general expansion, capacity at Johnstown was to be reduced, partly in response to tighter state and federal environmental standards but also to reflect changes in demand. Billets, bars, rods, and wire, its main products, were lines in which foreign suppliers and mini mills had made particular progress. The decision was made to close some of the rolling mills and to replace the open hearths with cold metal practice in electric furnaces, a step that would remove the pollution problems associated with iron making, coke ovens, and sinter plants. Annual steel capacity would fall from 2.3 million to 1.0 million tons. Less than a year later, this program was revoked in favor of maintaining existing levels both of steel making and employment. Some have attributed this surprising turnabout in policy to the fact that Lewis Foy, newly appointed chairman, could not face such a drastic reduction in the economic mainstay of his hometown. But there were continuing fears that even this change of policy might prove to be no more than marking time before the whole operation was declared redundant. The company itself was so concerned about Johnstown's longer term future that, in 1975, a study of the situation was begun under the chairmanship of Walter Williams, recently returned from the shipbuilding division as a vice president for the steel group with responsibility for manufactured products. The study group considered a range of options, including installation of basic oxygen converters or electric furnaces as well as the prospect of operating only rolling mills (using imported steel, possibly through a joint venture with a Canadian company) or struggling on with the existing situation. For a time, the uncertainties seemed to be dispelled. It was announced that $200 million would be invested in the works and that, instead of cold metal electric furnaces, it would at last be equipped with two BOF converters. This would mean continuing operation for the blast furnaces and their ancillary processes. Unfortunately, soon after this apparent reprieve, the outlook worsened as a result of completely uncontrollable external circumstances and darkening business prospects.

During February 1977, fires caused $15 million worth of damage at two coal mines in the Cambria Division. Five months later, there was severe flooding in the Conemaugh River valley, and the Johnstown works was very seriously affected. The vice president of steel operations learned of this flood in dramatic fashion, via a message from a Johnstown pay phone: "Just called to tell somebody in Bethlehem that the whole steel plant is covered with 20 to 25 feet of water." Steel production was curtailed until the end of September, but there were other, longer term implications. The coke ovens and blast furnaces were ruined, and the financial impracticality of reinstating them ruled out the use of the BOF process, even though work on installing this plant had already begun and commissioning had been expected for 1978. Overall clean-up and restoration expenses were put at an extraordinary $39 million. It was a most inconvenient time in which to have to bear such extra costs, for 1977 was a year in which

Bethlehem's steel output was 7 million tons or 30 percent below the level in 1973. Net income had been $168 million in 1976, but there was a net loss of $448 million in 1977. In fact, even while the flooding continued, the company, previously apparently so solicitous for the future of the area, announced that Johnstown capacity would be cut from 1.8 million to 1.2 million tons. Reverting to the earlier plan, management decided that the reduced output of steel would be made in electric furnaces. A partial compensation was that this seemed more appropriate in a plant concentrating on bars, which involved a wide variety of order sizes and specifications, whereas the mass production of a BOF plant was better suited to long runs of standardized products. A number of the existing rolling mills would be closed, with only those judged to have earning potential being rehabilitated.

The new electric furnaces about which there had been so much uncertainty in the late 1970s were in place by 1982. With only a handful of exceptions, they were the largest units of their kind in the industry. At this time, rod and wire operations at Sparrows Point were "consolidated" with those at Johnstown, which in fact meant their abandonment. Competitive conditions now proved harder and levels of production much lower than had been envisaged. Johnstown was still being run on what were called "traditional lines," and it was becoming clear that these lines were no longer viable. The works lost $72 million in 1984, more than 60 percent of the total for all of the company plants. In March 1985, Bethlehem Steel's bar, rod, and wire operations were formed into a separate division centered on Johnstown but including the thirteen-inch bar mill at Lackawanna. The latter had operated for less than ten years, but the four Johnstown bar mills were old, one dating from 1918, two from 1925, and one from 1963. Johnstown was effectively being converted into a mini mill, though its products were in many cases of a higher quality, and as part of this reorganization, it was provided with a new general manager from that section of the industry. Ted Leja had previously been president both of North Star Steel and of Georgetown Texas Steel. On the other hand, as compared with mini mills, his new works was still operating with USWA wage levels and work rules. These and the ethos of the mill could not be changed as readily as its management or the provision of a few items of new equipment. Considerable efforts were made to change old work practices and staffing and to produce what was called "a leaner, more cost efficient operation." There was some progress. An agreement with the union provided for a roughly 25 percent reduction in the work force, to twenty-two hundred, a cut of almost a quarter in labor remuneration, more flexible working practices, and greater "involvement" of employees. With co-operation on these points, it was projected that $50 million could be cut from the division's costs over the sixteen months of the agreement. Operations pro-vided an interesting insight into not only the "old plant" nature of Johnstown but also the traditional nature of the market that it supplied. Following a visit to Japan, Leja pressed for new equipment in the bar mills to meet stringent size specifications for bars. When automobile companies were approached, they revealed that, unlike Japanese firms, they had no use for bar rolled to such close tolerances.[8]

Despite more flexible management, lower wages, other cost reductions, and quality improvements, most of the gains made at Johnstown were quickly can-celed out by decreases in prices and volume.[9] Two years later, the unintegrated plant was hit by an additional burden, when operating losses increased because the rising cost of scrap was not fully offset by higher prices for bars. Although it was common to accuse overseas producers of dumping, in fact, mini mills were now the main source of the products competing with those from the Johnstown mills. An attempt was made to cut costs further, with the company announcing in 1990 that it was considering a "restructuring and modernization plan to improve its competitiveness." This was another scheme "dependent upon obtaining a more competitive labor agreement with the United Steel-workers."[10] The outcome was predictable. In January 1992, after more than a year of unsuccessful negotiations, the union proving inflexible, the decision was made to "exit" the bar, rod, and wire business "as promptly as possible, taking into consideration the requirements of our customers."[11] As late as 1988, bars, rods, and semi-finished steel made up 12.1 percent of Bethlehem's net sales; by 1993, the shares of those products was 1.2 percent. The company disposed of its saleable assets at Johnstown to Ispat, but the unions proved uncooperative. There were hopes that the new owners would follow through with earlier Bethlehem plans to install a continuous casting unit to improve efficiency. In fact, after 150 years as an important factor in America's iron and steel trade, most of the John-stown complex sprawling along the Conemaugh valley rapidly declined into an idle, unsightly shell.

Were slowdown and closure inevitable at Lackawanna and Johnstown, or might other policies have saved them? Retrospectively, one may come to either conclusion, but it is essential to recognize that those struggling with the situation at the time were limited both by the hard facts of their inheritance and by their inevitably partial knowledge of the way things would go over the next few years. There were some certainties but many imponderables. Bethlehem's decision to build a Chicago-area plant was a mortal blow to the long-term viability of production in the vicinity of Buffalo. The Lackawanna works was unquestionably a major operation, but, though periodically modernized in its various parts, it contained much old plant, had grown piecemeal, and was less well laid out or located than its newer and steadily expanding rival. Unless demand from the 1960s had continued to rise substantially rather than level off and then fall, it would become more and more marginal. Having recognized these inherent disadvantages, one can see that company policy toward Lackawanna was curiously hesitant. Johnstown had not been a growth point for steel in the twentieth century at all. After acquiring it in the early 1920s, Bethlehem had never undertaken any large-scale expansion program there.

Just below the attractive historic town center of Bethlehem as one comes down toward the bridge across the Lehigh River and to the steel works, the road passes a plain, unimpressive building. This was once a center of power and decision making independent of the company but very relevant to its future, for it was the old headquarters of the local branch of the United Steelworkers of America. Senior officials there and at union headquarters were often at odds with decisions made by the board or by top management. Eugene Grace had once proudly claimed that Bethlehem Steel was "more than a livelihood." Those who worked in the USWA local aimed to ensure that it provided at least that for its members. Unwittingly, they sometimes contributed to forces working against those ends and sometimes took positions that to an outsider seemed irrational and counterproductive. A minor illustration of this was provided by events in the company's limestone quarries. In the mid-1980s, Bethlehem wanted to sell the last of its quarries in the Lebanon area. Having found a purchaser, the company offered a deal to its quarry workers: if within, three years, the arrangement did not work satisfactorily, it would take them back into its own pension system. The workers held out for a five-year guarantee, and accordingly, Bethlehem closed the quarries and the workers lost their employment.[12] However, it must be stressed in mitigation of any charge of blank obscurantism on the part of the workers that many of their actions and attitudes were the result of a lack of recognition or due regard going back decades or indeed generations. In contrast to major, more complex steel centers such as Pittsburgh or Chicago, in a small community like Bethlehem, workers could see how well their managers lived, for the managers' fine houses were close by, on or near Prospect Avenue (or "Bonus Hill," as it was sometimes called). In 1988, Bethlehem Steel's top executives received an average 30 percent increase in their salary and bonus. Walter Williams alone received $611,000. It was scarcely a good foundation for the negotiation of a new labor contract in spring 1989.[13] During the 1990s, decisions made at this USWA local were important in helping to frustrate development planning for the Bethlehem plant.

This demise of the Bethlehem works had long been feared. The drift of company thinking had already indicated that the plant was no longer accorded a high priority. In the 1980s, $500 million was spent on installing large capacity continuous casting facilities at Burns Harbor and Sparrows Point, but, although pioneering work on the process had been undertaken there twenty years before, no concast unit had been installed at Bethlehem. During the six months' strike at U.S. Steel in 1986, the Bethlehem works made a great deal of money, but in the late 1980s, when $80 million was invested in a new electric furnace at Steelton, Bethlehem was again left out. The Bethlehem works reached a new low when its formerly successful and most distinctive line, heavy structural shapes, faced a declining market. To some extent, the problems it faced were related to changes in demand. Very few high-rise office buildings were now being built as more office space was provided in suburban office parks with low-rise, cheaper buildings using lighter beams. Construction planners increasingly used concrete pillars instead of I-beams, and for bridge work, more welded plate was used. In terms of outcomes, an important milestone or sign of the times in this section of the steel industry was the decision by the United States Steel Corporation to close heavy structural mills when it abandoned its Homestead works in the mid-1980s and the South Chicago works in 1992.

In retrospect, the elimination of Lackawanna can be seen to have been almost self-inflicted by Bethlehem Steel when it decided to build at Burns Harbor. The drawn out, erratic processes that led to closure at Johnstown were a response to a deadly combination: an increasingly unsuitable product range, obsolescent technology, and poor geographical location. In the case of the Bethlehem works, the matter was more complicated. It was affected by market changes, but above all it could not survive in competition with newer plants using a simpler complex of manufacturing processes. In the early years of a long maturing crisis, it seemed that steel from overseas would be the main threat, and clearly the import trade reduced the industry's capacity to modernize to meet later blows.

In 1957, Grace's last year in control of Bethlehem Steel, national shipments of heavy structural shapes and piling amounted to 7.4 million net tons, 9.2 percent of all steel products. Imports were below 300,000 tons. By the record year of 1973, domestic shipments had fallen to 7.1 million tons and 6.4 percent of all shipments; imports were 1.3 million tons. Between 1975 and 1984, domestic shipments fell from 5.1 million net tons to 4.2 million and imports rose from 900,000 to 2.2 million tons. However, from the late 1980s, imports fell off sharply. In 1992, 1993, and 1994, they averaged only 634,000 tons, but during the same years, Bethlehem's shipments of the same products fell annually and averaged 871,000 tons. Bethlehem was above all a victim of the mini mills.

In the mid-1970s, three rolling mills at Bethlehem had a combined rated annual capacity for 1.7 million tons of structurals. Nominal mill capacity for this category of products at Lackawanna then amounted to 2.2 million tons, though it is clear that it made very much less than that, but by how much is unknown. In 1984, the Lackawanna mills were closed, and the decision was made to spend $50 million to modernize the Bethlehem forty-eight-inch structural mill, the original Grey beam mill. Notwithstanding this major overhaul, the associated primary and finishing operations for heavy structurals were not modernized. To have included them in the improvement program would have required an outlay four times as large as what was planned. By 1990, both Bethlehem primary and structural mill operations were outdated. The two blast furnaces had been built in 1942 and 1955 and relined in 1983 and 1985, respectively. Together they could make up to 5,900 tons of iron daily, perhaps 2.1 million tons a year. The steel making capacity of the two-converter BOF shop was 2.9 million tons. Only two of the six batteries of soaking pits had been built or rebuilt since 1955. A thirty-two-inch blooming mill had been modernized in 1955; the forty-inch blooming mill was installed in 1907 and was not electrified until 1980. The forty-eight-inch Grey mill was a curious hybrid. It too had been built in 1907, and it was re-powered in 1920. It still incorporated steam powered bloomer and finishing stands.[14] With this aged leviathan, Bethlehem Steel faced a battle with well-equipped newcomers.

For decades it had been believed that the largest beams were best made where there was major integrated capacity, whereas mini mills produced steel of poorer quality, which limited them to noncritical grades of reinforcing bar, small angles, and shapes. Gradually, however, they improved the steels they made and began to make beams of smaller dimensions. Eventually, with improved designs of continuous casters, they made high-quality preformed shapes or "beam blanks" that could be transferred directly from the casters to the furnaces at the beam mill and then rolled into larger structural shapes. Compared with traditional technology, mini mill processes reduced both overhead and running costs through savings in capital investment, maintenance, labor, and energy. They operated with different work rule practices and wage incentives and, as compared with Bethlehem, little in the way of "legacy costs," which included benefits for retirees. Given such advantages, mini mills were soon invading the market for wider beams, the field that since before World War I had always been regarded as a Bethlehem specialty. In the competition that resulted, Bethlehem was further penalized by its far from optimum plant layout, the product of more than a century's evolution, in comparison with the greenfield sites and efficient layouts designed for the continuous flow of materials from steel plant to mills and to shipping bay.

In 1988, Nucor and a Japanese collaborator, Yamato, opened a $220 million structural mill at Blytheville, Arkansas, which was able to produce 600,000 tons of twenty-four-inch wide flange beams. By 1995, Blytheville had been equipped to roll wider beams. That year, it shipped 1.95 million tons of products, including H-piling, standard sections, and wide flange beams measuring up to forty inches in width. Its two finishing mills were backed by two continuous casting machines and two electric furnaces, yielding a steel capacity of 2.4 million tons. Barges delivered up to 85 percent of the scrap for these furnaces to Blytheville's dock on the Mississippi. Here was a new, slim, thoroughly modern contender for the structural business. By 1998, there would be two more important mini mill structural works: a Chaparral Steel plant south of Richmond, Virginia, well placed for access to the James River and rolling beams up to thirty-six inches in width, and a smaller Nucor plant near Charleston, South Carolina, producing narrower beams.

Production at Blytheville was reported as requiring one man hour per ton of product as compared with about five hours at Bethlehem. Costs of production were reduced by concentrating on only a limited range of sections, carefully selected as those most widely used. The Nucor chairman, Ken Iverson, claimed his new plant would have a fifty-dollar per ton advantage over integrated producers, and he predicted that it would gain 20 percent of the market. Another estimate in the early days of Blytheville, from someone who knew the Bethlehem mills, was that costs of production in the former would be at least one hundred dollars a ton below those in integrated mills. As things turned out, this new works proved able to sell its product even into the Bethlehem area and still make profits on the transaction.[15] A few years later, Chaparral estimated that it could produce more than 1 million tons of wide flange beams with only four hundred employees. Even before this mill entered the competition, Bethlehem had been forced to withdraw from it.

Rather than follow the lead of U.S. Steel and give up heavy structurals, Bethlehem chose to fight. A number of studies were made of the possibilities for making its operations more competitive. These exercises had certain themes in common, especially the replacement of the time-worn and costly mineral-iron-steel–primary mill route with a process dependent on scrap-based electric steel furnaces and continuous casting. There were two possible ways of achieving this change: build new facilities at Bethlehem or obtain the steel from the existing electric furnaces at Steelton. Either route, but especially the former, would involve large capital outlays, and these were difficult to provide given that in the six years through 1990, Bethlehem's net income totaled only $23 million. In short, the company lacked the funds to carry through the more radical solution alone. The alternative might be found in cooperation with others. In January 1991, Bethlehem Steel Corporation signed a letter of intent with the British Steel Corporation to examine the possibility of a jointly owned, equal share venture that would have involved most of the Bethlehem Steel structural and rail mill operations. The blast furnaces and oxygen steel plants at Bethlehem would close, but electric furnaces and a continuous casting machine to produce "beam blanks" would be installed in the existing BOF shop to supply the two structural mills. Major mill alterations would be involved. The alternative was to combine this works with Steelton as a 1.5-million-ton joint operation, whose steel supplies would be drawn from the Steelton electric furnaces. In either case, large capital outlay would be needed for plant upgrading. British Steel would invest on the order of $300 million; Bethlehem Steel accounts would provide for a $550 million restructuring charge to cover its share of the proposed expenditure. Negotiations lasted for some two years, including the months before the public learned of them. British Steel representatives were in Bethlehem for months, and Walter Williams made numerous trips across the Atlantic. For a time, all seemed to be going well, but a major stumbling block proved to be obtaining satisfactory arrangements with the USWA not only for new staffing levels and working practices but a cut of about two thousand in the work force. This was a bitter prescription, but it was hoped by those involved in planning the project that the union would see this as a last, best hope of being able to sustain the beam business for the long term. Interviewed in London early in July 1991, Bob Scholey, chairman of British Steel, refused to reveal detailed plans. In his typically blunt fashion, however, he identified the problem: "They [the USWA] have got to understand that both us and Bethlehem are after world competitive costs. We are both hopeful that we will get a sensible response from the USW—*then* we will unveil our plans." On another occasion, he traveled to the United States for a meeting with Bethlehem, only to find that the head of the local union district had refused to attend. Without an agreement with the union, funding could not be obtained, but the union was reported as turning this situation on its head, claiming that British Steel did not have the money to close the deal. After numerous meetings, it was concluded that the necessary changes could not secure union acceptance, and on 11 November 1991, it was announced that negotiations had ended in failure. Scholey later summed up the long discussions with a comment suggesting that if the union had not walked away, a deal could have been made.[16]

Immediately following the breakdown of the talks with British Steel, the Bethlehem Steel Corporation announced its intention to end existing iron and steel operations at Bethlehem as well as track work—but not rail making—at Steelton. No timetable for the slowdown was set, but it was already under way. In 1981, employment at the Bethlehem works had been about eleven thousand; by the end of summer 1992, it was around four thousand. Eleven months after the failure of the British Steel plan, Walter Williams retired as chairman.[17] For the next period, the fight to preserve the structural steel business, and with it the Bethlehem plant, lay with Williams's successor, Curtis Barnette. As a non-steel man again became head of the firm, Roger Penny was appointed president and chief operating officer.

In spring 1993, having at last reached an agreement with the USWA for a two and a half year wage freeze for its structurals division, Bethlehem created a new, wholly owned subsidiary, the Bethlehem Structural Products Corporation. Then, in a memorable meeting in the Hotel Bethlehem, with union representatives and members of the work force present, the company announced a modernization program for the plant, a scheme that at last would equip it with its own long-coveted electric furnaces and also provide for continuous casting of beam blanks and improvements in finishing mills. In the long term, investment might amount to as much as $250 million, but the first phase of the plan would involve the installation of the continuous caster and was expected to cost $105 million. In short, completion of the whole project would require $145 million in addition to what had been authorized. Once more, it seemed for a time that the future of the Bethlehem works would be secure, but in view of the figures indicated above, it seems an open question as to whether the scheme had been realistically costed. At any rate, Nucor president John Correnti, in the course of a visit to Lehigh University, derided the Bethlehem Steel plan to add a large electric furnace plant. He was reported to have said, "It's a joke. We'll kill them."[18] It was an ominous repetition of Lewis Foy's private reaction to Japanese competition twenty years or so before. In this instance, the birds came home to roost much more quickly.

Late in 1993, Roger Penny visited Blytheville. He was impressed by what he saw, including the fact that the operators were making good progress in developing their ability to make heavy structural shapes. He returned home convinced that his own company could not compete with this plant without making more radical changes than previously announced, including the improvements in finishing mills. By this time, however, the market outlook was becoming unfavorable, which made it less practical to make these improvements. Annual demand for H- and wide flange beams was now in the range of 3.0 to 3.6 million tons, but national capacity was about 4.2 million tons. Bethlehem's results in fall 1993 were adversely affected by operating problems and competitive pressures. The outcome was that the company decided on retrenchment. In January 1994, the company arranged a meeting with union leaders in the corporate office. Amid bitter comments from enraged workers' representatives, the chairman revealed that his board had reconsidered its decision of June 1993 and had decided that it would not go ahead with the modernization program. The strong trend to lighter beams was given as justification for the change of plan. Production of heavy wide flange beams would be phased out by 1996, but the forty-four-inch structural mill would be modified and upgraded at a cost of $50 million so that Bethlehem could concentrate on light and medium beams, from six to twenty-four inches in width, which now made up 80 percent of demand for the product. Instead of spending on a beam blank caster, new steel capacity, and other investments that had been planned, the company would revert to drawing on Steelton for blooms for the surviving Bethlehem beam mill. The works would use slabs from Sparrows Point for rolling sheet piling. Under the new arrangement, 2,000 jobs would be lost; there had been 4,340 at Bethlehem in

1990. Even now, it appeared there were some vestiges of hope, unless the words used were merely aimed to soften what was already seen as an inevitable collapse. Experience soon began to destroy those vestiges. In 1994, the company as a whole made a profit of $80.5 million, but operations at Bethlehem were estimated to have lost on the order of $90 million. Even after this, in the early weeks of 1995, the president of the Structural Products Division went so far as to suggest they might be able to introduce a better organization, one that would "create a customer-driven structural business along market lines."[19] This quickly proved to have been the last, forlorn, hope.

In accordance with the new scheme, Bethlehem's blast furnaces, oxygen steel plant, and the small electric furnace shop that had supplied the forge were closed in November 1995. Even more dramatic, during that same last quarter of 1995, sooner than originally scheduled, production ceased in the forty-eight-inch mill, the upgraded original Grey mill that had operated for eighty-seven years. The following year, another $25 million was spent to improve remaining operations, but results in these departments were now dependent on outside supplies of semi-finished steel, and there were added costs for transportation, inventory, and reheating so that the results were commercially unsatisfactory. By early fall 1996, the decision had been made to sell or close the whole structurals department. The "combination mill" ceased production in March 1997. Even then, there seemed to be possibilities of a last-minute reprieve when a group led by a former plant manager made an attempt to buy the mill and keep it open, figuring they might save more than two-thirds of the jobs. The offer was rejected by the board on the grounds that it would require Bethlehem Steel to guarantee a supply of blooms from Steelton. Large-scale production on the Bethlehem site ended. All that remained was a coke plant, which closed in March 1998, and the forge, now operated independently as Lehigh Forge.[20]

15

HOPE AND HOPE DASHED

Trade and Rationalization during the 1990s

IN 1995, TWO FORMER HEADS of Bethlehem Steel, Donald Trautlein and Walter Williams, now sixty-nine and sixty-six, respectively, were asked for recollections of their experiences. Trautlein, under whose leadership some thirty-five thousand jobs had been lost, emphasized the progressive nature of cutbacks: "Every time you made a tough decision, you'd try to think, 'Well this is it' but it doesn't work out that way." Williams referred to the conflicting thoughts and emotions surrounding the challenges and plant closures of his period of office: "You say, 'Gosh, darn it, if we can just get everybody working together we can turn this thing around.' You don't just give up; there is a constant hope, constant effort to make it work. Then, when it doesn't, you finally realize the game's up and you take action."[1] One of the dangers in paring back operations was that the process broke up an interlinked complex and exposed other departments to the same pressures; in other words, there was a domino effect. During the

1990s, notwithstanding the efforts of management, the situation of the company worsened further. In the ten years through 1999, on net sales of $44.94 billion, only four years showed a net income; the net loss over the whole period was $1.92 billion. For U.S. Steel in the same period, the respective figures were $59.44 billion, seven years showed a net income, and the overall net loss was $400 million. U.S. Steel was now able to stop payments to its pension fund because of surpluses from Marathon; Bethlehem continued to make substantial payments. As before, the Bethlehem record contained a number of good years, expectations of improvement, and a looking ahead to sustained better times, which again and again proved to have been rekindled only to be disappointed.

The last years of the Williams chairmanship were difficult. Raw steel output in 1990–1992 averaged 10.5 million tons; in steel products, 1988 proved to have been the last year in which shipments exceeded 10 million tons. Net annual income in 1987–1989 had been $274 million. The following year there was a $463 million loss, and for the following two, the loss averaged $608 million. In marked contrast with the relative euphoria of his welcome six years before, Williams had come to be regarded both by management and labor as a leader who needed to be replaced. For a time, there had seemed a possibility that the leadership of Bethlehem Steel would pass to Tom Graham, who had achieved such wonders in rationalization and improved returns as president of U.S. Steel. But Graham had not responded positively, in part perhaps because he realized how bad the situation was at Bethlehem but possibly also because he thought he might become the U.S. Steel chairman. However, in 1989, Charles Corry had succeeded David Roderick as chairman. Graham retired from U.S. Steel in 1991, and the following year, after briefly occupying the top post at Washington Steel, he became president at Armco. In early fall 1992, at the end of three successive years of net losses totaling more than $1.6 billion, Williams retired from both the Bethlehem chairmanship and as a director. Though two years under the now accepted retirement age of sixty-five, it was later recalled (whether in his own words or as described by another is not clear) that Williams was "totally disappointed, totally disillusioned, and worn out." There seem to have been three leading contenders for the chair at that point: Roger P. Penny, the fifty-five-year-old vice president in charge of steel operations (the post Williams had once occupied); Gary L. Millenbruch, the fifty-four-year-old chief financial officer; or Curtis H. Barnette, Bethlehem's general counsel and secretary. The board chose Barnette, and Penny became a director, president, and chief operating officer, the last position being a new post. Barnette had been with Bethlehem Steel since 1967. He had come from a legal background and had served the corporation in that capacity. Although he lacked technical expertise in steel, he proved able in mastering the various details of the business and was willing to learn from others by conducting his board as a cabinet government. His tenure as chair was to be longer than that of any of his predecessors since Grace, but he operated in radically less favorable circumstances, except for those through which Grace had to steer in the early and mid-1930s. In fact, for reasons largely beyond not only his own but company control, Barnette's incumbency proved a frustrating period.

From the start, there were strong indications of change ahead. At a farewell event for Williams, Barnette mentioned that the Bethlehem and Steelton works would need to show promise if they were to be modernized. To some, it seemed significant that on the same occasion, when asked about the company's future, Penny spoke only of Sparrows Point and Burns Harbor.[2] In its early years, the new administration gained successes in its efforts to improve the company's circumstances. The company immediately exited the bar, rod, and wire market, closing facilities for these products at Johnstown, Lackawanna, and Sparrows Point. In 1992, Barnette took up again Trautlein's aim of reshaping the administration of the company, molding the various separate activities into "business units" with increased authority and responsibility for production, marketing, and financial performance. It was hoped that this move would provide both greater flexibility and more accountability. The four main works now became the focal points of separate units. This was a major cultural shift, for until then Bethlehem Steel had always been marked by its strong, centralized corporate control, with large staff groups organized by specialty. Corporate staffs were now significantly reduced. On the other hand, the number of directors was considerably increased.

In 1992, results showed an improvement. Steel production and shipments were up, the utilization rate improved, and the size of the net loss fell. After 1993, there was a return to profits. Annual capital expenditure in the eight years under Barnette averaged $340 million as compared with $400 million over the previous eight, but the outlay was now concentrated on a much smaller operation, one less than two-thirds as big in raw steel capacity as in 1984. The main reductions in company size had been completed down—to 11.5 million tons of steel by 1993, falling to 10.5 million after 1995 with the closure of another plant,

	Table 15.1 Bethlehem Steel Corporation and United States Steel Corporation data, 1979–1999							
	Bethlehem Steel				US Steel			
	Steel shipped (million tons)	Sales ($million)	Net income ($million)	Employees (thousands)	Steel shipped (million tons)	Sales ($million)	Net income ($million)	Employees (thousands)
1979	13.4	7,137	276	97.7	21.0	12,929	(293)	171.6
1985	8.8	5,118	(196)	44.5	12.9	19,283*	313*	79.6
1990	8.9	4,899	(463)	29.6	11.0	6,073	310	24.7
1995	9.0	4,867	180	19.5	11.4	6,475	301	20.8
1999	8.4	3,915	(183)	15.5	10.6	5,470	51	19.3

Sources: Bethlehem and U.S. Steel annual reports for the years indicated.

*Includes sales and income from Marathon Oil.

before again rising by 800,000 tons because of the absorption of a small, but in quality terms, important rival. Operating rates were high in the first half of this period but fell for most of the later years. More disturbing, after two years of profits, 1996 yielded a loss, before a return to profitability in 1997. The following year showed a decline from the 1997 level, and by 1999, Bethlehem was again in deficit. Even so, whereas the net loss in 1992 had been $0.137 for every dollar of sales, the loss in 1999 was only at the rate of $0.046. Over these eight years, raw steel production was down by 10.8 percent, steel shipments by 7.1 percent, and employment by 37.8 percent.

For years, Bethlehem Steel had narrowed the production gap between itself and U.S. Steel; shipments by the end of the century were almost 80 percent as large. But whereas Bethlehem was heavily in the red, U.S. Steel was now making modest profits. Both the industry and the company continued to be plagued with the same problems as during the hard years of the 1980s, many of them beyond management's control. The difference from the previous decade was that the strenuous attempts then taken to slim down and modernize were now shown to have been inadequate, perhaps incapable, of solving the essential problems of old-style industrial structures. It was recognized that there were too many major companies, often in the "wrong" locations, and that the long-championed virtues of fully integrated operations must be questioned. Even so, through much of the 1990s, traditional causes continued to be blamed for the industry's ills. For all big companies, there was a serious problem of perception. Looking back a few years later, Williams recognized it clearly enough: "We were all stuck with our basic steelmaking—just too much to write off and too much to shut down."[3]

In the early 1990s, Bethlehem Steel had three integrated works and one other steel plant. At the end of the decade, it had two integrated and two scrap-based steel plants, one a recent acquisition. From the early 1980s on, closure of capacity had more or less kept pace with decreased output. This reduced the commercial standing of the company. From 1981 to the end of 1985, it had lost $1.9 billion, and the book value of its shares had fallen by 70 percent, but the shrinkage in capacity meant that in relatively good years it could still record high operating rates. For example, whereas the 10.7 million tons of crude steel produced in 1983 amounted to 49.4 percent of its installed capacity, 9.4 million tons in 1999 meant a utilization rate of 83.2 percent. In some sections of operations, slimming down proceeded more quickly than capacity reduction. This applied especially to the work force, always weak in such a situation. In 1973, when Bethlehem still had wide non-steel interests, it employed 118,000. Twenty years later, 20,700 workers were on its payroll, and by 1999, there were only 15,500. Circumstances in the early 1990s forced the unions to make more concessions. For example, in spring 1993, employees at the Bethlehem works accepted a freeze in wages through 1995, in the vain hope of helping to save their plant. In the light of this unhappy experience, when later asked for further concessions, they refused. Other problems from the 1980s continued to trouble the industry and the company.

In his first annual report to stockholders, Curtis Barnette referred to "subsidized and dumped foreign steel," and in six of the seven subsequent reports he spoke of "'unfairly traded steel [imports]." The only occasion on which this problem was not highlighted in his annual comment was 1995, a year of reasonable profits. The report for 1996 more or less echoed the opinions expressed by Trautlein over a decade earlier: "There is excess world capacity for many of the products produced by Basic Steel Operations. Many foreign steel producers are owned, controlled, or subsidized by their governments. Decisions by these foreign producers to continue marginal facilities may be influenced to a greater degree by political and economic policy considerations than by prevailing market conditions."[4] Indeed, while earning the high regard of top executives in other steel companies, Barnette was said by some to spend too much of his time lobbying in Washington for further relief for the industry from the foreign steel influx. His successor, Duane Dunham, would begin the new millennium by stating in his first quarterly report, "import levels are too high because unfair trade continues."[5]

Even in the mid-1990s, mini mills escaped a similar regular indictment in Bethlehem published reports, although their share of national capacity and output was increasing more rapidly than ever and their advance was now unmistakably at the expense of the majors.[6] In 1990, mini mills made up about 20 to 25 percent of national steel capacity; by the end of the decade their share was nearly half. They could make satisfactory profits at prices that meant heavy losses to integrated rivals. In 1991, six of the largest steel firms estimated that they lost twenty-seven dollars on every ton of steel they shipped; at the same time, mini mills were making profits of about ten dollars a ton.[7] Their lower costs enabled them to enter and succeed in trades that integrated producers were being forced to quit. Some of them had moved on to higher value lines, including structurals and plates, and beginning in the early 1990s, a few of them began to invade what had become the very citadel of the majors: the rolling of thin flat-rolled products. Compared with 1981, steel output for 1992 by U.S. Steel, Bethlehem, LTV, National, Armco, and Inland had roughly been halved. Over the last five of those years, capacity at these six majors was cut by 11.7 million tons per year. In the same period, there was an annual increase of 5.3 million tons at mini mills. In the first quarter of 1991, Bethlehem reported a net loss of $39 million; for the same quarter a year later, it lost $45 million. In these same periods, net income at Nucor was $14 million and $16 million, respectively. By early 1994, costs at mini mills were estimated to be 25 to 50 percent lower than those in integrated works. Their advance was relentless. In 1990, when Nucor first produced as much as 3 million tons of steel, Bethlehem made almost 11 million tons. By 1997, their respective outputs were 9 million and 9.6 million tons. Two years later, Nucor made 800,000 more tons of steel than Bethlehem and had taken its place as the second ranking steel company.[8]

As at other companies, Bethlehem Steel operations continued to be burdened and curtailed by the tightening of environmental standards. From the 1980s on, coke manufacture has provided an outstanding example of the impact of pollution control. In 1982, a new eighty-oven coke plant, costing $165 million, was completed at Sparrows Point. Its environmental quality controls alone cost $15 million. Seven years later, Bethlehem agreed with the Maryland Department of the Environment to spend $92 million over the next five years for "technologically advanced controls to further reduce air and water pollution, mainly from the coke ovens."[9] By the end of 1991, operations at this installation had been halted so as to enable the company to assess the most cost-effective method of introducing an emissions control program to enable it to meet more exacting environmental standards. It was anticipated that suspension of operations would last two years, during which coke would have to be brought from the ovens at Bethlehem or purchased from outsiders. Early in 1994, however, the company concluded that it would be impossible to recover the remaining book value and necessary future investment if the coke plant was rebuilt. Accordingly, though only twelve years old, this extremely costly plant was written off. When, in March 1998, coke production ceased at the Bethlehem ovens, China took over as the main source for the fuel used at Sparrows Point. Four months later, at Burns Harbor, Bethlehem detached itself from ultimate responsibility for environmental problems there—and also secured a useful influx of financing—by selling off its No. 1 battery of ovens. It continued to operate the battery, though now nominally purchasing its product.[10]

Assaults on profitability from outside in the form of high levels of imports, growth in mini mill output, and environmental constraints were met by a continuing struggle to maintain the company's place. It disposed of further unused or unprofitable assets in the form of mineral reserves, remaining "non-core" or peripheral manufacturing operations, and lines of steel production that were no longer viable, thus causing more plant closures. In the past, it had been axiomatic that the long-term existence of major integrated operations required huge, controlled reserves of iron ore, coking coal, and limestone. In sharp contrast, it was now recognized that a large part of these holdings would probably never be used and that in the meantime they tied up a great deal of capital and could conversely be treated as realizable assets. Income from their disposal could offset operating losses or contribute to outlay on new facilities to help the company become more competitive. In the mid-1970s, Bethlehem owned three iron ore operations (in Berks County, Pennsylvania, at Marmora, Ontario, and the mines of San Felix, Venezuela) and had major interests in six others (two in the upper Great Lakes region, one in the eastern part of the Ozark mountains in Missouri, two in the Quebec-Labrador ore districts of Canada, and the other in Nimba County, Liberia). By 1982, it was involved only as a part owner in five ore operations, one of which, in Brazil, was a new one. Investments in Liberian ore were sold in 1984. Within seven years, the ore interests were reduced to three, situated in Minnesota, Canada, and Brazil. By the end of the 1990s, after selling its share in the Iron Ore Company of Canada, Bethlehem Steel retained only part interests in Minnesota and Brazil.

The same process of withdrawal occurred in fuel. As late as 1981, Bethlehem controlled eighteen coal mines and thirteen coal cleaning plants in Pennsylvania, West Virginia, and Kentucky and produced 7.7 million tons of coal, much of it of metallurgical grade but including also considerable tonnages of steam coal and even small amounts of anthracite. (Given the company's nineteenth-century roots, it is interesting to note that, at this late stage, trials were carried out at Bethlehem in the use of anthracite in the blast furnace. The results were mixed and nothing significant followed.) Company-owned mines provided 95 percent of the coal it used. Into the mid-1980s, expansion was under way in coal, notably in a sector quite separate from its core interests. Low-sulphur steam coal was by this time in greater demand in order to cut sulphur emissions from power stations. Eager for revenue and responding to the opportunity this seemed to provide, Bethlehem opened a 250-million-ton deposit in its High Power Mountain complex in Nicholas County, West Virginia. The first trade shipments were made in October 1985. But the following year, in the process of disposing of what it had now come to regard as peripheral assets, Bethlehem announced its intention to sell this operation, along with other West Virginia low-sulphur steam coal reserves, and 174 million tons of coal in eastern Kentucky. After another five years, it resolved to dispose of most remaining coal operations and reserves. By May 1994, the closing of Mine 33 in Cambria County marked the end of Bethlehem coal mining in Pennsylvania. It retained two West Virginia operations: the steam coal mine at High Power Mountain (the sale of which was not completed until 1997, eleven years after it had been decided on) and the Eagle Nest metallurgical coal operations in Boone County. Eagle Nest was sold in the third quarter of 1996, supply contracts being arranged for part of Bethlehem's future requirements.

By the mid-1990s, Bethlehem Steel had two main operating departments. The first, Basic Steel Operations, consisted of four divisions: Burns Harbor, Sparrows Point, Bethlehem Structural Products (the Bethlehem works), and Pennsylvania Steel Technologies (Steelton). The second, Steel Related Operations, contained the CENTEC Roll Corporation, BethShip, and BethForge. The last of these suffered severely in the early 1990s largely as a result of the brief peace that followed the end of the cold war, for about one-third of BethForge business had been with the Navy Department, mainly for forgings for nuclear powered vessels. It subsequently diversified more fully into the production of electricity generating equipment, primarily for export to developing countries, where the increase in demand was much higher than in developed countries.[11] In 1997, the BethForge and CENTEC divisions were sold to the West Homestead Engineering and Manufacturing Company. By becoming the independent Lehigh Forge, the forging operations survived all other operations on the Bethlehem site. In 1997, Bethlehem finally abandoned the shipbuilding industry of which it had for so many years been a national leader. In this instance, the process of withdrawal had been under way for decades. In 1940, one-quarter of all Bethlehem Steel Corporation billings had been for shipbuilding, but by 1965, the value of property, plant, and equipment in shipbuilding and repairing amounted to only 2.76 percent and, by 1984, to 1.85 percent of the corporate total. As the trade collapsed, the company disposed of its yards one by one. The sale of the Sparrows Point yard in October 1997 marked the end of the division. The income yielded by asset sales of all kinds varied greatly from year to year, but from 1990 through 1999, it equaled more than one-quarter of the company's total capital expenditure.

During the 1990s, Bethlehem became involved in more joint ventures with other companies. Early in the decade, it took a half share in a 270,000 tons' capacity galvanizing line at Jackson, Mississippi, with Sparrows Point being the source of supply for the company's share of the plant's requirements of cold rolled coil. In 1995, it acquired a 45 percent interest in the building of a new light gauge cold rolling plant at Portage, Indiana, near its Burns Harbor mill, and five years later, it paired with LTV in an equal-share hot dip galvanizing project in Columbus, Ohio, designed to serve the automobile industry.[12] There was a new openness to the idea of mergers or the collaborative operation of sections of its own plants.

After the company withdrew from structurals, it fought successfully to hold its market position in the two remaining heavy lines. In both lines it did so in part by acquiring major rivals, eliminating one and absorbing the capacity of another even at the cost of some of its own plant. Although national rail production had shrunk to relatively small dimensions, since returning to the trade in the first decade of the twentieth century, Bethlehem had been an important player. Manufacture of rails had long been concentrated at Steelton. In the mid-1970s, rail mill capacity there was more than 1.1 million tons, but in 1980, Bethlehem produced only 190,000 tons and Steelton ranked well behind U.S. Steel's

Gary plant and still further behind the Colorado Fuel and Iron Company works at Pueblo, Colorado. After contributing a considerable part to Bethlehem's losses in 1983 and 1984, Steelton operations were improved by investments in the electric furnace shop, installation of an $85 million continuous caster, and $18 million worth of modifications to the rail making plant to enable it to roll long and head-hardened rails. It was given another fillip when U.S. Steel withdrew from rail production, closing its Gary and Ensley mills and deciding against a contemplated new mill at the South Chicago works. In the early 1980s, Wheeling-Pittsburgh Steel decided to install a rail mill at Monessen, Pennsylvania, but by December 1986, it had announced that it too was pulling out of the trade. Bethlehem resolved to buy the Monessen mill, and even though at the time it indicated that Steelton electric steel and continuous caster operations could supply its needs as well as those of its own mill, the motivation seems to have been to remove a competitor, with no real intention to run the acquired mill. During the 1980s, American railroads largely bought foreign made rails, and Steelton never reached expected rail production levels. Rail demand was depressed through 1987 and 1988, and although Bethlehem completed the Monessen purchase, it had decided by 1992 to sell the equipment there while at the same time considering further modernization at Steelton, conditional on "obtaining competitive employment cost" through a new agreement with the USWA.[13] In 1998, Steelton made 382,000 tons of rail products. There were now serious threats to its continuing viability not only from Colorado Fuel and Iron but also from mini mills. In 1999, Bethlehem output of rail products fell sharply to only 2.7 percent of its sales. That year, whereas the company operated 83 percent of its overall steel capacity, at the Steelton works the utilization rate was only 42 percent. National rail consumption had fallen, but costs were down due to low scrap prices. By late 2001, the rapidly growing EAF (mini mill) firm Steel Dynamics was completing a new structurals/rail mill at Columbia City in Whitley County, Indiana.[14] With an annual capacity of 900,000 to 1 million tons and a central location in the rail network, it seemed that this competitor's new mill could make Steelton (itself effectively a mini mill) peripheral in rail markets in the early twenty-first century, just as its Pennsylvania Steel ancestor had become in the ruthless rail struggles of the late nineteenth century.

For many years, the national market for plate had been much larger than for rails. In the mid-1970s, Bethlehem operated five plate mills, with an annual capacity of 500,000 tons at Johnstown, 1.14 million tons at Burns Harbor, and

1.16 million tons at Sparrows Point. There was another small universal plate operation at Seattle. Closure in the West and operational slowdown at Johnstown concentrated production at the two biggest works. Although Sparrows Point was earning plaudits in the mid-1990s from consumers of the material from its 160-inch sheared plate mill, its operations were older and less sophisticated than those in the newer Burns Harbor mills. The Sparrows Point mills had prospered by supplying their own facilities and independent shipyards but were not well equipped to produce the range of properties required in more modern markets. In May 1998, in a surprise move, the company revealed that it had purchased the Lukens Steel Company. Its origins were much older even than Bethlehem's, and in range and quality, though not in tonnage terms, it was the nation's outstanding plate making concern, covering both carbon and alloy grades. But though Lukens steel had a high reputation, in recent years the company had been in bad shape, and interestingly, the initiative for the link seems to have come from it and not from Bethlehem. The Lukens board at this time was deeply divided, and one party sought out a merger partner as a means of at last resolving the internal dispute. The anticipated cost of the acquisition was $490 million for Lukens equity and $250 million for assuming its debt. Fortunately, the management culture of the two companies proved to be so similar that the processes of combination and coordination were greatly eased.[15] The Lukens works at Coatesville and Conshohocken and Lukens's raw steel making capacity of 900,000 tons became key considerations in Bethlehem's plate business, for they increased its carbon and alloy plate capacity by about 50 percent and added stainless products to the mix. Inevitably, this merger was followed by further concentration. During 1998, Bethlehem closed the 160-inch plate mill at Sparrows Point and Lukens's 206-inch mill at Coatesville, thereby enabling it to increase utilization rates at Burns Harbor and Conshohocken, which until then had been operating below capacity. By the late 1990s, plate accounted for 21 to 22 percent of Bethlehem's finished steel shipments as compared with 9 to 11 percent twenty years earlier.

Though Bethlehem was now the nation's largest plate producer, operating experience showed it was by no means secure in the business. In mid-1998, the plate market was strong, causing the Bethlehem chairman to make the cheerful comment, "It's a good time to be No. 1 in the plate business." In the course of that year, however, plate imports increased by over half and net income from all Bethlehem activities fell 57 percent below the level in 1997. During 1999, plate prices fell "significantly"; in another section of the annual report, the adverb used was "precipitously." Part of the problem was attributed to global over-capacity and part to "record levels of unfairly traded steel imports." In February 1999, with four other firms, the company filed anti-dumping suits against plate producers in eight countries. But, as with rails, new capacity at home also contributed to the problem, and again the competition came mostly from mini mills. By 2000, Nucor was completing a new plate mill in North Carolina, and in 2001, Ipsco finished a mill at Mobile, Alabama. By late 2001, the Nucor mill alone was expected to be operating at an annual rate of 800,000 tons, roughly equal to 40 percent of Bethlehem's plate capacity.[16] Clearly leadership in plate could not promise a smooth future course for the business.

Although investment in plate and rails was important, for Bethlehem Steel, as for most major companies, sheet and tin mill products became dominant in tonnage terms and absolutely crucial to their survival. Shipments of light flat-rolled products accounted for less than 25 percent of the company's shipments as late as 1975. By 1990, they were 49.3 percent, rose to 63.1 percent in 1993, and had reached 71.0 percent in 1999.[17] Before the construction of Burns Harbor, Bethlehem's two great centers of production for light flat-rolled steel were Sparrows Point and Lackawanna. By the mid-1970s, the company had two hot strip mills at Sparrows Point with a nominal combined annual capacity of 5.2 million tons, while the hot strip mills at Lackawanna and Burns Harbor had annual capacities of 2.5 million and 3.5 million tons, respectively. Apart from considerations of operational efficiency, the geography of demand for sheet, strip, and tin mill products had indicated that Lackawanna was least suitably located, and its elimination concentrated Bethlehem's increasing dependency on this product at its two largest, lowest cost plants. In this area too Burns Harbor possessed outstanding advantages. It was in the center of the prime market, it had a highly efficient, low cost primary end, and its mills were high quality, high output computerized mills suited to premium products requiring special properties, uniform gages, and very clean surfaces. Although Burns Harbor became the company's main focus for plate manufacture, its sheets and its strip and tin mill products were vital to continuing success there. At Sparrows Point, the very survival of the plant depended on them. In the-mid 1980s, $60 million had been spent on modernizing its sheet, tin mill, and plate operations, and in the early 1990s, another $200 million or more was invested to "completely" modernize the hot strip mill. In 1999, Bethlehem authorized a new cold mill complex for sheet products at Sparrows Point, which produced superior quality products and proved highly cost competitive.

This vital range of products proved highly vulnerable. It was subject to volatile price changes, keen competition from overseas, important incursions since the early 1990s from EAF mills, and the effects of an unrelenting struggle to improve quality and reduce costs by most other long established producers. Mini mills were now rapidly increasing their output of strip mill products, and even more importantly, they were gradually improving their grade so as to more fully compete with material from the fully integrated operations. By the end of the 1990s, Nucor had three hot strip mill operations. Steel Dynamics, which began operations only in 1996, claimed within a few years that part of its output of hot band from its 2 million tons per year mill at Butler, Indiana, was of such high grade that for some applications it could be used as a substitute for competitors' cold-rolled band. In 1996, the Bethlehem management estimated that over the next several years, up to 10 million tons of additional flat-rolled capacity might be built, mostly by mini mills.[18] As mini mill tonnages increased and quality improved, a few existing large, integrated strip mill firms withdrew from business, but most chose to make further investments to enable them to stay in contention. Thus in 2000–2001, among other developments in this sector, National Steel was upgrading its Ecorse, Michigan, and Granite City, Illinois, strip mills, Inland improved the eighty-inch Indiana Harbor mill, and LTV upgraded operations in Cleveland and East Chicago.[19]

As indicated, Burns Harbor was now Bethlehem's most vital operation. For years, expansion of its rolling capacity meant it had to make large purchases of slabs from other Bethlehem plants or from competitors in the Chicago area. In 1994, when steel demand was at a high level, other domestic producers could not supply its shortfall, and up to 1 million tons of steel slabs were purchased from plants scattered around the world—a steel import trade in this instance beneficial to the company.[20] Two years later, the need to bring in slabs was reduced when Burns Harbor's steel capacity was increased by another 400,000 tons. In 1994, Burns Harbor shipped 5.1 million tons of steel products, Sparrows Point shipped 2.9 million, and Steelton together with the rapidly dwindling Bethlehem plant contributed 1.3 million tons. Sparrows Point operated at a loss during the four years from 1990 to 1993 but returned to profit in 1994. It did well in the mid-1990s, but in 1999, whereas Burns Harbor managed to operate at 95 percent of capacity, for Sparrows Point the rate was only 76 percent.[21]

Notwithstanding years of rationalization and large expenditures for modernization, Bethlehem Steel had not reached a steady state by the late 1990s. By this time, its steel capacity was about 11.3 million tons (5.6 million at Burns Harbor, 3.7 million at Sparrows Point, 1.1 million at Steelton, and 900,000 tons from the Lukens mills). In 1999, 71 percent of production was light flat-rolled products, 20.9 percent was plate, 2.7 percent was rails, and the remaining 5.4 percent was either other rolling mill products or other products and services.[22] After net losses of more than $1.6 billion during the first three years of the decade, the company had been profitable again in 1994 and doubled its profits the following year. In 1996, it lost almost $310 million and over the next two years made net profits that almost compensated for the loss in 1996, but in 1999, Bethlehem lost $183 million. The annual report for 1999, issued early in 2000, boldly carried on its cover the words "A New Century for Bethlehem Steel." In retrospect, it was noteworthy that the statement was so vague, providing no indication of what type of future might be expected. A letter to stockholders announcing that Barnette would hand over in April to a new leader contained no more hint of triumph or rejoicing than the modest statement that the new chairman and chief executive had the experience required "to lead Bethlehem successfully into its Second Hundred Years."[23] It failed to indicate that the company's second century would not really begin until December 2004.

16

INTO THE ABYSS

IN 2000, DUANE DUNHAM, employed by Bethlehem Steel since 1965, president of the Sparrows Point division in the mid-1990s, and then head of commercial and business development, became chairman of the company. At fifty-eight, he was the youngest of the three top executives who might have replaced Barnette. Dunham had become a director only during 1999, when he took over as president and chief operating officer from Roger Penny, who became vice chairman before retiring in January 2000 at sixty-three.

During 2000, the company commissioned the new $600 million cold sheet mill it had been building at Sparrows Point. This was to be the last major development project the company was able to celebrate. Although Bethlehem had continued to strive to improve efficiency, reducing costs of operation by almost $300 million in little more than three years from mid-1998, it was a measure of the depths of the company's misfortunes that over the same period, slower national economic growth and keener competition among steel suppliers

Curtis H. Barnette and Duane R. Dunham, early 2000. *Courtesy Bethlehem Steel Corporation.*

meant that annual revenues fell by more than four times as much as their savings through cost reductions. The net loss in 2000 was $118 million. Already Bethlehem was exploring prospects for partnerships or mergers with other steel makers at home and overseas. The new vice chairman, Gary Millenbruch, was in consultation with many of the world's leading companies, and some of these "very serious talks" went on for several months. At home they negotiated with U.S. Steel (on several occasions), as well as with AK Steel and Wheeling-Pittsburgh. Largely because Bethlehem's labor contracts and pension burden were major stumbling blocks, there was no positive outcome.[1] Early in 2001, Tom Graham, though now seventy-four, was invited to give his advice for the revival of Bethlehem fortunes. He made a number of visits, but circumstances were rapidly moving toward a crisis point.

Although conditions were volatile, the general drift of prices was downward. Pressure on flat-rolled product prices from overcapacity, both worldwide and domestic, caused extreme uncertainty in the marketplace. At the end of 2000, the world export price for hot band—the basic material for the whole range of sheet and tin products—was $175 a metric ton. By May 2001, it had risen to $205, but expert steel analysts then estimated it could fall back to $180–$190 within the next few months. In July 2001, domestic prices for hot and cold rolled sheet were, respectively, 20 and 21 percent lower than a year before, but prices were still moving downward. By August, the decrease in domestic prices since May 2000 was said to be 29 percent for hot band and 24 percent for cold rolled band.[2] By the third quarter of 2001, Bethlehem shipments of steel products of all kinds were 117,000 tons less than the levels of the third quarter of 2000, average prices were some $40 a ton lower, and sales, $160 million lower. A net third quarter deficit of $35 million in 2000 had become a loss of $134 million a year later, or more than $1.4 million a day.[3] Such a drain on company resources could not long be sustained. The economic disruption following the terrorist attacks on New York and Washington on 11 September 2001 worsened an already desperate situation.

Bethlehem Steel was now caught in a crisis of unprecedented severity. The consequences were equally exceptional. On 24 September, Dunham, who had been chairman and chief executive for only fifteen months, was transferred to the posts of president and chief operating officer without public warning and replaced in his former positions by Robert S. Miller. Millenbruch resigned. The company announcement of the change at the top optimistically described Miller as a "turnaround expert," and even Dunham managed to put a favorable gloss on the situation, saying of the man who had so abruptly displaced him, "We have bolstered our senior management team with the kind of expertise only a few people familiar with our industry could bring to the company." In point of fact, Miller was a newcomer to the steel industry, knew very little about Bethlehem, and had been called to the job with almost no warning. After working at the Ford Motor Company, in the early 1980s he had saved Chrysler from collapse and in the following ten years had been credited with rescuing some seven other ailing companies. Now he spoke darkly of "resistance to change" at Bethlehem, though he failed to identify from what quarter this inertia came. He considered their remaining operations to be efficient but explained that the ability to prove this was impaired by the burden of payments to retirees. Bold in setting out his aims, he was less clear about how they would be attained: "I have seen first hand the miracles that can be accomplished when management, labor, and government all come together. I intend to see that happen here at Bethlehem."[4] The real strength of those brave words was soon tested. At the beginning, Miller maintained that it would be possible to avoid seeking Chapter 11 bankruptcy; on 17 October, however, Bethlehem followed many other steel companies in filing for this form of protection from creditors. That year it would lose $1.9 billion. Federal court proceedings revealed it had debts of $4.5 billion, about $300 million more than its assets.

Could Bethlehem have avoided this disaster? Any attempt to answer such a question must first take into account the fact that almost every other major integrated company also had to file for bankruptcy with the exception of U.S. Steel. This company had been financially helped at a vital time in the 1980s by its link with Marathon, had had more than other steel companies in the way of disposable assets, and had passed through Tom Graham's ruthless overhaul. There seems no doubt that union contracts hamstrung the major companies in competition with both foreign and EAF producers, both of which, though for different reasons, benefited from lower labor costs. The USWA had often resisted efforts by the companies to modify labor contracts that restricted their capacity to adjust to the new, more difficult trading conditions, but on the other hand, when the union did make concessions, it sometimes found that the company had failed to do its part. The integrated companies could and did reduce labor costs and restraints on their own freedom of action by making savage cuts in the size of their work forces, but this in turn increased their burden for the provision of pensions and health care and further alienated employees. Clearly, major steel firms were caught in a no-win situation. All that may perhaps be said about their unenviable position was that it was the end result of many decades of unhappy relations between capital and labor, however caused. In short, the harvest of the "management versus workers" tradition was at last being reaped.

There were other, wider considerations. In the decades following World War II, the iron and steel industries of various other advanced industrial economies had been rebuilt and new countries had entered the list of important producers. They did so with the best modern technology, in many instances adopting from the start wholly new processes of production such as oxygen steel making. Often this technologically advanced plant was in new works constructed on "greenfield" sites and in tidewater locations. Except for the Fairless and Burns Harbor works, no new fully integrated facility was built in the United

States in this period. It is true that heroic efforts were made to modernize existing plants and a great deal was achieved. However, though the major companies, including Bethlehem, recognized the attractions of brand-new plants equipped with the latest technology, they were, with the exception of Fairless and Burns Harbor, unable to justify the expenditure to construct them. There were three main reasons for this failure. First, after the end of the rapid, sustained expansion of the market and the industry after the late 1950s, such a wholesale shift would have required the scrapping of much of the existing capacity. Second, the capital outlay would have been so great that the finances of these companies would have been ruined, as the new heads of U.S. Steel had recognized in 1979, when they rejected a plan for a new works at Conneaut, Ohio, on Lake Erie. Finally, the industry did not have the government support that might have canceled out or at least compensated for this financing problem. In short, the long-established, major, fully integrated operations in the American steel industry were now the victims of the same free enterprise economic philosophy and relatively unfettered commercial policies that in earlier years had given them such a unique boost. As one Bethlehem chief executive wrote in a private communication to the author, "I still think we did the best possible considering labor, imports, financial road blocks—but it didn't work."

One must conclude that apportioning blame for this dire situation is not only unprofitable but almost impossible to do fairly. It is easy to identify factors but not their relative weight. It seems there were at least some shortcomings in technology. Keen competition had been offered not only from rivals overseas but also from both long established and relatively new steel makers at home. Social costs, essentially health care and pensions, had long been a heavy burden. Management and unions, though engaged in mutual recriminations, had both fallen short if judged by their contribution to a continuing viable industry. There has been some dispute about the quality of the top leadership at Bethlehem Steel, but as one person in a good position to observe commented, the individuals in the leading posts over the last decade had been intelligent, hardworking, and loyal employees who had striven to save the company. Their deficiency was that they had failed. No one factor had brought the giant low; together they had succeeded in doing so.

The next step in crisis management involved an attempt to stabilize company finances. This was not helped by a collapse in investor confidence as soon as bankruptcy was declared. At the close of business on Monday, 15 October

2001, Bethlehem shares were at $1.20 on the New York Stock Exchange; by that time the next day, they were worth twenty-two cents. Although it was acknowledged that there would have to be further job cuts in pursuit of essential increases in productivity, announcement of the course to be followed in the next stages of the rationalization process was delayed until late fall. It took a new direction. On Tuesday, 4 December, Bethlehem Steel Corporation and the United States Steel Corporation revealed that they had been engaged in talks regarding a possible consolidation, a major regrouping that was envisaged might also include Wheeling-Pittsburgh and possibly National Steel and Weirton Steel. Thomas J. Usher, chairman and chief executive of U.S. Steel, seems to have initiated the discussions, and from the start it was clear that that corporation was not only the largest but also the strongest party involved. Active cooperation from the United Steelworkers of America in making concessions on working conditions and wage levels would be essential for a successful merger. It was also stressed that the plan would require backup from the government to check the flood of imports. Another prerequisite for progress was a reduction in the impact on company finances of the costs of pensions and health care for retired steel workers, possibly by the government taking up the burden of current outlays in these fields, the industry being expected to provide only for future calls. At this time, Bethlehem had some 14,700 workers but was contributing to the financial support of about 73,700 former employees. Thirty years before, it had nearly five employees for every pensioner; now there were five pensioners for every employee. In relation to both imports and social costs, the Bush administration proved accommodating.

In March 2002, the federal government introduced new, much higher tariff barriers against imported steel, and in December, the federally supported Pension Benefit Guaranty Corporation (PBGC) took over a now insolvent Bethlehem pension fund. Organized labor, those major integrated producers left outside the merger negotiations, and the EAF sector were either skeptical of the benefits or overtly hostile to the proposed amalgamation. As one leader of the latter group, Keith Busse of Steel Dynamics, put it, in what was clearly for him a knock-out blow against such a scheme, "I think it's corporate welfare and I'm against it."

Miller's public response to the proposed merger with U.S. Steel put the best possible gloss on what for Bethlehem could only be a corporate disaster, even if it enabled it to avoid complete collapse: "The devastation we are witnessing may have created the window of opportunity to once and for all fix what has been a recurring problem frustrating steel industry and government officials alike for more than a quarter of a century."[5] There were important unanswered questions. Even assuming this merger could be achieved with the active help and perhaps the financial involvement of the government, could the combined elements of the merger, the exclusion of yet more foreign steel, and even a solution for the "legacy cost" of heavy bills for payments to retirees really solve the problems of the industry and specifically of Bethlehem Steel? If it did solve those problems, how many jobs would have been sacrificed? Unquestionably, such steps in the direction of rationalization would help, at least for a time, but could they fully cancel out the industry's burden of old capacity that, however modernized, would remain in old-style locations related to raw material flows and to marketing patterns now partly or largely outmoded? Even after all this had been done, the industry would still have to compete in a new globalized economy in which there were so many more recently built tidewater operations, with excellent access to the world's richest mineral resources and at least equally good plant, equipment, and layout as well as continuing advantages from cheaper labor. In short, would not this or alternative mergers prove to be merely putting off a day of reckoning?

Even into the early twenty-first century, some commentators continued to claim that American mills had technology as good as or better than that of their main overseas rivals, though for the equipment used throughout the iron and steel works as a whole, if not for individual units within these plants, this seemed at least doubtful. If major further improvement were found necessary, it was questionable that the steps taken or anticipated during fall 2001 would make investment in integrated steel making more attractive to the public or to institutional investors; full modernization would remain difficult to finance. Moreover, as some recognized when the scheme was revealed, improvement of operations would be conditional on the elimination of some of the existing capacity. Which plants would have to close in order to achieve an efficient realignment of production? In the Chicago area, how would Burns Harbor and Gary compete or cooperate? Would an amalgamation that included the flat-rolled product capacity of both Sparrows Point and Burns Harbor mean that U.S. Steel's Mon Valley complex would have to close and that at long last bulk steel making would cease in Pittsburgh? If any large-scale pruning of plants occurred, would not the mini mill sector, already claiming to account for about half of present production, take the opportunity to expand further? If so, the result would be that, rather than being able to continue to blame its commercial problems on "unfairly traded" foreign steel against which the government might now take effective action, the outstanding threat to the continuing lives of the old-style "majors" would at last be seen to be that of the efficient, new-style steel industry competing from within the national economy. No government support could be sought against this domestic rival. There was no question over the quality of most of the material produced by the major companies; in Bethlehem Steel's last years, Burns Harbor cold rolled sheet on more than one occasion won the Supplier of the Year Award from General Motors. But how could they get their costs down sufficiently to compete? (In 2002–2003, the mini mills were at least temporarily hard hit by increasing costs for energy and scrap; at Nucor, these extra costs amounted to a four-dollar increase per ton of steel for energy and nineteen dollars per ton on the price of scrap. Even so, that company remained profitable. World scrap prices roughly doubled by spring 2004, largely because of purchases by a rapidly expanding Chinese steel industry, but the mills proved able to pass some of these extras on as "surcharges.") Two weeks after the unveiling of the proposed U.S. Steel/Bethlehem consolidation, Robert Crandall, economist at the Brookings Institution, summed up the situation: "There's no danger that we're going to lose the steel industry— we are just losing the Midwest-based, iron ore- and coal-integrated industry to smaller companies located all over the country."[6]

The proposal for merger foundered, with U.S. Steel moving on to what was for it a more logical realignment of production by acquiring National Steel and thereby at last obtaining the dominant position in the Detroit area. Other major producers found various routes to at least temporary survival. For instance, by the beginning of 2002, Wheeling-Pittsburgh had a $27.2 million rescue plan that included state loans of $5 million from West Virginia and $7.2 million from Ohio. Meanwhile, Bethlehem Steel remained in turmoil. In the last quarter of 2001, it had lost $97.3 million. Then it was announced that from January 2002, Dunham would retire as president, chief operating officer, and director.[7] By mid-2002, the outlook was still unclear. In early June, U.S. Steel stock was at $13.97, having recorded a high in the previous fifty-two weeks of $15.51 and a low of $9.09; Bethlehem stock was at $2.70 in mid-2002.[8] Government acceptance of the U.S. International Trade Commission's enhanced protection plan for the industry was under attack. In February 2002, thousands from Bethlehem and other plants demonstrated their support in Washington, but eventually the administration approved only a 30 percent increase in duties on imported steel rather than the 40 percent they demanded. Moreover, some results from increased protection had begun to seem counterproductive. A study by the Consuming Industries Trade Action Coalition predicted that the ITC recommendations would cause the loss of eight jobs in steel-using industries for every one saved in steel and might cost U.S. citizens between $1.9 billion and $4 billion a year.[9] In addition, as had been the case twenty years earlier with important Japanese firms, the new protection policies provided outsiders with an incentive to seek a position inside the protective barriers of U.S. industry. Some of their plans involved Bethlehem Steel.

During fall 2001, it was reported that CSN and CVRD of Brazil, the French giant Usinor, and Thyssen/Krupp were among those who were interested in the possibility of taking over Bethlehem. In March 2002, Guy Dolle, chief executive of the large new European group, Arcelor, formed by an amalgamation of three existing firms (Usinor, Arbed, and the Spanish company Aceralia), announced that his firm might try to buy control of ailing operations in order to get a foothold in the American market. Bethlehem seemed receptive to such interest, Miller having revealed that its preferred restructuring strategy was to join with strong global companies at each of their plants so as to bring in new capital and technology.[10] In May, the Dolle group approached Bethlehem with the suggestion that the two companies form a joint venture to run Burns Harbor. A key consideration would be reduction in its work force of fifty-five hundred.

In the course of 2002, prospects of a link with Arcelor faded. Instead, by November, Bethlehem was in talks with a new conglomerate formed in February that year to take over, reconstruct, and make money out of bankrupt steel companies. It did so according to a simple prescription, though it was one that would cause loss or suffering to many: purchase companies for fifteen to twenty cents on the dollar, cut their labor forces even more severely than had been done in the past, and insist on "improved" contracts with those workers who were retained. The International Steel Group (ISG) had acquired LTV in April 2002, and in October, it added the failed Acme group headquartered in Chicago. In January 2003, Wilbur Ross, head of ISG, proposed a $1.5 billion acquisition of Bethlehem Steel, and the Bethlehem board approved the sale on 8 February 2003. For the whole company, the purchase price was just double what Bethlehem Steel had paid five years before for Lukens. Three months later, for cash, common stock, and the assumption of its debts, Bethlehem Steel Corporation was brought into ISG and lost its independence.

The new owners of the Bethlehem operations announced they would reduce the work force to eight thousand, just half the level in 1998. They managed to persuade the union to accept a major reduction in the number of job categories. The USWA, which had been unwilling to make new arrangements with Bethlehem Steel because of its deep distrust of the corporation, proved ready to negotiate with the company's new masters. Paralleling its new arrangements with labor, ISG introduced a new, leaner management structure. There would now be three layers of command between the CEO and the shop floor as compared with the eight that Ross said he had inherited.[11]

ISG made clear that it would continue operations at Burns Harbor, which Ross's collaborator, the steel man Rodney Motte, had recognized as the chief prize of the purchase. Motte had previously been vice president of Nucor and general manager of its Hickman, Arkansas, mill. His high regard for this operation vindicated the high claims that Bethlehem had made for it over the years. Sparrows Point was also designated to continue. ISG proposed to close the Steelton works, but the U.S. government would not permit it to do so on grounds of national security. The reason for its intervention was that the modern and efficient melting shop there was capable of casting the large ingots required by Lehigh Forge, now independent, expanding, and undertaking major improvements. Lehigh in turn was needed to provide the forgings for a new generation of larger, faster, deeper-diving nuclear submarines for the U.S. Navy. In this way, more than a century after the military needs of the nation first saved Bethlehem Iron operations, they again proved key to the survival of two units of its oldest former inland plants in eastern Pennsylvania.

On 31 December 2003, the ISG plan of liquidation for Bethlehem became effective, and just a year short of its centenary, the Bethlehem Steel Corporation formally ceased to exist. Its stock had reached a low of five dollars in spring 2000, when Dunham took control, but it closed on that final day at just under one cent. The 136 million shares in the company became valueless.[12] It had been believed that the ISG absorption of Bethlehem Steel would create the biggest steel company in North America. Its size was increased further by the absorption of Weirton Steel in May 2004, but U.S. Steel's acquisition of National Steel and Nucor's large-scale expansion frustrated this hope of national leadership. Then, on 25 October 2004, it was announced that ISG was to join with the other rapidly growing focus of reorganization of the industry, Ispat International, to create what it was claimed would become the world's largest steel company. As these various changes of alignment occurred, neither the government assumption of the burden of "social costs" nor its agreement to provide more protection against foreign steel proved satisfactory for long. Ten months after taking over pensions, the PBGC informed the now almost seventy-five thousand Bethlehem pensioners what payments they could expect. Younger retired workers and those who had hoped to leave after completing thirty years of service were badly disappointed. Shortly thereafter, in response to pressure from the European Union, Japan, and other leading steel producing countries, as well as to an adverse judgment from the World Trade Organization and to protests from major steel using industries and areas at home, the Bush administration withdrew the punitive import duties in early December 2003. They had been expected to apply for up to three years but had been in place only twenty-one months.

In the meantime, the steel industry had entered a period of booming trade. The dollar was now weaker against the euro, so imports from Europe declined. Above all, there was the boost from the unprecedented economic growth and steel demand in China. If this recovery had occurred a year or even months earlier, it might have "saved" the Bethlehem Steel Corporation. According to ISG, by 2004, the former Bethlehem plants were shipping about 9 million tons of products and their revenues amounted to $5 billion. When this upward impetus eventually stalled, it seemed likely that individual Bethlehem properties would be sold one by one. It was symbolic of the depth of the change of circumstances already achieved that soon after taking control, ISG was already trying to find a buyer for the Martin Tower, Bethlehem's former headquarters, which thirty years before had cost $35 million. By 2007, the building was empty and scheduled for conversion into apartments. Perhaps what happened at Sparrows Point was even more eloquent of change in status and reduced circumstances. At the end of the 1950s, its rated steel capacity was 8.2 million tons; by the early twenty-first century, it could make about 3 million tons. In 1975, it employed twenty-eight thousand, but by 2007 its work force was only twenty-four hundred. Its current owner had made no major new outlay on it, and accordingly, workers there welcomed the announcement in February 2007 that the Justice Department would require its sale in order to meet antitrust requirements. A few months later Sparrows Point was sold to Esmark, which, in 2006, had acquired Wheeling-Pittsburgh.[13]

Most of the remaining parts of Bethlehem Steel seem likely to survive in some form, even if under strange names. When the promoters of Saucona Iron or Bethlehem Iron gathered before the Civil War or when, in December 1904, Schwab launched his new Bethlehem Steel Corporation, the future promised expansion for leaders with vision and energy. By the time Lewis Foy addressed those celebrating the corporation's seventy-fifth anniversary, prospects were already less certain, but Bethlehem was still a major industrial concern. Then, over the years, this huge industrial group, which had grown from a single-plant firm with origins in the 1850s, began to shrink as it cast off once important operations. It had finally become a remnant, operating under a succession of alien names. Altogether, it was a sad ending for a company with such a distinguished past.

EPILOGUE

The Roots of Decline

IN SPRING 2004, THE ONE-HUNDREDTH anniversary year of the Bethlehem Steel Corporation that had just been absorbed into the International Steel Group, *Fortune* magazine published an article titled "The Sinking of Bethlehem Steel." It suggested that the process of decline to the company's extinction had taken up almost half its life, that is, the sources of its ultimate collapse can be traced back at least to the mid-1950s, at which time there was little or no outward indication of decay. In 1955, Bethlehem was eighth in the Fortune 500 list of companies, Eugene Grace was in his last years in undisputed command, and output, ranging between 13.0 million and 13.5 million tons of steel shipped, was far higher than ever before. In 1957, the year in which illness finally forced Grace to begin to retire from active control, revenues were a record $2.6 billion. But seen in retrospect, there were already a few disturbing signs. Net income per dollar of sales had reached postwar peaks of 8.5 percent in both 1950 and 1955 and had then started to decline. More ominously, profitability as measured by return on equity (ROE) was low. Things soon worsened. Over sixteen years, beginning in 1958, the average ROE for Fortune 500 companies would be 11.2 percent; Bethlehem averaged 7.5 percent. Steel was no longer a growth or a glamour industry that attracted investors. Even in 1973, a year of record steel output and shipments of products, the Bethlehem ROE was below 9.7 percent. Much later, with severe pruning of the business, this index improved in good years, though there were now many years of often crippling losses. As it slimmed, Bethlehem was hit by heavy costs for plant closures, including severance pay for those laid off and benefits for newly retired workers.

The replacement of outmoded technologies involved abandoning uncompetitive plants, making large-scale investments in new facilities, and updating old ones. These policies were pursued despite the difficulties of the times. For instance, in the years 1982 through 1986, net losses totaled $2.09 billion, but over this period, Bethlehem undertook capital expenditures of $2.05 billion. In many ways, the results of investment on this scale, were, as proudly displayed in the annual report for 1987, spectacular. Costs per ton of products were reduced 24 percent, the tonnage of steel continuously cast rose from 1.6 million to 6.6 million tons, yield of finished products per ton of raw steel improved from 73 to 80 percent, and annual output of finished steel per employee rose from 220 to 410 tons or by 86.4 percent. The last of these transformations owed a good deal to drastic reductions in the work force. In January 1982, Bethlehem had 79,600 employees; by the end of 1987, there were only 34,100. This increased the number of its pensioners and in so doing exposed another long-term weakness.

At the end of 1957, the company had 10,045 pensioners. During that year, its average monthly employment was 164,859. Seventeen years later, at the end of an excellent year, employment was 122,000 and the number of company pensioners had increased to 35,139. By the end of 1987, following the impressive gains in productivity listed above, the work force was down to 34,000, scarcely half the 67,600 pensioners then receiving benefits. Ten years later the respective numbers would be 16,400 and 70,400. By that time, all benefit costs—pension provision, health benefits, and so forth—totaled well over half as much as salaries and wages. They had become a major burden on competitiveness. As such, they were in considerable part a result of a policy error made in earlier years. For many years, industrial companies had considerable freedom as to how they financed their pension plans. At U.S. Steel, it had been decided to contribute largely to the pension fund, list these contributions as deductible expenses, and receive the appropriate tax reductions. Bethlehem opted for a different course. Arguing that money could better be spent on plant modernization, it had, as time would reveal, underfunded its pension plan, even making a public virtue of this contrast with U.S. Steel, claiming it was reflected in product improvement. (In fact, as seen above, for many years Bethlehem had dissipated its capital resources by spreading investment too widely, each plant receiving something, and many projects proving to have only short-term viability.) As the number of pensioners mounted in both companies (the merger talks in late 2001 revealed that the pensioner/worker ratio was in fact marginally worse at U.S. Steel), what was crippling Bethlehem Steel remained a bearable expense at its larger rival.[1]

Most important of all as a barrier to the successful transformation of Bethlehem Steel, as well as to that of much of the rest of the traditional industry, was a more general though less tangible factor, one that began to be discussed under the heading of "legacy" or "inheritance." This was in part material, in part psychological; the latter was probably the more important. Bethlehem was a major steel concern, with an immense amount of plant. It could not readily scrap most of that capacity, for the economy still needed steel. But could steel users have obtained more of it elsewhere, as the drift toward imports seemed to indicate? Understandably, the company and other domestic producers opposed this idea, for a sudden and far-reaching change in this direction would have rendered their assets valueless. Strategically, too, it was probably unacceptable. Moreover, there were human as well as physical assets to be defended —skilled and unskilled workers, management, directors, and those whose investments were tied up in the business. In such circumstances, was it not inevitable that the company would struggle on? In a free enterprise "market" economy, capital and enterprise are able to migrate from one industry and company to others, but in the individual firms into which they are at various times invested, they inevitably become more or less immobile. Both capital and entrepreneurship in that sense become fixed assets. It is unrealistic to expect that those placed in positions to manage and defend those assets should be willing to make them over into something completely different unless they are otherwise faced with absolute collapse. Even then, it probably requires the freer mind-set of those who take over failed enterprises to reshape structures radically enough to make viable what has defeated the efforts of a long-established hierarchy of control. *Fortune* exposed some of this problem when it quoted an interview with Walter Williams: "We were all stuck with our basic steelmaking —just too much to write off and too much to shut down."[2] This was the material obstacle to change: too much legacy in plant. There was another, deeper barrier. Its nature was illustrated by the story of a conversation between a Pan Am executive and Jack Welch, then at General Electric. Asked whether GE might be interested in buying the Pan Am hotel subsidiary, Intercontinental, Welch was said to have responded, "You're selling the wrong business. You should be selling the airline." The Pan Am executive's reply was, "We can't. That's our business."[3] The fact is that industries and great firms are far more than simple business propositions. In that fuller sense, it must be concluded that in the end, the Bethlehem Steel Corporation was a victim of its own illustrious history.

STATISTICAL TABLES

Table A1. Annual pig iron capacities of the largest works
in the anthracite districts, 1857 (thousand tons)

UPPER SUSQUEHANNA DISTRICT	
Pennsylvania Iron works, Danville	24,720
Lackawanna works, Scranton	23,200
LOWER SUSQUEHANNA DISTRICT	
Lebanon furnaces	15,200
SCHUYLKILL DISTRICT	
Phoenixville	16,000
EASTERN GROUP	
Poughkeepsie, NY	16,000
Port Henry, NY	16,000
LEHIGH DISTRICT	
Lehigh Crane, Catasauqua	42,784
Glendon Iron Works	28,440
Allentown Iron Works	25,760
Cooper furnaces, Phillipsburg, NJ	25,760
Thomas furnaces, Hokendauqua	21,280

Source: S. H. Daddow and B. Bannan, *Coal, Iron, and Oil, or the Practical American Miner* (Pottsville, PA, 1866).

Table A2. Rolling mills in the United States, mid-1850s

	Number of mills	Production (tons)
New England	25	68,605
New York		
Rensselaer Co.	3	33,778
Other counties	9	17,050
New Jersey	9	29,796
Pennsylvania		
Eastern counties	46	122,575
Cambria Co.	1	17,808
Allegheny Co.	19	90,779
Other central and western counties	15	22,067
Ohio & Ohio Co., West Virginia	22	75,047
Michigan	2	10,332
Indiana	1	12,000
Missouri (St. Louis Co.)	4	7,050
Delaware & Maryland	10	13,949
Southeast*	20	44,229
Total	186	565,065

Source: Based on J. P. Lesley, *The Iron Manufacturer's Guide to the Furnaces, Forges, and Rolling Mills of the United States* (New York: American Iron Association, 1859), 219–62.
Note: Data for mill numbers and average production of finished iron are from 1855–1857.
*The Southeast designation here includes the states of Kentucky, Virginia, Tennessee, North Carolina, South Carolina, and Georgia.

Table A3. Westward trends in various factors affecting the iron trade
in the late 1850s and 1860s

	1856	1860	1869–1870
PROPORTION OF PIG IRON MADE (%):			
Using Great Lakes iron ore	under 1	9	24 (1869)
Using coke or bituminous coal	8.5	13.3	28.9 (1869)
SHARE OF NATIONAL RAIL MILEAGE (%):			
New England and Mid-Atlantic[1]		33.8	29.2
North-central and west of Mississippi		37.3	49.6
PERCENTAGE GROWTH IN VALUE OF MANUFACTURES, 1860–1870 (%)			
New England and Mid-Atlantic			120
Nine north-central states[2]			257

Source: Based on *BAISA*, 13 July 1870, 353; U. S. Department of Commerce, Census of Manufactures, various years; W. T. Hogan, *An Economic History of the American Iron and Steel Industry*, 5 vols. (Lexington, MA: Lexington Books, 1971):113.
[1] In addition to New York, New Jersey, and Pennsylvania, the Mid-Atlantic includes Maryland, Delaware, the District of Columbia, and West Virginia.
[2] Michigan, Indiana, Illinois, Wisconsin, Minnesota, Iowa, Missouri, Kansas, and Nebraska.

Table A4. Value of manufacturing output by states or groups of states,
1860–1900 (millions of dollars)

	1860	1870	1880	1890	1900
New England	469	1009	1103	1496	1873
New York and New Jersey	455	954	1334	2065	2786
Pennsylvania	290	712	744	1331	1834
Michigan, Minnesota, Wisconsin, Indiana, Illinois	164	533	916	1851	2615
New England, New York, New Jersey, Pennsylvania as % U.S. total					
			59.2	52.2	49.9

Source: U. S. Department of Commerce. Census of Manufactures, various years.

Table A5. Production of pig iron by geographic sections, 1872–1898 (thousand gross tons)

	1872	1880	1885	1890	1895	1898
East[1]	1217	1610	1312	2342	1390	1431
Western Pennsylvania	387	772	1081	2561	3549	4435
Central[2]	849	1502	1874	1956	6019	7787
South[3]	127	238	539	1554	1491	1785

Source: AISA and F. W. Taussig, "The Iron Industry in the United States," *Quarterly Journal of Economics,* 14 February 1900.

[1] Includes New York, eastern Pennsylvania, and New Jersey.

[2] Includes Ohio, Indiana, and Illinois.

[3] Includes Alabama, Georgia, Tennessee, Virginia, and Maryland.

Table A6. Bessemer works and rail mills built to 1876

1864	Wyandotte, Michigan (experimental plant, abandoned 1869)
1865	Troy, New York (experimental at first)
1867	Pennsylvania Steel Company, Steelton, Pennsylvania
1868	Freedom Iron and Steel Company, Lewistown, Pennsylvania (failed 1869)
1868	Cleveland Rolling Mill Company, Cleveland, Ohio
1871	Cambria Iron Company, Johnstown, Pennsylvania
1871	Union Steel Company, Chicago, Illinois
1872	North Chicago Rolling Mill Company, Chicago, Illinois
1873	Joliet Steel Company, Joliet, Illinois
1873	Bethlehem Iron Company, Bethlehem, Pennsylvania
1875	Carnegie, McCandless and Company, Edgar Thomson works, Pittsburgh, Pennsylvania
1875	Lackawanna Iron and Coal Company, Scranton, Pennsylvania
1876	St. Louis Ore and Steel Company, Vulcan works, St. Louis, Missouri

Source: Swank, J. M. *History of the Manufacture of Iron in All Ages* (Philadelphia: The American Iron and Steel Association, 1892), 411.

Table A7. Features of the Bessemer rail trade, 1876–1898

	National output (thousand gross tons)	Avg. price ($ per ton)	Percentage produced by:			
			Bethlehem	E. Thomson	Other Pa mills	Illinois mills
1876	368	59.25	8.2	8.8	32.4	32.4
1880	864	67.50	9.0	11.6	30.7	26.6
1885	964	28.50	13.9	13.1	41.1	28.5
1890	1,871	31.75	8.9	17.8	43.4	28.0
1895	1,300	24.33	5.2	25.0	36.3	25.2
1898	1,978	17.62	1.3	28.4	23.5	27.8

Source: Based on Bethlehem Iron and Carnegie Steel company records and on AISA annual statistical reports.

Table A8. Output of finished products at leading eastern works,
1901 and 1913 (thousand tons)

Company	1901	1913
Bethlehem	18	704
Cambria	467	1,193
Lackawanna	333 (Scranton)	544 (Buffalo)
Pennsylvania/Maryland	515	539 (1911)

Source: Iron Age, 22 October 1914, 951.
Note: Bethlehem's own figure for 1913 was only 606,000 tons.

Table A9. Steel amalgamation under discussion, December 1921

Companies involved in projected merger	Raw steel capacity (thousand net tons)	% of U.S. total
Midvale Steel and Ordnance	3,241	5.7
Lackawanna Steel	2,061	3.6
Youngstown Sheet and Tube	1,680	3.0
Republic Iron and Steel	1,562	2.8
Inland Steel	1,120	2.0
Steel and Tube of America	1,008	1.8
Brier Hill Steel	672	1.2
Total	11,344	20.1
OTHER LEADING COMPANIES		
United States Steel	25,424	45.0
Bethlehem Steel	3,603	6.4
Jones and Laughlin	2,957	5.2
Colorado Fuel and Iron	1,275	2.3
Others	11,894	21.0
GRAND TOTAL	56,497	100.0

Source: Iron Age, 8 December 1921, 1492.

Table A10. Bethelehem steel shipments by major categories, 1930 and 1955 (million tons)

	1930	1955
HEAVY PRODUCTS		
Structurals	1.90	2.65
Plates	0.90	1.40
Rails	1.10	0.65
Other	0.85	0.55
Total	4.75	5.25
LIGHTER PRODUCTS		
Sheet and strip	c.0.20	4.40
Black plate and tinplate	0.25	1.35
Wire rods, wire, and wire products	0.35	0.95
Pipe	0.25	0.68
Bars	1.40	2.75
Total	2.45	10.13
GRAND TOTAL ALL PRODUCTS	7.20	15.38

Source: Bethlehem Steel Corporation. 25 Years Debenture Prospectus, April 1963.

Table A11. Bethlehem Steel Corporation production of crude steel by plants
in the Northeast, 1940 and 1959 (thousand net tons)

	1940	1959	% Increase
Sparrows Point	3,490	5,363	53.7
Lackawanna	2,732	3,791	38.8
Bethlehem	1,796	2,119	18.0
Johnstown	1,667	1,522	-8.7
Steelton	693	812	17.2
Total	10,378	13,607	31.1

Source: Bethlehem Steel, quarterly reports.

Table A12. Estimated labor costs as a percentage of sales for leading American, European, and Japanese steel companies, 1957 and 1960

	1957	1960
Bethlehem Steel	38.1	42.8
U.S. Steel	42.2	46.0
Republic	35.1	38.6
National	30.7	33.5
August Thyssen	10.6	10.6
Usinor	17.3	15.9
Colvilles	17.1	17.4
Fuji	12.4	14.9
Yawata	12.2	11.2
Nippon	16.4	16.1

Sources: USWA International Affairs Department, April 1959, and International Metal Workers Federation, report, May 1962.

Table A13. Annual capital spending and receipts from asset sales at Bethlehem Steel Corporation, 1985–1995 ($millions)

	Capital spending	Receipts from asset sales	Major assets sold
1985	322	115	In part from sale of Seattle plant
1986	228	386	Kusan, Tull, Buffalo Tank, Lane Metal, Met-Mex Penoles, Beth. Int. Eng., part of Homer Research Labs
1987	153	88	Coal in eastern Kentucky, Beth. Supply Div., surplus land at plants
1988	304	47	Penn. limestone quarries, remaining Kentucky coal, Michigan dolomite, rail axle plant
1989	421	38	Beaumont shipyard, wire rope operations
1990	488	73	Two of the four Great Lakes ore carriers, etc.
1991	564	84	Freight car division, etc.
1992	329	125	Coal reserves and wire mill from Bar, Rod, and Wire Division
1993	327	15	
1994	445	32	Mainly remaining assets of Bar, Rod, and Wire Division
1995	267	18	
1996	259	8	
1997	228	192	Iron Ore Co. of Canada, High Power Mountain, and steel related sales
1998	328	309	Largely Lukens peripheral businesses
1999	557	184	Mainly Lukens stainless activities

Source: Based on Bethlehem Steel, annual reports.

Table A14. Bethlehem Steel output of structurals, plate, rails, sheet/tin mill products
1980, 1985, 1991–1999 (thousand net tons)

	Structurals	Plate	Rails	Sheet and tin mill products
1980	1,163	1,230	n.a.	3,169
1985	791	694	n.a.	3,649
1991	745	1,089	n.a.	4,054
1992	870	1,205	254	5,356
1993	766	1,230	324	5,689
1994	620	1,300	259	6,122
1995	602	1,360	287	5,940
1996	334	1,340	307	6,121
1997	114*	1,340	378	6,249
1998	-	1,940	382	5,679
1999	-	1,760	227	5,975

Source: Based on Bethlehem Steel, annual reports.

Note: The figures given here understate the tonnages involved because the percentages of total net sales from which they are calculated refer to *all* Bethlehem sales, including those other than finished rolled steel. They do, however, provide a reasonably satisfactory guide to proportionate tonnages of each product and a satisfactory indication of year to year changes.

* Production of structurals ceased March 1997.

Table A15. Bethlehem Steel Corporation statistics of operations,
employment, and finances, 1905–1999

	Steel capacity (thousand net tons)	Steel production (thousand net tons)	% operating	Steel shipped (thousand net tons)	Avg. employees	Revenues ($millions)	Net income (loss) ($millions)
1905	213	115	54.2	55	4,882	14.7	2.4
1906	213	136	63.8	112	5,755	17.5	0.8
1907	280	182	65.1	132	7,110	28.4	1.6
1908	571	373	65.3	214	5,703	16.8	0.4
1909	571	556	97.4	415	8,783	22.3	0.8
1910	571	538	94.2	404	11,034	26.3	2.0
1911	739	636	86.1	460	11,802	30.2	2.0
1912	739	733	99.1	525	11,965	33.9	2.1
1913	950	834	87.9	606	15,032	44.5	5.1
1914	1,109	670	60.4	460	15,586	47.7	5.6
1915	1,109	820	74.0	580	22,064	147.6	17.8
1916	1,897*	1,847	97.3	1,301	47,013	217.9	43.6
1917	2,866	2,565	89.5	1,900	64,772	301.9	27.3
1918	3,228	2,608	80.0	1,817	93,964	452.2	15.9
1919	3,340	1,843	55.2	1,270	81,695	283.8	15.4
1920	3,396	2,286	67.3	1,663	65,105	275.8	14.5
1921	3,396	1,033	30.4	806	36,435	151.7	10.3
1922	3,999*	2,527	63.2	1,868	33,816	134.8	4.6
1923	7,821*	5,332	68.2	3,978	62,350	276.8	14.4
1924	8,512	4,949	58.1	3,623	57,049	246.6	8.9
1925	8,512	5,986	70.3	4,291	60,098	276.6	13.9
1926	8,512	6,902	81.3	4,828	66,072	308.4	20.2
1927	8,512	6,262	73.6	4,448	61,978	275.2	15.8
1928	8,848	7,256	82.0	5,082	62,039	297.9	18.6
1929	8,960	8,224	91.8	5,837	64,316	350.1	42.2
1930	9,643*	5,953	61.7	4,342	60,993	265.4	23.8
1931	9,643	3,718	38.6	2,826	49,564	190.5	0.1
1932	10,685	1,808	16.9	1,496	50,807	105.7	(19.4)
1933	10,483	2,940	28.0	2,071	49,657	126.1	(8.7)
1934	10,483	3,655	34.9	2,602	63,645	173.8	0.6
1935	10,483	4,177	39.8	2,832	66,619	198.7	4.3
1936	10,483	6,713	64.0	4,636	79,686	294.1	13.9
1937	10,483	8,142	77.7	5,778	98,775	424.5	31.8
1938	11,247	4,873	43.3	3,368	82,680	271.9	5.3
1939	11,247	7,959	70.8	5,535	95,029	414.9	24.6
1940	11,469	10,705	93.3	7,663	118,439	603	49

Table A15. (continued)

	Steel capacity (thousand net tons)	Steel production (thousand net tons)	% operating	Steel shipped (thousand net tons)	Avg. employees	Revenues ($millions)	Net income (loss) ($millions)
1941	11,981	12,155	101.5	8,972	165,678	962	34
1942	12,700	12,452	98.0	8,922	238,272	1,498	25
1943	12,900	13,016	100.9	9,188	289,232	1,906	32
1944	12,900	13,262	102.8	9,461	260,481	1,750	36
1945	12,900	11,832	91.7	8,546	202,095	1,329	35
1946	12,900	10,012	77.6	7,285	143,732	792	42
1947	12,900	12,807	99.3	9,403	132,557	1,035	51
1948	13,800	13,411	97.2	9,993	144,670	1,315	90
1949	14,200	12,597	88.7	9,217	131,183	1,271	99
1950	15,000	15,116	100.8	10,933	136,146	1,445	123
1951	16,000	16,406	102.5	12,139	152,578	1,799	106
1952	16,800	14,116	84.0	10,290	153,357	1,701	91
1953	17,600	17,663	100.4	12,713	157,380	2,095	134
1954	18,500	13,810	74.6	10,227	135,784	1,667	133
1955	19,100	18,821	98.5	13,554	144,853	2,115	180
1956	20,000	18,322	91.6	13,199	150,126	2,343	161
1957	20,500	19,123	n.a.	13,536	164,859	2,625	191
1958	n.a.	13,393	n.a.	9,686	140,474	2,024	138
1959	n.a.	14,257	n.a.	10,268	126,874	2,079	117
1960	n.a.	15,941	n.a.	11,419	138,344	2,209	121
1961	n.a.	14,944	n.a.	10,045	128,000	2,057	122
1962	n.a.	14,677	n.a.	10,391	122,000	2,097	89
1963	n.a.	16,109	n.a.	10,987	120,000	2,116	102
1964	n.a.	19,436	n.a.	12,762	121,000	2,265	148
1965	n.a.	21,032	n.a.	14,319	130,000	2,601	150
1966	n.a.	21,275	n.a.	13,849	133,000	2,692	171
1967	n.a.	20,525	n.a.	13,056	131,000	2,619	130
1968	n.a.	20,372	n.a.	14,394	131,000	2,863	160
1969	n.a.	21,768	n.a.	14,481	130,000	2,928	156
1970	n.a.	20,586	n.a.	13,838	130,000	2,935	90
1971	n.a.	17,439	n.a.	12,577	116,000	2,969	139
1972	n.a.	18,334	n.a.	12,494	109,000	3,114	135
1973	n.a.	23,702	n.a.	16,627	118,000	4,138	207
1974	n.a.	22,281	n.a.	16,256	122,000	5,381	342
1975	22,742	17,489	76.9	11,865	113,000	4,977	242
1976	23,531	18,872	80.2	12,829	105,000	5,248	168
1977	22,204	16,609	74.8	12,405	100,000	5,370	(448)

	Steel capacity (thousand net tons)	Steel production (thousand net tons)	% operating	Steel shipped (thousand net tons)	Avg. employees	Revenues ($millions)	Net income (loss) ($millions)
1978	21,544	18,808	87.3	13,075	94,500	6,185	225
1979	22,403	19,401	86.6	13,436	97,700	7,137	276
1980	21,487	14,998	69.8	11,081	89,200	6,743	121
1981	22,088	16,721	75.7	11,572	83,800	7,298	211
1982	22,103	10,521	47.6	8,154	66,900	5,260	(1,470)
1983	21,644	10,692	49.4	8,744	52,800	4,898	(163)
1984	17,997	12,166	67.6	8,925	51,400	5,392	(112)
1985	17,605	10,440	59.3	8,792	44,500	5,118	(196)
1986	16,001	10,417	65.1	8,470	37,500	4,333	(153)
1987	15,990	11,545	72.2	9,361	34,400	4,620	174
1988	16,009	12,855	80.3	10,303	32,900	5,489	403
1989	16,006	12,181	76.1	9,779	30,500	5,251	246
1990	16,065	10,924	68.0	8,865	29,600	4,899	(463)
1991	15,907	10,022	63.0	8,376	27,500	4,318	(767)
1992	16,000	10,544	65.9	9,062	24,900	4,008	(449)
1993	11,500	10,303	89.6	9,016	20,700	4,323	(266)
1994	11,500	9,817	85.4	9,262	19,900	4,819	80
1995	11,500	10,449	90.9	8,986	19,500	4,867	180
1996	10,500	9,447	90.0	8,782	17,800	4,679	(309)
1997	10,500	9,559	91.0	8,802	16,400	4,631	281
1998	11,300*	10,191	90.2	8,683	15,900	4,478	120
1999	11,300	9,406	83.2	8,416	15,500	3,915	(183)

Source: Bethlehem Steel, annual reports.

* Indicates a year of important steel acquisitions, bringing in additional capacity. Figure shown is therefore average capacity for year, in contrast to the usual practice of showing capacity as of 1 January.

From 1940, revenues and net income are recorded to the nearest $1 million.

CHAIRMEN AND PRESIDENTS OF THE BETHLEHEM STEEL CORPORATION, 1904–2003

CHAIRMEN

1916–1939	Charles Michael Schwab
1945–1957	Eugene Gifford Grace
1960–1964	Arthur B. Homer
1964–1970	Edmund Fible Martin
1970–1974	Stewart Shaw Cort
1974–1980	Lewis Wilson Foy
1980–1986	Donald H. Trautlein
1986–1992	Walter F. Williams
1992–2000	Curtis H. Barnette
2000–2001	Duane R. Dunham
2001–2003	Robert S. Miller

PRESIDENTS

1904–1916	Charles Michael Schwab
1916–1945	Eugene Gifford Grace
1945–1960	Arthur B. Homer
1960–1964	Edmund Fible Martin
1964–1970	Stewart Shaw Cort
1970–1974	Lewis Wilson Foy
1974–1977	Frederic W. West
1978–1980	Richard F. Schubert
1980–1986	Walter F. Williams
1992–1999	Roger P. Penny
1999–2000	Duane R. Dunham
2001–2002	Duane R. Dunham

NOTES

Introduction

1. H. N. Casson, *The Axioms of Business*, 3rd ed. (London, 1925), 9, 182.

2. E. H. Chamberlain, *The Theory of Monopolistic Competition* (Cambridge, MA: Harvard University Press, 1956).

3. F. Redlich, "'New' and Traditional Approaches to Economic History and Their Interdependence," *Journal of Economic History* 25, no. 4 (December 1965): 480–95.

Chapter 1. *The Early Years and the Decline of the Anthracite Iron Industry*

1. Quoted in F. W. Taussig, *The Tariff History of the United States*, 8th ed. (New York: G. P. Putnam's Sons, 1931), 128.

2. *Niles Register*, 2 August 1834, 386.

3. H. M. Jenkins, *Pennsylvania: Colonial and Federal*, vol. 4 (Philadelphia: Pennsylvania Historical Publishing Association, 1904), 89, 90; *Niles Register*, 2 August 1834, 286.

4. *Niles Register*, 12 January 1833, 316

5. *Niles Register*, 7 July 1827, 310; 10 January 1835, 315. See also L. Metz, "The Arsenal of America: A History of Forging Operations of Bethlehem Steel," *Canal History and Technology Proceedings* 11 (March 1992): 233–94.

6. Ibid., 24 January 1825, 262.

7. Ibid., 10 October 1840, 96; C. D. H. Stapleton, *The Transfer of Early Industrial Technology to America* (Philadelphia: American Philosophical Society, 1987), 173–76.

8. Professor Wilson, Report on the New York Exhibition, xxxvi, 1854. British Parliamentary Papers, London.

9. *Journal of the Franklin Institute*, 3rd ser., 12 (1846): 131; L. Metz, conversation with author, March 2007.

10. See also S. W. Roberts on the early history of the Lehigh Coal and Navigation Company in *Bulletin of the American Iron and Steel Association* (hereafter *BAISA*), 21 May 1875; W. Firmstone, "Sketch of Early Anthracite Furnaces," *BAISA*, 8 and 15 January 1875; O. Williams, "Fifty Years of Anthracite Pig Iron Making," *BAISA*, 10 July 1889; "Fifty Years of Anthracite Pig Iron," *BAISA*, 12 February 1890; S. Thomas, "Reminiscences of the Early Anthracite Pig Iron Industry," *BAISA*, 1 August 1900. On this period see also C. L. Bartholomew and L. E. Metz, *The Anthracite Iron Industry of the Lehigh Valley* (Easton, PA, 1988); L. Metz, "The Arsenal of America: A History of Forging Operations of Bethlehem Steel," *Canal History and Technology Proceedings* 11 (March 1992): 233–94.

11. U.S. Dept. Commerce, *Historical Statistics of the United States* (Washington, DC: GPO, 1960), 427.

12. J. L. Ringwalt, *Development of Transportation Systems in the United States* (Philadelphia, 1888), 132; J. P. Lesley, *The Iron Manufacturer's Guide to the Furnaces, Forges, and Rolling Mills of the United States* (New York: American Iron Association, 1859); P. Temin, *Iron and Steel in Nineteenth-Century America: An Economic Enquiry* (Cambridge, MA: MIT Press, 1964), tables C-6, C-13; S. H. Daddow and B. Bannan, *Coal, Iron, and Oil or the Practical American Miner* (Pottsville, PA, 1866), 698.

13. *Iron Age*, 2 January 1896, 52; F. W. Taussig, "The Iron Industry in the United States," *Quarterly Journal of Economics* (February 1900): 145.

14. N. M. Butler quoted in *AISI Yearbook* (1930), 527.

15. Temin, *Iron and Steel in Nineteenth-Century America*, table C-3.

16. *Iron Age*, 13 January 1887.

17. *Quarterly Journal of Economics* 3 (1888–1889): 499; Temin, *Iron and Steel in Nineteenth-Century America*, 201–206.

18. American Iron and Steel Association (hereafter AISA), *Directory of the Iron and Steel Works of the United States and Canada* (1908); Metz conversation with author, March 2007.

19. E. B. Leisenring to J. K. Taggart, 23 December 1887, Hagley Library, Wilmington, Delaware (hereafter HL), file 1764; Metz conversation with author, March 2007.

20. E. V. d'Invilliers, "The Iron Mines and Limestone Quarries of the Great Valley in 1886," *Annual Report of the Geological Survey of Pennsylvania for 1886* (Harrisburg, 1887), 1416.

21. R. Ackerman, "On the Iron Manufacture of the United States," *Iron* (UK), 21 July 1877, 67, and 28 July 1877, 98.

22. J. T. Whiting, "Microscopic and Petrographic Studies of Blast Furnace Materials," *AISI Yearbook* (1938), 58; A. Sahlin in J. S. Jeans, *American Industrial Conditions and Competition* (London: British Iron Trade Association, 1902), 404, 405; Work Projects Administration, *Technology, Employment and Output per Man in Iron Mining* (Philadelphia: Bureau of Mines, Dept. Interior, 1940), 208.

23. *BAISA*, 1 June 1892.

24. Ibid., 10 January 1896, 1 March 1906.

25. Ibid., 10 March 1896, 1 April 1896. For later changes in the industry, see list of works dismantled since 1904 in AISA, *Directory of the Iron and Steel Works of the United States and Canada* (1908).

Chapter 2. *The Establishment and Growth of Iron and Steel Making in Bethlehem*

1. A. Cotter, *The Story of Bethlehem Steel* (New York: Moody, 1916); J. Fritz, *The Autobiography of John Fritz* (New York: Wiley, 1912), quoted in W. R. Yates, ed., *Bethlehem of*

Pennsylvania: The Golden Years (Bethlehem: Bethlehem Book Committee, 1976); *National Cyclopedia of American Biography, s.v.* John Fritz; L. Metz, *John Fritz* (Easton, PA: Center for Canal History and Technology, 1987), 20.

2. W. H. Jaques, "Description of the Works of the Bethlehem Iron Company," *Proceedings of the U.S. Naval Academy* 15 (1889).

3. R. H. Sayre to J. Fritz, 1 May 1860, National Canal Museum, Easton, Pennsylvania (hereafter NCM); A. Wolle to J. Fritz, 7 May 1860, NCM; Metz, "Arsenal of America," 257.

4. Fritz, *Autobiography,* 139–41; Bethlehem Steel Company booklet, *The Properties and Plants of the Bethlehem Steel Corporation,* 1925.

5. Bethlehem Iron Company minutes, 4 December 1864, HL.

6. Ringwalt, *Development of Transportation Systems,* 198; Temin, *Iron and Steel in Nineteenth-Century America,* app.; Bethlehem Iron Company minutes, 17 July 1865, 9 August 1865, 13 September 1865, HL.

7. V. S. Clark, *History of Manufactures in the United States* (New York: McGraw-Hill, 1929), 2:75; *Guide Book of the Lehigh Valley Railroad and Its Several Branches and Connections* (Philadelphia: J. B. Lippincott, 1873), 42, 43.

8. S. L. Goodale, *Chronology of Iron and Steel* (Cleveland: Penton, 1931), 161.

9. Fritz, *Autobiography,* 150, 151; L. Metz, *John Fritz,* 24, 25.

10. J. Fritz, "Progress in the Manufacture of Iron," American Society of Mechanical Engineers, 1 December 1896, quoted in *BAISA,* 1 January 1897; *Pittsburgh Evening Chronicle,* 1 September 1871; R. W. Hunt at dedication of the John Fritz Laboratory, Lehigh University, 1910, quoted in *BAISA,* 1 August 1910.

11. *BAISA,* 15 October 1873. On this period see especially Metz, "Arsenal of America," 237–42.

12. *BAISA,* 19 July 1871.

13. Ibid., 10 September 1875; A. Holley and L. Smith in *Engineering* (UK), 19 April 1878, 295.

14. Fritz, *Autobiography,* 162–65.

15. U.S. Dept. Commerce, *Historical Statistics of the United States* (1960), 428.

16. *BAISA,* 29 December 1869.

17. Ibid., 7 May 1873.

18. AISA, Report of the American Iron and Steel Association for 1874, 54, 57.

19. *BAISA,* 15 October 1873.

20. Edgar Thomson works construction data sheets quoted in J. F. Wall, *Andrew Carnegie* (New York: Oxford University Press, 1970), 318.

21. *Iron* (UK), 28 October 1876, 559.

22. Bethlehem Iron Company minutes, various dates, HL; Yates, *Bethlehem of Pennsylvania,* 115; Clark, *History of Manufactures in the United States,* 2:328.

23. Bethlehem Iron Company minutes, 22 June 1875, 27 June 1876, 26 June 1877, 25 June 1878, HL; Ringwalt, *Development of Transportation Systems,* 210.

24. *BAISA,* 28 May 1874; Ringwalt, *Development of Transportation Systems,* 210.

25. *Journal of the Iron and Steel Institute* (UK) (hereafter *JISI*), no. 1 (1913): 485.

26. A. Carnegie to J. Fritz, 8 December 1877, quoted in Wall, *Andrew Carnegie,* 336.

27. *Engineering and Mining Journal* (hereafter *EMJ*), 8 January 1876, 33; 9 September 1876, 172; Yates, *Bethlehem of Pennsylvania,* 116; Bethlehem Iron Company minutes, 11 September 1872, 9 October 1872, 28 January 1880, HL.

28. Bethlehem Iron Company minutes, 13 November 1872, 12 November 1873, 26 September 1877 (first quote), 25 June 1878 (second quote), HL.

29. Ibid., 26 March 1879, 24 June 1879, HL.

30. F. Ellis, *History of Northampton County, Pennsylvania* (Philadelphia and Reading: P. Fritts, 1877); Holley and Smith, in *Engineering* (UK), 28 October 1881, 427.

31. Clark, *History of Manufactures in the United States,* 2:291.

32. AISA, *Directory of the Iron and Steel Works of the United States and Canada* (1890).

33. Fritz, *Autobiography,* 192; A. Sahlin in Jeans, *American Industrial Conditions and Competition,* 400.

34. A. Holley and L. Smith, "Works of the Bethlehem Iron Company," seventh in a series on American iron and steel works in *Engineering* (UK), 24 August 1877, 139.

35. Fritz, *Autobiography,* 150–53, 161.

36. Clark, *History of Manufactures in the United States,* 2:63–65; Holley and Smith, "Works of the Bethlehem Iron Company," 139.

37. Fritz, *Autobiography,* 162–65, 184; *Iron Age,* 24 January 1889; see also B. E. V. Luty, "Changes in the American Iron Industry since the Iron and Steel Institute Meeting of 1890," *JISI,* no. 2 (1904): 416–25.

Chapter 3. *Failure in Commercial Steels, 1880–1899*

1. Goodale, *Chronology of Iron and Steel,* 196, 216.

2. E. C. Potter, "Rails, Past, Present and Future," address to Western Railway Club, Chicago, reported in *Iron Age,* 17 February 1898, 14; *Pittsburgh Dispatch,* 25 November 1893.

3. H. U. Faulkner, *American Economic History* (New York: Harper, 1960), 520.

4. *Iron* (UK), 22 December 1882, 529.

5. E. B. Leisenring to J. K. Taggart, 23 December 1887, HL, file 1764.

6. Goodale, *Chronology of Iron and Steel,* 192, 212; D. Brody, *Steelworkers in America: The Nonunion Era* (Cambridge, MA: Harvard University Press, 1960), 11.

7. Bethlehem Iron Company minutes, 16 June 1880, 26 June 1880. HL.

8. Ibid., 28 June 1881, 27 June 1882, HL.

9. Bethlehem Iron Company annual meeting report, 26 June 1883, HL.

10. Ibid., 10 June 1884, HL.

11. Ibid., 23 June 1885, HL.

12. *Bethlehem Times,* 24 June 1885, quoted in *BAISA,* 1 July 1885.

13. Bethlehem Iron Company annual meeting report, 22 June 1886, HL; W. W. Thurston to A. Carnegie, 30 December 1885, U.S. Steel archives, Pittsburgh and Annandale, Pennsylvania (hereafter USS).

14. Bethlehem Iron Company annual meeting reports, 28 June 1887, 26 June 1888, 25 June 1889, HL.

15. *BAISA,* 22 July 1891.

16. Bethlehem Iron Company annual meeting report, 26 June 1894, HL.

17. F. W. Leinbach to A. Carnegie, 21 December 1893, vol. 23, Andrew Carnegie Papers, Library of Congress (hereafter AC/LC).

18. Bethlehem Iron Company annual meeting reports, 27 June 1893, 26 June 1894, 25 June 1895, 23 June 1896, HL.

19. Ibid., 22 June 1897, 28 June 1898, 27 June 1899, HL.

20. J. Greenhough and H. G. Prout, "Railways," *Encyclopedia Britannica* (1902), 131, 132, 140.

21. Evidence to Stanley Committee of the U.S. House of Representatives investigating United States Steel Corp., cited in *Iron Age,* 17 August 1911, 367.

22. Fritz, *Autobiography,* 173–75; *EMJ,* 22 May 1886, 369; *BAISA,* 23 June 1886.

23. H. Grey to J. Fritz, 28 December 1897; Union Bridge Company to J. Fritz, 17 January 1898, John Fritz Papers, NCM.

24. M. G. Mulhall, *The Dictionary of Statistics* (London: Routledge, 1899), 415, 532, 801.

25. H. H. Campbell, *The Manufacture and Properties of Iron and Steel* (New York: Hill Publishing, 1907), 442, 443.

26. D. B. Tyler, 35, 46, 47; C. H. Cramp comments in Report of the Industrial Commission, vol. 14, 1901.

27. Bethlehem Iron Company minutes, 8 November 1894, HL; C. M. Schwab to H. C. Frick, 20 December 1894. Henry Clay Frick Papers, Archives of Industrial Society, University of Pittsburgh (hereafter HCF).

28. Bethlehem Iron Company minutes, 30 January 1895, HL.

29. *Iron Age,* 21 January 1897, 3.

30. Bethlehem Iron Company annual meeting report, 28 June 1898, HL.

31. Carnegie Steel Company minutes, 11 January 1898, 1 February 1898, AC/LC.

32. Bethlehem Iron Company minutes, 25 January 1899, HL.

33. Carnegie Steel Company minutes of Board of Managers, 10 January 1899, AC/LC 60.

34. Bethlehem Iron Company annual meeting report, 27 June 1899, HL; Jeans, *American Industrial Conditions and Competition,* 141, 199.

35. Jeans, *American Industrial Conditions and Competition,* 176, 555; Fritz, *Autobiography,* 176.

Chapter 4. *Armaments and Ores*

1. Bethlehem Iron Company, "A Statement concerning the Price of Armor Plate and Congressional Action on the Subject" (South Bethlehem, 1898), 9; *BAISA*, 7 November 1883; see also W. R. von Aaken, "Notes on a Half Century of United States Naval Ordnance 1880–1939" (Washington, 1939), 2, 5.

2. Yates, *Bethlehem of Pennsylvania*, 74; summary of Gun Foundry Board report, *BAISA*, 20 February 1884, 4 June 1884, 11 June 1884.

3. H. F. J. Porter, "How Bethlehem Became Armament Maker," *Iron Age*, 23 November 1922, 1339–41; Fritz, *Autobiography*, 182–84; W. H. Jaques, "Description of the Works of the Bethlehem Iron Company," *Proceedings of the U.S. Naval Institute* 15, no. 4 (1889): 538–39.

4. Bethlehem Iron Company minutes, 30 October 1885, HL.

5. Ibid., 25 November 1885, HL. See also Metz, "Arsenal of America," 246, 247, 258; Bethlehem Iron Company minutes, 16 April 1886, HL.

6. R. W Davenport, "Production in the United States of Heavy Steel Engine, Gun and Armor Plate Forgings," *Transactions of the Institute of Naval Architects and Marine Engineers* 1 (1893): 70–90.

7. Bethlehem Iron Company annual meeting report, 22 June 1886, HL.

8. Goodale, *Chronology of Iron and Steel*, entry for 1888; *BAISA*, 7 April 1891, 20 January 1897.

9. E. G. Grace, *Iron Age*, 31 October 1912, 1032.

10. *BAISA*, 5 January 1887, 12 January 1887; Bethlehem Iron Company annual meeting report, 28 June 1887, HL.

11. Bethlehem Iron Company annual meeting report, 25 June 1889, HL; Jaques to Fritz, 26 October 1887; J. M. Gledhill to Fritz, 14 December 1887; O. F. Liebert to Fritz, 5 May 1890, all in Fritz Papers, NCM.

12. Bethlehem Iron Company annual meeting report, 25 June 1889, 24 June 1890, 23 June 1891, HL; Bethlehem Iron Company minutes, 20 January 1891, HL.

13. *EMJ*, 26 April 1890, 477; Metz, "Arsenal of America," 259–62; W Jaques, "Description of the Works of the Bethlehem Iron Company"; *Harpers Weekly* 14 (March 1891), quoted in *BAISA*, 15 April 1891; Bethlehem Iron Company, "A Statement concerning the Price of Armor Plate," 11.

14. Bethlehem Iron Company minutes, 24 September 1890, HL; obituary of Jaques, *Transactions of the Institute of Naval Architects and Marine Engineers* (1916): 217; Bethlehem Iron Company minutes, 8 November 1894, HL.

15. *EMJ*, 26 January 1889, 94.

16. Bethlehem Iron Company minutes, 27 September 1893, HL; Metz conversation with author, February 2007; R. Linderman to Fritz, 14 February 1895 and letter of Fritz, 25 September 1895, Fritz Papers, NCM.

17. Bethlehem Iron Company minutes, 25 November 1896, HL; Bethlehem Iron Company annual meeting report, 27 June 1899, HL.

18. Bethlehm Iron Company, "A Statement concerning the Price of Armor Plate," 11; Bethlehem Iron Company annual meeting report, 28 June 1898, HL.

19. Bethlehem Iron Company minutes, 23 June 1896; annual reports for 1891–1895, HL.

20. "Armor Plate Inventory 1896," report from Navy Department, 18 July 1896, in Benjamin Franklin Cooling Papers, box 1592, HL.

21. R. H. Sayre to Secretary of the Navy, 6 April 1897, in Bethlehem Iron Company, "A Statement concerning the Price of Armor Plate," 29; R. P. Linderman in ibid., 30, 31.

22. H. C. Frick to A. Carnegie, 7 September 1891, HCF.

23. Bethlehem Iron Company minutes, 27 March 1895, 29 May 1895. HL.

24. BAISA, 10 October 1894.

25. Bethlehem Iron Company annual meeting report, 25 June 1895, HL; BAISA, 10 May 1896; Bethlehem Iron Company annual meeting reports, 23 June 1896, 22 June 1897, 27 June 1899, HL.

26. Wall, Andrew Carnegie, 648.

27. Quoted in S. Whipple, unpublished notes of interviews with Charles M. Schwab, 1935–1936, 135, HL and NCM.

28. H. C. Frick to C. A. Stone, 19 December 1894, HCF.

29. A. Carnegie to R. P. Linderman, 25 February 1895, quoted in Wall, Andrew Carnegie, 649.

30. Engineer (UK), 24 April 1898, 387.

31. Bethlehem Iron Company minutes, 8 November 1894; Bethlehem Iron Company, annual meeting report, 28 June 1898, HL.

32. BAISA, 20 March 1896.

33. "The Armor Plate Question," BAISA (1897): 10; BAISA, 1 December 1897.

34. BAISA, 15 February 1898.

35. EMJ, 3 August 1889, 99.

36. BAISA, 25 December 1889, 21 October 1891.

37. Ibid., 7 April 1891; Hope quoted in L. Metz, John Fritz, 34.

38. Quoted in Jeans, American Industrial Conditions and Competition, 178–79.

39. AISA, Directory of the Iron and Steel Works of the United States and Canada (1898).

40. Bethlehem Iron Company annual meeting reports, 1896–1898; Bethlehem Iron Company minutes, 30 November 1898, HL.

41. A. Carnegie, "Steel Manufacture in the United States in the Nineteenth Century," New York Evening Post, 12 January 1901.

42. Iron Age, quoted in U.S. Bureau of Statistics, Monthly Survey of Commerce and Finance, August 1900, 203.

43. Clark, History of Manufactures in the United States, 2:197, 198.

44. Ibid.; U.S. Bureau of Statistics, Monthly Survey of Commerce and Finance, August 1900, 205.

45. AISA, Annual Report for 1888, 30, 31; 1890, 36; *Iron Age,* 30 January 1901, 20.

46. Clark, *History of Manufactures in the United States,* 2:64, 65; Iron and Steel Institute, *The Iron and Steel Institute in America,* 83; Goodale, *Chronology of Iron and Steel,* 228; A. Sahlin in Jeans, *American Industrial Conditions and Competition,* 406–408.

47. Clark, *History of Manufactures in the United States,* 2:196.

48. *Iron Age,* 8 September 1904, 31.

49. H. M. Howe, "Iron and Steel," *Encyclopedia Britannica* (1911), 811.

50. Bethlehem Iron Company minutes, 31 March 1880, HL.

51. Ibid., 25 February 1880, HL.

52. Bethlehem Iron Company annual meeting report, 27 June 1882, HL.

53. Iron and Steel Institute, Iron and Steel Institute in America 1890, 77; Fritz, *Autobiography,* 162–65, 184.

54. Bethlehem Iron Company annual meeting report, 26 June 1883; Bethlehem Iron Company minutes, 27 June 1882, HL.

55. *BAISA,* 4 April 1883; *EMJ,* 24 March 1883, 157.

56. Bethlehem Iron Company annual meeting reports, 23 June 1885, 22 June 1886, 24 June 1890, HL.

57. U.S. Geological Survey, *Bulletin and Annual Report* 3 (1894): 57.

58. Bethlehem Iron Company annual meeting report, 25 June 1896, HL; *BAISA,* 20 August 1897.

59. *BAISA,* 6 April 1887.

60. Campbell, *The Manufacture and Properties of Iron and Steel,* 442.

Chapter 5. *Reorganizing and Redirecting Bethlehem Steel*

1. Jaques, "Description of the Works of the Bethlehem Iron Company," 538–39.

2. Obituary of R. W. Davenport, *Transactions of the American Society of Mechanical Engineers* 25 (1904): 1127, 1128.

3. Sayre diary quoted in Yates, *Bethlehem of Pennsylvania,* 182.

4. A. Hewitt to R. H. Edmonds, 17 September 1896, in A. Nevins, "Selected Writings of AS Hewitt" (New York: Columbia University Press, 1937), 359, 361, 362; *Iron Age,* 6 January 1898, 19.

5. A. Carnegie quoted in *Iron Age,* 17 November 1898, 10.

6. A. Carnegie to Carnegie Steel Company, 5 April 1898, AC/LC 50; A. Carnegie to Carnegie Steel Company, 28 September 1899, quoted in *Iron Age,* 5 June 1913, 1396.

7. Jeans, *American Industrial Conditions and Competition,* 178, 179. See also ibid., 5.

8. *Iron Age,* 6 January 1898, 19 (emphasis added).

9. *JISI*, no. 1 (1909): 482.

10. H. C. Frick to A. Carnegie, 9 September 1891, HCF.

11. H. C. Frick to Carnegie Steel managers, 5 May 1898, USS.

12. Bethlehem Iron Company minutes, 29 March 1899, 24 April 1899, HL.

13. *BAISA,* 10 July 1901; Bethlehem Steel Company minutes, 16 August 1901, 27 August 1901, HL; Memoir of R.W. Davenport (1905), 78.

14. *BAISA,* 10 September 1901; Yates, *Bethlehem of Pennsylvania,* 192, 193; Cotter, *The Story of Bethlehem Steel,* 6.

15. E. B. Aldefer and H. E. Michl, *The Economics of American Industry* (New York: McGraw-Hill, 1942), 124; *BAISA,* 10 September 1895; Mitchell, *Abstract of British Historical Statistics,* 1962.

16. Jeans, *American Industrial Conditions and Competition,* 254.

17. T. R. Heinrich, "Industrial Restructuring and the Decline of the Cramp Shipyard of Philadelphia, 1900–1927," paper presented at the fourth annual conference of the Industrial Working Group on Industrial Restructuring, Osaka, Japan, 25–27 August 1993, 13; *National Cyclopedia of American Biography,* 5 (1907), *s.v.* W. Cramp.

18. A. Charles of Camden in *Shipbuilder* (UK), spring 1908. For an excellent summary of shipbuilding, see Clark, *History of Manufactures in the United States,* 3:141ff.

19. Heinrich, "Industrial Restructuring and the Decline of the Cramp Shipyard," 13; K. Warren, *Triumphant Capitalism: Henry Clay Frick and the Industrial Transformation of America* (Pittsburgh: University of Pittsburgh Press, 1996), 288–94.

20. *BAISA,* 10 September 1901, 1 February 1902.

21. C. M. Schwab quoted in New York News Bureau, 19 October 1904, quoted in R. Hessen, *Steel Titan: The Life of Charles M. Schwab* (New York: Oxford University Press, 1975; reprint, Pittsburgh: University of Pittsburgh Press, 1991), 167.

22. Bethlehem Steel, brochure of ordnance material, 1904.

23. C. M. Schwab, "What May Be Expected in the Steel and Iron Industries," *North American Review* 534 (May 1901): 655, 661, 664; Morris, *The Tycoons* (New York: Times Books, 2005), 295.

24. Quoted in "Forging America: The Story of Bethlehem Steel," supplement to the *Morning Call* (Allentown, PA), December 2003, 29.

25. E. G. Grace, "C. M. Schwab," paper presented at the first C. M. Schwab Memorial Lecture, American Iron and Steel Institute, New York, 21 May 1947, 24, 27.

26. C. M. Schwab quoted in *BAISA,* 10 May 1907; Bethlehem Steel minutes of directors meetings, 18 June 1906, 17 July 1906, 4 September 1906, 27 November 1906, NCM.

27. E. C. Sholes and T. C. Leary, "Eugene G. Grace," in *Iron and Steel in the Twentieth Century,* ed. B. E. Seeley (New York: Bruccoli Clark Layman / Facts on File, 1994), 173.

28. C. M. Schwab, letter to Bethlehem Steel Corp. stockholders, 2 March 1931, NCM.

29. Grace quoted *Iron Age,* 22 April 1917, 1017.

30. Bethlehem Steel Corp. minutes of special meeting of directors, 7 June 1907; minutes of special stockholders meeting, 1 November 1909, NCM.

31. Bethlehem Steel Corp. minutes of special meeting of directors, 11 January 1910, NCM.

32. Bethlehem Steel Corp. director's minutes, 19 September 1912, NCM.

33. *Iron Age,* 16 May 1912, 1215.

34. A. Johnston to E. Grace, 19 July 1906, HL.

Chapter 6. *War Materiel, Ships, and Commercial Products, 1904–1914*

1. Bethlehem Steel Corp. minutes of special meeting of directors, 19 January 1905, NCM.

2. *BAISA,* 1 April 1905; Bethlehem Steel Corp. minutes of directors meeting, 3 September 1907, NCM.

3. Cotter, *The Story of Bethlehem Steel,* 30, 45; Bethlehem Steel Corp. annual report, 1913.

4. Bethlehem Steel Corp. annual reports for 1906, 1907; *Iron Age,* 25 May 1905, 168; *Times* (UK), 7 December 1906.

5. Bethlehem Steel Corp. annual report for 1908; *EMJ,* 29 October 1910, 885.

6. Clark, *History of Manufactures in the United States,* 3:68. For a useful general discussion of open hearth and Bessemer steel, see H. H. Campbell, *The Manufacture and Properties of Structural Steel* (New York: Scientific Publishing, 1896), chap. 12.

7. Notebooks of E. G. Grace as general superintendent, NCM.

8. *BAISA,* 1 November 1910.

9. U.S. Congress, tariff hearings before the Committee on Ways and Means of the House of Representatives, 60th Congress, 1908–1909, vol. 2, metals and manufactures of metals, 1828; Temin, *Iron and Steel in Nineteenth-Century America,* app.

10. H. N. Casson interview with E. H. Gary, quoted in *BAISA,* 15 November 1906.

11. *Iron Age,* 2 February 1905, 401; *BAISA,* 15 February 1905, 1 March 1905.

12. Bethlehem Steel Corp. annual report for 1905; annual statement reported in *Iron Age,* 3 May 1906, 1479; *BAISA,* 15 March 1906.

13. E. G. Grace notebooks, NCM.

14. Bethlehem Steel Corp. annual report for 1907; *EMJ,* 20 June 1908, 1252.

15. W. H. Sellew, *Steel Rails: Their History, Properties, Strength and Manufacture, with Notes on the Principles of Rolling Stock and Track Design* (New York: Van Nostrand, 1913), 382; AISI annual statistics.

16. Bethlehem Steel Corp. annual reports for 1909, 1910.

17. Ibid., 1909; *BAISA,* 1 November 1910.

18. *Iron Age,* 31 October 1912, 1034.

19. U.S. Congress, tariff hearings, 1908–1909, vol. 2, 1659.

20. *Iron and Coal Trades Review* (UK), 20 January 1896.

21. L. H. Miller, "Steel Construction," *AISI Yearbook* (1925), 85–95.

22. Recalled in letter from H. Grey to C. M. Schwab, 27 October 1908, HL.

23. Pamphlet of the "H" Column Steel Company, March 1905, HL.

24. Grace, "C. M. Schwab," 50, 51.

25. *Iron Age,* 25 March 1909, 1005; Bethlehem Steel Corp. annual report for 1909, 24.

26. Carnegie Steel Company minutes of directors' meetings, with reports by H. Bope for 14 January 1907, 12 and 19 October 1908, 16 November 1908, 14 February 1910, 19 December 1910, USS.

27. Warren, *Triumphant Capitalism,* 245ff; H. C. Frick Coke Company, minutes, 22 November 1899, USS. On the economics of supply for iron making materials, including coke, see tabulation of freight rates by H. S. Snyder of Bethlehem Steel in 1907, file 1770, HL.

28. *Iron Age,* 30 April 1914, 1083.

29. *Coal and Coke Operator,* 17 February 1910, 110, 3 March 1910, 16 June 1910, 38, 8 July 1912; *EMJ,* 6 August 1910, 276.

30. *Coal and Coke Operator,* 19 February 1914, 121, 9 April 1914, 238.

31. *EMJ,* 16 February 1907, 355; memo of A. J. Johnston, HL; Taussig, *The Tariff History of the United States,* 236, 300.

32. *Iron Age,* 23 January 1913, 249; Goodale, *Chronology of Iron and Steel,* 253; *EMJ,* 23 October 1915, 694.

33. Bethlehem Steel Corp. annual report for 1907.

34. U.S. Geological Survey, *Bulletin and Annual Report* 3 (1894): 66, 67; letter to H. S. Snyder, 26 November 1909, HL.

35. *EMJ,* 18 October 1913.

36. U.S. Geological Survey, *Bulletin and Annual Report* 3 (1894): 66, 67; DSIR Advisory Council (UK), 1918; *BAISA,* 15 October 1909; Vattier in *JISI,* no. 2 (1912): 334; Harold Blakemore and Clifford T. Smith, eds., *Latin America: Geographical Perspectives* (London: Methuen, 1971), 534, 535; *JISI,* no. 1 (1913): 703; Bethlehem Steel Corp. annual report for 1912, 19.

37. C. M. Schwab to A. Johnston, 21 November 1908, HL; Bethlehem Steel Corp. annual report for 1908.

38. Clark, *History of Manufactures in the United States,* 3:64.

Chapter 7. *Wartime Activity, Expansion, and Mergers, 1914–1923*

1. Bethlehem Steel Corp. annual meeting report, 7 April 1914, NCM.

2. *Iron Age,* 19 April 1917, 991.

3. U.S. Steel, finance committee minutes, 3 June 1914, USS; M. I. Urofsky, *Big Steel and the Wilson Administration* (Columbus: Ohio State University Press, 1969), 90, 91; *New York Times,* 6 August 1914.

4. Urofsky, *Big Steel and the Wilson Administration,* 90, 91; Schwab quoted in *Iron Age,* 8 April 1915.

5. Investors Public Service, Inc., 8 June 1917.

6. Schwab quoted in *Iron Age,* 8 June 1916, 1396.

7. Goodale, *Chronology of Iron and Steel,* 265; Bethlehem Steel Corp. annual reports for war years; *Iron Age,* 1 November 1917, 1036. There is an interesting but confusing record of Bethlehem's war work in J. K. Mumford, "The Story of Bethlehem Steel 1914–1918," Bethlehem Steel Corp., 1943, unpublished manuscript, chap. XI, "Weapons of War," NCM.

8. *Iron Age,* 21 January 1915, 201; *New York Times,* 31 December 1915; *Iron Age,* 24 February 1916, 496.

9. Cotter, *The Story of Bethlehem Steel,* 35.

10. E. G. Grace, quoted in *Iron Age,* 22 August 1918, 472.

11. *Iron Trade Review,* 30 September 1915, 611, 612; G. G. Eggert, "William Ellis Corey" in *Iron and Steel in the Twentieth Century,* ed. B. E. Seeley (New York: Facts on File, 1994) 96, 97.

12. H. C. Frick to A. Carnegie, 9 September 1891, HCF.

13. *BAISA,* 23 January 1901; Jeans, *American Industrial Conditions and Competition,* 300; memo on plant costs and incomes c. 1909, HCF.

14. *BAISA,* 2 March 1892, 9 November 1892; F. W. Wood of Maryland Steel, reported in *Iron Age,* 16 October 1913, 859.

15. *New York Times,* 6 October 1915, 16 October 1915, 27 October 1915, 30 October 1915; *Iron Age,* 23 December 1915.

16. *Iron Trade Review,* 10 June 1915, 1177, 1178.

17. Urofsky, *Big Steel and the Wilson Administration,* 92; *Iron Age,* 24 February 1916, 1961; *Moody's Industrial Manual; EMJ,* 16 October 1915, 654.

18. C. M. Schwab to Stockholders, 2 March 1931, quoted in W. T. Hogan, *An Economic History of the American Iron and Steel Industry* (Lexington, MA: Lexington Books, 1971), 543–44; *Iron Age,* 24 February 1916.

19. Bethlehem Steel Corp. minutes of directors meeting, 18 July 1916, NCM; *Iron Age,* 20 July 1916, 146; *EMJ,* 22 July 1916, 202; Cotter, *The Story of Bethlehem Steel,* 39, 41; *EMJ,* 6 January 1917, 37; *Iron Age,* 22 August 1918, 472.

20. Bethlehem Steel Corp. minutes of directors meeting, 17 October 1916, NCM.

21. Bethlehem Steel Corp. annual report for 1918.

22. Ibid., annual reports for 1919, 1924.

23. Ibid., annual report for 1920.

24. *BAISA,* 10 April 1902, 50; memo on operations in rival plants to U. S. Steel c. 1909, HCF; *Iron Age,* 14 April 1910; Sholes and Leary, "Lackawanna Steel Company," 267, 268; Hogan, *An Economic History of the American Iron and Steel Industry,* 900.

25. *Iron Age,* 18 May 1922, 1369.

26. Note on the formation of the Midvale Steel and Ordnance Company in Investors Public Service, Inc., 8 June 1917.

27. Bethlehem Steel Corp. minutes of special directors meeting, 24 November 1922, NCM.

28. Dewing, *Financial Policy of Corporations,* 172; Bethlehem Steel Corp. records.

29. Bethlehem Steel Corp. annual report for 1922.

Chapter 8. *Bethlehem Steel in the 1920s Boom*

1. AISI, *Directory of the Iron and Steel Works of the United States and Canada,* 1920.

2. Bethlehem Steel Corp. annual report for 1924; minutes of quarterly meetings of directors, 25 July and 24 October 1929, NCM.

3. Committee on Recent Economic Changes, *Recent Economic Changes: Report of the Committee* (New York: McGraw-Hill, 1929), 54, 59.

4. Grace quoted in Hogan, *An Economic History of the American Iron and Steel Industry,* 917.

5. *Iron Age,* 18 December 1924, 1597.

6. W. H. Voskuil, *Minerals in Modern Industry* (New York: John Wiley, 1930), 186; *EMJ,* 6 January 1917, 89, 22 September 1917, 540; *Blast Furnace and Steel Plant* (January 1931): 111; C. M. Schwab, interview in *Iron Age,* 7 January 1926, 11.

7. *Iron Age,* 3 November 1927, 1230.

8. Bethlehem Steel Corp., *The Properties and Plants of Bethlehem Steel* (Bethlehem, 1925).

9. Bethlehem Steel Corp. annual report for 1929, March 1930.

10. G. A. V. Russell, "Notes on visit to the United States and Canada, February–April 1941," United Steel Companies, Sheffield, England, 1941, 52, 129.

11. *Iron Trade Review,* 31 January 1928; *Iron Age,* 1 January 1925.

12. *Iron Trade Review,* 13 December 1928, 1542; Goodale, *Chronology of Iron and Steel,* passim.

13. Schwab quoted in Whipple, unpublished notes, 1935–1936, 170; Grace quoted in Bethlehem Steel Corp. annual report for 1924.

14. *Iron Age,* 21 August 1924, 448; *New York Times,* 2 April 1930, 38; Hogan, *An Economic History of the American Iron and Steel Industry,* 907; Bethlehem Steel, *The Properties and Plants,* preface; *New York Times,* 21 October 1928.

15. Grace to Bethlehem Steel Corp. special directors meeting, 24 November 1922, NCM. On rationalization at Bethlehem Steel, see also annual reports and *Fortune,* April 1941, 146.

16. *New York Times,* 2 December 1925.

17. *Bethlehem Review,* 15 October 1926, 3.

18. *Iron Age,* 1 January 1925, 10–17, 1 January 1931, 100.

19. U.S. Congress, Transport Investigation and Research Board, *Economics of Iron and Steel Transportation* (Washington, DC: GPO, 1945), 125; *Iron Trade Review,* 3 January 1929, 83; Goodale *Chronology of Iron and Steel,* 310; *Fortune,* September 1930, 124, 126.

20. *Iron Age,* 30 May 1912, 1348, 1349, 18 December 1924, 1603, 15 October 1925, 1032, 12 February 1931, 583, 11 August 1938, 56; *Fortune,* December 1930, 136.

21. *Iron Age,* 12 February 1931, 583.

22. Ibid., 30 April 1931, 1468.

23. Hogan, *An Economic History of the American Iron and Steel Industry,* 906, 907.

24. *Blast Furnace and Steel Plant* (January 1928), 63, 64, 73. On the growth of Ohio River steel transport in the 1920s, see *Iron Trade Review,* 9 May 1929, 1273, 1274.

25. *Iron Age,* 14 August 1924; *New York Times,* 13 November 1931; A. R. Burns, *The Decline of Competition* (New York: McGraw-Hill, 1936), 89n.2.

26. Burns, *The Decline of Competition,* 89.

27. On the general history of western plant promotion and failure, see annual reports of AISA (AISI); *JISI,* no. 1 (1882): 268, no. 2 (1882): 726, 727, no. 1 (1888): 414, no. 2 (1922): 304, 305.

28. Report of the United States Industrial Commission, vol. 13, 1901, 456; *Iron Age,* 20 May 1915, 1129.

29. *Iron Age,* 24 May 1923, 1481.

30. Ibid., 13 August 1925, 445; H. G. Moulton, C. S. Morgan, and A. L. Lee, *The St. Lawrence Navigation and Power Project* (Washington, DC: Brookings Institution, 1929), app. E, 373, 374.

31. *Iron Age,* 14 June 1917, 1464, 1 July 1920, 10, 27 November 1924, 1417.

32. Ibid., 22 August 1912, 406.

33. Ibid., 15 March 1928, 749, 24 May 1928, 1473.

34. Ibid., 30 November 1922; *Iron and Coal Trades Review* (UK), 15 December 1922, 883; *Iron Age,* 20 August 1925, 477.

35. *Iron Age,* 20 March 1930, 876; C. E. Fraser and G. F. Doriot, *Analyzing Our Industries* (New York: McGraw-Hill, 1932), 249–60 and passim.

36. Bethlehem Steel Corp. annual report for 1931. The details of the hearings were fully covered each day in the *New York Times.*

Chapter 9. *Retrenchment, Reconstruction, and War, 1930–1945*

1. H. W. Broude, *Steel Decisions and the National Economy* (New Haven: Yale University Press, 1963), 56, 57, 107; *Fortune,* April 1941, 140.

2. Bethlehem Steel Corp. minutes of special directors meetings, 25 July and 24 October 1929, NCM; *New York Times,* 24 January 1930, 34, 2 April 1930, 38.

3. *Iron Age,* 14 April 1932, 910; *JISI,* no. 1 (1933): 54.

4. Fraser and Doriot, *Analyzing Our Industries,* 271.

5. *Iron and Coal Trades Review* (UK), 7 April 1933, 541; *Fortune,* March 1936, 176, 177.

6. Bethlehem Steel Corp. annual reports for 1930s, and notes to tables of operating data.

7. Russell, "Notes on visit to the United States and Canada," 35, 36.

8. Hogan, *An Economic History of the American Iron and Steel Industry,* 1120.

9. *Fortune,* April 1941; *Iron Age,* 7 February 1935, 37, 14 October 1937, 328. On East Coast outlets for sheet, see *Iron Age,* 6 January 1938, 74; on shipments to the West Coast, see U.S. Congress, *Economics of Iron and Steel Transportation,* 46, 111; on basing point changes, see E. G. Grace to Temporary National Economic (Monopoly) Committee (TNEC), part 19, 10611, 10612.

10. *Iron Age,* 22 April 1937, 82.

11. Russell, "Notes on visit to the United States and Canada," 9.

12. A good general survey is in *Iron & Steel Engineer,* April 1938.

13. AISI, *Directory of the Iron and Steel Works of the United States and Canada,* 1920, 1938.

14. *Iron Age,* 7 March 1940, 87; E. G. Grace to T. R. Johns of the Industrial Collieries Corporation, Johnstown, 1 December 1939, Pattee Library, Penn State University, University Park, PA.

15. *Fortune,* April 1941.

16. Grace quoted in "When 'The Steel' Falls Silent," *Morning Call* (Allentown, PA), supplement, November 1995, 8.

17. Bethlehem Steel Corp. report to stockholders, 1 March 1946, and annual reports for 1914–1919, 1940–1945, NCM.

18. *Fortune,* April 1941, 65; *National Cyclopedia of American Biography, s.v.* E. G. Grace; "Bethlehem Ship," *Fortune,* August 1945.

19. *Iron Age,* 16 February 1939, 84.

20. *Bethlehem Review,* December 1939, 5.

21. *Fortune,* August 1945; *National Cyclopedia of American Biography, s.v.* Grace; *Iron Age,* 6 January 1944, 149; "Forging America,"73; *Fortune,* April 1945, 125.

22. Bethlehem Steel Corp. annual report for 1939.

23. *Fortune,* April 1941, 150.

24. *Iron Age,* 22 April 1940, 79.

25. Theo L. Hills, *The St. Lawrence Seaway* (London: Methuen, 1959), 70. See *Iron Age,* 5 August 1943, 96, 97, for a slightly different account of the wartime destruction of the ore fleet.

26. "Forging America," 71.

27. *Iron Age,* 9 October 1941, 97.

28. Ibid., 3 February 1944, 91.

29. Ibid., 1 November 1945, 100.

30. *Fortune,* February 1958, 51. An informative insight into this situation is provided in E. F. Martin, *Bethlehem Steelmaker: My 90 Years in Life's Loop* (Bethlehem: BMS Press, 1992), 81, 92–95.

Chapter 10. *Material Supplies, Growth, and Competition in the East, 1945–1957*

1. A. Johnston to E. G. Grace, 22 August 1945, file 1770, HL.

2. *Fortune,* May 1953, 103; A. Homer to Senate Subcommittee on Anti-Trust and Monopoly, 14 June 1955, in U.S. Congress, Senate Judiciary Committee, *Hearings before the Subcommittee on Antitrust and Monopoly* (Washington, DC: GPO, 1957–1958), 6, 10.

3. A. Homer to Senate Subcommittee on Anti-Trust and Monopoly, 1957, 664.

4. *Fortune,* April 1941.

5. H. G. Cordero, ed., *Iron and Steel Works of the World* (London: Quin Press, 1952) and 2nd ed., 1957.

6. *Iron & Steel Engineer* (January 1955), 117, 118, February 1947, 77. On the postwar ore situation generally, see "Iron Ore Dilemma," *Fortune,* December 1945.

7. See H. E. Johnson, "World Iron Ore," paper presented at the annual meeting of the American Iron Ore Association, Minneapolis, 1964.

8. On early developments in Quebec/Labrador, see the article by W. H. Durrell in *Iron & Steel Engineer* (November 1952), 87; Johnson, "World Iron Ore," passim; Hills, *The St. Lawrence Seaway.*

9. W. K. Buck, "Iron Ore in Canada," Canadian Government Department of External Affairs, Paper 81, March 1956; *Bethlehem Review,* March 1959, 4, 6; *Iron Age,* 9 February 1950, 110; *New York Times,* 15 November 1958.

10. Bethlehem Steel Corp. annual report for 1959; *Times* (London), 27 October 1969.

11. *Fortune,* May 1945, 272; Blakemore and Smith, eds., *Latin America,* 534; United Nations, *Survey of World Iron Ore Resources: Occurrence, Appraisal, and Use* (New York, UN Dept. Economic and Social Affairs, 1955), 24; *Bethlehem Review,* March 1955, 10, March 1957, 12.

12. *Iron Age,* 8 June 1944, 98, 1 November 1945, 100, 21 October 1948, 118, 3 March 1949, 149; *Fortune,* April 1962, 242.

13. *Iron Age,* 7 January 1954, 248.

14. U.S. Congress, House of Representatives, Subcommittee on the Study of Monopoly Power (Washington, DC: GPO, 1950), Study of Monopoly Power, part 2A, 847.

15. Bethlehem Steel Corp. minutes of directors meeting, 22 January 1951, NCM.

16. *Iron Age,* 1 February 1951, 122, tabulates the steel industry expansion schemes.

17. Ibid., 1 February 1962, 122; *Fortune,* March 1953, 104; W. Isard and R. E. Kuene,

"The Impact of Steel upon the New York–Philadelphia Industrial Region," *Review of Economics and Statistics* 35 (November 1953): 289–301; *New York Times*, 27 January 1956, 33, 36; *Iron & Steel Engineer* (February 1959).

18. J. B. Lovis, conversation with author, March 2007; *Time*, 11 November 1957, 60.

19. Bethlehem Steel Corp. minutes of directors meeting, 31 October 1957, NCM.

20. A. Homer quoted in *Iron Age*, February 1958.

21. Martin, *Bethlehem Steelmaker*, 82; personal recollections in October 2003 of a long-term employee of the Bethlehem works who was about forty when Grace retired.

22. Bethlehem Steel Corp. minutes of special directors meeting, 31 August 1959; minutes of directors meeting, 28 July 1960.

23. *Fortune*, February 1958, 51.

24. AISI, *Directory of the Iron and Steel Works of the United States and Canada*, 1957, 1964; A. Homer in *Bethlehem Review*, March 1958, 1; J. Strohmeyer, *Crisis in Bethlehem: Big Steel's Struggle to Survive* (Bethesda, MD: Adler and Adler, 1986). Martin, *Bethlehem Steelmaker*, 80–104, contains many insights into the circumstances of the top management at Bethlehem Steel in this difficult period.

Chapter 11. *Steel Making in the Far West and Midwest*

1. *Iron & Steel Engineer* (October 1957), 95–99; *Iron Age*, 10 April 1958, 79; Kaiser Steel, annual report on western steel consumption; *Fortune*, April 1963, 214.

2. Grace quoted in *Iron Age*, 2 August 1945, 100; see also *Iron Age*, 8 November 1945, 96; Fuller quoted in *Iron Age*, 1 November 1945, 80.

3. M. Barloon in *Harper's Monthly*, May 1947, 149.

4. T. H. Kirkham and W. S. Walker, "Report of a tour made of certain steelworks in the United States and Canada" (UK), 1946, 14.

5. "Bethlehem Steel in California," pamphlet c. 1966.

6. *Steel*, 14 May 1962, 24; *Iron & Steel Engineer* (January 1964), D-4; *Bethlehem Review*, March 1960, 6.

7. *Steel*, 17 January 1966, 29; *Iron Age*, 20 January 1966, 51; Lovis conversation, March 2007.

8. *Iron Age*, 2 January 1947, 75.

9. Ibid., 17 May 1956, 51–53.

10. Testimony of C. H. Weikel, assistant to the president of Bethlehem Steel, reported in *New York Times*, 30 April 1958, 53; *Fortune*, April 1962, 246.

11. *New York Times*, 9 May 1958, 33, 36. For an independent assessment of the increasing advantages of the Chicago area for steel making, see H. W. Johnson, vice president of Inland Steel, in *Blast Furnace and Steel Plant* (March 1957), 333.

12. Martin, *Bethlehem Steelmaker*, 135.

13. G. R. Reiss in *Youngstown Vindicator*, 16 September 1965.

14. A. Homer to Senate Subcommittee on Anti-Trust and Monopoly, 14 June 1955, in U.S. Congress, Senate Judiciary Committee, 6, 10; Grace quoted in *New York Times*, 12 December 1956, 1; Hogan, *An Economic History of the American Iron and Steel Industry*, 1689–92.

15. A. Homer to Senate Subcommittee on Anti-Trust and Monopoly, 14 June 1955, 8; *Iron Age*, 20 December 1956, 38, 39; *New York Times*, 17 September 1957, 47, 18 April 1958, 32; report of Proceedings, U.S. District Court, Southern District of New York; *Harvard Business Review*, March–April 1959, 16.

16. Bethlehem Steel Corp. minutes of directors meeting, 11 December 1956, NCM; Martin, *Bethlehem Steelmaker*, 136.

17. Bethlehem Steel Corp. annual reports for 1958, 1959.

18. Martin, *Bethlehem Steelmaker*, 134.

19. *Fortune*, June 1957, 145, April 1962, 246.

20. Evidence of W. Adams and J. B. Dirlam to Senate Finance Committee, quoted in *Mining Journal* (UK), 14 June 1968, 482; *Iron Age*, 14 July 1967, 101.

21. *New York Times*, 7 January 1961, 22.

22. Jones and Laughlin, annual report for 1963.

23. *Iron & Steel Engineer* (October 1971), B-18; L. Metz in conversation with the author; *Blast Furnace and Steel Plant* (June 1969), 485.

24. Martin, *Bethlehem Steelmaker*, 138, 139.

25. *Iron & Steel Engineer* (January 1965), D-65, (January 1966), D-47.

26. *American Metal Market*, 10 December 1968, 8, 27 June 1969, 2.

27. Martin, *Bethlehem Steelmaker*, 140–42.

Chapter 12. *Shipbuilding, Steel, and Labor in Bethlehem's Peak Years*

1. M. Borrus, "The Politics of Competitive Economies in the United States Steel Industry," in *American Industry in International Competition: Government Policies and Corporate Strategies*, edited by J. Zysman and L. Tyson (Ithaca: Cornell University Press, 1983), 61.

2. *German International*, August 1958, 23.

3. Broude, *Steel Decisions and the National Economy*, 257, 258; *Steel and Coal* (UK), 1 November 1963, 845.

4. *Blast Furnace and Steel Plant* (June 1964), 527; Bethlehem Steel Corp. minutes of directors meeting, 22 June 1966, and report for second quarter of 1966, NCM.

5. Bethlehem Steel Corp. minutes of directors meeting, 26 and 27 October 1966, NCM.

6. *Blast Furnace and Steel Plant* (April 1965), 326.

7. Ibid., (January 1961), 58.

8. Martin, *Bethlehem Steelmaker*, 121.

9. D. Todd, *Industrial Dislocation: The Case of Global Shipbuilding* (London: Routledge, 1991), 1; S. Donches, conversation with author, March 2007.

10. *Fortune*, April 1962, 106.

11. Bethlehem Steel Corp. annual report for 1962, 4.

12. Ibid., 1972.

13. Todd, *Industrial Dislocation*, 18.

14. Author's conversations with L. Metz in Bethlehem, March 2007.

15. Reuters report, 16 October 2001, the day Bethlehem Steel applied for Chapter 11 bankruptcy protection.

16. Hogan, *An Economic History of the American Iron and Steel Industry*, 1705.

17. Bethlehem Steel Corp. annual report for 1973, 1.

18. *Wall Street Journal*, 7 December 1973.

19. *American Metal Market*, 18 October 1972.

20. Quoted in "Forging America," 95.

21. *Fortune*, January 1976, 107.

22. Bethlehem Steel Corp. annual report for 1977; *Fortune*, 13 February 1978, 130.

23. Bethlehem Steel Corp. annual report for 1974, 2.

24. "Forging America," 92, 93.

25. "Forging America," 83; Hogan, *An Economic History of the American Iron and Steel Industry*, 1686.

26. "Forging America," 86.

27. *Bethlehem Review*, January 1959, 1.

28. Ibid., March 1959, 1; "Forging America," 86.

29. *Metal Bulletin* (UK), 21 June 1971, 44; W. Adams and H. Mueller, "The Steel Industry," chap. 3 of *The Structure of American Industry*, ed. W. Adams, 6th ed. (New York: Macmillan, 1992), 113–14.

30. L. Foy quoted in "When 'The Steel' Falls Silent," November 1995.

31. Bethlehem Steel, *More Than a Livelihood* (film, 1979).

32. Bethlehem Steel Corp. annual report for 1979, 2, 3.

Chapter 13. *Responding to Crises in the 1980s*

1. *Financial Times*, 23 May 1980; author's conversations with retired staff in Bethlehem, March 2007.

2. *A Brief History of Bethlehem Steel Corporation* (Bethlehem, 1963 and c. 1991).

3. *Mining Annual Review*, 1980; *Financial Times*, 9 June 1987.

4. *Economist*, 16 May 1992, 119, 120.

5. *Mining Annual Review*, 1985, 1986.

6. *Chief Executive,* March–April 1989, 46.

7. Quoted in *Iron Age,* 23 November 1967, 68.

8. Strohmeyer, *Crisis in Bethlehem,* 73.

9. *Chief Executive,* March–April 1989, 44; R. Preston, *American Steel: Hot Metal Men and the Resurrection of the Rust Belt* (New York: Prentice Hall, 1991), 12, 13; author's conversations in Bethlehem, March 2007; Bethlehem Steel former executive, correspondence with author, August 2007.

10. "Forging America," 85; see also K. Warren, "Anglo-American Productivity: Early Episodes and an Anniversary in Steel," *Steel Times* (UK), 29 October 1965, 552–53; Bethlehem Steel, *More Than a Livelihood.*

11. *Financial Times,* 19 May 1989.

12. "Forging America," 92; Bethlehem Steel Corp. annual report for 1967, 3.

13. *Financial Times,* 23 May 1980, 17 August 1983; *Mining Annual Review,* 1985, 325; Bethlehem Steel Corp. annual report for 1987, 7.

14. *Financial Times,* 2 October 1985; M. Reutter, *Sparrows Point: Making Steel The Rise and Ruin of American Steel Might* (New York: Summit, 1988), 437; Metz, conversation with author, March 2007.

15. Bethlehem Steel Corp. annual report for 1985, 2.

16. D. Trautlein to Senate Judiciary Committee, 1 July 1983; Trautlein to House Subcommittee on International Economic Policy and Trade, 15 September 1983.

17. Bethlehem Steel Corp. annual report for 1991.

18. Bethlehem Steel Corp. internal memo on capital budgeting, 30 January 1984.

19. First Boston Corporation to Bethlehem Steel, 2 April 1986.

20. Booz Allen report on the situation and prospects of Bethlehem Steel, 1986.

21. *Economist,* 3 February 1990, 79.

22. *33 Metal Producing Industry Magazine,* May 1989.

23. *New York Times,* 29 March 1986; Bethlehem Steel Corp. annual reports.

24. *Financial Times,* 20 November 1981.

25. Bethlehem Steel Corp. annual reports for 1981, 2, and 1982, 2.

26. Ibid., 1986, 3.

27. Ibid., 1985, 8.

28. *Morning Call* (Allentown, PA), 5 and 12 February 1987.

Chapter 14. *Paring Away the Unviable*

1. The author learned of this suggestion in conversations at Bethlehem in March 2007.

2. Cordero, *Iron and Steel Works of the World,* 1974.

3. Thomas E. Leary and Elizabeth C. Sholes, *From Fire to Rust: Business, Technology,*

and Work at the Lackawanna Steel Plant, 1899–1983 (Buffalo: Buffalo and Erie County Historical Society, 1987), 109.

4. Ibid., 131.

5. Bethlehem Steel Corp. annual reports for 1977, 3, 5, and 1981.

6. Ibid., 1977, 1, and 1978.

7. New York Times, 18 March 1983.

8. Morning Call, 29 March 1985; New York Times, 20 April 1985. I am indebted to a former senior planner at Bethlehem Steel for an assessment of Johnstown at this time.

9. Bethlehem Steel Corp. annual report for 1985, 8.

10. Ibid., 1990, 2.

11. Ibid., 1991, 3.

12. Author's conversations in Bethlehem, March 2007.

13. Globe Times (Bethlehem), 4 April 1989.

14. J. B. Lovis, The Final Years: Closure of the Steel Plant at Bethlehem, Pa. (privately printed, 2007).

15. Financial Times, 19 May 1989. See W. T. Hogan, Global Steel in the 1990s (Lexington, MA: D. C. Heath, 1991), 50, on the beam mills at the EAF operations of Northwestern Steel and Wire Company.

16. R. Scholey reported in Daily Telegraph (UK), 2 July 1991. Reported in discussions in Bethlehem March 2007.

17. Morning Call, 3 September 1992; referred to in "The Sinking of Bethlehem Steel," Fortune, 5 April 2004.

18. "Forging America," 105.

19. Bethlehem Review, February 1995, 22.

20. New Steel, February 1997, 9; "Forging America," 108; "When 'The Steel' Falls Silent."

Chapter 15. *Hope and Hope Dashed*

1. Quoted in "When 'The Steel' Falls Silent."

2. Morning Call, 3 September 1992.

3. W. Williams quoted in Fortune, 5 April 2004.

4. Bethlehem Steel Corp. annual report for 1992; Bethlehem Steel/DE, SEC filing, 31 December 1996.

5. "An Executive of Distinction," Pittsburgh Post-Gazette, 5 May 1998; Bethlehem Steel Corp. first-quarter report, 2000.

6. Mini mills were, however, now recognized in fuller statements such as the annual performance returns. There is an excellent and concise description of the position of mini mills in Bethlehem Steel/DE, SEC filing, 31 December 1996. Even in that docu-

ment, the force of the competition they provided was softened: they "provide significant competition in certain product lines" and "are increasingly able to compete directly with producers of higher value products."

7. Hogan, *Global Steel in the 1990s*, 30; *Economist*, 16 May 1992, 119, 120; Bethlehem Steel/DE, SEC filing, 31 December 1996.

8. *Financial Times*, 29 April 1992; *New Steel*, January 1994, 29.

9. Bethlehem Steel Corp. annual report for 1989, 17.

10. Bethlehem Steel Corp. annual report for 1981; *Iron & Steel Engineer* (February 1982), D-3; Bethlehem Steel Corp. annual reports for 1991, 14, and 1995, 15; "Bethlehem Steel" in Moody's Investors Service, *Moody's Industrial Manual* (New York: Moody's Investors Service, 2000).

11. *Bethlehem Review*, February 1995, 24.

12. Bethlehem Steel Corp. fourth-quarter report, 1993; Association of Iron and Steel Engineers (AISE), *Developments in the North American Steel Industry in 2000*, February 2001.

13. Bethlehem Steel Corp. annual report for 1991, 3, 15.

14. Bethlehem Steel/DE, SEC filing, 1999; *New Steel*, September 2001.

15. Author's conversations in Bethlehem, October 2003 and March 2007.

16. Bethlehem Steel Corp. annual report for 1999, 5, 13; survey of steel industry capital spending in *New Steel*, September 2001.

17. Bethlehem Steel Corp. annual reports for 1975, 1990, 1993, and 1999.

18. Steel Dynamics Web site, www.steeldynamics.com; Bethlehem Steel/DE, SEC filing, 31 December 1996.

19. AISE, *Developments in the North American Steel Industry in 2000*, February 2001.

20. *Bethlehem Review*, February 1995, 7.

21. Bethlehem Steel/DE, SEC filing, 1999.

22. Moody's Investors Service, *Moody's Industrial Manual*, 2000.

23. Bethlehem Steel Corp. annual report for 1999.

Chapter 16. *Into the Abyss*

1. "Forging America," 109.

2. Steel Dynamics Web site, "Steel Success Strategies," 19 June 2001, www.steeldynamics.com; Dow Jones, http://www.marketwatch.com, 15 October 2001.

3. Bethlehem Steel Corp. quarterly report, 30 October 2001.

4. Bethlehem Steel Corp. press release. 24 September 2001.

5. R. S. Miller quoted in *Pittsburgh Post-Gazette*, 5 December 2001.

6. R. Crandall quoted in Reuters, 17 December 2001.

7. *Steel Times International*, December 2001–January 2002, June 2002.

8. *Daily Telegraph* (UK), 5 June 2002.

9. *Steel Times International,* February 2002.
10. Ibid., November 2001, 48, March 2002, June 2002.
11. *Fortune,* 5 April 2004.
12. *Morning Call,* 1 January 2004.
13. Ibid., 25 February 2007, 7 April 2007.

Epilogue

1. *Fortune,* 5 April 2004.
2. Williams quoted in ibid.
3. *Fortune,* 5 April 2004.

SELECTED BIBLIOGRAPHY

Archival Collections

Bethlehem Papers. Hagley Library, Wilmington, Delaware.

Bethlehem Papers. National Canal Museum, Easton, Pennsylvania.

Andrew Carnegie Papers. Library of Congress, Washington, D. C.

Benjamin Franklin Cooling Papers. Hagley Library, Wilmington, Delaware.

Henry Clay Frick Papers. Archives of Industrial Society, University of Pittsburgh, Pittsburgh, Pennsylvania.

John Fritz Papers. National Canal Museum, Easton, Pennsylvania.

U.S. Steel Corporation Archives. U. S. Steel Corporation, Pittsburgh, Pennsylvania.

Whipple Papers. Hagley Library, Wilmington, Delaware.

Government Documents

United States Congress. *Hearings before the Joint Economic Committee on Steel Prices, Unit Costs, Profits and Foreign Competition* (Douglas Committee). Washington, DC: GPO, 1963.

———. Transport Investigation and Research Board. *Economics of Iron and Steel Transportation.* Washington, DC: GPO, 1945.

———. House of Representatives Subcommittee on the Study of Monopoly Power. *Study on Monopoly Power.* Washington, DC: GPO, 1950.

———. Senate Judiciary Committee. *Hearings before the Subcommittee on Antitrust and Monopoly.* Washington, DC: GPO, 1957–1958.

United States Department of Commerce. *Historical Statistics of the United States.* Washington, DC: GPO, annual.

United States Department of the Interior. *Minerals Yearbook.* Washington, DC: GPO, annual.

United States Federal Trade Commission. *The United States Steel Industry and Its International Rivals.* Washington, DC: GPO, 1977.

United States Industrial Commission. Reports. 13 vols. Washington, DC: GPO, 1899–1901.

United States Temporary National Economic Committee. *Investigation of Concentration of Economic Power.* Washington, DC: GPO, 1939–1940.

311

Books and Articles

Aaken, Wilbur R. Van. "Notes on a Half Century of United States Naval Ordnance 1880–1939." Washington, D. C.: Self-published, 1939.

Adams, W. "The Steel Industry." Chapter 5 in *The Structure of American Industry,* ed. W. Adams. 3rd ed. New York: Macmillan, 1961.

Adams, W., and H. Mueller. "The Steel Industry." Chapter 3 in *The Structure of American Industry,* ed. W. Adams. 6th ed. New York: Macmillan, 1992.

Aldefer, E. B., and H. E. Michl, *The Economics of American Industry.* New York: McGraw Hill, 1942.

American Iron and Steel Institute (AISI). Annual Statistical Report.

———. *Directory of the Iron and Steel Works of the United States and Canada.* New York: AISI, various years.

———. *Steel at the Crossroads: The American Steel Industry in the 1980s.* Washington: AISI, 1980.

———. *The Steel Import Problem.* New York, 1968.

Armstrong, G. S., and Co. *An Engineering Interpretation of the Economic and Financial Aspects of American Industry.* New York: G. S. Armstrong, 1952.

Auerbach, P. *Competition: The Economics of Industrial Change.* Oxford: Basil Blackwell, 1988.

Barron, C. W. *They Told Barron.* New York: Harper, 1930.

Bartholomew, C. L., and L. Metz. *The Anthracite Iron Industry of the Lehigh Valley.* Easton, PA: Center for Canal History and Technology, 1988.

Blakemore, Harold, and Clifford T. Smith, eds. *Latin America: Geographical Perspectives.* London: Methuen, 1971.

Borrus, M. "The Politics of Competitive Economies in the United States Steel Industry." Chapter 2 in *American Industry in International Competition: Government Policies and Corporate Strategies,* ed. J. Zysman and L. Tyson. Ithaca: Cornell University Press, 1983.

Brody, D. *Steelworkers in America: The Nonunion Era.* Cambridge: Harvard University Press, 1960.

Broude, H. W. *Steel Decisions and the National Economy.* New Haven: Yale University Press, 1963.

Burns, A. R. *The Decline of Competition.* New York: McGraw-Hill, 1936.

Campbell, H. H. *The Manufacture and Properties of Structural Steel.* New York: Scientific Publishing, 1896.

———. *The Manufacture and Properties of Iron and Steel.* New York: Hill Publishing, 1907.

Casson, H. N. *The Romance of Steel.* New York: A. S. Barnes, 1907.

Clark, V. S. *History of Manufactures in the United States.* 3 vols. New York: McGraw-Hill, 1929.

Committee on Recent Economic Changes. *Recent Economic Changes: Report of the Committee on Recent Economic Changes*. New York: McGraw-Hill, 1929.

Cordero, H. G., ed. *Iron and Steel Works of the World*. London: Quin Press, 1952 (1st ed.) and 1957 (2nd ed.).

Cotter, A. *The Story of Bethlehem Steel*. New York: Moody Magazine and Book Company, 1916.

———. *United States Steel: A Corporation with a Soul*. New York: Doubleday Page, 1921.

Daddow, S. H., and B. Bannan. *Coal, Iron, and Oil, or the Practical American Miner*. Pottsville, PA, 1866.

Davenport, R. W. *1905 Memoir*. New York: G. P. Putnam and Sons, 1905.

Dewing, A. S. *The Financial Policy of Corporations*. New York: Ronald Press, 1934.

Ellis, F. *History of Northampton County, Pennsylvania*. Philadelphia and Reading: P. Fritts, 1877.

Faulkner, H. U. *American Economic History*. New York: Harper, 1960.

Ford, Bacon, and Davis. "Reports on the Operations of the United States Steel Corporation." 200 vols. Unpublished. 1936–1938.

"Forging America: The Story of Bethlehem Steel." Supplement. *Morning Call* (Allentown, PA), December 2003.

Fraser, C. E., and G. F. Doriot. *Analyzing Our Industries*. New York: McGraw-Hill, 1932.

Fritz, J. *The Autobiography of John Fritz*. New York: John Wiley, 1912.

Glover, J. G., and W. B. Cornell, eds. *The Development of American Industries*. New York: Prentice Hall, 1941.

Goodale, S. L. *Chronology of Iron and Steel*. Cleveland: Penton Publishing, 1931.

Grace, E.G. "Manufacture of Ordnance at South Bethlehem." *AISI Yearbook* (1912), 175–77.

———. "C. M. Schwab." Paper presented at the first C. M. Schwab Memorial Lecture, American Iron and Steel Institute, New York, 21 May 1947.

Hauck, W. A. "Report on possible steel expansion program as requested by the President." Washington, D. C.: U. S. Office of Production Management, 1941.

———. "Steel Expansion for War." Reprint by *Steel* June 1945.

Hessen, R. *Steel Titan: The Life of Charles M. Schwab*. New York: Oxford University Press, 1975; reprint, Pittsburgh: University of Pittsburgh Press, 1991.

———. "C. M. Schwab." In *Iron and Steel in the Twentieth Century: The Encyclopedia of American Business History and Biography*, ed. B. E. Seeley. New York: Bruccoli Clark Layman, 1994.

Hills, Theo L. *The St. Lawrence Seaway*. London: Methuen, 1959.

Hoerr, J. P. *And the Wolf Finally Came: The Decline of the American Steel Industry*. Pittsburgh: University of Pittsburgh Press, 1988.

Hogan, W. T. *An Economic History of the American Iron and Steel Industry*. 5 vols. Lexington, MA: Lexington Books, 1971.

————. *Global Steel in the 1990s.* Lexington, MA: D. C. Heath, 1991.

Iron and Steel Institute. *The Iron and Steel Institute in America in 1890.* London: Iron and Steel Institute, 1891.

Jane, F. T. *Fighting Ships.* London: Sampson, Low Marston, 1914; reprint, London: David and Charles, 1968.

Jaques, W. H. "Description of the Works of the Bethlehem Iron Company." *Proceedings of the U.S. Naval Institute* 15, no. 4 (1889): 538–39.

Jeans, J. S. *American Industrial Conditions and Competition.* London: British Iron Trade Association, 1902.

Jenkins, H. M. *Pennsylvania: Colonial and Federal.* Vol. 4. Philadelphia: Pennsylvania Historical Publishing Association, 1904.

Jones, E. *The Trust Problem in the United States.* New York: Macmillan, 1922.

Kuchta, D. *Memoirs of a Steelworker.* Easton, PA: Canal History and Technology Press, 1995.

Lamoureux, N. R. *The Great Merger Movement in American Business, 1895–1904.* Cambridge: Cambridge University Press, 1985.

Leary, Thomas E., and Elizabeth C. Sholes. *From Fire to Rust: Business, Technology, and Work at the Lackawanna Steel Plant, 1899–1983.* Buffalo: Buffalo and Erie County Historical Society, 1987.

Lesley, J. P. *The Iron Manufacturer's Guide to the Furnaces, Forges, and Rolling Mills of the United States.* New York: American Iron Association, 1859.

Loomis, C. J. "The Sinking of Bethlehem Steel." *Fortune,* 5 April 2004.

Lovis, J. B. *The Blast Furnaces of Sparrows Point: One Hundred Years of Iron Making on Chesapeake Bay.* Easton, PA: National Canal Museum, 2005.

————. *The Final Years: Closure of the Steel Plant at Bethlehem, Pa.* Privately printed, 2007.

McCallum, E. D. *The Iron and Steel Industry in the United States.* London: P. S. King, 1931.

Martin, E. F. *Bethlehem Steelmaker: My 90 Years in Life's Loop.* Bethlehem: BMS Press, 1992.

Metz, L. *John Fritz: His Role in the Development of the American Iron and Steel Industry and Legacy to the Bethlehem Community.* Easton, PA: Center for Canal History and Technology, 1987.

————. "The Arsenal of America." *Canal History and Technology Proceedings* 11 (March 1992): 233–94.

Miller, L. H. "Steel Construction." *AISI Yearbook* (1925).

Misa, T. *Nation of Steel: The Making of Modern America, 1865–1925.* Baltimore: Johns Hopkins University Press, 1995.

Mitchell, B. R. *Abstract of British Historical Statistics.* Cambridge: Cambridge University Press, 1962.

————. *International Historical Statistics: The Americas and Australasia.* London: Macmillan, 1983.

Morris, C. M. *The Tycoons.* New York: Times Books, 2005.

Mulhall, M. G. *The Dictionary of Statistics.* London: George Routledge, 1899.

Mumford, J. K. "The Story of Bethlehem Steel, 1914–1918." Bethlehem Steel Corp., 1943. Unpublished manuscript.

Paskoff, P. F., ed. "Iron and Steel in the Nineteenth Century." *The Encyclopedia of American Business History and Biography.* New York: Bruccoli Clark Layman, 1989.

Porter, H. F. J. "How Bethlehem became Armament Maker." *Iron Age,* 23 November 1922, 1339–41.

Preston, R. *American Steel: Hot Metal Men and the Resurrection of the Rust Belt.* New York: Prentice Hall, 1991.

Reutter, M. *Sparrows Point: Making Steel—The Rise and Ruin of American Industrial Might.* New York: Summit, 1988.

Ringwalt, J. L. *Development of Transportation Systems in the United States.* Philadelphia, 1888.

Schroeder, G. G. *The Growth of Major Steel Companies, 1900–1950.* Baltimore: Johns Hopkins University Press, 1953.

Seager, H. R., and C. A. Gullick. *Trusts and Corporation Problems.* New York: Harper Brothers, 1929.

Sellew, W. H. *Steel Rails: Their History, Properties, Strength and Manufacture, with Notes on the Principles of Rolling Stock and Track Design.* New York: Van Nostrand, 1913.

Sholes, E. C., and T. C. Leary. "Eugene C. Grace." In *Iron and Steel in the Twentieth Century,* ed. B. E. Seeley. New York: Bruccoli Clark Layman / Facts on File, 1994.

Stapleton, C. D. H. *The Transfer of Early Industrial Technology to America.* Philadelphia: American Philosophical Society, 1987.

Strohmeyer, J. *Crisis in Bethlehem: Big Steel's Struggle to Survive.* Bethesda, MD: Adler and Adler, 1986.

Swank, J. M. *History of the Manufacture of Iron in all Ages.* Philadelphia: American Iron and Steel Association, 1892.

Taussig, F. W. *The Tariff History of the United States.* 8th ed. New York: G. P. Putnam's Sons, 1931.

Temin, P. *Iron and Steel in Nineteenth-Century America: An Economic Enquiry.* Cambridge, MA: MIT Press, 1964.

Tiffany, P. *The Decline of American Steel: How Management, Labor, and Government Went Wrong.* New York: Oxford University Press, 1988.

Todd, D. *Industrial Dislocation: The Case of Global Shipbuilding.* London: Routledge, 1991.

Tyler, D. B. *The American Clyde: A History of Iron and Steel Shipbuilding on the Delaware from 1840 to World War I.* Newark, DE, 1958.

Urofsky, M. I. *Big Steel and the Wilson Administration.* Columbus: Ohio State University Press, 1969.

Voskuil, W. H. *Minerals in Modern Industry.* New York: John Wiley, 1930.

Wall, J. F. *Andrew Carnegie.* New York: Oxford University Press, 1970.

Warren, K. *The American Steel Industry, 1850–1970*. Pittsburgh: University pf Pittsburgh Press, 1988.

———. *Big Steel: The First Century of the United States Steel Corporation, 1901–2001*. Pittsburgh: University of Pittsburgh Press, 2001.

———. *Industrial Genius: The Working Life of Charles Michael Schwab*. Pittsburgh: University of Pittsburgh Press, 2007.

———. *Triumphant Capitalism: Henry Clay Frick and the Industrial Transformation of America*. Pittsburgh: University of Pittsburgh Press, 1996.

"When 'The Steel' Falls Silent." Supplement. *Morning Call* (Allentown, PA), November 1995.

Yates, W.R., ed. *Bethlehem of Pennsylvania: The Golden Years*. Bethlehem: Bethlehem Book Committee, 1976.

INDEX

Bethlehem Steel Corporation *(cont.)*:
plate production in the 1990s, 254–56; progress between 1945–1957 compared with other companies, 159, 160; and the purchase of the Baltimore Sheet and Tin Plate Company in 1916, 111; and the purchase of the Lebanon and Reading works in 1917, 111; and purchase of the Lebanon and Reading works rationalized, 121; and purchase of Williamsport Wire Rope Company in 1937, 138; and rail making reorganization during last years, 253, 254; and rationalization of rail capacity in the 1920s and 1930s, 122, 138; and recession during 1914, 103; and recession during 1958, 164; rescue plan in 1993, 242; run-down and closure, 237–44; and the run-down of interests on the West Coast, 197, 198; and the sale of fabricating capacity for structural steel, 198, 207; and the West Coast during the post–World War II years, 165–69; and the West Coast steel industry in the 1920s, 128–30; and World War I armament orders, 104, 105

British Steel Corporation: and the 1991 plan for cooperation with Bethlehem in reconstruction of structural and rail operations, 241, 242

Burns Harbor, Indiana works: construction of, 173–77; exceptional efficiency of, 186, 268; expansion of in the 1970s, 200; expansion of in the 1990s, 257

Canada, iron ore from: and Bethlehem Iron, 61; and Quebec/Labrador and Marmora, Ontario ore post–World War II, 154, 201, 251, 252

Carnegie, Andrew: comments on Bethlehem operations in 1877, 27; offered stock in Bethlehem Iron in 1893, 36; pessimistic assessment of Bethlehem Steel prospects in 1901, 58, 70

Carnegie Steel Company: and the armor plate trade, 49; collusion with Bethlehem in armor, 52, 53, 55

Catasaqua, Pennsylvania iron works, 7, 8, 14

charcoal: use and limitations as a blast furnace fuel, 5

Chicago, Illinois: as growth area for steel consumption post–World War II, 170, 171

coal: and Bethlehem purchase of the Elkins and Jamison companies in 1919–20, 112; reserves sold in the 1980s and 1990s, 252; situation in the 1920s and early 1930s, 119, 135; supplies for Burns Harbor, 175

Coatesville, Pennsylvania works: in the 1920s, 121

coke: advancement as furnace fuel, 33; for anthracite iron district in the 1870s and 1880s, 12; and byproduct ovens for Bethlehem works, 96, 97

Consolidated Steel Corporation, 1918, 111

continuous casting: Bethlehem's early experiments with, 216; for Burns Harbor and Sparrows Point, 217; for Johnstown, 233; the United States lags in, 207

Cornwall ore banks: in late nineteenth century, 12; the 1970s closure of, 200

Cort, Stewart: chairmanship, 196; reveals expansion plans in 1973, 197

Cramp Shipbuilding Company, Philadelphia, Pennsylvania, 40; development after the 1880s, 74, 75; involvement in Vickers' 1901 bid for Bethlehem Steel, 72; and warships for Russia, 55

Crandall, Robert: on the changing pattern of the U. S. steel industry, 266

Davenport, Russell W.: career at Bethlehem, 68–70, 72; as expert metallurgist at Bethlehem, 49, 50

Delamater Iron Works, New York, 44

Detroit area: steel consumption in the 1950s, 171

Dolle, Guy: and Arcelor's interest in acquiring part of Bethlehem Steel in 2001, 267

Dunham, Duane: chairman in 2000, 258, 259; president in 2001, 261; retires in 2002, 266

Edgar Thomson works, Pittsburgh, Pennsylvania: compared with Bethlehem in 1875 and 1878, 23; compared with Bethlehem in the 1880s, 34; ore supply for, 59

electric furnace steel: and Johnstown in the 1980s, 235; in the 1950s, 184

El Tofo iron ore: early developments in and Bethlehem Steel's acquisition of, 99; exploitation of, 112, 119; interrupted supply in World War II, 146; run-down in the 1950s, 155, 156

Employee Representation Plan: from 1919 to the late 1930s, 201

Erie Mining Company, 153, 154

Experimental Negotiating Agreement (ENA), 1973–1982, 206, 207

Fairless Works, Morristown, Pennsylvania: building and competition from, 158, 159

First Boston Corporation: report on Bethlehem Steel operations in 1986, 222, 223

Fore River shipyard, Quincy, Massachusetts: and acquisition by Bethlehem Steel in 1913, 86; the history of, 86; in World War II, 144; post–World War II, 191; and the sale of, 191

Foy, Lewis: chairman in 1974, 199; on long term implications of Japanese competition, 208; outlook in 1980, 209; and reprieve for Johnstown works, 234; retirement in 1980, 210

Frick, Henry C.: open mindedness about eastern steel prospects in the 1890s, 71

Fritz, John: early career and movement to Bethlehem, 17, 18, 20; emphasis on high quality of products, 23, 24, 27; plans for production of structural steel, 39; withdrawal from Bethlehem Iron, 50

Gimbel department store, New York: as an example of the superiority of Grey beams, 94, 95

Grace, Eugene G.: at Bethlehem Steel in 1899, 69; career and character, 79, 80, 132, 133; recollections of the 1905 changes in management, 79; resignation, 160–62

Grace mine, Berks County, Pennsylvania: development of, 154, 155; production ended at, 201

Graham, Thomas C.: and proposed cooperation of U.S. Steel and Bethlehem Steel, 224; as possible Bethlehem chairman, 246

Great Lakes iron ore: and competitiveness of the East in late nineteenth century, 12, 13

Grey, Henry: and development of the universal beam mill, 39

Grey mill, at Bethlehem works: installation by U.S. Steel Corporation in the 1920s, 122; and Lackawanna mill in 1927, 124; the 1995 closure, 204; pre–World War I, 90, 91, 93–95

Gun Foundry Board: in the early 1880s, 44, 45

Hewitt, Abram S.: and pessimistic assessment of eastern steel prospects, 70

Hogan, William T.: and the 1971 evaluation of Bethlehem Steel, 195

Holley, Alexander L.: on anthracite fuel and Bethlehem ore supplies, 30, 31; on Bethlehem plant and improvements in 1881, 22, 23, 29; and development of the early Bessemer industry, 21

Homer, Arthur: and opinions on labor costs, 204, 205; and presidency of Bethlehem Steel, 149; reaction to suggestions of foreign technological leadership, 216; replaces Grace, 161–63; retirement, 181; run-down in shipbuilding, 190; and shipbuilding successes in World War II, 149

Homer Research Laboratories, 216

Homestead works, Pittsburgh, Pennsylvania: Bethlehem plate mill moved to in 1899, 41, 42

Howe, Howard M.: on pattern of ore supply in 1911, 60, 61

importing iron and steel to the United States: in the 1950s and 1960s, 183, 184; in the 1970s, 207; in the 1980s, 211–13; in the 1990s, 249

Inland Steel: compared with Bethlehem Steel in the 1930s, 136, 141

International Steel Group (ISG): acquires Bethlehem Steel Corporation in 2003, 267, 268

iron ore: and anthracite furnaces in late nineteenth century, 12, 13; and Bethlehem Iron in the 1870s and the late nineteenth century, 28, 30, 31, 33, 58–64; and Bethlehem Steel in the early years and the 1920s, 97, 99, 119; and Sparrows Point costs in the 1930s, 141; and tariff duties and imported ore, 59, 60, 97

Iron Ore Company of Canada: Bethlehem Steel and, 154; interest sold in 1990s, 252

Japan, competition from, 188; and costs in the 1970s, 207, 208; and possible joint ventures between Bethlehem and Japanese firms in the 1980s, 223

Jaques, William H.: and Bethlehem's entry into the armaments business, 45; joins Bethlehem Iron in 1887, 49

Jeans, J. S.: low opinion of eastern prospects in steel, 71; praises Bethlehem engineering shop in 1902, 57

Johnston, Archibald: at Bethlehem Iron, 68, 69; as director in 1905, 78; on need to drive men in 1906, 82; 1945 letter to E. G. Grace, 150

Johnstown works: acquisition by Midvale Steel and Ordnance, 1916, 109; Cambria Steel compared with Bethlehem Steel, 1901–1913 and 1913–1915, 100, 104; during the 1920s, 114, 124; during the 1930s, 140; and merger with Bethlehem Steel Corporation, 114, 124; run-down, 1975 study, and closure, 234–36

Jones, Reginald H.: and the Bethlehem board in the 1980s, 195

Juragua Iron Company, Cuba: early developments, 62–64; improvement of operations, 85, 89, 97

Korean War: and the steel expansion program, 158

Kottcamp, Edward, H.: and the rationalization of the steel sector, 1982–1986, 220, 228

Krupp, Alfred: and Bethlehem developments in armaments, 44, 51

labor, wages, conditions, and relations: at Burns Harbor and Lackawanna, 231; and E. G. Grace and the Employee Representation Scheme, 133; in the 1930's depression, 137; and the 1980s concessions by labor, 214; pre–World War I, 82, 83; post–World War II, 201–7; through the 1990s, 249; in the twenty-first century, 262, 268
Lackawanna Iron and Steel Company / Lackawanna Steel Company: disposes of Lebanon, Pennsylvania properties to Bethlehem Steel in 1917, 111; in 1890s, 38; and movement to Buffalo, 38; post–1902, 112, 113; purchase by Bethlehem in 1922, 113; reorganization in the 1920s, 123; strip mill, 1936, 140; victim of Burns Harbor competition and emerging crisis in the 1960s and 1970s, 176, 177, 186, 187, 230–33
Lake Superior ore supplies: to eastern works, 59
Lehigh canal, 4, 15
Lehigh Forge: forge operations in late years of Bethlehem Steel, 244, 252, 253
Lehigh valley: anthracite coal mining and shipments, 4; anthracite iron industry in, 7, 8; use of coke in furnaces, 11
Lehigh Valley Railroad, 5, 16
Leja, Ted: at Johnstown in the 1980s, 235
Liberia: and iron ore, 155, 251
Linderman, Garrett: alleged opposition to armaments business, 45; and Cuban iron ore, 62, 63; and rail production in 1885, 36
Linderman, Robert P.: and the armor plate business, 52, 53; career at Bethlehem and 1903 death, 68, 69
Lukens Steel Company: acquired by Bethlehem Steel in 1998, 255; in the nineteenth century, 40

markets: distribution in late nineteenth century, 13, 25; in the East in the early twentieth century, 88, 89; post–World War II, 156, 157, 170
Martin, Edmund: depended on by Homer for steel expertise, 163; oversees building Burns Harbor173, 174; record of grand opening of Burns Harbor, 177; remarks about Japanese competition, 188; retirement, 181; on second attempt to merge with Youngstown Sheet and Tube, 171; speech on future of Lackawanna in 1970, 231
McClintic-Marshall Company: acquired by Bethlehem in 1930, 126

McIlvain, Edward: on board and executive committee in 1905, 76; resignation in 1906, 78
Meigs, John F.: negotiates Russian orders in 1894, 49, 54
Midvale Steel Company / Midvale Steel and Ordnance Company: competition in armor before 1914, 87; competition in armor in World War I, 107; purchased by Bethlehem Steel in 1922, 113, 114
Millenbruch, Gary: assessment of Donald Trautlein, 227; possible successor to Walter Williams in 1992, 246; talks in 2000–2001 with domestic and foreign companies on cooperation or merger, 260; withdrawal in the fall of 2001, 261
Miller, Robert S.: chairman in September 2001, 261; on proposed merger with U.S. Steel Corporation in 2001, 264
mini mills, 194, 212–15; and advances in heavy structurals, 239–43; and competition in strip mill products, 215; plate and rail production, 254, 256; progress in the 1990s and early twenty-first century, 250, 266
Monessen (Wheeling-Pittsburgh) rail mill: bought by Bethlehem Steel and closed in 1992, 254
Motte, Rodney: and ISG takeover of Bethlehem Steel, 268

New Jersey iron ore, 12
Nucor: early history, 213; in the 1980s and 1990s, 214, 250; strip mills, 257; structural steel production, 240, 241
Nucor / Yamato structural mill, Blythesville, Arkansas, 240; and the 1993 report on Bethlehem, 243

open hearth furnaces: advancement of in the early twentieth century, 87–88

Packer, Asa: and the establishment of iron making in Bethlehem, 16, 17
Pea Ridge, Missouri: iron ore operation, 175, 201
pension funds: at Bethlehem and U.S. Steel, 246, 264, 269; lack of adequate planning for as factor in Bethlehem Steel failure, 272, 273
Pennsylvania Steel Company: acquisition by Bethlehem Steel in 1916, 108, 109; in the development of Sparrows Point, 38, 64
Penny, Roger: appointed head of steel operations, 228; chief operating officer and president, 242; conclusions from 1993 visit to Blythesville, structural mill, 243; possible suc-

cessor to Williams, 246, 247; retirement in 2000, 259

Pinole Point, San Francisco Bay: in the 1960s, 168, 169

railroad freight charges: and the steel industry pre–World War I, 89

rails: Bessemer rails in early 1870s and after the 1873 crisis, 24, 25; iron rail production at Bethlehem, 19–21; and the late nineteenth century crisis at Bethlehem Iron / Bethlehem Steel, 36, 37; market in late nineteenth century, 32, 33; pools in the 1880s and 1890s, 36, 37; rail production from open hearth steel in early twentieth century, 90, 91

Redington, Pennsylvania: test ground for ordnance, 49

Return on Equity (ROE): as measure of long term decline at Bethlehem Steel, 272

Ross, Wilbur: acquisition of Bethlehem Steel for ISG in 2003, 267–68

San Francisco works, 167

Saucona Iron company, 16

Sayre, Robert, H.: at Bethlehem Iron Company, 17, 18; career, 68; disagreement with Fritz in the 1890s, 50

Scholey, Bob: on British Steel's planned venture with Bethlehem Steel in 1991, 242

Schneider and Company, Le Creusot: and Bethlehem Iron armament plans, 44, 45

Schubert, Richard: passed over for chairmanship, 195; role in Washington, 218

Schwab, Charles M.: and the bonus scheme at Bethlehem, 80, 81; buys Bethlehem Steel in May 1901, 72; comments on Sparrows Point, 71; death in 1939, 143; plans for improvement and change at Bethlehem Steel, 77, 78; report on Bethlehem operations in 1894, 41

scrap: availability and price in the East before World War I, 88; availability and price in the Great Depression, 135; availability and price on the Pacific Coast, 166

shafting, manufacture of: in the late 1880s, 46, 47

sheet, tin plate, and other thin flat-rolled products: in the early 1920s, 118; in the 1930s, 138–41; in the 1990s, 256, 257

Shipbuilding: at Bethlehem Steel to 1914, 85, 86; in the 1920s, 117; and post–World War II cutbacks and closures, 149; shrinkage and end, 188–93, 253; in the United States in the nineteenth century, 39, 40, 73–75; in World War I, 106; and the World War II boom, 144–45

Snyder, Henry: secretary and treasurer of Bethlehem Steel in 1905, 76

Sparrows Point shipyard: early development, 109; in the 1970s, 191, 192; sold in 1995, 193

Sparrows Point steel works: before 1916, 38, 64, 108; changing status and 2007 sale, 269; compared with Burns Harbor, 224; expansion from 1916 through the 1920s, 110, 111, 124; major expansion in the 1950s, 159; in the 1960s, 186; plate production in the 1990s, 255; as possible link with Fairless works in the 1980s, 224; as a strip mill in 1937, 140, 141; strip mill operations in the 1980s and 1990s, 256, 259

steel industry: and concentration of operations in late twentieth century, 219; and consumption trends in the late twentieth century, 193, 212; and environmental costs in the late twentieth century, 212, 250, 251; and post–World War II expansion, 151

Steelton works, 64, 108; and changes in the 1960s, 187

strikes, 83, 202, 203, 206; and clause 2B at Bethlehem Steel, 203; and their impact on the future of the American steel industry, 183, 205

strip mills: Bethlehem Steel installs in the 1930s, 140; products in 1950s, 170; and reconstruction and competition during the 1980s and 1990s, 257

structural shapes: at Bethlehem Iron and other eastern works in nineteenth century, 38, 39; business during the 1920s, 125, 126; declining significance in the 1970s, 198; run-down at Bethlehem and U.S. Steel, 238–44

taconite: development and cost implications, 153, 154

Taylor, Frederick W.: at Bethlehem, 68

Thomas, David and Samuel: and decline of the anthracite iron industry, 14; and establishment of anthracite iron industry, 6; and growth of anthracite iron industry, 7

Tidewater Steel Company: and false rumor of Bethlehem acquisition in 1905, 90

Tracey, Benjamin: visits Bethlehem in 1889 and 1891, 57

Trautlein, Donald: chairman in 1980, 210; course of business under, 217; on frustrations of plant rationalization process, 245; international trade testimony in Washington in 1983, 218, 219; and Lee Iacocca's influence on his ideas in the 1980s, 225; plant rationalization and modernisation, 220; retirement in 1986, 227

Tull Industries: purchase and resale of in the 1980s, 226